Touched By All Creatures

Touched By All Creatures

Doctoring Animals in the Pennsylvania Dutch Country

by

Gay L. Balliet

with veterinary input by
Edgar Balliet, VMD

New Horizon Press
Far Hills, New Jersey

Requests for permission should be addressed to:
New Horizon Press
P.O. Box 669
Far Hills, NJ 07931

Balliet, Gay L.
Touched By All Creatures: Doctoring Animals in the Pennsylvania Dutch Country

Interior Design: Susan Sanderson
Illustrations by Linda George

Library of Congress Catalog Card Number: 98-66169

ISBN: 0-88282-169-5

New Horizon Press
Manufactured in U.S.A.

2003   2002   2001   2000   1999 / 5   4   3   2   1

Dedication

To my parents,
Ralph and Anna Eckensberger

In memory of
Gramma Eckensberger

Author's Note

These are my actual experiences and history, and this book reflects my opinion of the past, present, and future. The personalities, events, actions, and conversations portrayed within the story have been reconstructed from my memory and research, press accounts, letters, and the memories of participants. In an effort to safeguard the privacy of certain individuals, I have changed their names, and, in some cases, altered otherwise identifying characteristics and locations. Events involving the characters happened as described.

Each morning like a New born Man issues with songs & Joy,
Calling the Plowman to his Labour & the Shepherd to his rest.
He walks upon the Eternal Mountains raising his heavenly voice,
Conversing with the Animal forms of wisdom night & day,
That risen from the Sea of fire renewd walk o'er the Earth.

William Blake
The Four Zoas

Acknowledgments

I would like to acknowledge all my creature friends who have touched our lives in so many ways and now are gone. We miss you dearly: Merry, Nicky, Abby, Diane, Timmy Lee, Beverly, Brian, Sticky Bun, Marvin, Sophie, Little Sophie, Gadney, Broccoli, Allen, Hailey, Susan, Lyle, Lyla, Marshall, Blackie, Blackie II, Blackie III, Robert, Heidi, Annie, Missy, Jessie, Mindy, the Volcano litter: Irazu, Poas, Arenal, Spittin' Po, Robin, Terry, Louise, Stevie, Spike and my sweet Lucy.

Contents

Introduction

Experience with me the extraordinary realm of caring for and doctoring the wonderfully strange as well as familiar animals in the colorful, quaint Pennsylvania Dutch country where my husband and I are a mobile veterinary MASH team. In this still young and innocent part of America, people live simply without haste and perfunctoriness, valuing animals and the marvels of the natural world. These present-day American farmers, cowboys, zookeepers, equestrians and small pet owners are the heroes of these stories. Recalling their tales transports me from my mundane daily jobs of cooking up a pot of kasha and veggies, scooping out the cats' litter boxes or blowing dust off knickknacks accumulated through the years to almost an otherworldliness, as I remember assisting Edgar on his veterinary calls.

I daydream of times past when I waded knee-deep through the white and drifting snow of a buffalo range lugging buckets of obstetrical equipment to attend a birth; or others, when I sat peacefully atop a straw bale in a cob-webbed barn holding up a tiny kitten for Edgar's examination. Those days were all of a new, enriching grain and now, in memory, are like rare pieces of priceless amber.

I think back to the animals we have cared for: the foal Edgar resuscitated and a miniature donkey named Pedro who lives today because of Edgar's concern for a life that perhaps others would have written off. To his owner's delight, Pedro walks around his pasture, albeit slowly and deliberately, with the help of a prosthesis. I think of Tonto, an impish llama, and his goat and sheep friends; a lame bull that lead us on a wild chase through woods and pond; the rare Hobird, a newly discovered species more human than feathered, and the baboon whose wounds we stitched.

We are indeed inhabitants of an extraordinary world. Being in the veterinary field allows us contact with the inexplicable and contemplation of the unknown, for veterinary care has its moments of mystery. When the unknown is revealed, such as in a diagnosis of a rare but treatable disease, the wonder is the thing, the "objet d'art"—the different universe. When Edgar, flummoxed by conflicting symptoms, works out a solution as to why a sheep has a strange head tilt or a horse has shed half its weight in a year, the unfolding of the mystery gives us a feeling of accomplishment, the realization of the importance of luck, the strength of hope and the greatest personal feeling of all—the joy of knowing a doomed animal will have another chance at life. Conquering the unknown in the field of veterinary medicine offers, in a way, a sense of the power of otherworldliness, along with a sense of deep personal commitment and selflessness.

Like human characters, our pets and barnyard friends delight us with their antics. For example, our pet ram lusted after me as if I were one of his own kind. (I wasn't that impressed, but Edgar laughed like mad.) Yet I found it hilarious when the ram bowled Edgar into a pile of curled garden hose. Our pot-bellied pig, Lowell, can force a laugh from the most dour onlooker when he performs his pirouette as I give him the command, "Baryshnikov" and communicates with his audience through a score of varied vocalizations.

Ours is also the unique world of the Pennsylvania Dutch farmer. Sometimes misconstrued as thickheaded, strict and unyielding, the Dutchman or woman values hard work and self-reliance to the point of unrelenting self-discipline and self-deprivation. The Pennsylvania Dutch foster strong family ties and pride themselves on their frugality and endurance during adversity. They are a tightly-knit group, protective of their own and quick to defend their simple and unpretentious lifestyle. They value their animals and pride themselves on raising prizewinning pigs and steers and showing them at the county fairs throughout Pennsylvania. At the Kutztown and Allentown Fairs we have observed them tidying their animal's stalls with mild obsession and showering the dairy cows and pigs with cool water on a searing day. Most farmers care for their animals in much the same way they care for their own families—fastidiously—for to them the word "livestock" takes on an added dimension—humanness.

The Dutch people maintain close-knit family ties and yet are sociable and hospitable to guests and other visitors. Their cooking is famous. They will load up the table with mounds of sauerkraut and potatoes, pig's stomach stuffed with sausage and potatoes, souse (pig parts in a gelatinous base), tripe (beef reticulum or stomach in jelly), liver pudding, blood sausage, and scrapple (a gray conglomeration of cornmeal and pork scraps). Meals are accompanied by drafts of good amber beer chased with a mug of apple cider. Anyone enjoying these morsels as a steady diet has to be unique, stalwart, and equipped with an iron stomach.

To this world my husband and I belong, not just in spirit but also in heritage. We are both of Pennsylvania Dutch stock. My family names are Eckensberger and Weinsheimer, and Edgar's side boasts names like Dimler, Edelman, and Ochs. We are fairly thrifty, except when a Victoria's Secret catalogue arrives and lures me into replacing my rather plain underwear with extravagant lingerie. We also like to dip into the mysteries of Dutch food, consuming with passion apple schnitz, summer bologna, red beet eggs and potato salad, pot pie, pickled pig's feet and other fatty delights. Dinners at our house are big indulgent affairs suitable for the voracious Dutch appetite. Our favorite dishes are huge pots of beef with boiled potatoes, onions and carrots; meat pies; piles of corn; and yards of sausage. For those so apparently serious and self-disciplined when it comes to work, a good laugh comes just as naturally. We laugh big, deep belly laughs, like my Gramma Eckensberger, who bellowed and held her abdomen after a particularly good joke. We are a hearty, plump, affable group that appreciates fatty foods and good friends.

Our language is different from Standard English and defines our Pennsylvania Dutch individuality. At times both Edgar and I slip into the Dutchy accent and phraseology, using expressions such as "get out" (pronounced "get awt" and meaning, "I can't believe it!"), and "Say!" (pronounced with a lilting, musical "Sa-a-a-ay!" and meaning "I agree with you"); and "Geez" (pronounced "cheese" and meaning "Gee whiz" or "Gad" or "Egad"). There is also "Oy," meaning something like "Wow!" or Yikes!"

Edgar and I are good representatives of the Dutch except for our ties to the scholarly world and the fact that our life is a bit more complex than that found on the farm; we do not view these as necessarily positive characteristics. But the horses, cows and pigs regard us as being on the same plane as they are. They are always our friends and sometimes our patients. The animals we care for are both livestock as livelihood and pets for pampering. The people who own them are hard-working and appreciative of our diligence and caring. The animals respond, as do most humans, to kindness and genuine thoughtfulness. Whether the animal patient is a pig or a parrot, most of our human clients appreciate our attentiveness and care to their vulnerable creatures which is nearly equal to their own.

We offer ourselves to the unique world in which we live and work. Ours is an offering of selflessness, of openness and a desire to learn, aid, experience and share a part of an individual's life, be that individual a distraught client, a sickly pig or a lame horse. This different world, in contrast to that of people who reside desk-bound in the city or computer-bound in the suburbs, is the world that entices, holds and nourishes us. It is a world of unforgettable experiences, intriguing situations and memorable characters we want to share with animal lovers everywhere.

Prologue

Driving through the Pennsylvania landscape, the imagination wanders back to America's colonial days. Much of Pennsylvania's western and northern sections remain virgin forest, and these forests, covered with acres of mountain laurel, protect species of deer, bear and fowl. As we sped down the road, banked high by a cliff on one side, I wondered about the early explorers who had probably beat out the initial cow path that became this road. What historical ghosts lingered here at wood's edge as our truck dipped into shade and out again into patches of sunshine?

This richly heritaged area recalls the settlers who battled the Indians. Many of the old stone farmhouses still have secret cellar ways where the family hid during Indian attacks. The house walls are one and a half feet thick, the basements have dirt floors and sometimes there are even two kitchens—one for summer and one for winter. So many of these homesteads still have springs running through their springhouses. Abandoned smokehouses and huge stone bake ovens for baking bread still adorn these old lots as do separate cold cellars, which are used today for storing the garden's harvest.

The Lehigh Valley's historical sites and natural formations have Indian names: Monocacy Creek—meaning "river of many large bends"; the towns of Mauch Chunk; Catasauqua—"the earth thirsts"; Hokendauqua—"searching for land"; Tamaqua; the Nockamixon Lake, and the Delaware River. Thinking of Indians and early American settlers, we streaked along the wooded road toward the game preserve, thankful it wasn't winter and snowing.

The Trexler Lehigh County Game Preserve delights people of all ages. During the warmer months the eleven-hundred-acre park comes alive as families tour the winding preserve road in their cars, taking pictures and searching out the elk, deer and buffalo on the range. The natural world here is an exotic escape into stretches of forest, marshland and plains. Scores of birds, including black swans, as well as camels, llamas, antelope and punky-haired yaks reside within this natural environment.

Cedar-shake huts shaded by towering ash trees serve as high-class accommodations for any fox, bobcat or raccoon and line the narrow macadam road that leads to the picnic area, the petting zoo and the pony rides. What had always intrigued me as a child (and still does) is the ford we all had to drive across to leave the preserve. Even more thrilling was the horse auction held every September when the wild palomino year-lings were sold to the public.

Early in his career, Edgar became the official veterinarian for the game preserve. To date he has assisted with numerous births and with a buffalo suffering heat stroke. It is a far different workplace from the small animal vet's office in many cities and makes Edgar's and my commitment to this place and our human and animal friends here even stronger.

One summer afternoon Edgar was to vaccinate the preserve's sheep against tetanus. The job entailed catching, injecting and marking each individual of the thirty-member flock. One had to be quick, sure-footed and a little crazy to climb inside a pen full of manic sheep.

My job was to draw a pink chalk line down the back of each sheep after Edgar injected it. About five assistants helped us with the round up, tackling the woolly go-carts and then pinning them against the fence so Edgar could give the shot. As we worked, a great dust cloud built up inside the pen as harried sheep and people fell over each other in the confusion. But one lone creature stood, unruffled, in the center of the melee—it was not a sheep but a llama. His name was Tonto.

In the midst of all the commotion, Tonto stood, alone and digni-fied. At one time, he had been a favorite in the children's petting yard. Tonto is medium-sized and white and black in color. He fears no animal or human. In the petting yard, he had stood perfectly still through any disturbance, unperturbed while little kids tugged playfully on his wool.

Throughout the vaccinating, Tonto stood at attention. In the middle of the park, head upright on his tall neck, he followed the stam-peding sheep with curiosity in his big, curly-lashed eyes and appeared to be entertained by his harried cousins who climbed over each other all around him. Cool and nonchalant, he strutted calmly through the fren-zied throng. Then suddenly, as the din of the stampede increased and as the dust swirled, Tonto became wild-eyed and began to hop like a springbok, prancing, dancing on tiptoe amid the bleating sheep, his head erect, ears forward, eyes glittering.

Just then Edgar captured and vaccinated a sheep and signaled me to mark it. Running over to the sheep struggling in his arms, I started to draw the chalk line down its back. A tremendous weight landed on my back. Spinning around to see what it was, I yelled, startled, as Tonto's white and black face with flaming eyes stared at me. Tonto was glaring into my eyes, and by then his front feet were resting on my shoulders. His eyes, crystal bright with excitement, dared me to a challenge. I was no martyr. I ran screaming, pink chalk marker dangling from my clenched fist. Tonto galloped after, relishing my terror.

I sprinted to the gate and grabbed for the latch but missed it as Tonto dug into my derriere with his sharp front hooves. My screams were lost amid the din of the frantic sheep, but I finally scrambled out of the dusty pen and came to safety on the other side of the fence. Tonto screeched to a halt on his side of the fence. Then, with complete aplomb, he turned back to the herd.

Why had he attacked me? Why had he singled me out over the other people rushing about the pen? Along with my dirty and bruised hind end, I nursed my embarrassment at having run away from a petting yard animal.

Catching my breath, I eyed Tonto with suspicion, but now he stood angelically, as if nothing had happened. No one else had witnessed my struggle with Tonto—a fact I'm sure he was aware of. While everyone had been occupied by the frenzied sheep, Tonto seized the opportunity to become the wild thing he truly was and join in the fun. Now that the action was abating, he donned his cool and collected front and became again a respectable representative of the petting yard.

Of course, I was traumatized and when another incident occurred at the game preserve, this one involving the Green Guenon monkeys, I began to think the place might be jinxed. According to federal safety standards, monkeys must be tested for TB, a disease communicable to people. Zoo monkeys, in contact with people through wire cages, pose a potential threat to humans if they are diseased. The trick, however, is to administer the test by injecting the TB antigen into—of all places—the eyelid. The rationale behind injecting to test in the eyelid is logical: the monkey's eyelids are one of the few hairless places on its body, and because the results have to be seen by the veterinarian with the naked eye, the eyelid is the perfect place to administer the test. After the three-day waiting period, the vet need only look at the monkey's face to see if his eyelid is swollen or not.

Catching those quick, scrambling wall climbers would be tough, but injecting the fluid into the eyelid made a hard job nearly impossible. Many people don't realize wild monkeys are not the friendly, humanly-behaved, well-mannered little creatures that amuse us on television. On the contrary, a monkey is a wild animal with razor-sharp teeth and a vicious, defensive personality. This testing would be no picnic.

To help him, Edgar had rounded up two gamekeepers from the preserve together with Paul, a friend who would be attending vet school in September. In a room the size of a family bathroom, the monkeys sat on their wooden perches blinking calmly down at us. We five, armed with nets, heavy gloves, heavy coats and hats, looked ready to stave off a pack of pit bull fighting dogs. My job was to hand over the needles, syringes and TB fluid as Edgar needed them.

"They look like they're ready for us," Edgar said, drawing the TB antigen into a small syringe.

"And they don't seem very pleased," I contributed, visions of Tonto the llama dancing in my head.

As the gamekeepers and Paul put on the rest of their protective gear, Edgar and I looked up to the ceiling of the little cement room where the monkeys crowded together. We were met by a unanimous look of worry, and the monkeys huddled even closer, their little bodies pressed together for protection.

The monkeys came in all different sizes: the bigger ones were the old males, the middle-sized ones were the older females, and tucked either under a mother's arm or around her waist clung the little babies just born a month ago. The whole group, some hanging from a ceiling ledge and others on the wooden swings, sat hunched over—silent, with their tiny fingers gripping the concrete.

Now the three men, looking like Arctic explorers, eased carefully into the room, nets ready. Monkey heads lowered, primed, following the men as they slunk with poised nets to make the big snare. An erratic swipe through the air sent the monkeys flying overhead in every direction, and screams echoed off the walls of the tiny room. The men swung their nets with determination, aiming but missing. Chattering angrily, the monkeys ran in every direction.

Then it happened. As the monkeys raced along the ledge at the ceiling, they let fly their manure. Helplessly, the men dodged the fecal missiles. The monkeys couldn't have had a better defense, for the men cowered, defenseless, their arms shielding their heads.

"My God, what're they doing?" hissed one of the workers as he sniffed the air. Splotches of monkey shit shone on his shoulder. Before they could even react, each man was covered with monkey feces and urine.

"Oh, no!" Edgar stifled a laugh. "Just hurry and catch them; let's get the job over with."

The helpers began the chase once more, and once more the manure flew through the air, catching one of the guys in the face. "Yech!" he yelled, wiping his face and smearing it all over his forehead.

The monkeys, for sure, were more angry than frightened; after all, these same men fed them everyday, sometimes by hand, and talked to them all winter when they were housed inside. The monkeys had to know they would not be hurt; they were merely insulted that they were being treated like animals.

Suddenly Sid, the oldest male, became snagged in a net. Struggling and twisting around, his tiny fingers clawed the nylon net to find an escape hole. Then Paul waddled, thick with layers of protective clothing, over to the netted animal. He held it down, but despite his firm grip on the wriggling beast, the monkey twisted its skinny neck around to plant a bite right into his gloved hand. Even though Paul wore heavy gloves, Sid's little teeth sank into his skin; the man let out a tremendous yell and let go his grip. The monkey blinked up at his victim with curled lips.

When the men finally got control of him, Sid took his injection like a monkey.

Each monkey was then captured in turn. Mouths agape and eyes goggling, the monkeys screeched as needle after needle struck home.

Two hours and fourteen monkeys later, the men emerged from the concrete room carrying a stench that rivaled a retained placenta. They smelled of manure and urine, a smell so acrid it stung the eyes and nose. The fecal matter was clinging to their coats and caps in streaks and splotches. It was revolting.

"That was an experience I'll never forget," chuckled a worker, flicking a smudge from his shoulders.

"No shit," his friend answered, without realizing the pun.

"Next year when we have to do this again, I'm going to call in sick with the flu," said another, grimacing down at himself. At least they could laugh at themselves through the ordeal. As a way of making up, they fed the monkeys grain and crackers. The monkeys seemed to warm up somewhat, especially when we brought out the banana chips.

Three days later, we looked in at the monkeys in their concrete room. None had swollen eyelids. They backed against the farthest wall and huddled together, eyeing us. The monkeys did not have TB, but the price those men and animals paid for those findings was dear.

After checking the monkeys, Edgar and I drove out to the buffalo range and into another adventure. The visage of the craggy, furry-headed buffalo with its slim, well-muscled body can intimidate even the bravest zoological aficionado. Creased with deep folds of skin, the buffalo sports a beard that drapes a long and pendulous chin. Surely, only a buffalo could appreciate the beauty of another buffalo. Yet, despite its disconcerting countenance, the animal has a personality that, if not friendly, is inquisitive and sometimes downright meddlesome.

The buffalo is a nosy character—a kind of snoopy old woman of the animal kingdom. They plod in apparent boredom around their pen, nonchalantly licking up pieces of hay. They do not seem violent or aggressive, nor do they seem to have any drive or desire beyond hunger.

But the buffalo is a rare beast. Inside that powerful, chunky body and head lies one of the most curious and questioning animals. The buffalo has a kind of inquiring, mischievous attitude like a schoolboy witnessing a friend's scolding. This childlike behavior, this innocence, lies disguised beneath the buffalo's intimidating appearance.

As we drove up the road, we saw dark clumps lying here and there in the distance, the buffalo basking in the afternoon sun. They barely reacted to our stopping the truck right in their midst, being accustomed to vehicles delivering their daily meals. They lay chewing their cud, watching us without unconcern.

From the truck we watched from five yards away, observing their feeding habits and social behavior. In silence, Edgar and I watched the buffalo, grunting and snorting in great thunderous breaths.

They soon became restless. One rose from the ground, rump first followed by the supporting front legs. Then another labored to its feet. In minutes the entire herd was standing, and I must admit I grew uneasy being so close to those huge beasts.

As if staged for an Alfred Hitchcock movie, the buffalo herd descended steadily upon our truck, one sure slow step at a time. Edgar and I glanced at each other, hesitating to speak, lest we scare them and spook the "sedentary" beasts to action.

"What're they doing?" I whispered as one of them sidled slowly behind the truck.

"I don't know. I don't *think* they'll do anything. Maybe they're just being nosy," replied Edgar as a scratching sound rustled behind us.

"What was that?" I gulped.

Edgar, looking in his side-view mirror, said, "One of them is back there scratching himself on the back of the truck. Their hairs are like wire. They can probably remove paint with those stiff hairs; it's like taking a gigantic Brillo pad to the truck."

"I don't like this," I said, biting my fingernails. "It's eerie. If they wanted, they could topple us over."

Again a rasping sounded from behind as another buffalo backed up against the truck. Then the truck began to shake back and forth.

"What's that?" I hissed. "Let's get out of here! I'm scared!"

"There's another one rubbing his back on our truck. I'm sure he doesn't mean any harm, Gay. His back itches, that's all," said Edgar. In minutes the buffalo stopped his back scratching, and the rocking stopped, too.

Busy peering into Edgar's side-view mirror, I hadn't noticed a buffalo, nose to the ground, sniffing below my window. He was oblivious to our presence, and, for sure, he didn't see me gaping right at him. Head down, he sniffed and snorted the dirt underneath the truck, whipping up a huge dust cloud that rose to my window. Little did the animal realize that he had wandered to within a mere foot of my rolled-up window, humpedback parallel to my face. I was fairly certain, just by his innocent approach, that he meant no harm. Not once had he looked up to see where he was headed. But there he was, nevertheless, just inches away from me.

And then a strange feeling overcame me—an overwhelming attraction to the wild and primitive. Overshadowing any instinctive fear, I suddenly felt compelled to reach out and touch this wild animal. There was this compulsion to make contact and bond with something wild and possibly dangerous. I just had to touch that buffalo. I could not leave this earth without having done what most people have not. The feat clouded all other ambitions momentarily—even my childhood dream to be a ballerina.

With Edgar's guarded permission I slowly and very quietly rolled down my window. The buffalo sniffed the ground by the truck, unaware of my intentions, great humpedback within reach. Extending my hand out the window, I aimed for the very tip of that great, hairy back. Then I tweaked him and felt the sparse, wiry hairs—sharing at that moment a piece of the wild, a world unknown, a primal life force.

With that the buffalo's head rose from the ground. He snorted in my face, eyes wide as soup dishes, his nose flared. There we were, suspended for a moment, staring into each other's eyes with mutual fear. In a few microseconds that huge animal retreated from my window with the agility of a calypso dancer. He made one giant pirouette, and in a cloud of dust leaped back to the security of the shade trees and the other buffalo. And I, just as quickly, rolled up my window, spinning around to Edgar, wheezing, "Let's get out of here. This is too close for comfort. All I have to do is piss them off, and then we'll really be in trouble." With a turn of the key, we escaped the buffalo group under the trees. We left them hunkered together, staring after us as we faded from sight.

The buffalo were not the only disconcerting animals at the game preserve. My solitary sojourn into a pen full of hungry llamas and goats would delight the most dedicated horror movie enthusiast. One biting fall day after the preserve had been closed to the public for several months, Edgar needed to examine an old goat that was limping in the petting zoo. Driving up to the enclosure, we spotted a goat with a distinct hobble. As the other goats and sheep ran to newly opened hay piles, this goat brought up the rear with its painful walk. We opened the gate and walked into the long wire pen.

In the summertime the large petting yard entertains parents and children offering grain crackers to its hungry residents. Some animals are so stuffed by day's end that they refuse the crackers and are satisfied with a mere rub on the forehead or a pat on the back. No wonder the petting yard animals fear no people and behave sometimes like spoiled pet dogs.

By summer's end most of the animals are tired of the grain

crackers. Yet on opening day, after a barren winter without much human contact and without the tasty cracker treats, the floodgates are opened, and the Courtship of the Cracker begins. People charge through the preserve door, goody bags in hand, and the glut is on—to the delight of the inhabitants of the petting yard.

Edgar and I went to check out the lame goat though the day was well into the dead of winter—a season of dry hay and water and no special goodies. Little did we realize that the otherwise calm, respectful animals were ready to kill for a cracker.

Being an animal lover and bearer of animal gifts, I had salvaged a piece of leftover bun from our McDonald's lunch. I entered the pen with the tasty morsel in my hand.

Heads swiveled. What long-awaited delight did this strange person come bearing? As I marched toward the throng of hungry, pitiful souls, I held the bread chunk out in front of me, wondering which animal would reach for it. That was certainly not the smartest move I've ever made in my life.

Unfortunately, the animals were wondering the same thing. The entire herd of goats and llamas broke at once into a trot, heading right for me. From the other end of the yard, the beasts advanced, flying legs and bobbing bodies darting in and around each other, eyes alive with anticipation for that one crummy piece of bread to which I was hopelessly attached.

Still faster they came, kicking up dust, now a full stampede. No longer were these petting yard animals the epitome of calm and tranquillity. No—they had become a running mob, transformed by a mere hunk of bread. The woolly tidal wave was about to envelop and drown me. I turned to flee. Too late. They had the speed of a brush fire. My only recourse was to extend to them my single bit of bread, close my eyes, and brace myself for the hit.

It came. With lightning force, one of the animals snatched the bread from my clenched hand, and seconds later, pummeled by llamas and goats, I was on my back in the dust, face-to-face with the brazen llamas. Beset by the frenzied throng, I groped to a kneeling position as they pecked my jacket for more delights.

Now five giant llamas loomed overhead, crowding me, sniffing, prodding and tasting my coat. The goats, not as tall as the llamas, sucked at my knees, and one was tugging at my backside searching for hidden treasures.

I managed to get to a kneeling position. Concentrating on retaining my balance and protecting my face from the manic animals, I cried out to Edgar who was searching for the lame goat. Little did he realize that his crippled patient was probably in the midst of this pack of wolves in sheep's clothing, tearing away at my jeans along with the biggest and healthiest.

Rising painfully to my feet, I came nose to nose with a white llama swinging its head, demanding the grain crackers he knew I had stashed somewhere on me. I ran. I howled like a banshee, waved my arms and jumped back at them like a madwoman. It worked for a few minutes, just long enough for me to dart out the gate. Behind me I left about fifty puzzled and hungry llamas, goats and sheep.

Outside the petting yard I caught my breath, huffing and puffing. Would Edgar be the mob's next victim? Would I ever see him again? But in five minutes he strolled, undisturbed, through the gates, and with one glance at me he hooted, "I see the troops were a tad hungry. I ran to help you but turned my ankle. I didn't think they'd actually hurt you though."

"No, they didn't hurt me, but they knocked me to the ground. They're absolutely crazy for human food," I gasped.

As Edgar's eyes traveled down my body, he wrinkled up his nose, and his lips stretched out in a long, thin wail of laughter.

"What's so funny?" I demanded, and then I glanced down at my coat. Here and there were crease marks where llama and goat teeth had grabbed at my coat, permanently pleating parts of my jacket. A Kleenex hung from my pocket and dangled in shreds while the foil wrapper from a lifesaver pack draped over my other pocket. Worst of all, big splotches of dirt balls were clinging all over the arms and front of my coat. Juicy particles of dirt dotted my knees where the goats had been waging war. I looked pitiful. And yet, now that I had escaped with only a few black and blue spots on my rear end, I could only laugh—at first a snicker, then a giggle. Then I joined Edgar in a rolling belly laugh.

Part I

Tales of Innocence

"Pipe a song about a lamb."
So I piped with merry chear.
"Piper pipe that song again..."

William Blake
Songs of Innocence

1

All Creatures Large and Lilliputian

Edgar's and my fascination with animals and nature all began, as Fate decided, when we were too young to realize what it would all mean.

As far back as I can remember, I have had an affinity for all creatures, large and Lilliputian. Most of this fascination began at the age of six and was the result of my Gramma Eckensberger's keen insight and creative imagination.

I can still hear her loudly calling me by the pet name she gave me—a hybrid of Gay and, my middle name, Louise. Her voice still rings fondly in my ears.

"Gwee-ee-ee-eezer! Gwee-ee-ee-eezer!"

I flew to the picture window, parted the curtains and looked across our two-acre yard to my grandmother's grand, pink stucco home on the hill. There she stood on her flagstone patio that moist morning, a large, round woman in a white sundress speckled with bouquets of black-eyed Susans. As usual her flaming red hair was arranged in a haphazard French twist, strands of which stuck out like a sunburst.

Again she called. "Gwee-ee-eezie! Gwee-ee-eezie! I have something for you!"

She always had something for me—always some enchanting surprise. It didn't take much prodding for me, my parents' six-year-old only child with nothing to do, to race out the door and up to her large porch flanked by blooming lilacs and spicy verbena. It was spring, and my gramma's flowerbeds had already erupted into riots of ruby tulips, grape hyacinths and sun-yellow daffodils. And that was only the beginning. In summer the front yard would be festooned with a colored profusion of purple, yellow, red, blue and white wildflowers and not-so-wild flowers: bleeding hearts, snapdragons, daisies, roses, peonies, poppies and magnolias. Wherever there was an empty corner of ground, Gramma planted a bush, a tree or a collection of flowers.

Seconds later, I stood huffing and puffing before her raised porch. The great green garden umbrella was already open and poised luxuriously in anticipation of many summer picnics. Gramma smiled mischievously from an ample face and proffered her cupped hands.

Today's surprise.

"This is just for you," she said in a low, mysterious voice. "But before you see it, you must promise at play's end to put it back where it belongs."

I nodded, grinning with anticipation. Chewing my lower lip, I held out my hands as I had done many, many times before. I wondered what she held this time.

"Be careful," she said as she drew closer, bent over. I held out my small hands. "Don't drop it."

Then she made the exchange—from her closed fists to mine. At first I couldn't see what the mystery object was—there were too many fingers in the way. But I soon felt something warm and soft. Then I felt the little thing move. I quickly closed my fingers over it to keep it safe, but I wanted to see the object. Gradually I raised my hands and peeked inside the finger cave.

A tiny bunny. A baby animal so small it could fit inside a six-year-old's hands. There it sat tucked into a ball, its pink nose wriggling busily, looking as content as it made me feel inside. I held my breath so as not to scare the bunny and then brought the tiny animal close to my chest so that I wouldn't drop it.

"Look in her eyes," Gramma said. "She wonders who this little girl is."

Its ear twitched against my lips, and I giggled softly and whispered to it. One bright brown eye looked at me, and I stared into it,

trying to capture the essence of a tiny life so fragile and in need of protection—much like my own.

"What are you doing today, Bunny?" Gramma asked in a soothing voice. "Are you busy hunting for carrots?"

Watching the bunny closely, I listened carefully for an answer. But
it didn't say anything. It just twitched its nose and gazed curiously at us.

Gramma bent down and stroked the fuzzy animal along its
back, and its skin rippled under her touch. "What are you thinking,
Bunny?" To me she said, "Go ahead, talk to her for a little while, but
then you must put her back in the grass where she belongs so that she
can get back to her nest."

Very carefully, I walked over to a grass patch and sat down, all
the while cupping the young rabbit protectively against my chest. I must
have looked a little like Alice in Wonderland, minus the fancy frock and
patent leather shoes, as she conversed with her time-worried rabbit.
There I sat for many minutes whispering endless inquiries into the
bunny's ear. I asked her where in the flower garden she lived, how old
she was, and if I could see her again. Gazing into her clear chocolate
eyes, I became, for a few seconds, her bunny sister. I wrinkled my nose
against hers and touched my cheek to hers. We were friends, I thought,
and I knew she was thinking the same thing.

Shortly, under Gramma's instructions and watchful eye, I carefully lay the bunny in the grass at the corner of a flowerbed. The animal
hopped away, sniffing as it went, and sat camouflaged beneath a pink
peony bush. A few seconds later, it was gone.

A variation of that scenario replayed many times throughout my
childhood: Gramma's call, then my run to her porch, and always,
always, my grandmother's cupped hands with a mystery present.

Among these wondrous presents she so carefully placed into my
eager hands were a robin's egg, warm and sky blue; a large beetle of
some type with sticky feet and raspy nails; a spiked, fuzzy baby bird
fallen from a nest; a tomato worm that I really didn't like at all but held
anyway because Gramma insisted; a praying mantis; a walking stick; a
lady bug; and numerous butterflies and moths. With the present came
Gramma's advice—to always, always look into the animal's or insect's
eyes and offer conversation, and to touch its body and imagine how it
lived—in short, to walk around in its feet for awhile.

The mystery presents not only led me to appreciate nature and animals at an early age, but they also taught me to trust people. For example, Gramma never placed anything gross or nasty into my hands. I learned from these experiences that whatever she held in her hands would not harm me. Soon I realized that whatever she gave me to study she had found in nature, that it would probably be warm and moving, and that I would be able to hold it and talk to it for a few minutes before placing it back amongst the flowers where it lived.

My love for animals began with those offerings from Gramma Eckensberger's cupped hands. Those same hands, so kind and soothing to a six-year-old's skinned knees and hurt feelings, held delights of nature that were just as soft and giving as she. As with anything she imparted, Gramma always brought the "hand" animals down to my level, literally and figuratively. She never warned me about bites or gooey stuff leaking from them; if a caterpillar expelled "stuff" on my hand, she wiped it away before I even realized it, and if she didn't catch it in time, she let me know it wouldn't hurt me and calmly whisked it away with a corner of her apron. She taught me to respect animals and nature as I respected her and myself, to appreciate that each mystery present was an individual being with a life of its own to nourish and protect. I learned that not only was my own life and the lives of my parents and grandparents sacred, but that all life, down to the tiniest creature of the garden, was important.

About four years later, I graduated from bonding with garden creatures to appreciating those of a larger variety. The experience of horseback riding solidified my love for animals. But my introduction to horses did not revolve around private riding lessons taught by some snooty equestrienne newly arrived from the British Isles. I had no expensive riding habit, no saddle or bridle, nor a pony of my own—my parents didn't have that kind of money. What I did have was a little girl's huge fascination with horses.

So I was especially happy one day when my mother dropped me off at a local hack stable—Melody Ranch—for a "riding lesson." As I soon found out, it wasn't really a lesson—it was simply a half-hour ride in a hack string. Fifteen kids and a leader headed out on horseback at a walk, nose to tail, toward the distant woods. We were not allowed to let our horses step out of the lineup, and once the horses decided early on who was to follow who, that was the position we had to arrive back in.

The only advice the leader gave to improve my riding skills was to keep my heels down. I mastered that technique quickly, quite proud that I had learned to ride at last! When the half-hour was up, the leader, anxious for a cup of coffee, galloped us kiddies all the way back to the barn. I clung desperately to the saddle horn to keep from falling off and, obedient child that I was, frantically kept my heels down.

Every other Saturday I went horseback riding without ever learning how. Dangerous as it was, I even survived the dreaded mad sprints back to the barn. The leaders were only kids themselves, high school students working at the stable as a summer job. I didn't want to race my horse; I simply wanted to walk my equine friend through the woods.

What I really liked, however, came after the ride when I learned to take off the saddle and bridle and take care of my mount. I was able to spend quality time brushing down my favorite horse, Cindy, a short, stocky dark bay with a thick, rounded neck. I stroked her fur—talking to her all the while as Gramma had taught me with her mystery presents. I curried and scrubbed Cindy as she shifted in her stall. I picked out her hoofs, examining the frog for jammed stones or cuts. I combed out the mane and tail and polished her coat with a soft towel. When I was finished, the old hack mare shone like silk, ready for another stint in the hack string. After many months of hanging around the stable, I discovered I was actually happier petting and brushing the horses than sitting on top of them.

Although my parents were never wealthy enough to buy me a horse, they did surprise me with many other pets: turtles, hamsters, guinea pigs, chicks, tropical fish, a dog and kittens. I was never without the company of animals, a good thing since as an only child I lacked other companions.

At the age of ten, I was enamored by wildlife and domestic and barnyard friends, and dreamed of someday living in a cottage in a forest surrounded by the creatures I loved. I had no way of knowing that my future husband, who was just twelve years old, was busy playing with his own entourage of animals on his parents' farm just fifteen minutes away in a neighboring town. Growing up on a sheep and chicken farm, Eggie (a nickname for "Edgar") was adept at collecting the hens' eggs each morning, watering the dog and doing various other chores around the farm.

Just as my gramma's hands were instrumental in my first experiencing the animal world, Eggie's hands were similarly instrumental, only in a far different way. While my hands surrounded an innocent creature in a nurturing, emotional gesture, his hands labored at an early age to help with the farm work. His "touch" was practical, necessary and deliberate, while mine was more imaginative and interpretive.

Eggie's small hands could go places the bigger adults' hands could not. In particular, his small hands came in handy during the lambing season. Sheep are delicate creatures who often have trouble giving birth. In those days, a sheep farmer did not usually rely on the veterinarian to come to the farm but assisted ewes with difficult births himself. A few times when a mother lamb was having a problem, his parents called little Eggie with his small hands to help extract the unborn lamb.

Twelve-year-old Eggie marched importantly up to the struggling sheep, and with his mother holding the sheep's head and his father directing him at the back end, the young boy reached inside the animal with his small hand and felt for a leg. Under his father's watchful eye, he pulled, searched for another leg, and pulled again. Often Eggie brought a new lamb into the world that would have otherwise died.

Eggie's interest in animals extended to the farm dogs and cats, too. He would sit and play for hours with the cats, and his constant companion was his dog, Queenie, a German shepherd mix. Edgar had been born the year after his parents took in Queenie, and she lived for twelve and a half years. The two grew up together and shared many explorations to remote sites on the Balliet farm, including a rocky outcropping called Big Rock. There, the boy and his dog often sat looking over the Lehigh Valley, watching the trains run alongside the river, hearing the sounds of nature in the woods surrounding Big Rock, enjoying the solitude and each other's companionship.

At ten and twelve, so close and yet so far, we both were immersed in our animal friends. It was no one's guess that eventually we two would meet, marry and devote our entire lives to the well-being of animals in eastern and northeastern Pennsylvania.

2

An Interest
in Animals

As a teenager, I relinquished my dream of owning a horse while I lived with my parents. They felt it was too much responsibility, and couldn't afford one anyway. But I continued to talk to the caterpillars and other insects in the garden, cuddled my cats, accumulated scores of horse books for my library and found other teenage diversions.

My weekly trips to Melody Ranch dwindled to a few times a year, as I became more involved in activities at my high school, particularly being a majorette and hanging out with my girlfriends. I concentrated on schoolwork and existed for the next school dance where I assessed my chances with the football heartthrob.

Though I strayed, for a while, from the path of nature and skipped happily down the road of teenage fun and materialism, I still held, deep down, a love for animals which never faltered.

Unbeknownst to me, Eggie's life had also taken a turn away from animals as well. High school found him interested in wrestling. Though he still did farming chores at home and plowed fields for his father, he was amassing an excellent scholastic record for attending Penn State like many good college-bound boys in Pennsylvania. There he planned to major in very tiny animals—microbial critters. His interest in animals dwindled in his high school years, too, yet he had developed a keen enjoyment of the life sciences, of which animals are a part.

Like many teens, our relationship began with a chance meeting and a youthful attraction between a boy, this one eighteen, and a girl, in my case, sixteen.

Because of our mutual love of nature we got along like two peas in a pod. In summer when he was home from college, we spent time together at the Trexler Game Preserve and in my backyard just sitting and petting the cats. We also took long walks out to Big Rock with his family's German shepherd, Brandy. When we went to the Allentown Fair, we avoided the midway in favor of the animal exhibits where I talked, in Gramma Eckensberger fashion, to the roosters and rabbits in their cages. Edgar was never into talking to animals as I was, but he liked them, too. He tolerated my stopping at each animal to "schmooze" as it stood among its blue ribbons. He even stood patiently beside me as I watched the antics of the pigs.

What had begun as a boy-girl attraction soon ripened into an appreciation of each other's honesty and love for all creatures.

During those college years, our mutual interest caused us to enjoy other worlds far removed from civilization, from the malls, the movie theaters, the local teen hangouts. On our dates we gravitated instead to places like the Pocono Mountains, a forested honeymoon resort area, to enjoy the tapestry of autumn as it turned the surroundings into a patchwork of crimson, gold and tangerine. We often hiked the Appalachian Trail and the Hawk Mountain sanctuary, holding hands at the cliff's edge while black hawks soared the warm air currents.

We cruised through Lancaster County in our well-worn convertible, meeting Amish families going to market in their horse-drawn buggies. We stopped at flea markets along the road and listened to the chanting auctioneer taking bids on an antique chair or bottle. Homemade Pennsylvania Dutch wet-bottom shoefly pie and bags of homegrown peaches drew us to roadside stands where we sampled the sweet fruit before purchasing our own. As we sailed down the country roads, young and carefree, we were content with each other's company and satisfied with life.

One day, we decided to take a short drive to visit an animal tourist attraction in the Pocono Mountains. Along the roads flanked by forests we saw small summer cottages nestled along glacial lakes and came on all sorts of attractions: House of Miniature Dolls, candle and basket shops, Lake Wallenpaupak, Mount Pocono ski area, and many lakes, natural and man-made. Signs for antiques appeared everywhere, and billboards appealed to horseback riders, connoisseurs of fine food, fishermen and boaters—all enticing them to the area. We passed Mount Airy Lodge, a giant resort designed for honeymooners, boasting ski facilities, a lake for swimming and boating, tennis courts, racquetball courts and honeymoon suites with bathtubs big enough for two.

"Look, Edgar." I pointed to a Cape Cod house with brown scalloped valences and shutters. "There's Annie's Fudge House. Let's stop and get some."

In a few minutes we were feasting on some of the richest, sweetest, creamiest chocolate fudge I had ever tasted. From here, refueled with Annie's delicacy, we drove in search of the Pocono Wild Animal Farm.

From the main highway, we turned down a side road shadowed by pine and ash trees. On a large billboard, a zebra, wide-eyed and smiling, pointed its hoof at us mimicking the pointing Uncle Sam: "We Want You... To Visit the Pocono Wild Animal Farm. Entrance to Park Directly Ahead 500 feet."

"Well, here we go," Edgar said, pulling into a parking space. "It doesn't look very crowded today. Only a few cars here."

"Good," I said, climbing out. "We'll have the animals all to ourselves." I stretched, inhaling the good mountain air.

We bought our tickets, and when we came into the zoo area, were immediately greeted by a horde of pet goats and sheep whose wool hung in great pendulous chunks.

"Hey, hey, watch it," I scolded a brazen sheep sucking on the end of my wind breaker. "I don't have any crackers yet; keep your wool on."

Purchasing crackers at a little wood-shingled shack and turning around, I bumped right into a black, pointy-nosed alpaca, a South American relative of the llama. His flared nostrils pumped in and out— a detective sniffing out evidence—and he ran his muzzle over my jacket in search of the hidden crackers. Clutching the juicy morsels to my chest, I tiptoed away, crackers cupped between both hands. Within minutes another throng of strong, lusty fellows were ravaging my coat for goodies.

Edgar and I walked away with a faithful congregation trotting behind. In a while we began handing out bits of biscuits to the insistent beggars.

"Isn't this one cute?" I said, pointing at an approaching goat. As he munched the tidbit, dribbling crumbs, I scratched his wiry head, and he pointed his muzzle skyward, stretching his lips into a thin, contented smile. "Look, he likes me," I said. "This was a great idea, coming up here. I love these guys. They're so friendly."

"Yes, I guess so," Edgar said, offering a piece of cracker to a sheep poking him in the legs.

"What's going on over there?" I said, as a group of people galloped down the hill past the rhino pen.

"I don't know."

The men and women, running in panic, hurriedly dragged their kids through the in-gate. Then more people hurried past us, yelling a warning, "Hurry up! Get out!" One woman even pole-vaulted into a concession stand.

We stood there wondering what could be wrong and strained to see over the hill where the ruckus started. Soon, a small gray donkey came twirling over the hill like a miniature tornado, his hoofs flying about his head, his feet slicing the air. In a blind fury the animal scooted sideways then *WHOOSH!*—his back feet bit the air as he warned the unwary with brays and wild grunts.

"Here he comes! Run!" Edgar yelled as the enraged burro came pell-mell towards us. "Hurry the tree!" Edgar yanked me clear, and the donkey stormed past, searching for a more likely target. Then he disappeared over the next hill wreaking havoc amidst another group of people. "Wow," I said, slinking from behind the tree. "What's wrong with him? These animals are supposed to be tame."

Edgar dusted off his jacket. "I don't know, but he sure was mad; maybe somebody was teasing him."

Gradually, people came out of hiding from the parking lot and from behind trash cans and raccoon cages.

Resuming our tour of the zoo, we visited an emu, a cousin to the ostrich. He grunted and bellowed, blinking long eyelashes. His long neck went up and down like a submarine periscope, his eyes shifting back and forth for a cracker, which he broke apart with one clamp of his beak.

Then we moved on to an anteater trundling busily around its

earthen floor pen, sliding and poking its tubular elastic nose across the ground and into rocky crevasses in search of tasty morsels. Many old pieces of cracker lay in the dirt—obviously he'd rather suck on a big juicy bug instead.

We moved on to visit the rhinoceroses with their chunky cement block heads and eyes which can roll 360 degrees up, down, and around. These beady, glassy orbs rotate on end like the glossy tip of a roll-on deodorant. The rhino's petite mouth, set firmly between fleshy jowls, does not seem to fit such a large, cumbersome beast. When it chews, its lips munch daintily, deliberately, much as a grandma chews a chocolate cream.

As I threw a biscuit, the rhino, noted for its exceptionally poor eyesight, promptly stepped on it, crushing the flaky dough to dust. But he continued to blink at us through his mobile eyes. Could he possibly be remembering his old savannah grasslands where he used to romp, play and chew grass between sojourns to the river's edge? I wondered.

Enjoying the cool breeze, we surveyed the expanse of the zoo from a hilltop and watched the animals in their pens carrying on their daily routines of pawing, sniffing, sunbathing and looking out at passersby. Even though these animals weren't in their natural environment, at least they were well taken care of, free from predators and assured a daily meal. Somehow it made me feel better about their captivity.

"It sure is nice here," Edgar remarked, inhaling a welcome draft of air. "So peaceful and so calm, so tranquil. We should do this more often."

"I love it." I smiled and took Edgar's hand, leading him over to a bench under a tree. "Let's just sit here for a while and watch the people and animals."

We sat and talked as we watched families feed and pet the animals. We discussed Edgar's upcoming graduation from Penn State and his pending job with Air Products and Chemicals. We languished in the warm breeze. But it wasn't long before a dark cloud blew over our outing as a disturbance erupted in the big llama pen. A group of raucous army-jacketed kids, years younger than we, were teasing one of the llamas.

"Look at that!" I said, jumping from the bench.

"What's the matter?" Edgar said. He shaded his eyes to see.

"Those damn kids! Can't they let anything alone? They're teasing that poor llama!" I cried.

"How could they be teasing him? The llamas are separated from them by a tall fence," Edgar answered, squinting harder.

"Can't you see? They're tantalizing him with a cracker. First they offer him one, then, when he tries to take it, they snatch it away. I'd be furious, too."

Four boys hooted with laughter as the llama strained for the cracker. As the llama licked the very edge of the treat, the boys plucked it away, the llama's thin lips grasping at air. The kids laughed as, every time, without fail, they pulled it from the llama's reach. Like Sisyphus and the grapes, the llama yearned after the solitary biscuit. But it was no use: the boys had no intentions of giving it up.

"I can't believe anybody can be that nasty," I said, eyes glaring.

Edgar watched, "Yes, I see it now. They are teasing him."

"That poor thing. I'm going down there and give him a cracker," I vowed.

"You'd better watch out," Edgar warned as the kids swaggered away from the llama pen. "He looks mad, and his ears are back. He might spit at you."

"Nah, he won't. I'm going to give him the cracker those miserable kids wouldn't," I asserted, pulling mine from my jacket pocket. I stomped down the hill toward the pen, mumbling about the injustices of life and the cruelty of humans, damning those sorts into the everlasting pit of hell.

"Be careful," Edgar called.

"Don't worry," I yelled.

The llama stood, a pained expression on his muzzle, nose pinned against the fence, staring after the boys who had sauntered off with his cracker.

With only the best intentions, I approached that llama, extending my own meager cracker in friendship. "Here, Baby; here's a cracker for you," I cooed. But he had just been dealt a dirty deal and saw me as another human who was again going to whisk away a desired morsel at a moment's notice. "You can have this cracker, Baby," I coaxed. With that, he slapped his ears against his head, backed up two steps, eyes becoming slits, and spat full force all over me.

It took about five seconds until I realized what had happened. Then came the smell. A sickening stench of regurgitation enveloped me, a foul smell of sour, curdled milk and fermented food.

"AA-A-A-AR-CK!" I yelped, jumping from the pen and throwing my hands into the air. Glancing at my jacket, I saw pieces of half-digested food clinging here and there in blobs and splotches, releasing the grossest smell of putrefaction ever.

Then I discovered that the particles had hit me right in the face, for my left cheek felt warm and sticky. Gooey pieces of stomach contents hung in my hair, and I stared, cross-eyed, at something green clinging to my nose. The air around me reeked, and at any moment I thought I would surely puke.

"Help me!" I cried, arms outstretched, not wanting to touch myself and spread the vomit any further. "Hurry up, get this awful stuff off me!" I looked sideways and saw a saliva strand hanging in my long hair; it steamed with that horrid smell. I moaned, and my insides churned.

Edgar raced over to me and with assorted tissues and handkerchiefs he dabbed futilely, hardly able to stifle his amusement as giggles popped from his tight cheeks.

"Hurry up! Get it off! Get something to wipe me off. It's not funny! It's in my hair and everything!" I cringed, nauseated, my hands in the air. To no avail did he, between wails of laughter, weakly pick the particles from my hair and jacket. I was hopelessly jailed in a cocoon of llama barf, and I could only stand stick-still with my arms out to my sides.

"Hurry up, PLEASE," I begged. "Get it off me." I cringed in my scarecrow stance. With a Kleenex Edgar slid the gross chunks down and out of my hair.

"I am hurrying." Edgar hiccuped, trying to contain himself. "Phew! Do you stink! What a rose! And I have to drive all the way back home with you."

"You're all heart," I said. "Just remember that someday I may want to repay the favor." And as my loyal boyfriend, I reminded him, his allegiance to me should even cover the times when wild animals urp all over me.

Our day of abandon had come to an abrupt halt. As we began to drive home, my jacket had the whole trunk to itself, but I could not escape the odor that had settled in my hair. We drove at top speed with the windows and vents wide open. It wasn't until many years later that I could laugh at the fiasco I'd experienced at the Pocono Wild Animal Farm.

3

A Day to Remember

We dated each other exclusively for the next four years—through Edgar's graduation from Penn State and my own graduation from Muhlenberg College. His career interests led him into oral microbiology and a job as a senior research technician in the life sciences division of Air Products and Chemicals. My interests took a literary turn during college, and I graduated with a degree in English and a desire to land a teaching job somewhere in the Lehigh Valley.

At one point, the subject of marriage was mentioned. I delivered an ultimatum: "Yes, I would love to marry you, but you must promise to buy me a horse."

Edgar assumed a Shakespearean pose and sang, "Of course, of course. My bride shall have a horse."

I was high—high on the possibility of owning a horse and simply ecstatic with the idea of living with Edgar who was cute and kind and who cared about animals as much as I did.

In a simple ceremony we married in the chapel at Muhlenberg College. Then we set up home in a trailer park in the country outside the town of Bath.

We had so little money that the most economic abode was a mobile home. What an odd structure to live in—a rectangular crate twelve feet wide by sixty feet long. We often felt much like a pair of mice rattling around in a schoolboy's shoebox. Anyone who has never lived in a mobile home certainly has missed a memorable experience. In wintertime when the ground was frozen, the home shifted with the earth, throwing all the inside doors askew so that they couldn't be shut. During a windstorm the sheet metal roof clattered and shuddered like a percussion instrument. On nights like these we seemed stranded in a tremendous thunderstorm as the metal boomed and clashed to the wind gusts. Summertime would cause other problems for us in our "box," as it turned into the ideal sauna— a tropical paradise fit for a couple of parrots but hardly habitable for humans. In all honesty, though, it wasn't so bad. There's something to be said for coziness.

We had only lived there a year when I retrieved the letter in our mailbox that would change our lives completely: Edgar's acceptance to veterinary school. We celebrated for days, talked about train schedules to Philadelphia and the best route to the vet school, and began saving money that summer in preparation for the start of his courses in the fall.

Those years in the trailer were the "lean" years beginning in 1976 when Edgar began his veterinary studies at the University of Pennsylvania. Tuition was high, and I worked as an English teacher in my high school alma mater to help make ends meet. Paychecks were too meager and came less often than we needed them. We survived on macaroni and cheese casseroles, spaghetti and hot dogs. Weekends found us at both sets of parents, sponging the only protein we would see for that week. As for recreation, we seldom had any, but we enjoyed even the spare moments in which we held hands watching a sunset or took a walk amid nature. Edgar was studying, catching up on notes and going over lecture materials every free moment. Thinking back over those times, I realize that the free time we so seldom had then, we used more efficiently than we do now. We were young, thrilled by the pursuit of education and opportunity, and although we were poor, we were happy.

Edgar's daily schedule and timetable would have daunted the strongest person, but not Edgar. Today, he will admit to fleeting thoughts of quitting during those four years. I never realized the extent of his discomfort commuting to Philadelphia every day; I took for granted that his stamina and patience were incredible. Every morning at 4:00 A.M. we woke, feeling most times as if we had never gone to sleep. After breakfast, I kissed him goodbye, and he drove twenty minutes to a train station in Bethlehem. For two hours he rode the train to Philadelphia. From the train he rode the subway, and from the subway station, he walked the rest of the way to school.

Once at school he attended classes all day until 5:00 P.M., when he raced to catch the train to take him back home. Every night, he dragged himself through the door of our mobile home around seven or eight o'clock.

Then we wolfed down our dinner. By 9:00, I would finish the dishes, and he would begin his studies for the next day. Looking back on it now, I don't know how we did it for four years. I guess it proves that a person can put up with anything as long as he or she has a cherished goal.

Despite all the hardships and the unforgiving schedule, Edgar experienced many new and exciting things while in veterinary school. Luckily, I was able to share many of them with him.

Perhaps one of the most challenging courses taken by the veterinary students was anatomy. The course plunged him right into the nitty-gritty of body systems and functions. There were no "filler" courses like so many in undergraduate school. Each one would be valuable to the vet student after he or she had set up practice.

On the first day of class, Edgar and the ninety-nine other students began their intensive schooling, frightened and expectant, feeling like recruits on the first day of military basic training. Each one, having dutifully purchased his dissecting kit and anatomy lab book, sat at the lab bench wondering what the professor would talk about when he arrived: A course syllabus? The grading system? Deadlines and test dates?

Indeed, this was a different world from undergraduate or even graduate school. When the professor arrived, adorned in a tweed suit with a matching shirt and tie, he looked dressed more for a day on Wall Street than one in an anatomy lab. At once and with little acknowledgment of the students staring in awe, he led the group to a bleak, concrete-block warehouse and inside it to a large, cool chamber. As the professor opened the door the class saw rows of animal cadavers—horses, ponies, cows, steers—suspended from grappling hooks in the ceiling.

"Split up into groups of four and begin dissecting your animal. You will find all the information in your anatomy book. Be sure you identify all muscles, bones, tendons, nerves, veins and arteries of the circulatory system," rattled the professor in a detached monotone. Then he vanished through the steel doors until the next day.

Panic set in. Alone and abandoned, the students prepared to embark on a tour of the dead animals, hacking away at the bodies while educating themselves as to the locations of the various parts as outlined by their anatomy guidebook. Shocking enough, the eerie corpses dared anyone to make a first slice. Some had their eyes and mouths open, some were bent over, and others obviously had suffered an agonizing death.

According to Edgar, each student, more out of a fear of failing the course than a desire for learning, chose his animal—the pony, cow, pig, or goat that was a sacrifice for knowledge. In about twenty minutes and with books opened to page one, the first-year students had calmed their aversions and with newfound intensity, began to dissect. So began the first day of veterinary school.

For the first three years, a veterinary student suffered every test, academic and otherwise, imaginable—those challenging his or her intelligence, diligence and proficiency in the advanced sciences. Pathology, the study of gross and microscopic tissue, and pharmacology, the study of the interactions and reactions of drugs on the body, were only two of the subjects to be mastered. Courses like biochemistry, clinical microbiology and biostatistics tested the student's ability to grasp minute details and develop mathematical finesse.

However, Edgar learned the most his last year in school. As a senior he specialized in large animal medicine at the University of Pennsylvania's farm and teaching facility, New Bolton Center. An hour's drive from the Delaware border, the center lies amid lush pastureland and fields that lure crimson-suited riders to the foxhunt. White wooden fencing runs from one horse farm to another forming a continuous border between adjacent properties. Mirroring the English countryside, the rolling hills conjure visions of the baying of hunting hounds.

Many consider New Bolton Center one of the top equine and bovine medical facilities in the eastern United States. World-renowned doctors study and conduct research there. It is also a hub for performing specialized surgeries on large animals.

Besides having some of the world's best veterinarians, New Bolton's equipment surpasses most veterinary hospitals. There are two large animal surgeries. One is a concrete pit for cow surgery in which the animal lies on its back in a wooden V-shaped support—the cow resembles stuffing in a taco shell. Next to the bovine surgery lies the equine surgery room where horses are operated on while strapped securely to a tiltable table. All recovery rooms have rubber padding on the floors and walls to prevent injury to the awakening patient.

Another post-operative area, the equine swimming pool, has made New Bolton Center famous. This twelve-foot-deep, twenty-foot-in-diameter concrete pool resembles a fancy spa but is used primarily for an equine exercise and surgical recovery area. Still anesthetized from surgery, a horse is placed into a rubber raft, pulled along a ceiling track, and lowered into the pool. The water cushions and slows the flailing legs of the horse coming out of anesthesia, making it almost impossible for the horse to break or injure a leg. When not used as a recovery area, the pool rehabilitates debilitated or sore racehorses. The spa is considered excellent therapy for developing the heart and lungs, and race horse trainers, themselves in swimming suits, can often be seen leading their steeds down the ramp and into the water.

Peeking in on a horse's leg operation, we were amazed to discover similarities to human surgery. The horse, strapped to the surgery table, was intubated with a breathing tube and hooked up to an oxygen and anesthesia machine. A veterinary technician covered the horse in a green sterile surgery drape after clipping and scrubbing the surgery site. Then a team of surgeons wearing sterile greens, caps, booties and masks discussed the procedures they would follow. An anesthesiologist regulated the animal's breathing as technicians handed the sterile instruments to the head surgeon. Nearby was an x-ray of the leg lit up on a light screen. A surgeon pulled several pieces of shattered bone from the horse's leg. The surgical conversation reminded me of the television show, *Ben Casey*: the talking subdued, the doctors spouting medical jargon.

That day Edgar and I watched the procedure from afar until they started suturing the skin flaps together. We discussed the operation compared to an equally difficult one on a person. The surgical techniques and pre-operative procedures were probably similar. The prepping of the animal would require more time and work to make unclean animal hide almost sterile. The doctors observed all the conventions of sterility; an anesthesiologist was present, as well. This operation was accomplished with the same degree of cleanliness, precision and expertise as any performed on a human being. Yet, how different the costs would be. I bite my tongue when clients, who don't realize how similar animal surgery is to surgery on people, moan about the high cost of their pet's operation. The cost is comparatively reasonable—in fact, inexpensive—to help an honest, dear friend.

For the fourth year veterinary student, New Bolton Center had many conveniences, including student living quarters, a cafeteria and a modern library. The vine-covered Allam House built in the 1800s entertained lecturing VIPs and other visitors. Edgar and I rented a room there for the weekend of the senior ball as a treat after all our frugality of the past years. Nestled in a grove of pine trees, this great stone Tudor manor house recalls images of Renaissance England. It boasts two kitchens, one winter and one summer, neither capable of being used, but quaint just the same. The castle-like, winding staircases end before great arched doorways to the bedrooms. Our upstairs bedroom, furnished at the time with a Victorian canopied bed and two nightstands, overlooks the croquet-crisp lawn through cut-glass windows. Certainly this room was suited for royalty.

Feeling like members of the aristocracy, we followed the winding stone path back to the Allam House at two o'clock in the morning after the Senior Veterinary Ball. Feeling romantic, we unlocked the massive Tudor door and floated, as in a dream, up to our bedroom suite of a medieval time and place, my white gown trailing in the narrow stairway. It was fitting that knights and damsels graced our dreams there in our canopied bed.

Every year, New Bolton conducted an open house. As a public service, the students and faculty demonstrated the various new medical techniques and services of the university. Exhibits such as a simulated equine surgery, the heart room, a slide show of internal parasites and the equine swimming pool captured everyone's attention from young to old.

During his last year, Edgar was asked to display some of his grandfather's old instruments used in his veterinary practice during the early 1900s. Edgar brushed the dust and cobwebs from the two-foot-long molar extractor—which is still used today—the bloodletting knife and the caponizing set.

When a group of Boy Scouts came to our exhibit, Edgar explained that the old-fashioned treatment of a hoof ailment called "founder" was to snap the bloodletting blade against a main neck vein to drain about a gallon of blood from the horse. Letting the blood out relieved the pressure in the foot by relieving the horse's overall blood pressure. The scouts' eyes widened as they imagined the old-time veterinarian as a kind of merciful Dracula. "Since then," Edgar explained, "better methods for treating founder have been discovered."

The caponizing kit I showed had miniature surgical instruments for castrating roosters. This surgery set might have belonged to a doctor of Lilliput, so tiny were the instruments. A mother of four thought it quite amusing that a rooster could be castrated underneath its wing. Today the practice is done chemically.

During the open house of 1979, we had the unfortunate luck of having our display stationed next to a particularly odoriferous exhibit. Adjacent to our exhibit was a fistulated cow, the biggest attraction of the whole exhibition.

A fistulated cow has a hole about the size of a cantaloupe surgically cut into its side and through its stomach. Unbelievable as it seems, a plastic screw cap covers the hole and can be unscrewed at any time so that one can peer directly into the sloshing contents of the cow's stomach. The sole purpose of such a phenomenon is experimental. Scientists interested in testing different enzymatic activities of the stomach contents simply place certain chemicals through the fistula or capped hole. Then, after a period of time, they reach into the hole with a dipper and extract the stomach's contents for analysis.

Since this exhibit bordered ours, every time the strange cap was unscrewed to show the visitors, a smelly cloud of fermenting grass and gastric juices permeated the atmosphere, fuming over our display. Fortunately, we grew accustomed to the rank odor after a few minutes, but other people stepping in line for our display immediately sniffed the air, groaned wide-eyed with disgust and curiosity, and lunged right past our comparatively dull exhibit to see "What the hell stinks!"

The Boy Scouts were the most amusing. Approaching our layout, they suddenly became blind to us and, at once grimacing and holding their noses, ran yelling in the direction of the fistulated cow. When Edgar showed them the gaping hole in the cow, they set up a terrific cacophony, "We're gonna faint or get sick in a second." Some fled, wailing, from the room, hands cupping their mouths.

One brave scout, pinching his nose, peeked deep inside the hole, asking the demonstrator in a nasal voice, "Ith it alive?"

"Of course she's alive," the vet student said. "Don't you see her eating and making manure?"

"Yeah,…yech!" and out he ran.

But the highlight of the fistulated cow exhibit was an offer to put a hand inside the cavernous hole to feel the stomach lining and its contents. At this suggestion the entire scout troop recoiled, noses pinched, honking like a flock of disgruntled geese. Then the heckling started.

"Go ahead, you do it. You're not chicken," elbowed one youngster to another.

"Oh, no, I'm not gonna. You do it," squawked the other, falling back into the crowd.

"No way; I'm not dumb," said another.

"I'll do it," one boy sacrificed. The others pushed him to the front. Through the dead silence he sidled up to the cow. One would have thought he was going to the gallows.

"Okay, now we're going to put this plastic sleeve on your arm so you won't get messy," said Frank, the vet student, as he slipped the long rectal sleeve over the boy's arm. A groan rose up from the crowd of Boy Scouts. "Don't hold your nose," Frank admonished. "It's not that bad."

"Yeth, it ith; I can't thtand it. I mutht hold my dose," the boy said.

"What's your name? Her name is Fanny the Fistulated Cow," I offered.

"Randy," he said.

"Okay, Randy, now I want you to put your whole hand in there and feel the lining of the cow's stomach," Frank insisted.

Randy, with a grimace, stood on tiptoe and, arching his body as far away from the cow as he could get, inserted the sleeved arm inside the hole while his other hand clung to the tip of his nose. A smile erupted on his face as he felt inside. He marveled, "I feel it; it'th bumpy and thlimey." Fanny continued to eat and chew her cud with apathy.

"All right now, feel the bottom of it, and feel how it churns around this sea of grass."

Randy the lion-hearted dove his arm down into the cow's stomach until he was up to his shoulder in watery seaweed. He swished his arm around, feeling all over the inside.

"I feel a hole downd thith way," Randy said goggle-eyed. If he went down any farther, he'd have his ear in the soup. The rest of the Boy Scouts gravitated inch by inch around Randy and his cow, making a semicircle around Fanny.

"Yes, that's a passage from one compartment to another." A few groans rose up. "You see, the cow's stomach can hold approximately ten to twenty gallons of food. It has four compartments, and the food flows from one compartment to another, each one performing a very special function on the food," explained Frank.

"Wow, it feelth neat," bragged Randy as his arm swirled like an agitator in a washing machine.

Soon, many brave scouts, not willing to be outdone by one of their own, volunteered to "help" feel the cow's insides. From time to time, Fanny, chewing her cud, threw a glance at these little people gone crazy touching her innards.

And so ended New Bolton's open house, providing all with a different diversion from Saturday afternoon football games and horror movies. And certainly for all the Boy Scouts who were able to explore the depths of Fanny's stomach, it was a day to remember.

4

"My Bride Shall Have a Horse"

Edgar remembered. He scrimped and saved until he finally accumulated the $200 that bought my first horse, the one I'd dreamed of since childhood. His name was Nicholas. Edgar was just finishing veterinary school and we were still living in the trailer, so I had to board Nicholas at a dairy farm until we got our own place. It wasn't an ideal situation for Nicky who probably would have preferred equine company. But he did have a good home with good, green alfalfa for every meal and lots of corn cobs for snacks. One good thing was that he seemed to develop a calm and unflappable personality.

Later that year, we bought a mare named Merry so that we each had a horse to ride. Admittedly, we probably should have spent the money on more practical things, but our love of horses took precedence. "It won't be long," I told Edgar, "before we have our own home and barn, so it makes sense."

"Horse sense," Edgar joked.

Since we now had two horses, we asked Edgar's father if we could keep the horses at his farm.

With reservations, Edgar's father allowed our mare and gelding to stay in an old tractor shed. I say "with reservations" because Edgar's father did not care at all for horses, preferring sheep instead.

The reason for this intense dislike of horses was logical. Raised on a Dutch farm where an animal's worth was usually determined by the food it provided or the work it accomplished, Edgar's father came to the opinion of most Dutch farmers: any animal kept for pleasure or recreation not only was a waste of money but a downright sin. A Pennsylvania Dutch farmer would never own a horse for fun or as a companion, he said, because "Ef ya can't eat 'em or wear their fur, ya shouldn't have 'em." Horses for pleasure riding were our only frivolity—but one that grated on Edgar's father.

One day, while we talked with his parents around the kitchen table, Edgar's father, looking out toward the pasture, muttered in an almost inaudible voice, "Those horses irritate the hell out of me." Then he got up and stomped away. Throughout our horses' short stay at the farm, we tolerated complaints of those "miserable eating machines" chewing his pasture down to a nubbin. He especially objected to Merry who was pregnant and a nagging reminder of a two-horse squad soon to be three. He had visions of his sheep farm being ravaged and torn up by a frantic herd of high-spirited horses.

It was me who had made matters worse for my father-in-law when I indulged another favorite childhood dream and bred Merry. Now she was showing all the signs of an impending birth. At a head-on glance she stood in the pasture, long face melting into wiry legs. But on either side of her body hung two giant pouches where lay her growing foal. She resembled a Mexican mule with two huge watermelons slung over her back. Her disposition changed, too, as her burden became greater day by day. She clomped around the pasture searching for someone to pout at and threatened Nicholas with a kick if he passed too close by. Hot and uncomfortable, she rolled and swayed around the fields as though the very air annoyed her.

My father-in-law, too, seemed as irritable as she, for every time he saw the mare, he would not see one useless animal but two. It was almost unbearable. "What the hell do you want with another horse?" he demanded. "It's just more money down the drain, and you already need all the money you can get." Then he would trudge away while we hung our heads, as he expected we should.

During the next few mornings when I came to feed her, I was disappointed to find Merry sulking alone in the pasture, still pregnant and still irritable. The bun still wasn't quite baked—the time for the foal to be born had not yet arrived.

Then, late one night, the phone rang in our trailer. My head shot off the pillow, and I bolted upright in bed, trying to focus. Edgar sprang from under the covers like a discharged cannonball. He snatched the receiver.

"Edgar, this is Mom! You've got to come over quick! Merry's having trouble!" Her words, upset and distant, were almost indecipherable. "It's a beach!" she seemed to say. And she hung up.

Hearing her, Edgar immediately understood trouble was at hand. "My God! Hurry up!" he shouted. "Merry's having trouble. I think Mom was trying to say it's a breech birth."

Jumping out of bed, I snatched at the nearest clothing. I hopped around the room pulling on pants and searching for a top, thinking, *What if the foal dies before we get there? What if Merry dies? What if they both die?*

Edgar and I clambered into the truck and raced for the Balliet farm. As we rushed through the humid night, we considered all that could have gone wrong with the birth and all that could be done once we got there. I blamed bad luck and scolded myself for not sleeping overnight in the pasture with Merry. I felt guilty for having wanted to breed Merry, who was pushing fifteen years and hadn't had a foal in ages.

"Why did I take a chance on breeding her?" I moaned. "I should've known she'd have problems." The truck shuddered as it sped down the road, and stones flew as we slipped onto the shoulder.

"It's not your fault. A foal born in the wrong position can happen to a young mare as well as an older one," Edgar reasoned. "I just wish we could've been there when she was having problems. I just hope we aren't too late to save them both," he said, as he gripped the wheel and pressed harder on the accelerator.

Silence and worry followed us like ghosts. The fifteen-minute ride seemed, instead, an hour's race to the finish line, a losing battle with time. We passed Derhammer's farm where all the lights were out in the house, and we zoomed past the goat farmer, Mrs. Schell; there, too, the homestead was asleep.

At last we plummeted down the Balliet driveway, my hands poised on the door handle to leap out.

It was 1:30 A.M. on a night devoid of a moon to light the way. Blindly, we groped beneath the hooded sky. On top of the darkness, the terrain of the pasture—two hills that sloped toward each other and met in a valley below—didn't make it easy to find the mare. We ran to the pasture's edge, trying to make out a silhouette of a horse. My mind visualized Merry out there, somewhere, lying flat out on her side. Finally, we heard a high-pitched whinny—frantic and panicky. It was our mare.

Merry's cries punctuated the quiet night like fireworks, and I was further disheartened by her terror-stricken voice. "Hurry, Edgar," I whispered. A few minutes later we heard another voice, a human one: Edgar's father was yelling from the direction of the creek in the valley below. "It's all right. I have the foal, and it's okay. Quick! Come down here, and help me get it up the hill."

"My God," I said, clutching my chest, "It's okay. But why is Merry still screaming? What's wrong with her?"

"I don't know. Follow me and watch your step so you don't slip on one of these loose stones," Edgar cried, plunging toward the valley floor.

Running to the creek's edge, we saw a flashlight signaling. We raced toward the light and found the two—our newborn foal on shaky legs and the hero, Edgar's father, who embraced the foal with both arms.

Then we saw Merry up on the hill above us. She was squealing and whinnying because she couldn't get to her baby. We helped the foal up the steep hill and toward the shed where Merry came running to meet us.

Edgar lifted the baby into the stable where the floor was thick with good-smelling straw. In the light we examined and caressed our new furry wet gift while Merry nudged it protectively. Edgar, checking the sex, announced we had a baby girl, a filly, and we decided to call her Fancy, for indeed she was.

She stood on skinny, shaky legs, less than an hour old. Her body was thin but healthy looking, and she sported a shiny fur coat. But this young, freshly-made equine model looked, at the same time, old, for around her thin pink muzzle had grown long whiskers that resembled a grizzled old man. These hairs would help her feel for her mother's udder when she was ready to nurse.

Her eyes, big and set too wide apart for the size of her small head, glinted a kind of crystal translucent brown. She glanced curiously from her mother to the sides of the stalls, to the straw bedding, and to the three of us. She looked perplexed, and it was no wonder, for only moments ago she had been inside her mother's womb in darkness. Now she searched, inquired, and marveled at this new world, and we three, enthralled with this newborn's wonder at a world into which she was so rudely thrust, could merely watch in silence and awe.

She seemed as fragile as a china doll, as though she would crack if she fell against something. Even her fur had pale highlights to it, resembling the color of bisque. We knew, of course, that within a few months she would shed that coat for a new, more fashionable color, possibly bay like her mother or a rich mahogany brown like her father.

Edgar gave her and her mother a quick physical examination, and seeing that everybody was healthy, we left Merry and her foal to become acquainted with each other. Merry nickered, and Fancy tiptoed toward her on spindly legs.

I remarked, "Why do you suppose the foal should be so wet? The mother's fluids should've dried by now. And it doesn't feel like that slimy wetness of a newborn animal. I wonder why that is?"

"I know well why," interrupted my father-in-law with a smirk. "This whole night has been quite an experience..."

And for the first time I noticed what he was wearing. There he stood in a short, olive-green, terry cloth housecoat. His bony, sparsely-haired knees peeked out from under the garment, and in the stable light the veins in his legs glared blue with the cold. To complement his outfit, he wore a pair of corduroy, olive green bedroom slippers on his feet. They had soaked up water and mud blobs from the pasture, and straw was stuck all over them. Giggling, we pointed at his mucked-up booties.

Edgar's father laughed, "Yeah, yeah, go ahead and laugh at me. But remember I saved that cute little furry thing from certain death."

Edgar said, "What do you mean: 'saved her from death?' She looks fine to me."

"Ha! She's lucky, that's all. About one-fifteen I heard this whinnying in the pasture. I figured Merry was foaling so I woke Mom to call you. Then I took the flashlight, ran out to the pasture, and there was Merry on top of the steepest hill—about fifty feet up. She was running back and forth, looking down at the creek and snorting like crazy. I flashed the light around everywhere and couldn't find anything. Then, after walking around the pasture, I finally found her foal lying in the creek. The water was rushing all around her, and at first I thought she was dead." He paused to catch his breath. "So, I waded in to pull her out. Jean was still in the house and called me from out the upstairs bedroom window to see if everything was all right. I yelled that it was 'in the creek!'"

Then Edgar interrupted, "But when Mom called us, she said, 'It's breech!' We were really worried."

"Oh, no!" I laughed. "Bre-ee-eee-eech! Cree-ee-eee-eek!" I sounded out the words. "She must've thought your dad said 'breech.'"

"Yes, probably," Edgar's dad agreed. "Anyway, I quickly hoisted the foal out of the creek. She was still alive, but she was shivering and seemed really weak. Meanwhile Merry was calling to her baby from the top of the hill because she couldn't get down to her. In fact, she was so upset that I was afraid she'd come flying down the hill and land on top of me. Well, then I had a hell of a time dragging the foal out of the creek. Both of us were in the water and were muddy, and I kept slipping on the stones. What a mess! I finally got her out of the creek when you guys drove up."

"So Merry gave birth on top of the hill, and somehow the foal fell down and into the creek?" I shuddered.

"That's right, and that's a good fifty to sixty-foot drop at about a seventy degree angle," said Edgar. "Probably when the baby stood up, she fell and rolled right down the hill and into the creek. If you hadn't heard Merry, Fancy either would have drowned or her body temperature would've dropped in that cold water," Edgar determined. "She really could have died."

"I think so," said his father. "She was pretty weak when I pulled her from the creek."

How ironic that the man who had never cared for horses had saved our foal's life, and, that despite his lack of affinity for them, he had dashed from his snug bed into an icy-cold creek to save a horse and ruin his favorite slippers.

Shaking my head, I awakened from my trance to the sound of Fancy sucking her mother's milk and smiled. Then I turned to see my father-in-law also watching them with a smile on his face.

5

Edgar's
First Case

We kept our three horses at the Balliet farm for six more months until Edgar graduated from veterinary school. With that feat accomplished, he was instantly hired by a multi-vet practice in the area. Edgar would be their new large animal practitioner. I was still teaching school, so adding our two incomes together, we decided the time was right to build a house and barn in the woods adjacent to his parents' farm.

As a child I had always dreamt of living in a cottage in the woods, like Red Riding Hood's gramma minus the wolf. Of course Edgar's and my funds were limited but had they not been, we still didn't want a house that was intrusive or showy or a blight on the landscape. So, a cottage is exactly what we built—small and seeming to grow naturally out of the land around it. With its natural wood siding it sits harmoniously amongst the trees and boulders.

After about a month of learning the intricacies of the multi-vet practice, Edgar was to begin doing calls on his own. He anxiously awaited his first phone call.

Both anticipation and dread cloud the veterinarian's first case. Ideally, the first medical attendance would happen with the doctor marching right up to the animal patient, lifting an eyelid and diagnosing a rare but easily curable affliction. The owner, deeply and visibly appreciative, would then thank the good doctor and pay him in cash.

Afterward, in our idealized case, the owner's wife would rustle up some of her famous blueberry pie, which the rookie vet would then accept humbly beaming. Thereafter, the young vet would proceed with his rounds, confounding all with his diagnoses and cures of the animals he would treat—his successful future guaranteed.

Edgar's first case was not quite so ideal.

Early that Monday morning, the phone rang. I quickly answered, eager to be a part of it all. A hurried, breathless voice panted, "Is this the veterinarian's office? This is Mrs. Haus. I need help immediately. One of my cows is down in the creek. Something's terribly wrong; she won't get up—she's flat on her back. She just lies there groaning. She's going to die if somebody doesn't help her soon." Mrs. Haus's breathing sounded harsh and strained.

"All right, Mrs. Haus. Dr. Balliet and I will be out immediately. And keep calm; everything will be okay."

Toward the beckoning finger of the future, Edgar and I, our truck heavy with medical equipment, sped down the highway. Edgar's thoughts were transparent as we drove in silence down the road. The air was heavy, thick enough to cut. I could read his mind. He was thinking, *What could have happened to the cow in the creek? Could it be bloat? A calcium deficiency? A broken leg? A neurological incident?* Reviewing everything he knew about downer cows and treatment of hypothermia due to extreme cold, he gripped the steering wheel tighter. This would be the ultimate test—far harder than the examinations and oral grilling he had worried about while in vet school. This was real-life stuff; he had to save an animal, and there was no one to help him or bail him out of a muffed diagnosis. I watched his serious face. He was no doubt thinking, *What if I forget everything I learned over four years of vet school? What if I completely blank out?*

Edgar turned the steering wheel, and there were sweat marks where his hands had been. Now I began to worry. *What if he has no idea what is wrong with the cow? Should he fake it? What if there is nothing he can do, and he'll have to let the cow die a slow, painful death in the creek?*

Yes, even I had my doubts. No one should misunderstand: I love my husband and respect his intelligence, but I also know his imperfections and, on that day, I understood the weight of the situation.

I worried myself into imagining a grim picture: a lone woman was keeping a silent vigil by a cow prostrate at the stream's edge. The sobbing figure clutched her ragged, scraggly yellow hanky, patting and consoling the dying animal in the suffocating mist. As the long night began to break, the cow, in one long, thick, pitiful cry, heaved up her soul, and the woman, burying her face into the great furry hide, sobbed racking, heart-wrenching sobs for having relied on an inexperienced, rookie veterinarian.

I shook the evil picture from my head, and for the rest of the trip blared the radio to drown our worries.

Edgar wheeled onto the stone driveway as a distraught Mrs. Haus, in soiled work clothes and black, knee-high rubber boots, ran from her house. She pointed to the brown spot a quarter mile away down in the pasture. "Hurry! Hurry!" she pleaded.

Edgar opened the back of the Bowie unit—a truck body designed especially to house large animal tools, equipment and medicine. All was neatly and systematically arranged: the mark of a well-intentioned, well-organized, beginning, nerdy veterinarian. We had spent hours cleaning and polishing the used unit. It brimmed antiseptically with concoctions of drugs and salves and the rather barbaric-looking tools of the trade. In a large drawer, the steel hoof testers hung on a hook while yards of rubber hose used for drenching horses with mineral oil and others for administering enemas were coiled. There was also a mouth speculum for prying open a horse's jaw for dental work.

In another drawer, rolls of Vetwrap and other bandaging items such as cotton and adhesive tape were stored neatly along with a stainless steel bowl and cotton swabs for cleaning and wrapping wounds. A few stainless steel buckets sat in the drawer, serving as a temporary storage area for his brand new coveralls. On the far side of the Bowie unit was an array of smaller, shallower trays that held every bottle of injectable medicine—from antibiotics to steroids to hormones—known to veterinary medicine. Here, too, were rows upon rows of eye medicines, pills of every assortment and bute paste (animal aspirin in paste form). A refrigerator drawer held vaccines in disposable syringes packaged in cellophane and ready to administer. Another drawer held the deworming pastes used to eliminate ascarids, pinworms, strongyles and tape worms.

Finally, from the neatly packed Bowie unit, Edgar pulled out the drawer containing his bovine treatments. He reached for glucose, potassium and calcium. He also took out an electric cow prod that would come in handy to jolt the cow into standing, if it could. Ten minutes later, lugging buckets, tubes and trays of calcium and glucose, we trudged after Mrs. Haus into the marshy pasture.

Mrs. Haus squatted by the stream's edge, brow crinkled and muttering to her cow. From a distance the cow had resembled a brownish-gray boulder, a solitary island in a shallow, rushing stream. As we neared, the swampy pasture clawing at our boots, the tools and medical supplies weighing us down into the quicksand-like mud, Edgar and I saw the victim, wedged on her back between two large rocks. She lay motionless between the boulders, and her head was dipped back into the trickling water with her feet pointing skyward as if she were admiring the blue expanse overhead. The picture was surreal and unsettling. Here was a large animal made so vulnerable—her neck stretched out eerily, her body prostrate, her belly exposed to the sky.

"My God, Betsy's much worse than when I left her fifteen minutes ago. Oh, look at her poor little face," the woman cried, sniffing back tears. Indeed, Betsy presented a frightful countenance, her large eyes rolling toward her owner. "She looks so frightened, and I feel so sorry for her. I've been with her, bringing her something to eat, but she's too scared and weak to even eat carrots."

"Don't get yourself so upset now, Mrs. Haus," Edgar persuaded, stalling for time. He patted Betsy on the flank. "I'll do everything I know to get her up again."

"Oh, if she dies, I don't know what I'll do. She's been a good cow, and she's more of a pet to the family and me. You simply *must* do something to get her out of this creek. She was the kids' first Four-H project. She won second place at the Kutztown Fair." Mrs. Haus began to bawl in earnest.

My heart went out to my husband as I scrutinized him. *Why an emergency for his first case? Why couldn't he just be giving flu shots to a couple of docile ponies? The next thing I know, the woman will fall prostrate on the ground, and then for sure we'll be in trouble.*

"Yes, she does look quite poorly, Mrs. Haus, but try not to worry too much. First, we must position her better so that I can do an exam to find out exactly what's wrong," said Edgar, using his newly-attained professional demeanor to calm her as he placed his equipment precariously on the creek bank. Later, he confided that he felt like a jelly-filled donut at the prospect of failing. He needed time to think, to research his lecture notes, to browse with a cup of tea through veterinary journals and textbooks on the "downer cow" syndrome. But, of course that was out of the question. This was the time to put all he'd learned into effect, and hope he'd learned it well.

"Okay," the woman sobbed. "But you must help her—*somehow*! I'll go get some ropes."

Searching in a wooden box, Edgar found a cow halter and another rope. Climbing down the mud bank and into the stream beside the cow, he fitted a halter to Betsy's head and tied a rope around a back leg. After manipulating the rope and pulling Betsy's head over to the correct position, he and I yuxed her (a Pennsylvania Dutch term for jiggling or pushing with vehemence). We finally were able to turn the cow partially onto her left side. We were soaked. Mrs. Haus came running, ropes in hand.

"I still need to move her feet around so that I can examine her rectally," he said, reaching for the ropes. With the woman's and my help on the rope and using a fallen tree branch as a lever, Edgar got the cow's back feet into position. Suddenly the cow shifted, and we heard a terrific CRACK!

"What did you do!" the woman shrieked, her hands cupping her face. Edgar later said the air had gone out of his body. At that instant, Betsy, her eyes and nostrils flaring, opened her mouth wide, showing a large saliva strand stretching across it like a rubber band, and let out a throat-tearing moan.

Edgar stammered, apologizing, "I had to get her legs under her so I could examine her, Mrs. Haus. We really had no other choice."

I bit my lip.

Mrs. Haus glared through tear-brimmed eyes.

Just then Betsy cupped spindly legs under her and with a tremendous heave stood up. She clambered out of the creek and up the mud bank. Her owner ran to the cow's side and hugged her. "Thank God! How do you feel? Are you all right? Oh, Betsy, you poor thing," she wailed.

Edgar and I looked searchingly at each other and also silently addressed the celestial canopy.

Betsy was munching grass as if nothing had happened.

Edgar completed the examination then, by the stream's edge. He found nothing physically wrong with Betsy. But there was a clue that said, *Something is wrong with this picture*. In all the frenzy none of us had noticed the skid mark on the other side of the creek.

"You've gotta be kidding!" Edgar exclaimed, peering at the gouge in the mud.

"What?" I asked sloshing to his side, "what are you looking at?" Mrs. Haus gaped from atop the bank.

"See these skid marks? She must've just wanted a drink, came to the edge here, and slipped down the hill and into the creek. Just follow the track." He pointed.

There lay the evidence: skid marks in the mud. Betsy's feet must've scooted out from under her, sending her over the bank and smack onto her back between the two boulders. There she lay on her back until we came to her rescue. She had simply fallen and gotten stuck.

Then I said in my deepest bovine voice, "Help me. I've fallen, and I can't get up."

Edgar gave me a hand, and the sweat on his forehead began to recede as the tension eased. He patted Betsy on her side, "Good girl.... You'll be okay now."

As Edgar grabbed his various trays, bottles and tubes meant for the challenging case we'd anticipated, he stopped to watch his stiff patient hobble back through the muddy pasture to find the rest of the herd. Alongside him Mrs. Haus marveled, "Just look at her now, Doctor. Why, minutes ago I thought Betsy would be leaving us, but just look at her now. She's almost as good as new. You saved her life." Her eyes sparkled. "If you have some time, I just made a blueberry pie this morning. Could you and your wife stay for a piece?"

Edgar grinned. "Yes, I think we could spare time for some pie," he said. I nodded. Side by side, we and Mrs. Haus trudged up the steep hillside. She was happy because her pet was alive and well. Edgar and I were equally happy because the ice was broken and no one had fallen in: the patient lived; the owner was grateful. What more could a beginning vet and his beaming assistant ask for?

6

Pizza Pie Nevermore

Country life was the center of our universe. Edgar and I believed in its wholesomeness and loved the animals that "peopled" our daily existence. The superficiality of other, more cultivated roads did not attract either of us. So, little did I realize that I would become the pawn in a game of wits vs. stamina. It happened on a day I decided to forego riding my horse, Fancy, so that I could help Edgar with his calls. That afternoon marked the end of a particularly sunny, fresh country day. The car phone jangled, and a voice sounded in the truck, "Retained placenta at Stettler's dairy farm, Doc. Sorry about that—bet you guys thought your day was over."

I was a very active veterinary assistant at this point in Edgar's career. I wanted to be an integral part of his practice and was eager to help restrain horses for injections, ready to assist during piglet castrations and enthusiastic to hand Edgar his tools during large animal surgery. So, this day I looked forward to "curing" something called a "retained placenta." I had no idea what it entailed.

"Can I help with this one, too?" I asked, as Edgar turned the truck. We plunged into a ditch of weeds and milkweed pods and rolled out onto the highway.

With a Mona Lisa smile he said, "You might not want to assist with this call."

"Why not?" I wondered. "What is it?"

"It's exactly what the name says it is—a retained placenta. The placenta never came out of the cow after she gave birth to her calf. It's stuck inside the mother and generates bacteria, eventually becoming toxic. Removing it is not a very pleasant job. Of course, if you really want to help me, you can. I'm just warning you; it doesn't usually smell too great."

We drove for a while before I made up my mind. "What kind of assistant would I be if I can't stand a little odor here and there? You can't have your helper copping out on you just when you need her, right?" I said.

We rode along the blacktop road to Stettler's dairy farm with its 180 milking cows, two prizewinning resident bulls, an army of farm hands and three farm managers. The place was a small industry in itself and supplied local residents not only with milk and their own ice cream but a convenient grocery store and dairy bar.

A meandering, bubbling brook paralleled the road to Stettler's. Beside it, Holstein cows were basking beneath thick-branched willow trees; some were sleeping on their sides, some were knee-deep in the stream. Hundreds of cows dotted the meadow along the creek. Edgar drove through the gate and stopped at the milk parlor.

From the back of the truck Edgar pulled a long, clear plastic hose, a stainless steel pump and a bucket for antiseptic solution. "You sure you want to help me with this one?" he asked, coiling the hose around his shoulder.

"Yep, I'm sure. Give me something to carry," I said. We batted the curtain of flies that hung before the door to the milk parlor and walked inside the barn. There stood our subject, a black and white cow sporting a Rorschach design. A strip of bluish-red tissue hung from her back end. Beside her stood Curtis, one of the farm managers.

Curtis must have weighed 375 pounds or even more. Every inch of his clothes, from his blue-checkered shirt and his bib overalls to his red-striped sneakers bulged at the seams. Even his scalp looked tight.

Standing beside the cow, he patted her flank and whisked away flies with his baseball cap. He had a pillow face with deep-set, button eyes around which folds of skin were pulled taut, like tucks in an Amish quilt. Numerous creases and darts puckered his chin and brow. His face had a kind, grandfatherly look.

"Hey, Curtis, how's it going?" Edgar said as he put the equipment down beside the cow.

"Hi," I said, arranging the bucket of soapy water and rubber tubing side by side. "I'm Edgar's wife, Gay. A bit warm today, isn't it?" The cow swung its tail, and when the bluish-red strip of tissue flopped from side to side, flies erupted from it.

"Yop," the big man agreed, "and the flies are really badt, too." Trails of sweat snaked along the fatty crevices in his face. "Yop, it gets damn hot around this place, wit all the cows and manu-are." With much effort he dug a handkerchief from his pocket and mopped his brow. "But, then, I suppose vinter's chust as badt. Then the fingers don't move so gudt, and we haf a hell of a time keepin' the water tups unfroze."

Edgar rolled up his coverall sleeves and donned rubber knee-high boots. He looked as if he were going small stream fishing. "Curtis, you can take a break today. Gay's going to help me with this retained placenta." I smiled importantly, proud to attend. But there was the strangest glint in Curtis' eye.

"Vy sure, Doc. That's all right. She can take over my chob any-time naw," he laughed, and his belly jiggled like Jabba the Hut. Then he turned and went to the other side of the cow barn where he hitched him self precariously atop a tiny metal railing. He spread his legs over the rail as if settling in front of the television.

"Gay, see this thing here?" Edgar nodded to the bluish-red mass hanging from the cow. "That's our subject—our retained placenta—that's what I have to get out of her." Well, I obviously didn't think that thing belonged there. Flies danced all over it. Edgar inserted his rectal-sleeved arm into the vagina. After much tugging, he detached the rubbery tissue, and it splattered to the floor. That was no big deal, I thought.

"That was no big deal," I said. "Let's go get some ice cream at the dairy barn before we leave."

"Oh, we're not done yet," Edgar said. "Now, Gay, come around here in back of the cow with the antiseptic solution. Hook one end of the hose to the pump and begin pumping when I tell you."

I gathered my materials and shuffled closer, detecting a slightly pungent odor. "What's that smell?" I said suspiciously.

"That's the retained placenta," Edgar said. "I told you it wouldn't smell too great." He swirled his arm up to his shoulder around inside the cow.

"Hey, Curtis." Edgar smiled. "This is a real ripe one. It must've been in her for about a week." He fished his arm around, and Curtis giggled and jiggled from his far metal throne.

Humpf, I thought. Ripe? What did he mean by *ripe*? A sweet, juicy plum or a four-day-old roadkill? I sniffed the air carefully and decided it wasn't a plum.

"Ya, I've been smellin' her for qvite a vhile naw. Thought I'd better call ya when it finally didn't come awt," Curtis yelled. "Course, I would'a called ya sooner, but I vent to the Poconos to go fishing for a coupla days. Ah, I knew this vudt vait, anyhow. And I know you like them well done, how 'bout it, Doc?" He laughed, teetering on his iron perch.

I sniffed the air again, and a heavy gas penetrated my nostrils. My breath caught. "God, it's disgusting! Why does it smell so bad?" I coughed.

"Because it's rotting inside her," Edgar said nonchalantly.

"Of course," I replied, bending over the bucket and pushing the hose end on the pump. This procedure would be a sure test of strength, but I was no shrinking violet.

"No, no, don't stand over there. Come closer; the hose doesn't reach that far. Stand right here by me," Edgar ordered. I moved toward the cow's backside, trailing my bucket of antiseptic solution.

I am not ordinarily squeamish. I would assist in the bloodiest of operations, trip happily through a field of horse manure and am almost never revolted by rectal examinations. But as the week-old placental stench wafted past, I wasn't so sure of myself. I imagined particles of decaying placenta and blood fermenting inside that cow that resembled the fluids and muddy flows inside a volcano. And I could visualize those bubbles bursting quietly inside, throwing off that pungent, rancid odor that was unlike anything I had ever smelled in my life.

"Start pumping, and when I tell you, take the hose off the pump and hold it into the manure trench. Be quick about it cause this stuff will come gushing out as soon as we stop pumping," Edgar instructed. He manipulated the hose.

"What does that do?" I said.

"That siphons all that gook out of her. I get a suction going inside her uterus. Then, when you take the hose off the pump, the fluids drain off. It's the only way to get that bad shit out of her. Now bend down there, hook the hose to the pump, start pumping in the solution, then, when I tell you, direct the hose end down into the muck trench."

I looked down at the loaded manure trench, and suddenly felt that perhaps Curtis would have been better suited for this job. I was ready to make that suggestion when Curtis said, "Yop, I can remember when Dr. Harrington's wife used to help him wit this chob. She was real good at it, too. She really pumped away. Yes, sirree," Curtis squealed, bobbing on the iron pipe.

Now I couldn't refuse, not if Dr. Harrington's wife survived with little difficulty.

"Yop, she did a hell of a chob," Curtis insisted.

With gritted teeth, I began to pump, taking long, deep strokes, pulling the solution up and through the rubber hose. At last, with only a half-inch of water in the bucket, Edgar, holding his end of the hose in the cow, yelled, "Okay, let 'er go!"

With that, I snatched the hose from the pump and directed it into the already loaded manure trench. With terrific force a brownish-gray, heavy fluid burst from the hose, and as I bent over, my face only two feet from the trench, my nostrils snapped shut, recoiling from the hot stink. A kind of strangely sweet, but acid odor filled my nostrils. Never in my life had I smelled anything so putrefying. As if hit by ammonia fumes, I staggered back as still murkier fetid material flopped and flowed from the tube.

"Hold it closer to the trench! You're getting it all over the place!" Edgar shouted as I stood on tiptoe. The fluids splashed everywhere, and solid chunks landed and stuck to the concrete floor.

"I said, hold it in the trench!" he yelled.

Then Curtis began to laugh. I heard a giant roar and glanced at the huge man swinging effortlessly on the metal railing. He sang, "Oh boy! Oh boy! I can smell it all the vay dawn here—all the vay dawn here. That's a good one all right. Yes, sirree! I thought it vudt be gudt and stinky after all the time it vas in dere."

A sickly mist had begun to glaze my eyes. I burped a pint of gas.

Edgar poked me. "Gay. Gay! For Christ's sake, try to get it in the trench!"

I pointed the hose down, but seeing that chocolate-colored fluid with its chunky pieces and hearing them hit the trough and, worst of all, smelling that stench made me break out in a chilly sweat. Unable to stomach any more, I squeezed off my nostrils with my free hand and shut my eyes. Perhaps I could handle the smell without the picture or the picture without the smell; but I knew I couldn't handle both without blowing my entire lunch all over the barn.

Again Curtis boomed, "Yop, Dr. Harrington almost got sick one time doin' one of these chobs. It vas a pretty old one chust like this. He chust had hiss lunch before he came here. He alvays did hate to do these chobs. But vhile he drained the cow's uterus [he pronounced it *yoo-truss*], I thought I'd have some fun vit 'im. I said how that stuff looked chust like the pieces and chunks on a pizza pie." He held his belly. "It does, doesn't it, Mrs. Balliet?"

Sweat broke out on my face as I clung to the tube. My stomach curled itself up into a little ball ready to strike at something, and my jaws clenched tighter as I determined not to let the dam break. I eructed another quart of gas.

"...and how it looked like stewed tomatoes," Curtis continued happily. "Oh, man, was it ripe!" he cheered.

Fingers still plugging my nose, I glanced at Curtis and gave him a cold stare, hoping he couldn't see my green pallor. His eyes were little slits—devil's eyes. He was master of a nasty game. He wasn't merely conversing; he was detailing that story purely for my benefit. I was "It" in this game of "Gag."

His eyes sparkled mischievously. He tried to completely revolt me. He probably wished, yes, probably *prayed* for the flimsy female in front of him to lose her cookies all over his cow. I couldn't even speak for fear of getting sick but still clung to the spluttering gutter tube.

"Vy, dat night," Curtis continued unmercifully, "Dr. Harrington vent awt to a bar. Somebody there ordered a pizza pie, and, by cheez, that did it! He threw up little chunks right then and there all over everything, including the big pie as he gulped it down!" Curtis rocked on the iron piping, and his laughter filled the barn.

Edgar was busy manipulating the tube around inside the cow and wasn't even listening to Curtis. But my mind fell easy prey to the farmhand as I was hopelessly attached to that steaming hose, and my nausea continued to build. My only defense was to breathe through my mouth and close my eyes as Curtis brought his story to a roaring crescendo.

The hot and steamy air around me felt palpable. I had to re-direct my thoughts to less distasteful subject matter to win this battle against Curtis. So, as he built his story, I concentrated on Walt Disney's story of Snow White.

As hard as he blasted me with images of rotten tomato paste, greasy pizza pies and clumped spaghetti, I invoked mind control and visualized each of Snow White's seven dwarfs marching around the log cabin in my mind to the tune of "Whistle While You Work." I was deter-mined not to lose this game.

Finally, Curtis's story came to a screaming climax. Steaming superlatives, stinking metaphors, gross similes and exaggerations rock-eted from his mouth and ricocheted off the walls.

"Okay, Gay, we're done," Edgar said, grasping the hose from me as the last chunk dribbled from the end and flopped into the trench.

Suddenly the barn grew silent. There at the end of the barn, Curtis stood, slump-shouldered, a beaten, broken man. Somehow, I had done it; though I emerged weak and nauseous, I was unharmed. The only battle scar would be my total recall weeks later of the exact smell of that retained placenta. I tasted it in every steak sandwich I had for the next two months.

While Edgar and I packed the equipment into the truck, Curtis followed, head down. Edgar said, "That was a real bad one, Curtis. Next time call me before it gets so rotten."

Curtis nodded with little enthusiasm; his entertainment was over for the day. He was sweating a river, and the flies zoomed around his head once more.

As we headed out the driveway, Curtis made one last attempt to disgust me, "Hey, Mrs. Balliet—hope ya don't have pizza tonight!"

7

Spirit Food

Though the Curtis foray was a regurgitating one, learning to be part of a veterinarian team was usually not only balm for the spirit but the palate as well. Grateful animal owners brandished trays of donuts and steamy drinks after a winter's emergency in the pasture—like Mrs. Dougherty, whose cow, Daisy, Edgar saved from a bout of milk fever. After Edgar spent an hour dripping the IV calcium into Daisy's veins during a storm of freezing rain and sleet, Mrs. Dougherty slipped some delicious apple fritters through the truck window. "These are for you two," she said kindly. The pungent cinnamon aroma quickly filled the warming truck, and Mrs. Dougherty smiled at our grateful expressions, thanks enough, and carefully made her way back to the barn.

Some owners, like two Arabian horse trainers whose animals were our patients, had their own brand of refreshments just as they had their own brand of horses. Whenever we stopped at this particular farm, Sara, one of the owners, always offered the same beverage—diet A-Treat Cream sodas. The soft drink had been her favorite since she was a child, and that, she figured, necessarily made it our favorite as well. Edgar and I always looked forward to going to the barn. Sara and her sister, Susan, also made us privy to the fact that old-fashioned vanilla colas are served (upon request) at the Cozy Corner, a tiny restaurant that boasted fine Dutch soups such as cream of potato; ham, string beans and potatoes; and corn chowder. The next time we had lunch at the Cozy Corner, we each ordered vanilla colas and were immediately transported to the sixties. All we needed were a pair of bell-bottoms for me, and a Nehru jacket for Edgar.

Another pleasure of large animal veterinary work is being free to enjoy the pure, old-fashioned country setting. Edgar and I roamed the dew-jeweled, lush Pennsylvania countryside on our way to the farms and horse ranches and, on a whim, often stopped at a roadside ice cream stand for our favorite—peach frozen yogurt. But even more satisfying than sating the stomach was watching a distressed animal recover from its sickness or lameness. At other times there was another fringe benefit—comic entertainment.

One day we set out to attend what promised to be an uneventful case—a bull with a stiff hind leg. We parked in Bert Biechy's gravel driveway before his multicolored, multi-cornered house. For several minutes we waited in the truck and contemplated all the chicken houses, tool sheds, machinery sheds, the springhouse, the outhouse, the doghouse and general storage buildings. When no one appeared, we drove to look for Bert, our equipment bumping and rattling, slewing and banging against the truck bed. We stopped with a lurch as a large figure emerged from the doorway of one of the shacks. Slowly he started towards us, but I could not appreciate the man's size at that distance. Only after he had approached the truck, thus providing a comparison to something nearly as large, did I realize just how big this person was.

Bert looked to be about six feet tall by three feet wide. His belly, like a giant fleshy teardrop, fell from a barrel chest and flowed over his belt. A white T-shirt struggled to cover the moonish expanse. Bert strode toward us, tugging and pulling at his recalcitrant shirt which, at three sizes too small, was stretched to its limit. The effort was seemingly unconscious, the habit of every day and every hour. First, he pulled on one side, and the T-shirt obligingly covered that side of the stomach. But that caused an equal reaction on the other side so that the shirt accordioned up around the bulbous entity. Then that side received a tug that made the other hike up once again. Finally frustrated, Bert let go the shirt whereupon, with a pop, the edges of the tee flipped up like a window shade.

Bert's bearded face was as round as a cantaloupe. His eyes, tiny beads, seemed lost in that expanse, like pebbles in a desert. His medium-length, dark brown hair lay slicked perfectly around his melon head, leaving perfectly trimmed cutouts for his ears. His mouth, like the smooth, rosebud lips of a high school sweetheart, did not belong there beneath the curly mustache. Bert, indeed, was a picture of contrasts. He resembled something of the surreal—part fruit, part human.

"Hi, Mr. Biechy," Edgar called, leaning out the window. "How's James?" James was a pig Edgar had treated a month ago. James was more a pet than a livestock animal, and his lameness had worried us all.

"Vy, he's fine naw. Your medicine healdt that cut fine and dandy."

Bert rolled over to us and leaned against the truck. "Doc, Buster's awt on t'range. I tried to get him dis mornin', but the old guy knew somethin' vas cookin'. Wuldt ya mind drivin' me up to vhere he iss? I think he's awt by da voots, in da shade."

"Where did you say he is?" asked Edgar. Bert was hard to understand through his thick Pennsylvania Dutch accent.

"Da voots!" Bert bellowed as if the problem was with Edgar's hearing, not with the pronunciation. "DA VOOTS!" he yelled.

"Oh, the woods," Edgar said with a nod. He pointed to a mass of trees atop a steep hill beyond. "Climb in front with us. Might be a bit crowded, but it'll only be for a short while."

I squeezed over so that Bert could steer his belly into the cab. Soon we were rolling over pastureland in the direction of the distant "voots," shoulders hunched and arms clamped against our sides. With every lurch of the truck, Bert dug his fingernails deep into the dashboard to help stabilize the weight that, because of gravity and centrifugal force, he had not much control over. In time to the rolling and heaving of the truck, Bert's body ricocheted first off the door then off me. We smiled weakly, our bodies touching in a strangely intimate way that made us both uncomfortable. At last, on the valley floor and perhaps a mile away from the woods, Bert instructed us to drive straight up the hillside to meet the cow path at the top.

"You've got to be kidding!" Edgar shouted over the noise of the truck. "That hill must be at a forty-five degree angle. I'll roll this truck if I go up there."

"No-o-o, no-o-o-o, I do it all da time vit my truck. Dis shuldt make it too," Bert insisted. He tugged at the T-shirt and dug his nails deeper into the dashboard.

"Well, I'll try it, but this isn't a four-wheel drive, you know," worried Edgar. "Hang on, Gay."

I gritted my teeth.

Chugging up that incline, the three of us bent forward, we reached the top and turned left to meet the worn cow path leading to the woods. Still on an angle, the turn had set off a chain reaction in the truck cab. Though we were traveling in a horizontal direction, we were being pulled vertically downhill by gravity, riding almost totally on the truck's left tires. Bert, clawing to stay on his side of the seat, eventually lost the strength to hold on, and in minutes the forces of physics took over. Bert's impressive poundage slid atop me. And I, not a featherweight myself, in my helplessness slid too, landing against my husband. Bert and I smiled sheepishly at each other as our bodies, without our consents, melded together. Like Bert's, my fingers dug the dashboard in desperation. And then, when I could hold on no longer, I surrendered, too. Edgar, beneath our combined weight, peered bug-eyed at the path ahead. Nose to nose, Edgar and I faced each other, eyes popping under the force. Now the hill grew even steeper. As the pressure in the cab increased, we all gave up the senseless battle against gravity and leaned into the left side of the truck. I heard wheezing and realized it was my own, reacting to being crushed inside our truck that doubled as a compactor for humans.

For perhaps a mile, we followed the cow path, all three of us molded into one compressed lump, and at last we stopped at the edge of the woods. Falling from the cab into knee-deep fescue, we expelled our held breaths.

"There he iss!" Bert shouted, pointing toward a clump of bushes. Grabbing a long stick, Bert bounced off in the direction of the bull with Edgar and me right behind. Buster, a muscled Black Angus, turned his massive, cement-block head to us in warning.

Poking Buster with the stick, Bert, farmer turned matador, jumped back and forth, yelling like a demon possessed as he tried to rouse him back to the barn, "Hee-aw, ee-aw, hee-aw, yeouw. Get, go on, naw. Cluck, cluck, shooooo-oo-oo-oo-aw." He machine-gunned the bull with "ch-ch-ch-ch-ch," but Buster simply stared at him, emotionless. Edgar and I joined in.

Finally, probably perturbed by our war whoops and whistles, the bull began to pick his way out of the woods and onto the dusty cow path. Rusty barbed wire fence contained his escape to the left so that he could only go toward the farm. He trundled daintily down the path, skipping away without a care.

"Now, oncet he iss on dat path, he'll go back to hiss shedt where you can take a gudt look at him, Doc," Bert panted.

Large as he was, Bert ran off, graceful as a water nymph, stick in hand, coaxing the nonchalant bull all the way back to his shed.

Edgar said, "I'll help him get the bull. You try to drive the truck back to the farm."

"Okay." I watched him race off after Bert and Buster. The bull enjoyed his elusiveness and trotted away like a child at play, soon outdistancing his captors. Bert pursued, his belly jiggling with each step, his shirt hopelessly coiled up to his armpits. In contrast, Edgar, his spider-like legs reaching out, sprinted off in another direction to head the bull off. As his head bobbed over the horizon, I ran for the truck and drove it carefully down the leaning cow path and back to the farmhouse. Soon I could hear the men shouting from the valley floor.

Maneuvering around the outbuildings, I wheeled around to a large algae-covered pond surrounded by milkweed pods and wild wheat. I laughed. There Buster stood, elbow deep in the very center of the pond. At the water's edge, Bert and Edgar whistled and cajoled the bull, who stood calm and motionless, remote and safe, in the watering hole.

In my imagination Buster took on traits attributed only to the human race. He portrayed, all at once, the allegorical characters of disdain, satisfaction, mischief, challenge and, the king of all traits—smugness. The chase was at a standstill with the bull the obvious victor.

I got out of the truck and joined Bert and Edgar, who were clearly frustrated by the bull's escapade. Edgar observed, "Well, his leg couldn't be hurting him that much; he ran like hell from us. Since it doesn't look as if he's planning to leave this pond for awhile, I'll give you some analgesic powder to throw in his feed two times a day. That ought to take care of any pain or swelling."

Edgar caught his breath at the pond's edge. We stared at Buster, so relaxed now in the water, and Edgar laughed, "Well, I guess he's not so dumb. He knows damned well we won't race into that muck and try to drag him out of the pond. And look at him—just look at his expression."

Buster stood, his eyes drawn into slits and his muzzle into a smirk. He raised a leg and paddled the water, lapping it up and under his belly as if to say, "So there!"

"Hee's teasin' us, iss dat awld bugger," Bert said with a chuckle. But I contend the bull was laughing more with us than at us.

As we left the farm, I glanced back at the pond. For once the contest had resulted in a standoff—man and beast momentarily were equals.

8

The Dark
Presence

Many were routine calls like reproductive work, yearly injections for flu and rabies, Coggins tests, health surveys and dewormings. Edgar also played a significant part in diagnosing cases of abuse and animal neglect. Unfortunately, early on we saw enough of man's cruelty to animals, though the instances, thankfully, were not many. However, perhaps the most painful task we learned about in these times of new beginnings was that of euthanasia.

Any euthanasia case, from the arthritic, incontinent Labrador to the thoroughbred horse lying in agony with a shattered leg, puts a heavy burden not only on the owner but on the doctor as well. Often, the veterinarian alone is responsible for deciding when modern medicine can provide only an inadequate or temporary solution. And having made that decision, he is the one to draw the dark curtain on the animal.

Moments before the animal drifts off to sleep, the vet consoles her, telling her not to worry, that everything will be all right in a few seconds. And the animal, eyes blinking with trust as she had always trusted her owner, sinks limply, painlessly out of this world. The vet and the animal, two beings—one entity—are momentarily united against the fear and dread of the unknown.

Afterwards, the vet consoles the owner, the brokenhearted friend who will always cherish memories of his lost pet. And family members unite in grief, offering support for the sister or mother or son most affected by the loss.

Most people don't realize that the doctor also grieves. Many people don't know that the emotional pain associated with euthanasia becomes no less traumatic as the years pass because each case is an individual one with its own set of special circumstances. One cannot grow immune or acclimate himself to this kind of finality. Each pet is mourned separately, distinctly, by the owner and the doctor.

One such painful experience occurred one afternoon as we made our daily rounds, rattling our way over the parched August fields.

After bumping along a winding dirt road for some minutes, we came to the place. Now abandoned, it had once been an old egg farm. Rows of gray chicken houses, lined up like worn-out soldiers, leaned against each other; the processing shed, a long, low, dilapidated wooden building, spoke of a time long past and long forgotten. What history did the old boards hold? Did they whisper of workers madly sorting, grading and cleaning eggs and depositing them in rows in cardboard boxes for hours on end until the whistle blew for lunch? In contrast to this beautiful, Technicolor day, the sheds were brown, the driveway was brown, and a slight wind whipped up dust devils, tainting any colored object somber shades of gray.

Pulling up between Mr. Jacoby's house and the barn, we saw no one around. The house was meager by any standards, incredibly small and dilapidated—a shack. It was a remainder, clinging to a life of another time. The clapboarded shack hung low to the ground; wooden slats tipped and dangled precipitously over other slats; the entire building slanted to the right in a losing battle with gravity. The old man had been a hired hand on the old egg farm and as part of his payment was still allowed to live there. He raised pigs for years, but had recently sent them all to market and gone into the grain business.

Then we saw the old man walk slowly out of the house, the screen door slamming loosely behind him. He wore rags, and his gray hair drooped around the edges of his soiled cap. Motioning Edgar to follow, he shuffled into the barn, head down. A lump rose in my throat at his pained expression and lowered eye; Edgar, too, wore a defeated look. The horse had been getting steadily thinner, in spite of all his owner fed him, and the old man couldn't afford to pay for any in-depth health work-ups. Although there were no definitive tests, Edgar felt Star was slowly dying of liver and renal disease which he could do little about even if the old man could afford treatment. None of the good health and high spirits we had seen at other barns that day meant anything now. We all knew the old man's friend, companion and confidante of thirty years was about to be lost forever.

Edgar emerged from the barn and walked slowly up to the truck. Through the window he whispered, "The poor old horse is really in bad shape. He can't hold any weight, and he's getting weaker day by day. You'll see him when we bring him out. We're going to put him to sleep over there on that grassy patch—he'll be easier to bury." Edgar pointed to a spot about two hundred yards away.

I swallowed. "Are you sure?"

"Yes, I'm sure," Edgar said sharply. "That horse can't be treated. He's too old…his body is giving out on him. I can't do anything more." And with that, Edgar filled two syringes with the deadly pink solution and headed toward the grass.

The old man came soon after, leading his horse by a frayed rope. My eyes smarted. A large palomino gelding standing at least 16.2 hands, he had dwindled to mere skin stretched over a skeleton. He jiggled to the grassy plot. He walked loosely, the lack of muscle causing his limbs to merely flop in front of him. It hurt; it really hurt to see what probably had been a handsome horse, ending his life looking so undignified and wretched. But, what finally broke through my attempt at self-control was the expression in the horse's eyes. He actually looked expectant, as if he were going to do something and go somewhere interesting today. It was a look of quiet excitement, silent enthusiasm for whatever small treat lay ahead. His eyes bespoke a muted spark that still looked forward to the innocent, pleasurable moments on the farm. Surely he expected a walk to the apple tree at the end of the drive.

The horse moved, heavy step by heavy step, folds of skin rippling under the loose joints with every movement. Finally he and his owner stopped beside Edgar. There would be two deaths here today: the physical death of the horse and the emotional death of the man who was about to lose a part of himself.

I turned away, frantically blinking away the tears. *How does one prepare a friend for death? There's no past experience to fall back on. What actually lies beyond the Door? Animal or human, one must die alone—no one else can go along and help share the fear. What will my own demise feel like? The Door is opened a crack, but I'm afraid to peek in. Gramma, how was it?... Please, someone go with me. I think I can do it if I'm not alone.*

My eyes clouded over with tears as Edgar approached the horse. For a few seconds I could barely make out Edgar's profile beside Star's neck. I looked away again. Then there was a dull thud—it was over. I wiped my face on my sleeve, biting my lip. The horse lay on the grassy plot, tail spread out behind him, his emaciated body at peace.

The old man, head lowered, turned away, but I could see his face, strained red from the effort of courage. Without a word, he stumbled back to his shack, and the screen door banged hollowly behind him.

9

Lurking Around the Corners

It took me a while to recover from having to euthanize Star, the egg farmer's old horse. One of the things I hadn't bargained on in my enthusiasm for helping Edgar with his cases was the constant threat and appearance of death. I was beginning to think it lurked around each corner. I guess when our practice began, I had a childish notion that every sick animal Edgar touched would be restored to health and vitality. Those ideas were fantasies, I found out. Yet Edgar and I did pull off some nearly heroic feats.

One such feat that summer was a memorable case in which our patient narrowly escaped meeting the Reaper.

"Do you know what time it is?" I said, squinting at the fluorescent dial on my wrist after nearly nine hours of calls on our animal patients.

"No, how late is it?" Edgar tiredly asked as we rumbled along toward home in the practice's truck.

"It's quarter of eight, and I'm famished. We haven't had a thing to eat all day. Could we pick up something on the way home? I don't feel much like cooking after a day like this," I said, turning to him.

"Sure thing," he replied. "Let's go to the Gourmet Chalet."

"Great!" I said.

He whipped the truck around to the right, and I grabbed the

armrest to keep from plummeting into his lap. One thing I really didn't care for while assisting Edgar on his rounds was his driving. With every call, I was his captive audience to be jostled and tossed about like a limp puppet in the front seat. I had virtually no recourse, for criticism of his driving techniques only caused him to react in the extreme. If I said anything, he would get a crushed look on his face and then slow down to a mere crawl, stopping abruptly at every railroad crossing and yellow light.

As we sailed over a bump, the windows rattling, I shifted stiffly, for, sharing my already small space on the bench seat, were piles of papers, forms of all kinds, letterheads, receipts of bills, Coggins test results and tuberculosis test forms. Also, with each sharp curve or sudden stop, a reference book on veterinary medicine banged into my hipbone. On the floor beside my feet rested the x-ray machine. Beside that, like a mad thing, a roll of adhesive tape gyrated on the floor. Numerous times I felt the bandage scissors or rectal thermometer poking me as they vied for position in the squashed cab.

"We'll be there in twenty minutes. Do they serve this late?"

"The real question is, do they serve people that smell like horses?" Edgar laughed. We lumbered onto the shoulder and slopped back onto the road with a lurch.

"Guess we'll both smell like horses and eat like them, too."

So we headed to our favorite restaurant, passing our own home on the way where the horses stood cozy in their stalls, and the myriad of cats were tucked asleep in the hayloft corners. We passed the Sigley's house and saw a light glowing in the barn: probably Trudy, busy brushing her pony. We sped down the highway past fields of chest-high corn and turned off onto a tree-lined back road that was a shortcut to the restaurant.

During summer rounds, which is the busiest season for the large animal vet, my husband seldom ended the workday before dusk. The equine shows are in full swing, and horses injure themselves in various ways: cutting themselves in horse trailers, scraping themselves during a fall, or developing bellyaches or stiff joints from the stress of competition.

Trail riders also invade the hillsides in friendly bands during the summer. They ring up the vet for scratches, bruises and bee stings to their mounts, incurred from walking through thorny underbrush. Every horse owner enjoys his animal the most during the summer, brushing and grooming, riding and caring for him. And while all this activity is going on, strange lumps, bumps and rashes are found that were never noticed before. Then they call the veterinarian.

As we headed to the restaurant, the familiar crackling came over the radio, and a voice from the main office said, "Dr. Balliet, you have an emergency in Bally. A horse has fallen into a cold cellar. The people want you to tranquilize the animal so that it won't go crazy when they try to lift it out." Then the same voice chuckled, "Better you than me, Doc."

There was a long pause, and Edgar gazed through the sunroof. The emergency was all the way on the other side of the county. He sighed, picked up the microphone and droned, "Okay, call them and tell them I'll be there in about forty-five minutes."

"Oh, brother," I moaned, thoughts of a delectable dinner vanishing. "I sure hope the horse is all right."

"So do I." Edgar made an abrupt U-turn. We plunged into a deep shoulder and popped out again onto the country road. Edgar stomped the gas pedal to the floor, and once again I clung helplessly to the armrest.

"How could it have fallen into a cellar? Surely it couldn't have been in the house, could it?" I said, upsetting the mound of papers beside me.

"Who knows? People do strange things with their animals. You know that."

"Yes, that's true," I agreed. "Do you remember Mrs. Lash who stabled her two Arabians on the barn's second floor, a wooden floor? All that moisture from urine—the floor was half rotted away because of it. Then one horse almost lost a foot when it broke through the floorboards."

Edgar added, "Yeah, I was pretty worried until I got that call over with—I just couldn't figure out why the horse couldn't get up. When we went down to the potato cellar, one leg just dangled there above us. That was a weird one. Thank goodness it wasn't broken."

We had already seen numerous disasters. For example, the Martins tried to halterbreak their yearling the same day the farrier was coming to shoe him. What usually took people days or weeks to do, they hoped to accomplish in a total of fifteen minutes. The scared horse flipped over backwards striking its head on the concrete floor. A few hours later it was dead of head injuries. In another sad case a team of show horses was pulling a carriage through a competitive obstacle course. The driver had steered them across a corner of the lake; the horses panicked and swerved out to the center; and as the water got deeper, both horses, weighted down by the harness and carriage, disappeared and drowned. I rubbed the goose bumps on my arms.

We continued on our rescue mission, all visions of food and the day's end vanishing as we thought about past problems and agonized over the one that lay ahead.

We sped past Mrs. Henninger's farm shadowed in the evening twilight; Edgar and I had once gone there to clip her rabbit's front teeth. Mrs. Henninger had a barnyard menagerie, and tonight she jumped up from her garden patch and shook a menacing fist as Edgar startled her with the horn. But when she recognized us, she smiled and waved.

I couldn't smile back. I was imagining the trapped horse—a somber picture in which the horse, unconscious, lay prostrate on the basement's concrete floor while a sobbing woman with a yellow handkerchief stroked its head.

"I just hope it's all right," I said, my fists clenching a Kleenex.

The ride seemed to take forever. Finally, we lurched to a stop at the farm. A group of adults and teenagers gathered around the house's little makeshift porch. The people seemed quite fascinated by something on the porch, but we couldn't see what. "What are they doing?" I questioned. Edgar shook his head. According to the mailbox, we were at the right place. But surely this couldn't be where the horse was. They said it had fallen into a cold cellar, but Pennsylvania Dutch ground cellars are separate from the house, usually a hole covered by a single cellar-type of door. What could these people be staring at?

We started walking toward the group when one of the men turned around and motioned to us. The people parted, letting us through. The sight we saw on that porch seemed incomprehensible. Anxiously, I squeezed Edgar's arm.

There was the horse, swallowed up to its waist by a deep hole.

The only parts visible were the animal's head, shoulders and two front legs which lay stretched out in front of him on the wood porch floor. The rest, as if he had been bisected into two pieces, hung hidden somewhere below. How did he get in this predicament?

What did his poor legs look like down in that cavern? Had he cut them open in the fall, and were they bleeding? Was it possible they were just dangling by a sinew? Had the fragile leg bones been broken or snapped in two? Just what we would find down in that hole no one knew or could conjure.

We drew closer, scrutinizing the top half of the horse's body rising above the dark pit. Thank goodness he was not thrashing about. Panic had not yet set in, but, watching him, Edgar and I both knew that could happen any moment and its outcome would be disastrous. Innately nervous and skittish, a horse can contribute to its own demise. Thus, these owners had wisely requested a tranquilizer for the animal. If, when being hoisted out of the shaft, the thousand-pound animal should panic, it could become so violent that it might damage itself more and endanger those people rescuing him.

Peter, the owner of the horse, a small, wiry man in his early fifties, had gathered a rescue team which included a few relatives and a few burly neighbors. Everybody waited now for Edgar.

"Hey, Doc, we got a real problem here. Can you help us with it? Pride," he pointed a finger toward the horse, "fell through the floorboards over the cold cellar. He just sank right down into the hole."

Edgar nodded. "I've got the sleepy juice; all we have to do then is figure out how to pull him up out of that hole."

Edgar stood ready with the tranquilizer as Peter and his rescue team started rigging up a pulley system between the crossbeams of the rickety porch and Pride, who was now becoming agitated with all the activity milling around him.

Everyone voiced an opinion as to how to extract the horse from the shaft. "Rope will tear and break; you better use chains to lift him out," offered a neighbor.

"No, chains will hurt him if they slip, and they could break, too. Don't forget; you're dealing with a thousand-pound animal here," another argued. The hubbub continued.

"Put a board under his rear as he comes up the hole. It'll serve as a lever," Edgar enjoined.

I shivered. This rescue attempt might not even work at all. Such a skimpy porch roof might collapse under the horse's tremendous weight, and in a flash Pride would be swallowed entirely by the black hole.

"But," Edgar insisted, "it's our one chance for me to tranquilize him."

Finally, Peter hooked up the rescue gear—chains, pulley, wooden boards and a device called a come-along.

As Edgar bent to find the horse's neck vein, he said quietly, "It'll take just a few minutes for him to become limp, then you can winch him up. The drug's effect lasts about fifteen to twenty minutes. In that time you must get him out of there." And with that we watched the tranquilizer disappear into the vein.

Edgar patted Pride on his neck, "Be a good boy, and let us get you out. Okay?"

Within three minutes Pride became limp, but even though his head sank to the porch floor, he didn't fall through the hole.

Immediately, the men went to work, crawling over the horse, wrapping chains, straps and other ropes around his waist. As they began to winch up the cable in the come-along, the back end of the animal emerged from the chasm. Pride, loose as a rag doll, resembled a drunk, so motionless and unconcerned was he about the whole affair. The flimsy porch roof moaned and creaked angrily under his half-ton weight.

Shortly, the back legs appeared from the abyss—miraculously whole and unbroken—with only a few scratches. Of course, we could not know if anything major was wrong yet: that had to be determined by a thorough physical examination. The immediate problem seemed to be the porch roof beams which threatened to let loose. They were bending like rubber. Soon the back hoofs came clear, and with enthusiasm the men finished the task, covering the hole with wooden planks and lowering Pride to the ground. Miraculously the rafters held.

The owners were relieved. Hugging and petting the horse, they led Pride slowly into the yard. Though tranquilized, he could still walk.

He teetered, catching his balance after the effects of the anesthesia, but somehow he had suffered no major injuries in the accident—just minor scratches here and there.

"You were lucky, old boy," said Edgar. He turned to the owners. "How'd this happen?" he asked.

"Well," said Peter, pointing to a redwood table on the lawn, "see that picnic table over there? We always have it on the porch over this hole, but last weekend we had a family party and moved it out into the lawn. Well, we didn't move it back and forgot that Pride likes to walk onto the porch and look in the windows at us. That's just what he did today. My daughter Sally was in the house and saw his face in the window one minute, and the next minute it had disappeared. There was an awful crash, and then we found him. It was the most horrible thing I've ever seen. We didn't know what to do." The man shook his head, "At least he didn't go berserk when he fell in."

Once more the family gathered around the horse, and everyone, Pride included, appeared grateful.

Each of the family went about shaking Edgar's hand. It was ten o'clock when we pulled onto the open highway once again. All the good restaurants had closed; only the fast food places were open. Edgar and I were winding up another long day—hot, tired, and still hungry. Sometimes we couldn't help resenting the time and sacrifices his job demanded, but I didn't resent them this evening: we had helped save a life and made a family happy.

10

Jim Bob

Slowly we were learning, functioning as a team while Edgar became the veterinarian he wanted to be. So one morning, when Bridle and Saddle Farm called Edgar out to remove the wolf teeth from their two-year-old stallion, we both felt comfortable in using our ripening skills. Edgar and I were impressed the first time Jim Bob was escorted from his stall. A great, impressive hulk of a pinto saddlebred, Jim Bob was quite a sight: his regal head sat two stories high upon an elegant, giraffe-like neck which, with those well-developed muscles, told every passerby he had male hormones pulsing through his bloodstream. He was his owner's pride and joy, for Harry always brought Jim Bob from his stall to greet us, whether we were there to treat him or any of the other horses. Before we did anything at the barn, we always had to give a quick check to Jim Bob.

From his stall, Jim Bob began to strut, dramatically lifting up his front feet, holding his tail high and swishing it flirtatiously, all with a seeming air of nonchalance. And the fillies went wild—calling out and pounding the dirt with applause. Their whinnies were human wolf whistles at a Chippendale performance.

When not preoccupied with his mares, Jim Bob craved human attention and had his own method for acquiring it. His favorite game was to poke his tongue out a small opening in his stall in order to lure someone's finger into his mouth—the way an angler fish baits its prey. It was

Jim Bob's personal "taste test"—a device to entice human contact. We loved to tell this story when we stopped at the Cozy Corner for a bite.

One day we joined Mr. Heckinberger, one of Edgar's Dutch clients who raised Morgan horses, at the restaurant's corner booth. While enjoying a sauerkraut sandwich, he told us about one of his horse's antics. The story reminded me of the kind of games Jim Bob played.

"Say, Mr. Heckinberger, we know a stallion just like your horse."

"By Godt, not another character," he grinned.

I swallowed a spoonful of corn and potato soup. "Yep, every time Edgar and I walk into the barn, this stallion, Jim Bob, slips his long tongue through his grain hole. He does it just to get attention. He wants people to stroke it."

Mr. Heckinberger looked puzzled and interested, swallowing hard in expectation.

"It's so cute," I continued. "So coyly, so slyly does he stick his tongue out of his stall," and I made a face and stuck my tongue out at him to demonstrate, "that his pink tongue is the only thing a person notices jutting out into the aisle of the barn. It is the only piece of color in an otherwise brownish-gray barn. A person can't miss it."

Mr. Heckinberger giggled, and I heard a gurgle from Edgar who was agreeing with me through the juiciness of his cheese steak sandwich.

"Yeah, ya doan't say," said Mr. Heckinberger with a hiccup.

I continued. "He dangles it out of his stall like that fish, you know, that entices little fish into its mouth with its tongue. The unwary fish takes the bait and then *snap* goes the angler's lips over it." I made a smacking noise. "You should see it! Jim Bob's tongue must hang down the wall of his stall at least five inches. It's truly amazing."

I spooned up the last of my own delicacy. Edgar popped in the last fry and the rest of his coffee, and we said goodbye.

This day, we were ready for another of Jim Bob's "taste tests." Jim Bob had such a charming way—offering a slippery, pink welcome mat—tantalizing a softie such as myself for a touch. And he was smart. He didn't snap the trap upon first taste of the human finger. Instead, he baited me first by letting me stroke the tip of his tongue. As I became enamored by the silky tongue, flicking it back and forth and pinching it gently, laughing the while, I almost forgot about Jim Bob's "coup de grace." Suddenly the horse whisked his tongue back inside his mouth, and his lips snapped shut on my hand. If I had been totally unaware, my fingers would have suffered a terrible crunching between his teeth. But this was Jim Bob's game, and I outguessed his strategy this time. He had made it a contest, but I escaped unharmed.

Harry and his assistant scurried down the barn aisle in time to see me whisk my hand safely out of Jim Bob's mouth. "Almost got ya, I bet," Harry laughed, rushing to take the stallion from his stall. "Problems with his wolf teeth, Doc."

"Are you sure his wolf teeth are the problem with his bit?" Edgar asked Harry, sliding his index finger into Jim Bob's mouth.

"Yep, I know it," Harry said. "Just recently he won't work right off it, and I didn't change bits either. Seems he resents it. I've seen other horses have problems with those damned wolf teeth getting in the way. He's got 'em, too, and they gotta come out. Today."

"Okay," Edgar said, "but I can hardly feel them." The stallion's eyes grew wide as Edgar probed the inside of his mouth. Jim Bob only liked having people's fingers in his mouth on his own terms. "They're probably impacted; in which case they might indeed hurt him when you put the bit in. Of course, I'll have to sedate him first—use a local anesthetic—before I can go in there with the tooth extractor." Edgar pulled the savage little instrument from his dentistry bag.

Harry groaned, shifting his feet uneasily, "Hey, not the friendliest looking dental tool you've ever seen, is it?"

Edgar continued, thinking how best to approach this case. "I just hope I can find those little suckers right away," he mumbled, laying the tooth terminator back in its case.

Minutes later, Jim Bob stood immobile in his stall. "I didn't give him too much tranquilizer, so he won't be out for too long. We better get busy, Harry."

"Can I help you hold him, Doc?" Harry offered. Jim Bob's eyes were glazed, but Harry's were unusually bright.

With his index finger, Edgar probed the horse's mouth again while his other hand pried it open. Edgar grunted as he struggled to feel the gums, "No...no, Harry, I don't think so, not yet, anyway. Gay, hand me the syringe with the local in it."

Jim Bob's eyes suddenly opened wide. Edgar said, "Here goes. Everybody stand clear in case this jolts him. I don't want anyone getting hurt." He pulled the anesthetic into the syringe.

Then he stabbed the needle into Jim Bob's hard palate, at the same time injecting the surgical site. Jim Bob hadn't felt much, although his eyes opened wider, and he bobbed his head as if to say, "Did someone knock?"

"It's okay, good buddy. Go back to sleep, and tonight the tooth fairy will bring two nice, juicy carrots for you," Edgar coaxed. But Jim Bob's eyes foretold that he was more alert than we all realized. Possibly the tranquilizer hadn't had quite enough time to work.

"Now, let's check again to see where those nasty wolfers are," Edgar said as he slid his finger along Jim Bob's gums. Harry grinned with pride.

Just as Edgar probed Jim Bob's mouth, I heard a crunching sound. Jim Bob's eyes were closed to slits as if he were contemplating a mathematical equation, but, in contrast, Edgar's eyes were painfully wide.

There was silence preceded by a catch of breath.

Edgar's expression told it all. His eyes flicked open like sprung window shades. And then an inward look began to pulsate, to fume from the depths.

"What's wrong?" I blurted.

"Nothing, dear," Edgar squeaked, his eyes still bugged and staring. He withdrew his hand from Jim Bob's mouth, and the horse simply stood calmly, aware of nothing. Edgar took a deep breath and stretched out his hand.

I winced at the bloody thumb. The thumb itself was still in one piece, but Jim Bob had smashed the nail to a pulp. Edgar stared at the mashed stump, his eyes glassy. I wanted to console him and take the appendage into my care, offering candy and Bactine, but that might ruin his stoic image in front of his clients. So I said nothing.

"I have to bandage my thumb," he mumbled as we all stood holding our breath. Then he strode calmly down the aisle, his battle-scarred digit raised like a flag.

Harry and his assistant looked at me as Edgar disappeared through the barn doors. Finally, the trainer said, "Thought he was gonna cry."

"Edgar, cry? Never! Oh, no. You'd be surprised how many injuries he takes in a week of veterinary work. Why, that's minor compared to some of the things that have happened to him." I passed the incident off so nonchalantly that the group just shifted thoughtfully and shook their heads.

Shortly, Edgar walked back into the barn, his thumb wearing a huge bandage the size of a Tootsie Roll Pop. He waved it in the air, mummified in its bright pink bandage of Vetwrap. "I don't even feel it," he announced with a cracked smile.

I tried to ease the tension. "Quite a bandaging job you did on yourself! Ha ha! Think you'll be able to get it in the front door when we get home?" My audience laughed, but Edgar's eyes which met mine were cold sober. But with people to entertain, I was on a roll. "Ya know, Hon, they're doing construction down the road—they could use your thumb to help direct traffic." I got a few more laughs. "Hey, ya know what else? This could make us rich. You could stand on a city street corner with that wad and draw sympathy for quarters."

Harry and the trainer snickered, and Edgar smiled with vengeance.

"All right, now let's get to this job." Edgar recited the plan step by step. "The local should be working now, so he shouldn't feel a thing. We'll give him the general anesthetic and that will put him out of it for a while. I'll get the extractor in there and simply pull those teeth right out."

Harry cradled Jim Bob's head, the horse's nostrils quivering in and out in somnolent rhythm. Edgar retrieved the extractor, lifted the horse's head, and inserted the instrument up into the gums. Just at that moment Jim Bob jerked his head and smashed our plans for Edgar to be the practiced, expert veterinarian.

Edgar cried out.

"Oh, God!" he yelled as I watched his eyes wincing. "Why did he have to move like that—just as I was getting that tooth out! Now we've really got problems!" Edgar grimaced as he threw the tooth extractor to the ground.

Edgar's hands, stuffed inside Jim Bob's mouth, were blocking the view. His back was to me and so was Harry's as they both strained to see the problem inside Jim Bob's mouth.

Suddenly Edgar yelled, "I cut the palatine artery in his hard palate! Everybody out of the way!" With that, he took his hands from the horse's mouth and out gushed the purest red stream of blood I'd ever seen. The cardinal river pulsed from poor Jim Bob, a river released from the dam and fed from the heart.

The next moments were a blur as Edgar went into action. The orders flew. "Gauze pads, Gay! I've gotta stop that blood—gotta find and tie off that artery. He can bleed to death! Damn! Why did he have to move?"

The blood poured from Jim Bob's mouth like a fertile spring. With every second the horse's lifeblood spurted onto the floor, bringing him closer to oblivion. At the rate the blood was draining, Jim Bob would be dead within the hour. A body rapidly draining blood feels no pain, no suffering, just a slow mesmerizing sleep into the Garden of Darkness.

Luckily, with it all, Jim Bob stood tranquilized, his mouth agape, the bloody froth pouring out. "I've got to get a suture pack from my truck—gotta tie off that artery. Someone has to hold pressure on this bleeder. Gay, press your fingers on the artery. You should be able to feel it—it's vibrating."

I moved to Edgar's side as he let go. As a new stream hit the floor, he guided my hand to the mass of clotted blood where the throbbing originated. I searched for the maddened pulse; Jim Bob depended on me now.

Then I felt the artery that wasted its life down my sleeve and into my armpits. My ruined shirt didn't matter nor the slimy feeling down my arm. My mission was to locate that runaway vessel and keep it shut until Edgar got back. In the time it took to find the artery, clots had materialized along my arm to a thickness, at places, of half an inch. Jim Bob merely stood immobile with a pool of blood around his feet. The stream was beginning to slow.

Then as my fingers pressed the roof of the stallion's mouth, there was a voice of another world, an eerie drone. It was not a distant voice but very near, so muffled that it was almost inaudible.

It was Harry, his face white as a Crenshaw melon. He was clinging like a dead weight to Jim Bob's halter. He was supposed to be holding the horse's head, but it was the other way around with Jim Bob unwittingly steadying Harry. Harry moaned weakly, teetering on the brink of a faint.

"Harry, get out of here! The blood's getting to you," I said. Harry teetered on skinny, weak legs. "Go take a walk. I'm okay with Jim Bob. We'll be fine—now go away!"

Harry fled, abandoning Jim Bob's lead rope that I caught with my free hand before it fell into the bloody pool. Swaggering like a drunk, Harry careened down the barn aisle, grabbing onto the stall doors as he went. He would have to fend for himself.

Minutes later, Edgar was back, suture needle ready. His shirt cuffs were already caked with blood clots, but he was going in again. "Okay, let's see if the bleeding has stopped any." I released my hand from Jim Bob's mouth, and a freshet poured anew. "Damn," Edgar said, upset. "I have to find the artery and close it off." The tide of blood on the floor had grown to an area two feet in diameter.

I watched him intently.

"There. There, that's it!" Edgar removed his hand from Jim Bob's mouth. Miraculously, no blood followed. We held our breath and stared at the horse's limp jowl, his lower lip heavy with gobs of blood. Amazingly, we had stayed the river at its source.

Edgar smiled, "Look at that. It's amazing—just one suture to stop that horrendous torrent. It worked! I don't know what else we could have done short of standing here for a few hours holding pressure against it. Maybe, just maybe, we could've stopped the bleeding with pressure alone: but I just couldn't chance it."

I was already cleaning up Jim Bob's muzzle with gauze pads and hydrogen peroxide. He was beginning to come out of the anesthesia: we had stopped the bleeding just in time. He gazed with sleepy eyes, checking us out. Then he looked sideways at the black pool at his feet. Suddenly he trumpeted a snort and skidded onto his back legs.

I hung onto the lead rope. "Don't be silly, Jim Bob," I said. "That's your own blood you're afraid of." He relaxed but kept an iron stare on the puddle before him.

Momentarily all of us had forgotten a horse's natural fear of liquid things, that to them their reflection in a pool seems like a pit that could swallow them. That's why our horses always balk at a puddle and refuse to cross creeks. It is no different than a bottomless abyss to them. In time a trainer can condition that fear out of them, but their natural reaction is to panic.

But might I have underestimated Jim Bob's intelligence? Perhaps his fear at the sight of the bloody pool was not, as I had thought, the fear of falling down a pit in which vile things squirmed. Perhaps Jim Bob's realization extended beyond the superficial, beyond the physicality of a "hole." In fact, could he have realized he had narrowly escaped death, a fall into a pit more solid and final than that of an abandoned well? Who was to say if the animal understood death? Beyond the meadows of alfalfa, mares with his foals, visions of oat suppers, the gentle touch of another horse and the friendship of a human being, did he see reflected in his own pool of blood a blackness which only humans give themselves credit for understanding?

Jim Bob was nearly entirely out of the anesthesia when Edgar walked back to the truck to find Harry. I backed Jim Bob away from the black pool, slicked over and drying, and turned him down the barn aisle. He nearly pulled me to his stall—as if a great shadow menaced his back. For several minutes I talked to him and reassured him, telling him that nighttime was still many years away.

11

A Memorable Character

It was not only the quaint and rustic Pennsylvania Dutch countryside which intrigued us, but the droll and whimsical, as well as the increasingly exotic humans and animals we were getting to know which aroused both our curiosity and affection. A few weeks after our experience with Jim Bob, we were to meet one of the most memorable characters of all. It all started as a rather routine call to a farm with a lame horse.

"Come on, boy," Edgar coaxed the horse, using the hoof testers to try to find the sore spot. The horse jerked its foot away when the tester discovered the infected area; he had an abscess. With one slice of the hoof knife, Edgar would be able to drain away the pus and relieve the pressure. In minutes, the horse would be walking sound again.

"There it is, Gay," he said, pressing the area again with his thumbs. The horse flinched. "Okay, boy, we'll relieve that pain for you in a minute."

"Give me the hoof knife," Edgar insisted, as he stood, bent over with the hoof propped between his knees. I searched my pocket, felt the sharp blade and plucked it from my coat.

"Here it is."

Edgar reached for the tool, and just as he took it, the animal spooked, knocking the hoof knife from Edgar's hand and throwing

Edgar into the side of the stall. It happened so fast neither of us had any warning. The boards rattled under the impact. "Yow!" Edgar yelled, picking himself off the dirt floor, "What's the matter with him?"

The horse cowered against the wall, its head tilted eerily to one side. It was glaring, bug-eyed, at something behind the opposite stall wall.

"I don't know what's eating your brain, but we'll try it again, ol' boy," Edgar said, and again he propped the hoof on his knee. The horse stood still but continued to gape with bulging eyes at the wooden wall.

Just then a man wearing a blue and white trucker's cap that spelled *Mack Truck* peeked over the stall wall. His eyes sparkled from an old crinkled face; his gray, wiry hair bristled from beneath his cap like porcupine quills. "Hello-a," he said in a Dutch accent. "See ya got a hot-bludted one there."

Edgar looked with surprise at the apparition. Then suddenly the hat disappeared behind the wall, and a rickety old man lurched into the box stall with us. His lips looked cracked and dry. His face was adobe red and reminded me of one of those bizarre apples, dried and shriveled into the likeness of a person. His eyes, however, betrayed his sun-seared appearance; they were rheumy and lively.

"Yep, got a live wire there, naw don't ya? My name's Zirth from dawn the lane oncet ova," and his stubby finger pointed out the barn door.

"Howdy," Edgar said, finding the hoof knife in the straw. Edgar resumed tracking the abscess, gouging a tiny hole through the hoof sole. "Got to dig out the culprit a little better," he said, reaching for the hoof tester again. "How are you doing today, Mr. Zirth?" Edgar began. He had begun to feel more comfortable with his skills and was now able to converse while he worked. Edgar focused intently on the hoof. The elfin man seemed not to hear, and then a high hoot of recognition broke the air.

"You're in!" the man with the crevassed face blurted. "You're in!" he shouted. I wondered what Edgar was *in*. Maybe we were in a stall with a dangerous horse and weren't aware of it.

As I handed Edgar the hoof testers, he looked with a puzzled expression. "I'm in what?"

"No, no. You misunderstand me! Urine! Urine!" The voice resounded, bouncing off the stall walls and the cobwebbed ceiling, "Urine'll do it!" The horse gaped, wide-eyed, but Edgar clasped its foot as he excised the abscess. "Did you say, 'urine?'" Edgar asked with aplomb, as if the man had said something as innocuous as "bread box."

The small man with the fissured face cocked his head, smiled confidently, and raised an index finger. Edgar and I didn't know it, but we were about to be privy to a proclamation that would survive the annals of modern veterinary medicine.

"I said, rub on some urine." There was a long pause. For sure he was crazy. He continued, "Chust get yaself a quart of urine and rub dawn that leg, and that horse'll walk awt of this barn like there's nothin' wrong wit 'im." He nodded and drove his point home with a slap on the stall's edge. "Yep, works like a charm, oncet even."

"Urine, huh?" Edgar questioned, setting down the horse's leg. His eyes narrowed, and he cajoled the medicine man to tell more. "Yes, now what did I read about that new treatment in my recent veterinary journal, Gay?"

Edgar never passed up the chance to explore or be entertained by an odd character, and he had an extraordinary one here. Some clients like this one were versed in home remedies and incantations. When I was a kid, even my Gramma Eckensberger healed my brush-burned knee by rubbing her hand over it and chanting in Pennsylvania Dutch, "Haily, Haily, hinkle dreck." I couldn't understand the words. All I knew was that it had something to do with chicken shit, and that because of its powers, in forty-eight hours my sore would probably be gone.

Another folk remedy for a human life gone sour was to preserve a mare's milt. Milt is a round lump of coagulated protein, similar to egg yolk that is found inside a mare's placenta after giving birth. According to the Dutch, this milt ball sits in the foal's mouth for it to suck on all through its gestation. At the moment of birth, the foal spits it out into the placenta. This lump of protein is the source of good luck for the Dutch: they dry it out and save it. One of Edgar's clients has several milts lined in a row on a windowsill in the barn, and the last milt ball she recovered is now sitting atop her radio.

On a daily basis Edgar competed with the likes of Mr. Zirth—those advocates of natural and folk remedies that, if they couldn't cure the animal, were either harmless or could certainly kill it. Scores of Dutchmen treated their colicky horses with a few ounces of whiskey while others poured draughts of turpentine down their poor throats. Our neighbor, Mr. Derhammer, an inveterate pipe smoker, swears that a couple of large doses of tobacco kill his horses' worms. But the best treatment for ascarids that Edgar's ever mentioned has been diatomaceous earth purchased at any pool or spa supply company. The theory for killing the worms was explained thus: diatomaceous earth (being made up of tiny, rigid, razor-like diatoms, or fossilized algae, smaller than the eye could see) should be fed every day so that the sharp, angular edges could slice all those worms to pieces in the stomach.

Like Gramma Eckensberger, Mr. Zirth believed in folk remedies and natural medicine. No aloe vera for this guy. He was going right to the "gudt" stuff—URINE. I could imagine him concocting gooey medicinals containing everything from dandelion, catnip and wild mint to powdered pigs' feet.

"Uh-huh!" Mr. Zirth said. "It's great stuff!"

I rolled my eyes, and Mr. Zirth saw my faithless expression. "O-o-o-o-oh... don't you doubt it! Urine'll cure most everything! For example, it'll cure any skin condition, tendonitis or ligament [he pronounced it *lik-a-mint*] ails. Just let it soak into the skin, and then chust rub it in real gudt."

"How many times a day do you have to rub it in?" Edgar asked, as if he were planning on prescribing it for his next patient. He wanted to make Mr. Zirth talk.

"Ass many times ass iss necessary; it'll never hurt ya. It can't hurt."

Edgar winked at me. "I have a hang nail on my big toe." With a look of *Oh, if only I could get rid of this hangnail*, he queried Mr. Zirth on a possible remedy. "Do you really think urine would help it?"

"Sure vudt; you'd need to soak it all day maybe. But the next day it'd be gudt as new."

Mr. Zirth peeked suspiciously over the box stall and then bent low to the ground, to see if a medical spy might be afoot. Luckily the coast was clear.

"I'll tell ya somethin' I don't tell many people." His ruddy face cracked into a sneaky grin.

"What?" Edgar said, leaning toward him, for Mr. Zirth lowered his voice to a whisper so that only the horse and the two of us were privy to the information.

Mr. Zirth's eyes were tiny knife blades as he said, "The best kind of urine to get...." He stopped, stepped to the outside of the stall, and looked about.

"What? What is the best kind?" Edgar urged with growing excitement.

Kind? This was getting disgusting. Different kinds?

Mr. Zirth stepped gingerly back into the stall. "A pregnant woman's urine is the best!" With this proclamation, his finger vibrated importantly in the air.

"Get awt!" Edgar shouted, accidentally slipping into a Dutchy accent, his eyes wide. "Is it really?"

"Yessir!" Mr. Zirth threatened, "Ya believe me, ya hear. Course, sometimes it's a bit tough to findt. But, if ya can't findt a pregnant woman's urine, it's better to use urine from an oldt person rather than a young one."

I stifled disbelief, but Edgar was loving it. Here was a character to rival *Seinfeld*'s Kramer. "No, kidding! I have to remember that next time I get a pain in my leg."

"Yep, it don't work so gudt for arthur-itis, but it works like hell for most other stuff. Cheese, it's great for stroke and heart dis-ease, too."

This time I couldn't contain myself. He was going too far.

"Stroke! How's rubbing urine on yourself going to help a stroke?" I said doubtfully.

"Oh, ya don't rup it in; ya drink it!"

I gasped.

"Makes sense," Edgar remarked nonchalantly. I stared at my husband in horror.

"Hey, belief me, naw. It's not so bad as ya think. Ya have to drink it so that the urecate can get right inta the bludt stream."

My guts flipped against my ribcage, and my teeth clamped shut to stay the surge flowing up my throat.

"What?" I said. "Drink it?"

Edgar chuckled and added, "Well, it only makes sense, Gay. If it works so well by rubbing it in, what do you think it'll do if you drink it! By the way, what is *urecate*, Mr. Zirth?"

"That's the stuff that does the trick—ya know—the 'actiff ingredient.'"

Mr. Zirth could see he was winning half his audience, but he had yet to convince me. "Yah, right," he exclaimed, his eyes darting, demanding my full attention. Then he began the tough job of providing proof to back up his theories. "The doctors over in Europe use it all the time to cure internal bleeding. Oh, and I forgot—it's perfect for chlorosis."

"*Chlorosis*?" Edgar questioned with a frown.

"Yap, ya know naw—chlorosis of the liva."

"You mean *cirrhosis* of the liver?" Edgar said.

"Yap, that sounds gudt. Vy anyvay, like I said, the doctors over in Europe use it all the time for stroke and heart dis-ease."

"That's so?" Edgar replied. He began wrapping a bandage around the hoof, rolling the adhesive tape around the foot.

"Yap," the old man's lips flapped vehemently. "But I'll tell ya another secret." He paused and closed his eyes dreamily, like a child savoring the last of a candy bar.

"What's that?" Edgar coaxed, and he stopped work to give him his full attention.

"They flavor it!" he yelled, his finger slicing the air. The horse pulled back, its eyes popping, its mouth agape.

Taking the horse's foot back between his legs, Edgar nonchalantly replied, "That's a good idea."

"Yap, they flavor it with coffee or vanilla."

"Think I'd prefer the vanilla myself," Edgar said, inspecting the hoof. I swallowed a lump of bile that had risen in my throat like mercury in a thermometer.

Then the ragged old finger pointed again. "But," said Mr. Zirth, "but..." There was momentary silence. What was he going to say now? He let it out in one gushing breath. "But the best way to take it is without any flavoring at all, nothing artificial, just gudt, fresh urine."

Oh, Lord, I thought, *why is he going on so*? Then he sidled up to me and took a deep preliminary breath. He thought he'd already won

Edgar over. He was intent only on me now. I was the remaining safe to be cracked. Mr. Zirth needed me to believe his story for a complete victory.

Suddenly, I couldn't stop the daydream conjuring up in my mind as the stable in which we stood faded away. A paneled room with a long, leather couch came into focus, and a nameplate with the words *Dr. Balliet—Psychiatrist* floated down and settled on the oak desk at which I sat. I pulled a pen from behind my ear and tapped it against my chin, thinking, as a craggy-faced patient lay on a nearby couch, his hands working themselves into tight, nervous fists.

I uncapped the pen and leaned over my desk. *Now, Mr. Zirth, what seems to be the problem?* I recrossed my legs and swiveled my chair around to take in the city's panorama outside my skyscraper window.

A feeble voice said, *Vell, Docta, it seems people chust don't take me seriously. No one ever listens to me.*

A pigeon on the ledge outside the window maneuvered a stale bun between its feet. *Excuse me, Mr. Zirth, what did you say?*

His voice whispered from the couch. *I said, nobody ever listens to me. I chust don't know vy.*

What do you mean, nobody ever listens to you? I asked in my most soothing tone.

A nervous crack split the weak voice. *It seems whenever I have something important to say nobody beliefs me. Everybody beliefs everybody else, but they don't belief me.*

Why is that?

Chust cause it's me. I'm short and have a craggy face. People don't believe me cause I'm me.

Funny he should use the word *craggy*, I, as a psychiatrist, thought.

The crinkled, dried-apple face said, *Even my dog won't come when I tell him hiss dinner is ready. Ya see, nobody—no one—beliefs me.* His voice trailed away.

Very interesting. I scribbled some notes on a paper and chewed the tip of my pen.

Suddenly, a thin wail rose from the couch, disintegrating my dream.

A thick whisper rasped in my left ear. "Try it some time; it really works." Mr. Zirth winked, and his beady eye flashed under a scaly eyelid.

"All right, I'll try it," I said, swallowing another lump and a bit of pride. "But I draw the line at swallowing it," I said adamantly. "I have this back problem that flares up every now and then." And I placed a flat hand at the crook of my spine and stretched painfully against it. "I think I just might try the urine if it works as well as you say it does."

Mr. Zirth's face lit up like a Halloween pumpkin. His eyes danced, and all the wrinkles on his cratered face stood out as if in *bas relief.*

He was happy now. I was a player in this game now. "Yep, might even try it tonight, back seems a bit stiff right now." I winced.

He didn't say anything. He stood calmly, the grin easing into contentment. He offered no more directions on the medicinal purposes of urine. He merely sashayed proudly to a corner of the barn—*fait accompli.*

Even the horse Edgar had been working on looked relaxed, enveloped in the cloud of calm that radiated through the barn. Edgar threw a knowing look at me. He smiled. We, indeed, had met a memorable character.

12

The Invisible
Helper

On another summer day during our learning years, the heavy
August sun sulked toward the horizon. As early evening approached,
heat radiated from the ground and purple thistles slumped. Miragelike,
the laden oats, drying brown in the field, swayed in the warm moist
waves of air while a ladybug on a withered cornflower fluttered its
wings, like a spinster fanning herself.

An hour had passed since my weary husband disappeared
through the barn door, stainless steel bucket in hand, rubber hose slung
over his shoulder. The barn doorway stood impenetrable in the shadows, overgrown with cobwebs. "Poor Edgar," I commented to the fly sitting on the dashboard before me. "He must nearly be done in by now."
But I was really feeling sorry for myself. The fly swiveled its head
towards me. The car phone began to beep, so I flicked it on and heard
my mother's voice.

"Hi. I tried to get you at home, but I figured you were along
helping Edgar today. How are you guys managing in this heat?"

"Oh, we're doing okay. I should really be helping Edgar clean out
a couple of retained placentas, but it's just too hot...I can't stand it."

A brief silence followed. Then, "Well, why did you go along with
him if you didn't want to help?" The remark struck home, and I
cringed.

I lowered my voice. "Now wait a minute—it's just too sticky and miserable, and the flies will eat me alive in that barn." I swallowed, ashamed of my simpleminded, flaccid excuse.

"So-o-o-o-o," poured my mother's words.

"So-o-o-o-o," I said, "so-o-o-o-o my name is not written alongside his on the veterinary diploma, is it? Why should I have to suffer?" Another limp argument—I was feeling guilty.

She swooped in for the final attack: "Because you married him."

I winced. "Yeah right, and that makes us the Bobsey twins, huh? Haven't you heard of the feminist movement? Well, for the moment I've joined it."

"You're tough," the cool voice chided, and there was silence.

Certainly I wanted to help Edgar with his new career, but hot days like these were just unbearable. He was the doctor, no less a savior, to some clients. I was only an apparition in the background.

In truth, I was proud that people admired him, yet I would have liked a smidgen of recognition, too—a small compliment from someone would have helped stem the feeling of invisibility.

I sighed into the car phone.

"Gay?" came my mother's voice.

My conscience was beginning to ache. Was I wrong for sitting out on this call? Should I submit to the barrage of flies and nauseating stink that I knew brewed inside a barn full of cows with retained placentas? Was I pampering myself as a kind of vengeance for not commanding the respect Edgar seemed to be building wherever he went?

"It's not fair," I sputtered, trying not to sound like a whining wife, but sounding like one anyway. "He didn't get home until eight o'clock again, I had to eat supper alone in front of the TV; and then he was on the phone until nine. I fell asleep and...."

"Poor Edgar," the voice murmured. My mother was dealing the final, deliberately subdued, calmly driven blow. "He works so-o-o-hard." I frowned. A fly landed on my nose.

Summer was always a busy time for large animal veterinarians. It was something I was not entirely prepared for this early in his career. These days he had hardly any time to himself—nursing sick foals late at night, driving long distances for an ill goat or pig that I wouldn't drive even for a bargain on a "Liz" dress. Usually he pulled out of the driveway at seven o'clock in the morning and arrived back home at seven o'clock at night. Then he'd gulp dinner, call a few people for appointments for the next day and be called out for a late-night emergency.

My mother's voice scolded me once more, "Remember, you encouraged him to be a vet. Sometimes I think you love animals even more than he does."

An even heavier sweat broke out on my face. It was true. I knew my love of animals had inflamed Edgar with even more passion. We were both suckers for sick or injured creatures. Memories of a possum hit in the road stirred in my head. The jaw hung, slack and bloody, as the animal danced dizzy circles in the middle of the road. One eye had popped from its head and dangled from its bloody stump. Surely it would be facing a miserable end—dying of starvation—or it might be hit again while it stumbled blindly in the road. Instead, Edgar backed the truck up to the poor thing, affixed a syringe of T61 to a pole, and darted the animal with euthanasia solution. It died quickly and peacefully in a bed of thick grass and clover on the side of the road, and we drove home in silence.

"Gay, what are you doing?" my mother said.

"Uh, nothing. Maybe I should go see what's keeping Edgar so long."

"Yes, that would be good. So long. Oh, by the way, you're coming for dinner tomorrow. See ya then."

I hoped I wasn't too late to help Edgar. After all, when the steam boiled away, the stew was still wholesome and delicious. The essence was love, any way one wanted to serve it up. In his own way Edgar sacrificed things for me out of love. It was only right that I share his work today, too.

As I flung open the truck door, an eerie sound filled the air. A fly skidded to a halt on the back of my hand, and I brought the creature up closely for a look. His big fly eyes stared leadenly at me, somehow defiantly. How was it that a living creature smaller than a pea could succeed so brilliantly at tormenting and teasing an intelligent, superior being? He flew away, and I headed in the direction of the barn with the swarm of flies following.

As I reached the barn door, it flew open, nearly hitting me in the face. It was Edgar. Managing a weak smile, he shrugged the hose from his shoulder, emptied the pail into the stones under his feet and heaved his pumping equipment into the back of the truck. The flies zoomed onto the fetid wet spot.

"You must be beat," I said. "I was just on my way in to see if you needed help."

He wiped his forehead. "Unbelievable weather, isn't it. You okay?" He slumped into the driver's seat, slapped a fly from his nose and started the engine. "Can't wait for a shower," he said. "I just want to go home, get cool and watch TV for awhile."

He smiled sheepishly.

The smile had been conjured by my many lectures on the evils of couch potatoes and stagnation before the television set which would result in the eventual destruction of the human intellect and the untimely demise of the human imagination. This time, however, I didn't lecture him about destroying his brain. In fact, now I would even join him in front of the television set.

"In fact," he said, "why don't you join me, and we can,..." he wiggled his bushy eyebrows lustily, "vegetate together."

I scowled. "Vegetate in front of the TV? Turn our minds to pudding?... Terrific! Let's do it!" We sped down the lane.

Today, we had squished through foot-deep cow manure to test a herd of 128 cows for tuberculosis; Edgar had survived a swift kick to the shin from a hysterical heifer and a body press by a backyard horse. So passed many days like this one. After work we'd arrive home tired but with a feeling of well-being, muck from the collective barnyards clinging to our backs. From one week to the next Edgar sported a Band-Aid or Mercurochrome stain over an injury, his Purple Hearts won in tussles with recalcitrant patients.

Today, we had also nursed a panic-stricken thoroughbred through a bout with colic. We had worried about the animal's welfare and seen to its comfort and recovery. Over such cases as colic, death's shadow hovers, threatens; it is our elusive competitor in the support of life. We don't always win, but we give the animal every possible chance. For the most part, our clients appreciate that doggedness in search of health and life, whether their animal is a household pet or a member of the barnyard. We are all in it together, for the short or long haul toward physical and emotional well-being. Yet the country veterinarian's rewards are expressed, ultimately, in the eyes of the animal patient he is able to help—eyes that express calm and contentment, eyes that are free from pain. That is what makes our life so satisfying.

Our car bumped along the dirt lane and onto a main highway, rumbling past a bevy of Pennsylvania Dutch stone farmhouses and out-buildings. The metal pails and utensils in the Bowie unit banged in rhythm to the rock music playing on the radio. We passed Isaac Knecht's house, with the barn sheltering his two cows and many chickens leaning like a melting candle. The curtains lapped the hot air beyond the open windows. It looked so cozy as we drove past then, our tires rumbling over gravel and dirt: there had been a warm yellow glow through the curtains, the outline of a cat curled up on the windowsill enjoying the slight breeze.

Crouched behind the wheel of the truck, Edgar was an amusing but lovable picture. Stuffed into a pair of worn pinstriped coveralls, he resembled the Cook from the *Canterbury Tales* (minus the oozing pimple)—a connoisseur of sweat and grease—his hair clumped to his forehead, his nose, large-pored and swollen with the heat. Compared to the handsome, rugged young man who had escorted me down the aisle—a perfect specimen whose chiseled features and deep brown eyes could entice any woman—this man resembled *MASH*'s Corporal Klinger after a grueling KP duty. His work clothes looked like a gourmet salad garnished with an assortment of goodies, only these were composed of straw, mud, placental juices, blood and manure.

My attraction to Edgar now was not his looks but his kindness and devotion to the vulnerable creatures of this world. He would never allow an innocent to suffer, although, I must admit, sometimes with his busy schedule he forgets about my pain. I need to remind him that I hurt, too, sometimes, and require care and attention just like the animals. I still admired him for his allegiance to his patients—his delicate handling of the accident victim, his cajoling of the scared animal, his comforting of an animal about to die. I leaned over and brushed a dirt smudge from his temple, and he smiled softly. But the smile vanished as static sounded over the truck radio. It was followed by a familiar voice. "Dr. Balliet, a heifer is having trouble calving at Herman Zettlemoyer's farm."

Edgar let out a heavy sigh and turned the truck around in the direction from which we had just come. "What a day!"

"At least we are in the vicinity and not already home," I offered. "Better they get you now than when you're busy recuperating." He reached out and squeezed my hand gently.

Edgar stared blankly at the road ahead. He hadn't done that many calvings this early in his career. It was likely that he was remembering another problem calving of only a few days ago. The little fellow had been inside his mother upside down, and the presentation was breech. For hours Edgar strained against the heifer, shoulder-high into the cow's insides, pushing the calf and turning it an inch at a time to correct the bad presentation. It was a game of Ping-Pong, Edgar and the heifer the players with the poor calf in the middle. Edgar looked at me, and we stared anxiously at the open road ahead.

We plunged down Zettlemoyer's lane, scattering a flock of geese. As we shut off the truck, a roly-poly man with thick features and thinning gray hair came out of his white, wood-framed farmhouse and ran toward us. He smiled broadly.

Herman fairly sprinted to the truck as Edgar opened the door. His forehead was wet with sweat, but he appeared almost not to mind the heat. "Hi there, Docta Ed," he chirped in his thick Pennsylvania Dutch accent. "Haven't had the misfortune of seeing ya lately, say naw?" He laughed mightily.

"How are you, Herman? How's Emma?" Edgar climbed out of the truck and pulled the stainless steel bucket from the back while I lifted the obstetrical equipment from its corner.

Emma was one of our "sustenance" clients as I referred to clients who proffered food and drink. She always had something good cooking on the stove that she was enthusiastic to share with us. One time it was blueberry cobbler, another it was a homemade jar of sauerkraut. She was a saucy little plump lady who, like the rest of us Dutch people, knew that life without good fattening food was life hardly worth living.

"Vy, da vife's chust fine, naw. But Clara here does seem to be rather poorly at da moment. She chust can't push her calf awt, Doc. Chust seems a bit too big for da girl. Come, see naw."

Edgar and I followed quickly after Herman, who hurried over the straw-covered cobblestones and into the darkening barn. In a small stall off in a corner lay a cow straining and breathing hard. She pawed the straw in misery. She turned her head toward us as we shuffled through the straw, stirring up a fine, fragrant odor. Her eyes were narrowed into painful slits. When we approached, she lay her ears back in a submissive gesture.

Edgar ran his hand along Clara's sweaty flank, patting and soothing, "It's okay, girl. You'll be all right soon…. How long has she been trying, Herman?"

"Vy, abawt two hawrs naw. She don't seem to be doin' too much." He scratched his head.

"Well, let's just see what it feels like inside." Drawing a rectal sleeve over his hand and arm and lying down behind the cow in the fresh-smelling straw, Edgar talked to Clara in a low, bovine tone of voice. "Yes," he cooed, "we'll just take a look here for you, girl. Nothing for you to be upset about." He wriggled himself strategically behind her and secured a foothold on the stone wall.

Herman had crouched alongside Edgar and almost lay, himself, in the straw. "Yah, yah, take a gudt look there, Doc. Dis is my best cow. Take gudt care of her. She holdts a special place in my heart, Clara does. Just so happens she was born here on da day my youngest granddaughter vas born. She's von of my best milkas, too."

As Edgar's arm disappeared into the cow, his determined mouth relaxed into a smile. "Herman, I think we have a live one here yet, despite the long time Clara's been pushing. YOW! He just tried to bite me! Those little teeth are sharp!" Edgar laughed and resituated himself behind the cow.

Herman grinned proudly, apparently delighted at the prospect of the baby biting the hand that saves. "Vell," he said, "Clara culdt be a bit temperamental every oncet in a vhile too, naw." He chuckled into his checkered handkerchief.

Edgar searched deeper inside the cow. "The calf's definitely still alive, but I hope we can pull him out quickly—been in her just a little bit too long now."

Herman scratched his head, his booted toe digging the dirt. "Yah, vell, Doc, do vhat you can. Dat's all I can ask off you, naw. Like I saidt, Clara is von of my best milkas."

Locating a front leg, Edgar manipulated the calf inside its mother while I waited, ready with the calf puller, if he needed to extract the animal mechanically. Suddenly out of the corner of my eye, I noticed movement. But there were only the empty cow stanchions, bales of straw, an old rusty push lawnmower, a few pitchforks and a bucket. It was a dog, probably.

Edgar was struggling and slowly being swallowed by the deep straw bed behind the cow. Only his head and shoulders were visible as he wriggled to get a better grip on the elusive calf. Herman stood bent over, intent on the drama in the straw.

Once again I noticed movement to my left. Something fairly large had scurried behind a stack of straw bales. Then, slowly, from behind the bales appeared the top of a soiled, green baseball cap. Beneath the cap was the face of a leprechaun, pixie-like and angular. The face grinned at me like a wild thing.

A diminutive bony man in a torn red and black plaid shirt and green work pants straightened up, unnoticed by either Herman or Edgar. He propped a knee on a bale, intently watching the scene before him. He didn't come close nor did he say anything; he watched attentively. Then with a single-toothed grin he turned his attention to me. I waved, and he waved back—probably a farmhand, I guessed, a dairy helper.

Farm help is not easy to find; the farmers can pay very little, and the hours are inconvenient and long. Cows must be milked at the hour when their udders are full. The work is not the cleanest nor the most dignified, and during the summer the flies and heat make the dairy chores nearly unbearable. Consequently, a farmhand must be a person who can tolerate low wages and uncomfortable working conditions. He is usually somewhat disadvantaged, uneducated and travels from barn to barn, renting himself out to clean cow barns and help with the milking. While the typical farmhand may not be an intellectual, typically he is caring toward the animals, treating the cows and other beasts much like companions instead of animals of the barnyard. He also is usually a soothing sort, someone who can calm the anxious cows and make the more stubborn ones behave. Many Dutch farmers take farmhands into their houses, offering shelter, food and family life in exchange for work. Sometimes, several farms share the farmhand and pay him wages on a daily basis.

When the farmhand hiding behind the bales of hay felt more

comfortable with Edgar attending to Clara's situation, he turned his attention to me. Suddenly, the leprechaun began to sprint in a game of hide-and-seek from one straw bale to another, all the time grinning and waving before he disappeared out of sight. He was like a jack-in-the-box. First he crouched down behind one, then he popped up from behind another.

"Uh-oh. Problems," Edgar whispered.

Herman squatted down beside him; his fingers went to his mouth.

"Vat's wrong?" he said.

"This is a big calf, Herman. The shoulders are so big," Edgar paused and twisted his arm around inside the cow, "and Clara's so dry in here—no fluid left in her anymore. Gay, get a bucket of soapy water and the hose," he said.

When I returned, Edgar lay exhausted and immobile in the straw. He looked worried. "God, I've got to get this little guy out of there before its too late. Hurry, give me the bucket."

He attached the hose to the pump and set it in the bucket of soapy water in order to siphon the water into the cow's uterus. Herman chewed his lip as he helped steady the bucket.

Edgar's face was red, "Got to get him out," he grunted, "fast, before he suffocates. This soap will lube everything up."

Herman looked doubtful.

"We'll juice him up a bit—make the calf slippery as a fish—then he should just pop out. Look at that, Herman, we're giving your new calf a bubble bath before he's even born."

Herman knelt in the straw and mustered a smile.

"Good. That did it! Here he comes, Clara!" With a great last pull, Edgar slid the calf from its mother. It landed on the floor with a squish amid a tidal wave of suds and water. It gasped air.

"That was a bit hairier than I like," Edgar said. "He looks good, though. How do you like him, Gay?"

"I want one," I laughed.

Edgar turned the glistening calf upside down to evacuate the fluid from its lungs while Herman patted it with a dry rag. The solid black calf lay blinking and shivering in the thick, clean straw. Then

Clara rose, trembling, and bellowed for the calf to come near. As we all watched, the evening's prized newcomer struggled to rise. Within ten minutes, he arranged his shaky legs under him and stood up. He took two precarious steps toward his mother and careened with a grunt into the straw bed beside her. Again he tried to walk, raising his hind end first, then stiff-leggedly pushing himself up with his front legs while Clara bellowed encouragement. Finally the calf stumble-hopped to his mother where she briskly began licking him dry.

I couldn't help smiling. Here stood a new life, wet, confused, shuddering in the summer night—a being perfectly formed, an exact image of Clara. Only moments ago, it had been confined within its mother's belly unaware of the succulent grass and playful relatives that awaited him.

The calf moaned, then fell headlong into the straw. We laughed. "Gudt job, Clara." Herman positively glowed. "Vy, by cheez, I belief he'll be all right, Doc. He's a cute bugger, by Gawd."

"Give him a few hours to get over the trauma," Edgar suggested. "Both he and Clara should be all right now that he's not being pushed around anymore. So long, girl. Take care of your baby."

Gathering the chains and buckets, we three left the twilight-filled barn with its low, cobwebbed ceiling and musty odor. Mother and baby nuzzled each other; Clara grunted protectively when the calf bumped against her.

Equipment in hand, I glanced back at the straw bales for the little man who had been watching me. There was no trace of him, but behind the old lawnmower was a rusted, dark green, thick-wheeled bicycle propped up against a wall. It probably belonged to the farmhand, for Herman was hardly the bike-riding type.

Edgar started the truck, and I crawled in beside him. Herman, who had disappeared, came running back gripping a paper sack. He shoved it in through the window. "Vy, Emma chust pickdt some sveet corn dis afternoon. Wuldt you like a couple dussen?"

"Sure would love some, Herman," Edgar said peeking into the bag. "Tell Emma thanks, and tell Clara to take good care of her baby."

As we backed around, I spied the green hat peeking from behind a corner of the corncrib. I tweaked Edgar on the sleeve. "What's the name of the strange little man over there?"

Edgar looked back. "Oh, Jakey, the farmhand? He really likes animals. Herman told me that Jakey feeds the cows carrots and throws them grass clippings from the lawn mower. Herman says he's always fussing with the cows. In fact, the cows like him so much that if Herman needs help with a particularly grouchy cow, he sends Jakey to talk to her.... You know, I didn't even notice him around today, but then he is kind of shy and doesn't usually make himself obvious."

"Well, I noticed him. He was peeking at us from the hay bales."

Edgar laughed. "Usually he follows me around, sprinting from one corner to another. He has no family, except the farmers who take him in, but Jakey really has an uncanny way with livestock. He communicates with them clairvoyantly, I swear. In fact, if Clara weren't such a sweet cow, Herman probably would've had to get Jakey to calm her."

"An agri-psychologist," I smiled.

"No kidding! Believe it or not, he's a precious commodity in these parts. Old Mr. Fraisley swears Jakey's presence during milking time calms the animals into better milk letdown. He claims Jakey persuades the cows to give more."

Edgar steered the truck down the dirt road bordered by fields of oats, which were all of a sudden being whipped by the wind into waves. A thunderstorm was brewing, and the air held that heavy, sweet odor just before a downpour. Staring at the glistening charcoal sky before us, I envisioned the rain being sopped up by the thirsty crops and sun drawn animals. For a long time thereafter, the sweet smell of rain in the air reminded me of this place—and Jakey.

I patted Edgar's knee, and we drove home.

13

A Better Seat

While Edgar was learning the ropes of veterinary medicine and when I wasn't teaching high school level English or helping him with his calls, I was practicing my horseback riding. My riding instructor, Gale, helped me greatly improve my balance and confidence aboard Fancy. I vowed she and I would soon make our debut in the showring alongside some of Edgar's clients. After several months of practice, I felt I was making real headway as an equestrienne.

"Hey, you're not doing too badly," Edgar called as he pulled his truck alongside the riding ring.

"I feel a lot better," I agreed and urged Fancy into high gear. We sped around the ring, leaning into the turns. Like experts, we drew up beside the fence. "I really think I'm getting a much better seat, don't you think? Ha! *Seat*—get a load of that equestrian talk!" I laughed and patted Fancy on the neck. "Think we'll be ready for a show in three weeks?" Edgar's opinion was important; he knew a lot more about riding than I did. But in those three months of riding and lessons I thought my riding had improved drastically.

"Looks like it. You're going around that ring pretty slick now. What a difference from a couple of months ago!" He smiled broadly.

He was right. My stumbling block in learning how to ride was being able to admit that I couldn't ride. Once I did that and realized the reason I had to scrape myself off the ground several times wasn't the horse's fault, I was ready to make progress.

For many weeks, we practiced. The process was reciprocal: Fancy taught me how to ride, and I helped her polish her gaits. We spent many hot, grueling hours in the ring finding proper balance at the walk, collection at the running walk and perfection of the rocking-horse canter for which her breed is so famous.

Both of us were sweating and groaning, pulling muscles and stretching tempers. However, the hard work eventually brought results. Not only did I understand Fancy's way of thinking, but I became a better rider and she a fine athlete.

"It's a nice day, and I don't have any more calls. How about taking a little ride around the woods? I'll take old Nicky," Edgar suggested. We didn't ride him often, but he was the calmest and safest of the three to ride.

"Okay, you get Nick ready, and I'll meet you at the barn." Fancy and I cantered once more toward the far corner of the ring.

As the four of us ambled along the wood's path, I decided to show Edgar my new riding abilities and prove that I wouldn't kill myself falling off. "Would you like to race?" I winked, shaking Fancy up into a prancing walk.

Edgar ducked beneath an overhanging branch of a wild apple tree as Nick chugged through the weeds, his big sturdy hoofs impervious to the thorny brush. A faint perfume from the budding alfalfa scented the air, and swallows dove after grasshoppers we disturbed along the way.

"Race? Where to?" He smiled, always eager for a challenge. He urged Nicky into a faster walk.

"Just down to the point of the woods," I said, tugging at my T-shirt.

"Are you sure you're ready? Are you sure you ought to?" Edgar said with trepidation.

His worry was about me. Edgar would never refuse a race. He loves to win but hates to lose even more.

"Yes, I want to," I insisted. "Of course! You see how well I've been riding lately. We haven't had any mishaps in the past few weeks."

I felt superior. "Hey, let's see if *you* ought to!" And with that Fancy and I took off.

The race was on.

In the woods, Gadney, one of our tomcats, was perched, licking his paws, on a tree stump. He paused with a raised foot—surprised as we thundered past. We galloped past a patch of blue wild flowers and wild raspberries, and the wind stung my eyes to tears. Fancy was enjoying the race. Her hoofs thundered over the ground, her legs stretching before her, and her breathing was deep and rhythmical.

The ride was exhilarating. Fancy and I were one being, a composite of wind and motion. The sensation was so natural, so right. Released from my civilized chains for a time, Fancy and I were players in a fantasy world. I was a white-robed princess aboard my faithful steed as we galloped to our hidden castle within the forest's depths. And as the woods enveloped us, the brooding trees shrank back in deference to our goodness. We were escaping Edgar the Evil astride Nicholas, the scaly-hearted dragon. Only safety in our moss-covered mansion could save this Princess of Piety.

We fled through the dense brush, flying, soaring into the air. The clamor of Nicky's hooves sounded heavy behind as the ogre bore down upon us. I urged Fancy faster, and my hair flew back from my face. As we dashed over my imaginary drawbridge, I glanced back at my pursuer.

"AH-HA!" I shrieked in delight. "I've foiled you, you villain!" I only experienced one moment of triumph. Then the world slid out from under me.

My royal steed had stumbled into a groundhog hole. The disaster unreeled in horrific slow motion as Fancy disappeared from beneath me. Pitching forward, I grabbed the empty air then somersaulted over her head. With sickening force, I hit the ground, plowing a furrow with my face. For sure, I thought, the Princess of Piety was dead.

"Gay! Are you all right! Gay, are you all right?" The weeds rustled as Edgar rushed to my side. Arms clawed at me, and I gazed bleary-eyed at the figure before me. He shook me, and I uttered a feeble "okay." Then he hugged me as though I had just come back to life.

"I thought you broke your neck! You should have seen how you hit! My God! You rammed your face into the field. Then your body rolled over your head. Your neck was bent like a rubber hose. Oh, it was awful! I thought for sure you had broken your neck! Are you sure you're all right? How does your neck feel?"

"I guess I'm okay," I mumbled. How embarrassing—no princess of any status ever rolled grossly over her neck. "No," I said, getting more concerned as my fingers probed my face. "No! Oh, no, I think my nose is broken!" I winced, feeling it swelling already. My fingers danced across my face, searching for more bumps and lumps; they felt deep scratches, and blood was coming from somewhere on my cheek.

In a minute I knew the partial extent of damage by Edgar's grimace. "What are you looking at?" I cried. "Is it that bad?

He didn't answer, and the Dona of Demolition started to cry.

At least Fancy hadn't been hurt. She only had a couple of dirt smudges on her knees. We remounted and went back to the barn.

Back at the house, this Maharani of Mincemeat slunk to the mirror. My nose was puffed and my eyes were beginning to darken. I resembled a cross between a beaten Sugar Ray Leonard and Rocky the Raccoon.

X rays revealed a slightly shattered nose bone, which would heal on its own. Bottles of pain reliever lessened the hurt; and I had to live with my eleventh grade students' teasing, "Uh, Kemo Sabe, who is that masked woman?" I also avoided helping Edgar with his calls. I didn't want his experienced horse set clients to know I damaged myself like this from clumsily falling off a horse.

In time, my eyes and nose returned to normal size, but there was no cure for the worst hurt, the one that would keep me humble for quite a while. An Annie Oakley I still was not.

14

A Childhood
Dream

The raccoon mask I wore after Fancy's and my spill took several months to disappear. But it was only a few weeks before Fancy and I started training again.

Now I patted Fancy as we came down into a flat walk. "We're ready, girl. That was a great canter. Next week it's going to be you and me against the world." Fancy looked around, and her eyes were confident. I smiled. "North Sixty Ranch's horse show will have their first taste of a walking horse." Fancy shook her head. "We'll show them what a great ride you give."

Moving into the running walk, we circled the ring, its path worn bare from our constant practice. I was relaxed and proud on the most pleasurable riding breed anyone could want. Fancy was a limousine, and the wind gently tickled my face as we sashayed along.

As we approached the wood's edge, Fancy's knees pumped higher. Bruce, our orange-striped cat, darted out at us in play-attack, a glint in his eye. Fancy jumped and eyed her assailant, but I maintained my balance and composure. We resumed the running walk while I assured her the cat wouldn't swallow her in one gulp.

Then back down into an easy flat walk we came and then back up into her rocking-horse canter; it was easy and comfortable. We rounded the far side of the ring, and a voice called, "Looks better than ever!" It was Edgar.

"How about it?" I agreed. "Fancy and I are finally together, and I actually can feel the harmony Gale always talks about when a rider feels right on a horse." We halted as Edgar walked from the barn. He stood, hands on hips. Shadows sculpted him in chiaroscuro. He looked charming in the muted light.

"Yeah, you two have it together now, but, you know, you'll be competing against all different kinds of horses at North Sixty's show. It's going to be hard for a walking horse to place in a class with trotting horses."

That would be a major obstacle. Most other horses trot, but the walker is a sort of oddball with a different gait. The running walk is a fast walk, a four-beat gait with the feet hitting one at a time on their four corners; this is how the animal can glide so smoothly over the ground. In colonial times plantation owners used walking horses for their quick, smooth ride; the owners could stay in the saddle checking their fields for hours without tiring.

Walking horses are comparatively rare in the northeast. Quarter horses and thoroughbreds are more popular because of their versatility; but they trot, and it's a rough ride. The trotters would be my competition at the show. Although the running walk was noted for its grace and dignity, its very difference could ruin my chances at winning.

"Yes, the trotters will have the upper hand, and we'll be in the minority, but I only want to make a respectable showing there. I don't expect to win, really. My goal is to take Fancy into that ring and complete the class—actually *survive* would be a better word. Fancy will get accustomed to behaving herself around strange horses, and I want to stay on top of the horse, not fall off." Many horses rear and throw their riders into the dust at their first show. First shows are usually disasters.

"Oh, you won't fall off. When's the last time you went over the side?" he scoffed. He dared me to recall that foray into the woods.

Fancy shifted her weight, and I leaned over to straighten my socks that had accordioned around my ankles. "Two weeks ago," I kidded. His eyes bugged. "But I think I have this balance thing worked out now. The aim is to sit straight up and more toward the back of the horse, riding the rear end, as Gale would say. Before when Fancy spooked, I leaned forward into that protective fetal position. And that's what made me fall off."

I laughed, shaking my head, remembering how poorly I used to ride. Actually, it couldn't even be called riding back then. In the saddle, I had been a loose bag of joints and stuffing encased in a skin sack; I had no control over my body. Only by the disinterest of the Fates did I manage to stay in the saddle as though atop a beach ball. My legs were like putty, and my rather ample derriere moved like a greased thing in the saddle.

"Gale says she's never seen anybody have such an affinity for the ground as I do," I laughed. Fancy snorted.

"Don't worry about it. You say you've got the feel now, and you understand balance. Just keep your wits about you, and remember all that stuff in the showring," Edgar said and patted Fancy.

"I know. Sometimes I wonder why I'm going into this show business. Here I am thirty years old, a beginning rider on a three-year-old horse that has hardly ever been away from home, and I hope she'll be rational in the showring with a bunch of other horses. Sometimes I think I have more guts than brains. And every time I get dumped, I wonder when I finally will learn my lesson and give it all up."

He grinned and shielded his eyes from the sun, "You'll never give up, no matter what. I know you. Once you get onto something, you're obsessed with it. I would've quit by now. I can't take defeat," Edgar admitted, chuckling, stubbing his toe in the dirt. He looked at me with admiration, and I knew, too, I would never give up if only just so that he would be proud of me.

"I won't quit. Put it this way: I can't quit. I've got to do this thing, this showing—to like myself. You're a wonderful doctor—you're achieving something rare. When you walk up to someone, they respect you for that." He smiled. "But though I love teaching, for some reason I need to do this. It's like a childhood dream I can't relinquish until I achieve it."

The North Sixty Ranch bustled with activity the day of the show. People arriving at the show grounds drove their trailer rigs up the gravel road, spilling dust in their wake. Horses jigged in their vehicular compartments, sensing the excitement, curious as to the smells and sounds of other horses. Beautiful well-bred animals neighed from all kinds of trailers. There were two-horse trailers with dressing rooms for the rider, open stock trailers and huge, diesel horse vans that could accommodate as many as twelve animals.

The trailers were parked all around the grounds, and some of the horses tied behind the rigs munched hay nonchalantly. Some riders readied their animals for a class—applying hoof polish and brushing in coat conditioner for a sleek shine. In the distance, the hunter people in skintight jodhpurs and knee-high field boots, hunt jackets and hard hats galloped their thoroughbreds through the practice fields. It was like a summer fair, with different activities happening in each corner of the property.

Edgar ran a cloth down Fancy's chest, and I stood in my stirrups to check their length. "Calm down," Edgar said, pulling my pants leg over my boot. "You're a nundle of berves," he said smiling. But his smile faded too quickly. *That's not the right kind of smile,* I thought, adjusting my derby. *That's the smile of disaster; he's afraid for me.*

Fancy and I were ringside waiting for our class. Fifteen other horses and riders milled around also waiting. They shined with new tack, their manes and forelocks professionally manicured.

The riders, most of them anyway, wore passive expressions. Some, no doubt, debated trotting into the ring instead of walking in so as to catch the judge's eye. "Be flashy," I overheard a redhead on a black horse advising her younger friend. "Stay to the inside of the ring, and be visible. Remember to keep your eye on the judge so you can take it easy when he's *not* looking; then you can really strut your stuff when he *is* looking." While each rider devised a plan of attack that would insure a ribbon, I fantasized about hearing the announcer call Fancy's registered name, Gay's Merry Shadow, as a winner. But, Fancy and I didn't have to worry about the cute tricks. It would be all I could do just to keep my eyes straight ahead and maneuver Fancy and me around the ring in one piece. I'd have no time to look at the judge much less vie for his attention.

The horse show mothers, fathers, boyfriends and girlfriends stood outside the ring, giving advice, offering soda pop and dusting smudges from their riders' hunt boots. The fussing made me nervous. Out of the corner of my eye, I thought I saw a few of Edgar's clients and their horses, but I was too anxious to be sure.

Edgar straightened the coattails of the new saddle suit I had bought especially for this occasion. "It's okay, relax. It's only a horse show, remember that. You'll do fine." But I doubted him and his strained smile this time. I felt more and more apprehensive as the class before ours claimed their ribbons and exited. Then we were ordered into the ring.

I swallowed an imaginary orange lodged in my throat as the redhead confidently urged her black animal ahead. I gripped Edgar's hand. "I'm scared to death. My legs feel weak and flimsy. I need good, solid legs to balance with, but mine feel absolutely drained of strength. Look at all these horses," I whispered as they pranced ahead of me into the ring.

"They're older than Fancy, and their riders have probably been through this fifty times," he said. "Don't worry." I sucked my bottom lip.

Then I felt a stirring in my bowels, "I have to go to the bathroom."

Fancy moved restlessly. She shook her head as the other horses filed past her into the ring.

"No, you don't—don't be silly. You'll do all right," Edgar said. "But you don't have to go into the ring if you really don't want to. We can go right back to the trailer and go home and sip iced tea all afternoon." He would've liked that, I knew.

For a second, the idea sounded delicious—go home where I was safe and unthreatened to sip tea all afternoon. "No, I can't," I blurted, and into the ring Fancy and I went.

"Break a leg!" Edgar called.

We circled to the right at a flat walk. Fancy was coming alive under me, apprehensive with the unfamiliar horses snorting around us. On the right we passed a chestnut horse with white stockings. Its rider was a young girl with her hair in a bun; she sat confidently with a straight back.

Then we passed a gray Arab ridden Western style and tacked in a silver-studded saddle and bridle. It was jigging and sidestepping instead of moving in a straight line. Fancy sensed the horse's anxiety and called to it. Her ears flicked back and forth evaluating the situation. I moved Fancy to the left to give the Arab a wide berth.

Out in the open, I demanded Fancy's attention, driving her into the running walk at the announced "Trot" command. My apprehensions soon vanished as the initial sensation of being in the showring wore off.

The two of us were united, minds concentrated toward one goal: completing our first show without a mishap. Among the older horses for whom this was mundane work, we glided unobtrusively, doing our own thing and yet fitting in perfectly.

The judge signaled for the canter, and obediently, the loudspeakers gave the command, "Canter your horses, please. Canter, please."

Bringing her down into a walk and adjusting my weight for the correct lead, I signaled Fancy into the canter. As her back end pushed up from behind, I sat deep in the saddle, finding the rhythm of the gait. We had successfully made the sometimes-difficult transition from the walk to the canter.

A horse passed by on the left, rolling effortlessly past; but as more and more of the animals broke into a canter, Fancy's ears spun and pasted flat against her head. I swallowed hard. Then it happened.

I heard a loud snort—like that of an enraged bull—and at the same time, a pounding, out-of-control gallop coming from behind. It was the Western-style Arab giving its rider a rough time. He was startled. Fancy had heard it, too; and in her mind, no doubt, flashed the word, STAMPEDE!

In a panic Fancy leaped sideways to get away from the locomotive bearing down on her. Again I felt like a character in a cartoon—an Olive Oyl, gripping the steering wheel of her invisible car after it had been rear-ended from under her. But unlike Olive Oyl who "rode" the air until Popeye swept her to safety, I landed with a crunch in the sandy ring.

The crowd groaned. The announcer called in an urgent voice for all riders to stop their horses. Hitting the sand, I instantly wished for a pit to swallow me. I winced with the agony of the hurt, a hurt not so much of the body but of the mind—my pride needed an ambulance.

If only I could have disappeared, been whisked away by some sleight-of-hand so that the audience would have doubted their own eyes. How I wished to be a mole so that I could have burrowed into an escape hole or at least have been blind to the smirks. And I wished for a quick sunset into night so that I could slink unobserved into the nearby brush.

Unfortunately, I would not be blessed by luck or magic; there would be no earthquake to steal the audience's attention away from my disaster. I would have to face them all when I exited the ring. Furthermore,

Fancy was stamping her feet right next to me to assure me she was fine and that I could remount anytime. I was an immobile, very obvious heap in the middle of the ring.

Much as I felt like crying and running to Edgar, I couldn't—I was a grown woman, but I would've given anything to have been ten years old and allowed to leave the ring bawling my eyes out. The crowd would have understood and pitied me then; they would not have laughed.

Certainly everyone had to be in hysterics watching this cinder woman mopping the ring with her body. What a riot it must have been to see her roll all over the ground, gathering dust like a cowboy's spit-ball. There I was—a clod—my peepers blinking from beneath my dirty riding hat, like a spider peeking from its trap door. Yet I couldn't just lie there drawing attention. I had to remount as gracefully as possible.

Slapping my coattails as the dust cloud billowed around me, I gathered the reins and faced the judge, red-faced. My voice quaked, "May I please finish the class?" I really didn't know the protocol in a case like this. Was I allowed to finish the class? Why hadn't I looked it up in the rule book, just in case I did fall off?

Surprisingly, the judge nodded her head.

"Thank you," I mumbled, hoisting myself into the saddle.

"Walk your horses, please," the announcer called again. We came around at a flat walk, and I glanced up at Edgar who was watching from a hill. He shrugged. Tears welled up, but I blinked them back and kept smiling. I had to complete this class without falling apart.

"Now canter your horses, please," said the announcer. I signaled Fancy again, resolved that I had already blown any chance for a win. But I needed to finish *on top of the horse*, or I would never again enter a showring.

Fancy took the canter as calmly as if she had done this a hundred times before. We rocked past the judge, whose eyes bored into my back. Was I more relaxed now? After all, what had I to lose now? I had already done the worst. Not much else could happen to make me look more foolish.

But gradually, as I felt Fancy's relaxed back, my confidence began to return. The warm flow of self-respect started to slowly drizzle back. Fancy's easy canter took me past other horses and riders, past the announcer's stand, and the crowd at the rail. There was a fearlessness coming from her. Then the announcer ordered, "Walk your horses, please. Now line up in front of the ringmaster."

The dust began to settle as each rider walked his horse to the center of the ring. In the line-up, Fancy parked out, and I glanced down at myself. My dark green coattails and coat sleeves peeked out from the white dust, and my polished jodhpur boots resembled the shoes of a chimney sweep. Little did I realize that I had ridden the class with a quarter inch of dust in the brim of my derby. While my stubby braid lay askew under my hat, an ache began its slow thud up my back. The judge awarded the ribbons to the winners, and all the horses and riders exited the ring.

Edgar approached, head down. He hurt for me, and that made me feel even worse. When he did look up, I felt limp. As much as I tried to smile and pretend the whole thing didn't really matter, the traitorous tears welled up. Despite my frantic blinking, the tears trickled over the dam in final defeat. Edgar recognized the glassy look, but thank goodness few other people were around. Thank goodness the tears prevented my distinguishing any of Edgar's clients who may have been lurking in laughter. Thank goodness I could not see the show of pity for Doc's wife. There were no dramatic sobs, no moaning or groaning, just the salty tears pouring down my cheeks.

He put his arm around me and patted Fancy as we walked back to the trailer. "You had been doing so well, too," he said, but my eyes filled with water again and spilled down my face, running into the corners of my mouth and back out again.

I couldn't speak.

"Ya know," he said, "Ya know, I thought the judge was looking at you a lot before you, uh...fell."

"Sure she was," I spluttered. "You don't have to try to make me feel better."

"Yeah, I swear," he said. I avoided his glance. "Listen, I really thought she looked interested in you a few times. In fact, I thought at first you might place."

"Sure, sure," I said wiping the tears with the back of my hand. Even Fancy seemed depressed. She turned her head toward me, and her soft, deep-brown eyes peered sadly. "You didn't really think she was going to pin me?" I asked doubtfully.

"Yes, I really think so. Of course, when you fell, that automatically disqualified you." He looked sincere.

"Uh-huh, I know that," I sniffed. "At that point I only wanted to get back on and finish the class. I had to *at least* finish the class so I didn't make a complete fool of myself."

"Well, don't feel so down. There are plenty of other shows this year you'll be able to go in. After all, this was both your and Fancy's first show. Some of these other people have been showing since they were six-years-old."

"Like some of the teenagers, huh? I can't even compete with the little kids. I just wanted to make it out of the class alive and with some dignity."

"Well, you *are* alive," he kidded.

I smiled weakly. It was true. "Yeah, but my pride is wearing a shroud," I said.

We walked to our trailer where Fancy's halter hung on a rope. "Guess I'll hook her up, take off her tack and put my old clothes back on." I sniffed, unhooking the bridle.

Fancy dropped the bit from her mouth, and I smoothed her forelock in place under the halter and brushed a smudge over one eye. I loved her even if I couldn't stay on her.

"Everybody saw it," I moaned. "They all laughed when I bit it, didn't they?" I wondered if Edgar would try to spare me the truth.

"No, Gay...you're wrong on that one. I didn't hear anyone laugh. All I heard near me was concern for your safety. But no one was laughing at you."

I unbuckled the saddle and hoisted it onto its rack in the trailer; I crawled inside the tack room of the trailer to change.

My riding habit needed to be dry-cleaned and my blouse and gloves washed. The derby was ruined—probably a stiff brushing would remove the dirt and sand, but I didn't know about the dent. I hung the clothes, brooding over the mess I had made of them and my short-lived reputation as an equestrienne. I had let both myself and Edgar down.

I pulled on my jeans and zipped them. The sweat was beading up on my forehead inside the steamy dressing room. Fancy was munching hay and shifting at the back of the trailer. Pulling on a T-shirt, I heard rustling, then Edgar's voice.

"Gay, hurry up; you've got to see something," he yelled.

"Okay. I'll be right out." What could be so important?

He was staring at a yellow sheet of paper. His smile was mysterious.

"All right," I said. "What's that paper about?"

"This, my dear equestrienne," he waved the paper in front of me, "this tiny, minuscule piece of parchment...."

"All right already; what is it?"

"This, my loving wife, is the judge's sheet from the class which you just blew," he said, eyes merry, mouth sliced into a dirty grin.

I grabbed the paper, but he snatched it away as I lunged, arms outstretched, towards him. "Give it to me; lemme see it, please. Come on, let me have it!"

"On one condition," he said, holding the paper away from me. Fancy eyed the yellow bird and stretched out her neck, ready to bite it.

"What's the condition?" I asked, exasperated.

"The condition is," he paused, "that you promise to ride in the show next week."

"I can't promise that. I can't even stay *on* the horse let alone compete and do well. I don't want to make an ass out of myself again. No, I don't think I can promise that," I said truthfully.

"I'm sorry, but you're wrong. You did compete successfully— that is, up until the time you fell off," he said.

"What do you mean?"

He handed me the paper. "The judge was going to place you. It looks here that you might've gotten fourth or fifth place—out of fifteen riders."

I scanned the paper. There, sure enough, was my number jotted down on the side. Then it had been scratched out with the word *Fell* written behind it.

"So, you see, you are able to compete and do well, too. This was both your and Fancy's first show; and you would've placed, according to this paper. The only thing that fouled up the works was that you just happened to fall off." He grinned.

"My God, it's true," I squealed, staring at the numbers scrawled across the paper. "I really would've placed. I really would have—out of fifteen riders—my first show." I clutched the paper to my chest. "Wow! That's terrific! Fancy, did you hear that? We could have gotten fourth or fifth place!" I put my arms around Edgar's neck and kissed him. "Thank you...thank you; I love you."

"You can have that judge's sheet, if you want it. I already asked the show management. We can get a copy made and send it back, so you'll have a souvenir."

"I can't believe it!" I said. I stared into the sky, eyes fixed on a puffy cloud. I murmured, "I would've had fourth place—fourth place out of fifteen horses."

Somehow it didn't matter that I was grown up. It didn't matter that I had fallen off. That seemed only incidental. As far as I was concerned, my childhood dream had been fulfilled. And I, as do we all—somewhere inside—know that those dreams are the ones that really matter, no matter how old we become. I *had* been a winner in the class. The proof was on that little yellow judge's sheet.

That evening, after Edgar and I packed the equipment and put on Fancy's leg wraps and shipping blanket, we tucked her into the trailer and left. I proudly clutched the yellow paper all the way home.

15

Reilly, the Goat with Nine Lives

Chuck Kocher, one of Edgar's early clients, seemed a human mixture of opposites—a beady-eyed, mustached version of Harpo Marx with a tender love of animals. We first met him one rainy August afternoon when Edgar stopped to treat one of his sick horses. Despite his slapstick look, the man was an equine connoisseur and owner of one of the area's largest standardbred racing stables but had had a rugged earlier life as a carpenter and house framer. Upon closer inspection, I noticed his quiet, rhythmic patting of the ill horse's flank, his worried glance. He seemed to have a childlike, innocent love of life and its grace—a genuine concern for his animal's well-being and comfort. Hidden within him was the sparkle of youth, his pudgy cheeks puffing in and out with worry and indecision

"Vhateva ya say, Doc. Chust do vhateva ya can," Chuck's staccato voice pierced the air. The gnarled hands rubbed together, and his ebony eyebrows molded with worry into one.

"I'll be back tomorrow around nine o'clock to see how she's doing. Do you have enough penicillin until tomorrow? How about needles and syringes?" asked Edgar, returning equipment to the truck as the summer rain increased.

"Yes, I belieff I haff enough to last me, Doc," machine-gunned Chuck. He pronounced his words quickly and deliberately, with short

stops and abrupt enunciation. As we backed the truck around the barnyard and edged down the hill, he disappeared into the horse's stall
where he had kept a nightly vigil with his sick horse for the past week.

The man's unique concern for his animals had afforded us an
opportunity for knowing his essence, his inner workings. Other people
who know him might like him, but they may not know how much he
loves and appreciates his animals; they may not know that his pets are
his soft spot in an otherwise tough exterior. His menagerie consists of six
dogs, several cats, a barn full of horses, a couple of goats, a fox and a
raccoon. This is his family. The care Chuck gives his pets tops all others. More often than not, when the telephone rings, Chuck is on the
other end asking for the vet. The law of probability prevails: the more
animals one has, the more one needs to call out the vet. Likewise, we
also have our own cast of animal characters. Each cat, each horse, even
each fish has its own personality, and each will at sometime need medical attention. In Chuck we recognized all that we value: a need to recreate that symbiotic relationship between man and beast, the need to
reestablish those ancient ties to the primitive, the need to succor and
protect the innocent and dependent.

Once Chuck nursed back to health a ragged fox he found in a
trap. He also saved a fawn that was standing dumbly by its dead mother
in a roadside ditch, nudging the newly killed body—the only entity, the
only being it had known since birth. I admired the relationship that had
developed between this caring human and a wild animal. It was as if he
alone held onto some long-forgotten secret that somehow survived the
ages of "progress" and man's alienation from the natural world. Yet,
regardless of his scrupulous care, his pets fell victim to sickness and
accidents, too.

In truth, it seemed catastrophes lurked around every corner at
Chuck's place. Edgar went there so often that our familiarity with him
quickly reached a first name basis. Now, when Mr. Kocher called, he
said, "Hello, thiss iss Chuck. Iss Et home?"

His voice came out in spurts as though each word was shot
through a peashooter. One of the first times Chuck had called I had
trouble deciphering his speech. I wondered what "Et" was. Of course,
given a moment of thought, I realized that "Et," pronounced by a

Dutchman, was "Ed." Thereafter, I could readily translate Chuck's spic-cato speech: "Et" was "Ed," "lek" was "leg," and "neet" was "need."

One night about nine o'clock the phone rang. It was Chuck. The familiar voice exploded in my ears, "Hello, iss Et home?"

"No, I'm sorry, Chuck, he's out on an emergency, but he should be back shortly. Is there something wrong?" I asked, reaching for a pad and pencil.

"Yess, I think my goat, Reilly, neets some stitchess. Cudt ya haff Et call me vhen he gets back?"

"Sure, he'll be back soon. I'll tell him you've got a problem and have him call when he gets home. Bye," I said.

Then I heard a brittle, "Yeah, bye," on the other end, and he hung up.

Minutes later, Edgar pulled into the garage. After I relayed the message, Edgar phoned Chuck, telling him to bring Reilly over. A few stitches wouldn't take too long if the cut wasn't bad. But Edgar was to have a shock when the goat arrived, for it was no little suturing job, not something that only "neets a few stitchess," as Chuck had said. From out in the garage I heard Edgar yell, "My God, what happened! His whole scalp is almost completely off!"

Chuck, a survivor of many of his animals' disasters, said, mat-ter-of-factly, although still with a tremor of concern, "Vy, I think he godt inta one off the horse stalls and godt kickdt gudt in the hedt. He hass trouble valking, too, ass you can see." He put the goat down on the garage floor, and the dazed animal staggered drunkenly in a tight cir-cle.

Hearing all the commotion, I stumbled out to the garage to see what was the matter. It was unbelievable. A horse had surely kicked Reilly in the head as the border of a hoof outlined the laceration on the animal's scalp. The entire cut, shaped like a half-moon, must have been around five inches in length, leaving the scalp an oval flap of skin. It was disgusting, and what was worse was that a hard blow to the head surely spelled eventual death for the poor animal. Since the accident had just happened, the brain hadn't begun to swell yet, but within a few hours the pressure inside his head would certainly kill Reilly. Chuck looked concerned, yet it was a resigned kind of concern, one he had known many times before. He had had so many problems with all his animals that he was beyond being shocked by anything.

"Et, vhat do ya think ve can do for him?" Chuck shot out, holding the staggering goat by the leash.

"Let me take a closer look at him and see the extent of the damage," Edgar said, bending down to pick up the goat. He gently placed it on a table that folded from the truck.

And then Edgar shouted, "Damn! The skull is pushed down into his head about half an inch! He must've really been blasted. That's why he has trouble balancing himself; he's knocked silly." He peered into the gaping hole in the head. "Well, Chuck, I hate to have to tell you this, but it doesn't look very good. What will probably happen is that his brain will swell, creating so much pressure it will kill him. I can try to counteract the swelling by giving an injection of steroids, but there's no guarantee it will work. I've never seen a skull pushed down into the head like this." Edgar cupped Reilly's poor swollen face between his hands. After he gave his prognosis, a lump rose again in my throat. Poor Reilly.

"Vell, I knew he godt hidt pretty badt vhen I found him. Chust do vhat ya can, Et," Chuck said, petting the goat's side and steadying it. Cases like these always died in the end, no matter what good and conscientious care a vet and owner would give. Tears welled in my eyes. It hurt too much for me to see, and I went back to the house.

It took Edgar perhaps an hour and a half to suture Reilly's scalp back onto his head. I heard Chuck's car pull out of the gravel driveway and the door to the garage snap shut.

As Edgar came into the house, he said thoughtfully, "If the steroid injection works to keep down the swelling, he may recover, but it looks pretty bleak at this point. Poor Reilly…poor Chuck. He certainly has troubles with all his animals." Trudging upstairs, Edgar stripped the clothes from his back, muddied and bloodied from the night's emergencies.

The next morning, Edgar, with me following reluctantly, went to check Reilly: we were primed for disaster. To our surprise the goat was still alive, bandages still wrapped tightly around his pate like a cartoon character with a toothache. The only parts of his noggin visible were his muzzle and his eyes that peeped from the bandage—he looked lost in an icy cave. But, amazingly, he was alive, and he had regained some of his equilibrium.

Just then Chuck walked into the barn, a slight smile spreading across his lips. "Looks like he's going to make it, Et," he rocketed. His eyes, although happy, drooped—he had probably stayed up all night with Reilly, making sure he would not slip into a coma.

"Yes, sir, he looks terrific. I can't believe it. I'd say this fella has a pretty good chance of making it now. I'll just give him a few more injections to ward off any infection and swelling, and he should be in fine shape." With that, Edgar sprinted to the truck.

But a normal life Reilly was not destined to have. A few weeks later, a voice again machine-gunned me when I picked up the insistent phone. "Hello! Iss Et there?"

"Just a minute, Chuck. I'll get him," I said.

I heard the conversation from Edgar's end. "Oh, no, not again! How bad is it? Okay, I'll be up in a few minutes. Just try to stop the bleeding if you can."

"What is it? What happened?" I shouted, following Edgar down the hall as he flipped his jacket off the chair and struggled to put it on.

"It's Reilly. One of Chuck's dogs got him and chewed his hind leg to pieces." Edgar was out the door, and the truck roared from the garage.

A few hours later Edgar walked into the house. "How is Reilly?" I asked. "Pretty bad, I'm afraid. That dog almost took his leg completely off. It's all infected. I put in about thirty sutures, double-layered, too, but with that roaring infection, I doubt if this time he'll stand a chance. There could've been so much blood loss to the leg that it might just rot and die, too. Then we'll have to amputate, and still Reilly might not make it." Edgar pondered his bloodied fingernails. "That goat sure has had a rough life."

I chewed my cuticle, then asked, "How about Chuck? What was his reaction when he heard your diagnosis?"

"You know Chuck. He takes it all in stride. But I know he'll sit up all night with Reilly again like he did when he had the head injury. That guy is amazing. He'll do anything for his animals. He really takes good care of them. But I can't believe all the terrible things that have happened to that goat. If he lives through this one, it'll be a miracle."

And apparently it was a miracle, another one, because Reilly did live. In fact, with Chuck's non-stop care the goat was walking, a bit stiff-legged at first, within three weeks.

The next time when the phone rang, it forebode a terrible call. I picked the receiver up slowly. The voice blasted, "Hello, iss Et home?"

Again, I recognized the piston-like voice, "No, he isn't, Chuck. Can I help you?"

"I wudt like Et to come here when he gets home," Chuck said.

"What's wrong?"

"I just ran over Reilly vit my truck, and he's not breathing too gudt."

"Oh, no, not again!" I moaned. "I'll beep Edgar and tell him to get over there as soon as possible. Wrap him in a blanket, and keep him as still as you can till he gets there." I hung up, and my fingers danced across the phone buttons to tell Edgar of poor Reilly's plight.

"What! He ran over him with his truck? Call him back and tell him I'm on my way. What next?"

I called Chuck back. "Edgar will be there in about ten minutes. How's Reilly doing?"

"Oh, he's still alive. But he's breathing awful hardt. Seems he can't get hiss breath. He's flat awt, too. Won't even move." There was a pause. "I think maybe this time he's hadt it. I think I didt him in for gudt. But I chust didn't know he vass walkin' in back off the truck when I backt up." Chuck fired the words into the receiver. "I hope Et gets here real fast. I don't think he'll last too long."

"Well, don't worry, Chuck. He should be there any minute now. Hang in there."

I must've paced a rut into the hardwood floor until the faint outline of Edgar's truck raised a dusty trail up our driveway. I ran outside. "How is Reilly? Will he be all right?" I shouted into his window.

"He's in real bad shape this time, I'm afraid. Those other accidents were bad enough but not as bad as this. He's really battered up." Edgar closed his eyes. "I've done everything I know to do. Chuck will really have a few long nights ahead of him now. It'll be critical to see if Reilly makes it through the night. If he does, he might have a chance, but it sure looks hopeless at this point."

My hands went to my mouth again, "How's Chuck?"

"He's all right. He's resigned, I guess. Nothing seems to faze him anymore. But I bet he'll stay up in the barn with Reilly tonight."

The next day Edgar telephoned him. Again I could only hear Edgar's end of the conversation. "He is? That's good. Condition a bit better than last night? Okay, I'll be up shortly."

Miraculously, Reilly's condition remained stable throughout the next night. He was alive, but barely. I couldn't bring myself to go along with Edgar. I had become too emotionally involved with the goat and Chuck.

But the next day when Edgar called Chuck, I listened in on the other line. Chuck said, "Hi, Et. He's okay. He's looking better. I think maybe he'll make it ova the hump again." His voice sounded tired, but it still contained that staccato quality we'd recognize anywhere.

"That's great, Chuck. I'll be up sometime today to check him out again. Keep up with his medicine till I get there. Looks like you pulled him through again."

"Yep, Et. I'll see you later, then."

When Edgar came home that night, I immediately questioned him about the goat. What relief I felt after Edgar gave his revised prognosis, "Reilly will be good as new in a few weeks. The danger appears over. He'll be all right. Of course, Chuck is in about as bad shape as Reilly since he only slept three hours in the past three nights." Edgar chuckled. I could see satisfaction in his face, and I'm certain he could see it in mine, too. We both liked happy endings.

16

Ewes Growing Up

Fall flew by and icy winter took its place. During February and March, woolly sides swollen with their unborn, ewes begin dropping their lambs in singles and twins and, on rare occasions, in triplets. Nothing is quite so cute as a newborn lamb with its tightly curled wool and rather thick, stubby legs, seeming somehow unable to bend. The first days of life the lambs hop stiffly around the barnyard sorting out their different mothers and developing social skills.

The baby lamb sports corn-silky, floppy ears and a close-cropped furry face. Deep, dark, soft eyes peer, wondering, from under thick eyelashes. Unfortunately, a number of these innocent, docile creatures die every year from various birthing problems.

Such a problem affected us when one of Edgar's parents' ewes gave birth to triplets. Two of the lambs frisked around the barnyard while the other one slowly began to starve to death. Evidently the ewe could not supply enough milk for a set of triplets, and the two stronger lambs hogged what milk she had. Consequently, the third, a weakling from the beginning, was getting less and less nourishment.

One day, my mother-in-law noticed the one lamb "didn't seem right." She told us it looked skinny and hunched up. When he walked, he just stumbled sideways as if he were a drunk. When she came to the barn the next day, the sickly lamb lay in a dark stable corner, curled into a tight ball. The baby had dwindled down to mere bones covered with skin. Even with prodding the lamb wouldn't get up. Although he was still alive, he could only lie motionless, staring. He seemed to be awaiting death. Patting him to stimulate circulation, she whisked his limp body out of the sheep pen and brought him to us.

Not only was Edgar anxious to show off his growing veterinary expertise, but he and I were committed to saving sickly or dying creatures. Show us a mistreated cat needing a home, and we'll take it. Show us a healthy puppy soon to be put to sleep because the owners are moving and can't take him along, and we'll find it a new life. Show us an animal abandoned or orphaned, and I will raise it myself. We cannot tolerate inhumanity to animals; in our small way, we try to make up for the wrongs some people have committed towards the vulnerable creatures of our earth.

So, we offered to help the lamb. When Edgar's mother brought it to us, she knew the animal would get the best care available anywhere. Edgar immediately went to work on it, but it was too weak to stand or support its head, and it had a subnormal temperature: death was imminent. Edgar also discovered the telltale signs of dehydration as he pinched up a hill of skin on the lamb's neck only to see that it remained stiffly in place. Surely this lamb had little time left.

So Balliets' MASH unit went into immediate action. Placing a towel before the blazing wood stove in our living room, I set the lamb on it, stroking its shriveled body while Edgar set up an IV drip bottle. The lamb needed fluids and minerals to stabilize his functions. Soon the bubbles in the IV bottle began ticking to the top as Edgar pumped the life-giving salts and fluids under the skin. After we finished, the skin was bumpy with fluid-filled mounds all over the lamb's body, like sand dunes on a desert. But within an hour or so the lumps diminished as the fluid was absorbed by the dehydrated cells.

At the same time, I warmed a bottle of milk containing a touch of whiskey, a home remedy rather than a veterinarian's prescription, figuring this would perk him up if nothing else would. Holding his little head in one hand, I bottle-fed him with the other. It was extremely lucky he hadn't lost his sucking reflex, which contributes to the death of so many newborn lambs. Slowly and weakly, his lips began to pull on the rubber nipple, and, as the air bubbles flowed through the liquid, we both knew he was getting the needed milk.

For hours, Edgar and I guarded our woolly patient, running fluid under his skin and warming him before the fire. Slowly he regained his strength, raising his head with difficulty and peering, bleary-eyed, around the room. Noticing the strange animal before our fireplace, Timmy, our black tuxedo cat, trotted up to him and snuffled, his body arched, ready to spring back if the spooly-headed monster should attack.

Timmy, of all our cats, had the most curious personality. He was skinny, and with his bobby-socks legs set out away from his body, he looked like a bulldog. Although he appeared tough and unafraid and always nurtured his macho image, he was set to turn tail and run behind the hassock if the lamb was to make a sudden move.

Miraculously, by the night's end, the lamb's temperature was normal, and he even managed a few shaky steps around our living room, his tiny hoofs clattering across the hardwood floor. And when Timmy approached, too curious, stalking his prey from behind the sofa, the lamb, with great temerity, clip-clopped right up to Timmy and touched him on the nose as if to say, "Well, here I am. Now who are you?" Startled, Timmy jumped as if on a pogo stick and motorcycled behind the sofa again. Edgar and I laughed, but Timmy definitely didn't appreciate our mockery as he peeked from behind the couch.

To our relief, the lamb did survive the night, and within a week was completely back to normal. For one month the baby stayed in our warm basement and we fed him a bottle of warm milk every four hours. Day by day his strength grew until he grew too big to live downstairs. From then on he stayed in a pen built just for him in the barn.

By summer, the half-grown lamb we named Hiram was a big, forty-pound boy who skipped along after us as we did the daily barn chores. By now he was not only a barnyard animal but a companion. While trundling wheelbarrow loads of horse manure, I took care not to trample him as he scooted in front, jerking the wheelbarrow and me to a stop. In the garden he helped me weed, plucking the weeds with his delicate lips and then gobbling them down. Surprisingly, he did not pull the vegetable plants from the ground—only the crab grass, burdock and wild catnip. And when I took a siesta on a lawn chair, he plopped beside me and slept like an old dog. So, at four months of age, Hiram became the puppy we always wanted.

One morning while feeding the horses, I bent over to remove the wires from one of the hay bales. Suddenly, I felt a push from behind. A moment later I was picking myself out of the hay pile. With sprigs of hay sticking like porcupine quills from my hair and T-shirt, I wheeled around to find Hiram, a good sixty pounds now, backing up, nose to the ground, eyes in slits, ready to wage another attack against my bare, pale legs.

"What do you think you're doing?" I yelled, hopping to the side to avoid another crash with his oncoming head. Edgar was laughing at the other end of the barn.

"He's getting what they call *rammy*," Edgar joked. "I'm afraid our cute little puppy-dog lamb is not going to be so cute in a few months. Just the other day he slugged me in the legs when I took him for a walk. It's typical ram behavior, and it will probably get worse."

"Terrific," I mumbled as I watched Hiram bowl over a plastic bucket in a corner of the barn. "That explains why the wheelbarrow is overturned all the time. Do you think he's knocking it over just like he tried to knock me over?"

"Probably. And that's why your bicycle was in a heap in the middle of the driveway," nodded Edgar, chewing a piece of hay.

"Well, I'll be damned! I'll show him who's boss. He won't pull that kind of stuff with me! I'll get him with a broom!" I vowed, hands on hips I cast a threatening look at Hiram, busy munching alfalfa in a corner of the barn.

In a month, Hiram had become incorrigible, butting everything in sight: cardboard boxes, hay bales, piles of wood, buckets and the rototiller. One time he clouted a webbed lawn chair that was minding its own business in the middle of the yard. By the time the woolly maniac was finished, the chair lay in shreds like a defeathered chicken: the aluminum legs were bent and ripped from the seat, and the orange webbing was strewn across the lawn.

And he never overlooked a good wallop at one of us. Of course, Edgar had the strength to tackle him, wrestling him to the ground where he'd spank him with a firm hand. But I could only try to leap away when he decided to clobber me.

I must admit, though, it was funny seeing one of Hiram's attacks on Edgar. On one occasion, Edgar was bent over, coiling the garden hose around its storage cart, when the sheep began winding up at the other end of the yard. He dipped his head, aiming perfectly at Edgar's derriere, and as my husband looped the hose round and round the wheel, Hiram revved his engine, pawing the ground with his front feet, a look of concentration on his face. Then he shot loose like a pebble from a slingshot. I held my belly, straining with laughter as Edgar, usually so "together," sprawled amidst the loops of hose, scrabbling and fumbling like a roller skater atop a boulder pile. Then Hiram met his match. For hours later, the ram walked the barnyard with a handprint engraved on his fluffy back.

The situation was getting so serious that I was afraid to venture outside anymore. If I did, I had to sneak around the inside of the house first, checking the yard through the windows to see where the brute lay. Then I'd tiptoe to the barn, peeping around corners in dread of the woolly tank.

Finally, the day of reckoning came when we could no longer tolerate his bullying behavior. Edgar and I had noticed for a while that Hiram was acting studdish. He mounted plastic buckets and gasoline cans, probably envisioning in them voluptuous, woolly female bodies.

Imagine a ram's vision of his most beloved mate. There was Hiram's imagination ticking away: those ewes with their beautiful, slim, svelte legs beckoning to him as they winked from behind the hay bales. Who could dare tell what visions popped into his hot, little brain.

One sultry summer afternoon, as Edgar and I relaxed on the lawn chairs, Hiram trotted up to us, circling, looking, apparently, for a shady spot to rest. But something seemed to be irking him that day, for he did not lie down next to us as he usually did. On the contrary, he continued to pace around my chair, snuffling and snorting as if annoyed by a persistent mosquito.

"What's he doing?" I said to Edgar as Hiram sneaked, snorting, past my chair.

"I don't know. He's awfully restless," Edgar commented as Hiram slunk past me, sliding his nose along the edge of my chair.

We gaped at this sheep beside us who, for some reason, was acting so strange. What was wrong with him? Why did he continue to circle my chair, wide-eyed and preoccupied? And then I watched his eyes grow smaller and close to slits under his heavy eyelids. Without warning, he leaped from the ground and landed, all 150 pounds of him, in my lap. The air exploded from my lungs, and I struggled for breath, finally managing a weak scream, which, seconds later, mounted to a bloody curdle. I flailed like a tortoise on its back as he pinned me to the chair.

"My God, he thinks you're a sheep! The horny bastard is trying to mount you!" Edgar cried, roaring with laughter. "He's in lo-o-o-ve," Edgar sang.

"Ach! Get off! Get off me!" I shrieked, kicking. For some seconds we faced each other, the sheep doing what comes naturally and I trying to escape. As I screamed and squirmed, Hiram hopped back to the ground, astonished at this banshee. He gaped with a puzzled expression, as if to say, *Ain't I desirable, Honey?*

"That's it! That's positively the end!" I yelled. "We've got to find him a home!"

Edgar threw back his head and laughed.

"It's not funny. He thinks I'm a sheep!"

"You're right," agreed Edgar, still trying to stifle his laughs. He headed for the phone.

Within a few hours Edgar had found a good home for him—a substitute ram for a herd of ewes whose leader had just met his end. Now he would have his fill. He could live the "macho" life: he'd have his own harem of woolly beauties to dote on him. He could take them and his progeny on family picnics and to the country fair to see all the home-made jams, jellies and homegrown vegetables. Best of all, I thought, now he could have the real thing, instead of plastic buckets, gasoline cans and me.

17

Going Solo

Edgar's position with the multi-vet large animal practice had been invaluable. In fact, it was an intense, twenty-four-hour-a-day learning experience. However, after about one-and-a-half years he yearned to go solo to expand his practice and treat the many animals, exotic and tame, which lived in the area.

"Do it!" I said over breakfast one day.

But he was worried. "Your teaching salary is low," he said, "and we've got a mortgage to pay."

I crammed a jelly donut into my mouth. "So what. Let's take a chance. That's what you've always wanted to do, and I want you—I want us both—to do something that makes our hearts leap, not just plug along. I'm teaching, and maybe you could work part-time for a small animal hospital just to supplement our income while you start your own large animal practice."

"Gay, you're really wonderful," he said, beaming at me. "I'll give Paul a call to see if he can use help during small animal appointments some evenings. Okay, I'll do it."

Edgar bought an old pick-up truck, put an old Bowie unit on the back, and gave two weeks notice to the multi-vet practice. In those two weeks he worked night and day outfitting the new truck with drugs, medical supplies and surgical tools. He then sent notices to horse and dairy barns notifying them of his services. We both knew it was a bit tough drumming up business in the beginning since most large animal owners already had their veterinarians and didn't know about the new vet in town, but eventually word began to spread. And those who had used Edgar as part of the multi-vet practice wanted him exclusively now. Edgar felt a little guilty taking those clients, but it was their choice as to whom they felt would best tend their animals.

In addition to going out on his own, Edgar did manage a part-time position in the evenings doing small animal appointments at a clinic in Allentown. When I wasn't helping Edgar, I continued to teach high school English and took night classes towards a Ph.D., which would enable me to teach university-level English. Our joint earnings kept us afloat those first few months until Edgar's practice started growing. Soon, Edgar was averaging two to three calls a day, and things began looking brighter.

However, our new vet practice was built on a shoestring: no secretary/receptionist, no billing clerk, no vet technicians and no building from which to work. He and I did it all. Edgar and I took calls at home (when he wasn't doing rounds and when I wasn't teaching), and an answering service took messages in between. The base of operations was the den, and the medicines, bandage materials and other supplies we stored on shelves in the basement. He bought an x ray machine on an installment plan, as well as an autoclave, a microscope and a blood machine from a retiring veterinarian.

One day the flu kept me home from riding with Edgar; I felt like a piece of raw meat. Edgar altruistically offered to take my mind off my discomfort by volunteering me as his receptionist for the entire day.

"But I'm sick!" I burbled in self-pity. "I can hardly even stand up straight, and my throat is dry and raspy, and you want me to take your messages?" I quoted Edgar Allan Poe in desperation, "'Is there no balm in Gilead?'" My head felt like it was bursting under the sinus pressure.

"Ah, come on, Gayzie. Just take a few calls; we can save money by not using the answering service."

I propped myself dizzily on my elbows. "Only if you get me some ginger ale," I bargained. I'd only do him the favor if I got one in return,

I thought. He brought it to me instantly. "Okay, I'll answer the phone," I croaked, crashing back onto the sofa. A boll of mucus slid down my throat; I gagged and groaned to the cats, easing my inflamed body back onto the pillows. Edgar waved goodbye; I heard the truck start up in the garage, and he left for his first call.

I began to think about how different we were from each other, and how far we'd come through those differences. There is a universe and then another couple of galaxies of dissimilarity between my personality and Edgar's. He exudes a kind of pure, rugged individualism that qualifies him as a tower of strength, patience and willpower—resistant to the foibles of the human spirit. He strives for perfection, especially in the medical field. And he is naturally gregarious, perhaps to a fault. He instantly likes people and makes friends easily, trusting everyone, including those who are untrustworthy. He thrives on being liked and liking others. He relishes this kind of relationship with his clients, too. He comes as close to faultless as any person I've ever met, but his many virtues make me feel rather inadequate. He approaches matters with logic and calm reason while I react defensively and with melodrama.

While Edgar is natured like the bovines, I am more feline, in the jungle-cat sense of the word: territorial, protective of our home and ready to pounce on intruders and interlopers who feel threatened by our contemplative lifestyle. I am catlike in that I am curious and seek out experiences that enlighten and reveal the unexpected, the "other." Also, I am a not-so-radical feminist.

I approach people in much the same way people approach me. My motto is "What comes around goes around." It follows that if someone is generous, nice and honest with me, I will respond in like manner. But if he or she is cruel, snobbish, self-indulgent or egotistical, then I can beat him or her at the game. For this I make no apologies: one can only be what one must be. I am and always will be an existentialist—a defender of responsibility for one's own actions.

At times Edgar has actually appreciated my forthright approach to his clients, because, while he is averse to confrontation, I tend to dive into a battle asserting a kind of "territorial dominance." Yes, my husband and I resemble the unlikely partnership of a cow and a cougar, but the combination seems to work for us.

In fact, our odd mix of personalities worked quite well during those tense months when we were starting our own practice. In the first few weeks, we met a pushy cowboy at a local horse show. That day, the fancy, silver-studded show horses were being put through their maneuvers in the practice area. They and their owners sported the latest in expensive show apparel and shining leather equipment. Edgar and I were dazzled by it all as we walked to the showring and stopped to talk with Barbara, our farrier's wife, outside the practice gate. Suddenly, she looked up past us, her eyes wide, and shouted, "Watch out, don't run over our doctor!" Edgar hopped sideways, narrowly escaping being trampled by a horse and rider. The trainer atop the horse was practicing backing the animal and had unwittingly almost backed right over Edgar.

"Oops! Hi, Barb, how're ya'll doin'?" he said with a southern twang, pulling his horse up alongside us. "What did you say? Doctor? Who is he?" he said, pulling on the brim of his Stetson and frowning down at us.

Barbara introduced Edgar. "Alan, this is Dr. Balliet, our new veterinarian."

"Hello," Edgar smiled. He extended his hand. "Nice horse you have there."

But the cowboy ignored the offered handshake and without so much as a "Hi, there," straightened his shoulders, smoothed his shirt and began a tirade against all veterinarians that were not his. Had he known that Edgar's protective lioness was standing there, poised for the pounce, he might have weighed his words a bit more carefully. He chuffed, pulling importantly on his horse's reins, "Well, my vet is Dr. Harrington, and I wouldn't give him up for the world."

The shackles rose on my scalp. Poor Edgar, friend to all, looked as though he'd just been slapped. Then I attacked.

I snarled, my index finger pointing daggerlike at his face, "Dr. Balliet is every bit as good a vet as Dr. Harrington, if not better!" I stood, arms akimbo, red-faced and eyes blazing. The man gaped, slumped into his saddle and urged his horse quickly away.

Barb said, "Wow, I apologize for Alan. He overreacts sometimes." I stared with annoyance at the retreating horseman. Edgar stood, jaw slack, staring in disbelief at his wife turned protective tigress, but I caught a look of appreciation in his eyes.

Coincidentally, days later this same trainer called Edgar with an emergency. I answered the phone. "This is Alan Beam," he said. "I'm awfully sorry to disturb you, but I have a horse that's foundering, and I need the doctor's help right away." He continued in a sheepish voice, "You see, today is Dr. Harrington's day off, and, well...he's a personal friend of mine and all, but he wouldn't like to be disturbed on his day off and all...."

"That's all right; I'll relay the message, and Dr. Balliet will get back to you as soon as he can," I said. Within an hour, Edgar went to Alan's farm and put his horse right. Later, Edgar and I chuckled about the trainer who received some well-deserved training. Edgar has been attending Mr. Beam's animals ever since that day.

The memory faded, and my sick room came into focus again. I curled the afghan around my neck, squishing my body into the soft pillows of the sofa. The phone rang. I groaned. Dizzily, I got up from the sofa and snatched the receiver.

"Hello," I said, steadying myself, as Stevie, our black cat lying on the sofa, began to spin eerily around the room. I struggled to focus and make the sofa and cat come to a halt. I shook the fog from my head, and the cat mirage floated back to earth and settled onto the sofa.

"Yes, hello. Is this Dr. Ballot's office?" a woman's voice blurted over the other end.

"Dr. Ballot?" I stammered, blinking wearily. "Oh, you mean Dr. Balliet," I said, mopping my forehead in a wave of lightheadedness.

"Well, I want to know how much he charges to crop a Doberman's ears," she questioned in a staccato voice.

Nauseous with vertigo, I plunked my robed, aching body into a nearby chair. "I'm sorry, he doesn't usually work on small animals, but I can recommend a small animal hospital for you if you'd like."

Probably thinking she was talking to some uninformed receptionist who was unaware of the size difference between a miniature poodle and a Doberman, the woman bristled at my suggestion that her dog was a small animal. The receiver rattled, "A Doberman is NOT a small animal!"

I shook the reverberations from my ear and very calmly said, "Well, it certainly is compared to a horse or cow." A bead of feverish sweat raced down my neck.

Then a little peep sounded over the other end, "Oh, that's true. Good-bye."

I reeled miserably back to the sofa and fell asleep, visions of recalcitrant clients slogging through my head—in particular, a horse trainer who had forced Edgar's tolerance level to the ultimate test.

"Yes, definitely in the shoulder, Doc," the trainer said in my delirium. "I can tell by the way he moves. What do you recommend? I think perhaps a shot of cortisone in the joint might reduce the inflammation." The trainer pointed to the horse's shoulder. He stood in typical cowboy gear: Western hat, plaid shirt, leather chaps and pointy, leather-tooled boots. He tapped his toe in the dust.

"I really don't think it's the shoulder, Don," Edgar said. "His pain, it looks to me, is in his hoof. Let's check it out."

Searching through his farrier's box, Edgar found the hoof knife and began hacking away at the foot's hard sole. Flakes of horn slid away under the scraping, and after a time and with a quick gouge of the knife tip, a gray trickle of pus flowed onto the ground.

"Uh-huh, there it is," Edgar smiled. "The culprit was an abscess—that's all—certainly a lot better than a shoulder problem, and it's also much easier to treat. After I clean and wrap it, he'll be sound in a few days. Looks like you're in luck."

The trainer thumped his boot in the dust, hands sunk deep into his pants pockets. "Yes. Well, he very well might have an abscess, but I know there's still something wrong with his shoulder."

Edgar paused. "All right—maybe you're right. Let's see how he moves when he walks," Edgar offered.

The trainer snapped a lead rope to the horse's halter and took the animal off at a trot, but the horse showed no limp. Now that the pressure in the foot was relieved, he moved pain free.

The trainer, lips pursed, stopped, dejected and disappointed with the miraculous recovery. Then Edgar said, "I do think maybe he is a bit stiff in the shoulder, just like you said. Give him a day or two of rest, and that shoulder'll come around."

The cowboy flashed us a look of "I told you so" and with a smirk and hitch of his pants, led the horse to its stall.

I turned to Edgar and hissed, "Shoulder? It wasn't the shoulder, and you know it! You saw how soundly he walked after you got the pus out. Edgar, who's the doctor around here, anyway?"

"Dear," he winked, "after I fixed that foot, I needed to repair a damaged ego." He paused. "Now we *all* feel better, right?"

But that day I had trouble accepting his judgment, and I still feel the same way today. People should earn the right to authority, not simply demand it.

I woke up with a start, and the dream faded away. An hour later I began feeling a little better—the cats were no longer spinning. Edgar would be home soon, and he could listen for the phone while I sipped ginger ale.

18

Meet
Tucker Jones

Edgar wasn't the only veterinarian in the area who was struggling to build his own practice. So was a classmate of his, Tucker Jones. We had heard that Tucker had begun his mixed practice from his home, and we had time one day to visit him and see how he was doing. He lived on the side of a mountain that could only be navigated with a four-wheel drive vehicle.

"Look out!" I yelled and gripped the door handle, bracing myself. Edgar jerked the truck around a foot-deep pothole, veering off the dirt road and onto the muddy shoulder.

"It's okay. Just hang on. We'll be at Tucker's place in another half-mile." Edgar threw the truck into four-wheel drive.

We took another dive into a crevasse, and my head hit the ceiling of the cab. "Ow! A half-mile more of this torture? I can't believe Tucker has a half-mile of nearly unnavigable driveway. How does he get his own car up this way in winter?" I marveled, grabbing my armrest as we ricocheted off another bump.

"He doesn't. When the snow's real deep, he parks his car at the end of this road and walks the entire half-mile to his house." Edgar whipped the truck around another large pothole, and I held on with determination.

"Now, look for the sign," Edgar said, squinting.

"What kind of sign?"

"The sign to the nudist camp," Edgar replied.

"To the nudist camp?" I choked. "Why?"

"I told you, he lives by that nudist colony, Barely There Acres. Remember when I came up here one time, and just around a bend— look, that's it right there." I strained to see as Edgar continued, "I saw all these people sitting around a campfire—stark naked—they looked just as surprised to see me as I was to see them. There I was interrupting their powwow, driving right past their meeting with this big old truck. I felt a little awkward, to say the least. They were all naked as jaybirds."

We rounded the bend, and I craned my neck, hoping to catch a glimpse of a real live nudist. Edgar frowned. Unfortunately, there were no nudists today; the campfire was a rubble.

We continued clawing our way up the muddy road that was Tucker's driveway, navigating still another slippery hairpin curve. Finally, cresting over a grassy hill, Edgar stopped the truck.

"Gay, meet Tuckerland," Edgar proclaimed with a sweep of his arm. "This is the homestead of Tucker Jones, VMD."

Tucker Valley loomed below. The place was a bizarre mixture of woodland, pasture, vegetable garden, human habitation and animal refuge. The yard resembled a flea market with its array of junk: broken-down automobiles, tractors, wheels and other skeletons of long-deceased machines and appliances. Horses, cattle, chickens, dogs and cats roamed helter-skelter, and somewhere in the midst of all this was a mobile home.

Tucker lived in a trailer home just as we had while Edgar was going to veterinary school. Tucker's "box" was set haphazardly atop half of a house foundation from which a sewer pipe wound around and down into a septic tank. A rickety porch loaded with cats led down from the trailer's front door which was missing the lower glass pane. With his head protruding through the empty window space, a German shepherd, panting comfortably, surveyed the area. He had the best of both worlds—the great outdoors and indoor comfort.

The trailer's other three sides were hooked up to an electric fence that provided an enclosure for three horses and two shaggy, mud-smeared steers. Three other mangy German shepherds saw us and pointed their noses, howling—an inharmonious trio. A few chickens chased each other and pecked at the sparse grass that was Tucker's front lawn.

Bits of machinery and pieces of farm equipment slumped in the front yard. There were parts from an antique lawnmower, rusty plows and pieces of tractors which farmers had bartered for veterinary services. An assortment of tool sheds, old doghouses and chicken coops leaned in every direction. A broken-down, rusty, green Rambler sat contentedly in the front yard as we drove past and parked amid the maze of junk and confusion that Tucker called home.

"Tucker lives here?" I asked.

"Yeah, different isn't it? He sure has a lot of stuff lying around. Well, he just bought the property, and I guess a lot of this junk might be here from a previous owner. He probably hasn't had time to clean it all up, especially with starting his veterinary business."

A cat jumped on the hood of our truck and stared in at us through the windshield. By this time, we were surrounded by the three dogs, standing on hind legs, barking at our windows. One gray-muzzled shepherd saved his energy for one big yelp only after the others had finished their long, cacophonous chorus.

"Look, there's Tucker," Edgar laughed, waving at the front door.

"Hi, Ed," Tucker called. Then the apparition behind the door disappeared, and there was scrambling inside.

I climbed from the truck as a dog took a threatening stance at my feet. Easing past, I dashed to the front porch after Edgar. Suddenly, a yellow tiger cat raced ahead, and a puff of feathers spit into the air. The cackling was deafening.

"Cut that out!" Tucker scolded the old hen. "She's always chasing the poor cats." The chicken motorcycled around the side of the trailer, and the cackling died away. "Hey, how ya doin', Ed? Come on in."

We stepped onto the tiny, plywood porch. Edgar steadied me amid the sea of cats assembled there—seventeen of them on a three-foot-square porch: tigers, whites, grays and orange ones.

What struck me most was the missing windowpane in the front door. It gave all the cats, dogs and chickens easy access to the inside of the house; they could travel in and out of the trailer as the mood struck them. A cat dove from the inside to the outside just as we came up the steps. The upper pane was still intact but full of smudges. Behind the dirt and grease-clouded upper pane, Tucker smiled broadly, like a graveyard ghost, while his hairy knees protruded starkly through the lower opening.

Edgar pulled on the door handle, but the door stuck; he yanked harder, but it wouldn't yield. "You have to come in through the door—*through* it." Tucker smiled, pointing to the open window. Scrunching down, we straddled the opening, squeezing ourselves inside.

"Hi, Gay," Tucker grinned, "nice to meet you. I'm Tucker." His handshake was firm and friendly.

"Hi," I said. "I've heard a lot about y…." I gulped as one of the dogs poked his muzzle at my backside and bellowed.

The inside of his home was just as mind-boggling as the outside—practical hominess mixed with the tools of the veterinary trade. It was amazing. The usual furnishings of a living room were without pretension: a sofa dating from the 1950s; a flocked, slip-covered chair; an Early American cocktail table. Piles of newspapers, magazines, veterinary journals and textbooks lay cluttered everywhere. Used dishes and kitchen utensils were stacked high on a set of nesting tables. One could not see an inch of floor underneath all the books, blankets and tossed clothing. An ironing board stood amid all the junk and on it lay a cat, its body stretched out belly-up, its paws dangling over the sides.

Tucker noted our surprise. "You folks almost caught me in the middle of a spay job. I was just setting up when you came." He smiled and tapped the cat's eye for a reflex.

A tall man of about forty years, Tucker had a pleasing, easygoing manner in contrast to his sternly set, square jaw. He wore horn-rimmed glasses over a hawkish nose and had a black mustache. He was good-looking in a rugged sort of way. He was a Sasquatch on a smaller scale. One might picture Tucker—his long, lean, muscular body emerging from a Tibetan glacier—as a kind of mountain barbarian. Yet the savage grinned kindly at me. He was a rugged innocent, an ingenue of the woods. He had an honest look, and I liked him instantly.

"You're doing the spay on the ironing board?" I asked.

"Yeah, I'm doing small animals out of my home now since my landlord decided to sell the building I was renting." There was no bitterness in his voice. He tugged thoughtfully on his dark stringy mustache. "So, until I get another place, I'll have to do things as best as I can right here. It makes things a bit tight, I know, but so far it's been working out pretty well—I've been doing all right by my patients." He patted the cat.

He led us into the kitchen, but a bookcase loaded with veterinary textbooks and magazines blocked the hallway. Tucker turned sideways, sucking in his stomach and sidestepping down the hall, his back against the opposite wall. Edgar followed in the same manner, then I.

We slid into the kitchen, and Tucker proffered me a chair stacked high with business correspondence and various other stationery. I started to remove the papers to the kitchen counter also laden with dishes and other utensils when suddenly a flash of light lit up the room.

"What was that?" I yelped, almost dumping the papers.

"Oh, that's just my incubator. I had a cow with a uterine infection the other day, and I'm trying to grow the bacteria." He looked in at the agar plate. "Yep, there are some colonies growing out already. I'll have to check it this afternoon." Tucker stared at it as if he were reading a crystal ball.

Edgar smiled. I sat at the kitchen table, and Tucker made three cups of instant coffee. Edgar removed a stack of papers and magazines from another chair and sat down, hemmed into the corner by the roguish bureau.

"Would it be all right if I borrowed your x-ray machine today? Mine's on the blink. I need a picture of a hock that's stubborn to heal," Edgar said.

"Yeah, sure," he said. "How's your practice going?" Then a discussion followed which I could not really understand. Tucker offered his experience with lame hocks, and they debated various treatments: DMSO, injecting the joint, poulticing, etc. Tucker was an excellent vet, and I could tell he and Edgar had a lot of respect for each other's expertise.

"I'll get the x-ray unit for you. It's in the bathroom." Tucker squeezed past the elfish bookcase that seemed to come to life whenever one wanted to pass by.

"Tucker's a hell of a nice guy," Edgar said, sipping his coffee. He noticed me surveying the cluttered kitchen. "He's just a bit disorganized, you know, kind of slip-shod when it comes to neatness and having everything in its place. He's more concerned with his patients than with order. Don't let the looks here fool you; he's a real good doctor."

Then there came a noise, a quiet, low rumbling underneath my chair. My skin melted onto my seat. "Did you hear something?" A shiver rippled up my thighs, and goose pimples rose on my neck. Edgar was still as death, his eyes bulging. Again I heard what sounded like a foghorn in a mist.

"Maybe it's another cat," I said hopefully. I swallowed with difficulty. My imagination pictured a lion with incisors the size of my big toes.

Edgar offered, "Yeah, it probably was."

"BLA-A-AAA-AAA-H-H-H-HH!"

A gurgling yell shot from under me, and I hurtled off my chair and into the arms of that mocking bookcase. In the melee two dinner plates hit the floor, and toast crumbs flew into the living room.

"Jesus, it's a goat!" Edgar blurted, the color flowing out of his cheeks.

"Right under the kitchen table!" I said. The goat, like the cat, was spread in a semi-conscious state on the linoleum floor. This time a piercing cry parted its thin lips. I leaned against the bookcase, wringing my hands; no one knew what would pop out next in this carnival fun house. Would I meet the old laughing woman guarding the "Haunted Cove" behind the pantry door? Next I expected to see a boa constrictor slither from behind the furnace. This forebode shades of Stephen King.

A casual voice sounded from the living room. "I'm sorry, Ed. The leather strap on the x-ray unit ripped the other day, and I haven't had it fixed." Tucker squeezed past the snickering bookcase. He saw us staring under the kitchen table. "Oh, is he waking up? Had to take a lump from his left hind leg this morning. The owners should be able to pick him up shortly." He leaned over and patted the goat. A thin wail came from the goat's lips, reverberating in the tiny kitchen. Then the incubator light flashed on again, enveloping the stacked dishes on the kitchen counter in a pallorous light.

"Hey, Tucker, did you hear anything about your prospective clinic yet?" Edgar opened the centrifuge sitting next to the refrigerator.

"I should be hearing something on that today, as a matter-of-fact. Looks good, though. Good price—place does need a little bit of work. It will take a while to get fixed up. But it'll all come out in the wash. I'm not worried about it; working in the house like this does cause certain inconveniences, but I can put up with it for as long as I have to.

"Say," Tucker repositioned his eyeglasses, "I'd like you to look at something and see if you agree with my diagnosis."

He opened the refrigerator door, and a chemical odor rolled out. A carton of milk and the usual staples that belonged in a refrigerator stood on the first rack, but there was something alien on the second.

A large, gelatin-like lump, encased in a beige plastic garbage bag, flowed out over the shelf. Tucker pulled the large mass from the refrigerator, handling it delicately, and lowered the two-foot-long, three-inch-high blob onto the kitchen table. Then he rolled back the plastic edges. A strawberry-yellow cow's liver protruded from the bag, and a rank odor wafted into the air. I swallowed hard.

"I'm sending it to the lab today. What do you think?" The goat let out another groan. "This was a fairly young cow, too."

"It had to be some chronic thing: looks like it's gone through hell. Cirrhosis in a young animal? I really don't know what it could be. Guess it could be any number of things. Let me know what the lab says on that one," Edgar said thoughtfully.

I bent down to pet the goat; he didn't know where he was or what he was doing here. Likewise, I didn't understand any of the medical talk. Many terms were familiar, but I didn't know anything about pathology.

"Well, I'll let you get back to your spay." Edgar picked up the x-ray unit with the broken strap. "Let me know when you get your new clinic; I'd like to see it. Let's get going, Gay." He inched past the giggling bookcase and steered the x-ray unit out the gaping hole in the front door.

"So long, Tucker." I smiled. "It was nice meeting you," I said, tripping over a shoe. "Good luck with your practice." The cat still lay on the table, its pink tongue curled around its lips, its eyes still staring. I crawled through the door, and Tucker steadied me as I put a foot out the window opening and onto the porch.

"Watch your step there," he cautioned. The cats dove off the porch. The dogs, barking furiously, escorted us to the truck, and while Edgar carefully fit the x-ray machine into the back of the truck, I once again saw Tucker's hairy knees peeking out the lower window hole. From the blurry top window I could make out a ghostly hand waving back and forth. As Edgar started the engine and we backed around the driveway, one last high shriek from the goat echoed from the house.

19

And Beauty
Was His Name

Whether you are a medical doctor or a veterinarian, you learn friends have a way of seeking "free advice." In between doing a few large animal calls a day and small animal appointments a few nights a week, friends and relatives began bringing their pets to our house for treatment. Some of our friends' pets were really spoiled, too. One in particular was Beauty.

"Eggie," our family friend Harvey Horwith said thoughtfully, looking at my husband and rubbing his ruddy hand through his stubbled, gray beard, "What kind of shots do you think we should give Beauty?" Harvey was a friend of Edgar's parents of perhaps twenty years whom Edgar had come to regard as an uncle. Now retired from school teaching after having raised two children, he and his wife, Lucinda, concentrated their silver years on Beauty, a gray and white feline family member.

Beauty was the queen bee of the Horwith household. Her owners, particularly the softhearted Harvey, were wrapped neatly and tightly around her little paw. Harvey filled her needs for feline delicacies without question: she refused any food but hamburger or chicken with boiled rice. Whatever Beauty wanted, Beauty got. She picked her choice of the chairs for her afternoon naps, and since the cat didn't like to be left home alone, she accompanied them on day trips to Peddler's Village and New Hope. One time, they even took her to the Jersey shore.

Many pets are not treated with such indulgence. Some are starved by their owner's neglect and indifference. I abhor a person who takes advantage of an animal's vulnerability and trust. Animals are seldom mean or ill-tempered without good reason: they deserve humane treatment. Furthermore, animals are seldom moody, unless they are sick, and they are never vengeful. How sad that many become whipping posts for humans with marital problems, career disappointments and other of life's vicissitudes.

Certainly, the ideal relationship between an animal and its owner should be mutual, somewhat like a marriage, in which neither partner dominates the other, but learns to give and take by turns. Similarly, as people reinforce mutual treatment in each other, an animal also responds with respect and fairness when treated that way. A friendly assurance elicits a lick on the knee, a wag of a tail; an offer of sugar assures an appreciative nuzzle from a horse. Indeed, animals appreciate human kindness and generosity.

However, Harvey's relationship with his beloved kitty, Beauty, far exceeded the ideal mutuality between man and beast. Beauty, for sure, had the upper paw, mewing demands for her specially cooked tidbits and demanding nightly rights to Harvey's bed comforter, hand-sewn by an Amish woman from Lancaster. Likewise his wife, Lucinda, also indulged Beauty. They were as two grandparents with a newborn grandchild.

On the day Beauty and her parents arrived at our house for her first appointment, I spied her bright green, marble-round eyes as she peered out from her soft yellow baby blanket. Harvey cuddled her as I tucked the edge of the blanket under her chin. She gave me a kind blink and then drew her eyes back into a comfortable, lazy gaze. With a pleasing grunt Harvey hoisted the bundle of joy, a full twenty pounds of it, onto his left arm.

"So, what do you think, Doc, about the o-p-e-r—" his words trailed off. Harvey shot a glance at Beauty and clutched her close as if to shield her from the news.

"Sure, Harvey, I'll spay her now. When you bring her back to remove the stitches, we'll give her all her shots."

"Okay, okay, but be careful with her, Doc." Harvey nodded. The old man's jowls and lips jiggled and smacked as he rocked Beauty rhythmically in his arms.

Harvey kept talking to Beauty as if she had pre-surgery jitters. I looked at her more closely. To me, Beauty did not appear concerned at all about the affair. While he cooed and reassured her, Edgar began preparing the surgery area (our kitchen table) and the instruments: scalpels, scalpel blades, sterile spay hooks, clamps, etc. "I think it's time for you to leave, Harvey," Edgar finally said.

We were ready to begin the operation. Harvey's expression became anxious and his pallor white as Edgar drew the anesthetic into the syringe. But he didn't want to leave, so Edgar relented and let him stay with us. Edgar explained the effects of the tranquilizer. "It's okay, Harvey. Ketamine is a safe drug. It doesn't really make the animal go to sleep; you'll notice Beauty's eyes will be open, but she won't be aware of her body or have much feeling. However, a cat under Ketamine is sensitive to noise so we must be careful not to be loud." He continued, "When she comes out of the anesthesia, she might twitch a bit, but that's quite natural. I also buffered it with another drug to help her relax all over. Everything will go just fine, I'm sure."

"Gay, hold Beauty for the injection," Edgar said, turning to me.

"Uh…Eggie, I'd like to hold her if you don't mind?" Harvey interrupted.

"Sure…sure. Now, hold her tight there in your blanket, Harvey. The shot stings a little when it first goes in, and I don't want either of us getting bit."

"Okay, okay, Eggie. I think I have her pretty tight in her quilt." Harvey jostled the cat so that only one meaty leg was exposed. There on a gray patch of fur would be the target: a perfect bull's eye.

Once more Harvey patted the blanket. "It's all right, Beauty baby; in a few hours it'll be all over, and you'll feel good as new. Mommy and Daddy will take you home to your beddy, and we'll give you some hamburger when you're all better."

"Here goes, Harvey. Now hang on to her," Edgar said, and with that he darted the needle into Beauty's flank. The blanket jerked and stiffened, and a gurgling yell arose from within its folds. It was muffled, of course, but high-pitched and furious. Just as suddenly as it had come, it died as though someone had clapped a box over it. There was silence. Edgar and I relaxed. That was always the worst part: giving the stinging anesthesia.

"Eggie, Eggie," smiled Harvey as Edgar injected the last of the drug into Beauty's fleshy leg. "She's…she's…biting me." He said it calmly and softly, as if noting the total recorded rainfall for the year. Only his smile's twisted, ruptured quality made me aware that something was truly wrong. Silence.… Then, softly the voice said again, "A-a-a-ah, she's biting my hand…like hell, Eggie, like hell." Harvey whispered the words between gasps, yet he continued to smile, his teeth clenched.

The injection had lasted only a second, yet Beauty held on, her teeth clamped into Harvey's hand. We responded in slow motion mostly because he was still smiling: the proclamation just didn't match the physical response.

Finally the blanket went limp, and Harvey removed his hand. "Oh, poor Beauty, poor Beauty," Harvey moaned. He uncovered the cat, and now Beauty lay in his arms like a head of wilted lettuce, her eyes open and staring, her mouth gaping dumbly. Harvey proffered his injured hand. Four angry pin holes were stamped into his palm.

Edgar said, "My God, Harvey, you should've told me she was biting you. Well, I mean you did, but…I didn't think she really was biting you hard. You just didn't look it."

"Oh, she can be a little devil sometimes," Harvey admitted, blinking back the tears. "It wasn't all that bad, just a little nip is all." The ruptured smile cracked across his face as he braved the pain.

Edgar gently lifted Beauty onto the kitchen table and began to prep her belly. I unfolded the sterile instrument packet, careful not to touch anything inside. Next, I positioned Beauty just so, tying her legs with soft ribbons to the four table corners.

Edgar watched, his sterile hands raised, and then he started as I secured the last leg.

"What's the matter?" I said, opening the sterile glove package.

Edgar blinked, stared, and blinked again. He said, "We are doing a *spay* here, aren't we?"

"Certainly," I said with surprise.

Gingerly he lifted Beauty's tail and stared in horror.

"What's the matter?" I said again, bending over to the source of the problem.

"Don't you see them?" Edgar said, turning red.

"What?" I returned, following the direction of his finger. There, grinning at us, were two testicles, plump and furry.

"Harvey, Beauty's not a female—she's a male!" Edgar blurted out.

Harvey was struck as still as a mannequin. "No, that's impossible. Beaut is a girl!" Harvey said. "I'm sure she's a girl. She has been all these months."

Edgar pointed to the evidence.

"My God," Harvey said cupping his chin thoughtfully. "I could have sworn she was a girl. My Beauty, my Beauty...," he cooed. "My Beauty is a boy." Then he burst out in his characteristic wheezy laugh. We joined him too, as Beauty in all his newfound male identity lay spread out asleep.

Weeks passed before we heard from Beauty and Harvey again. This time the voice was frantic. "Eggie, it's Beaut. I think he's sick. He's behaving very strangely. I'm really worried about him."

Edgar asked what was wrong.

"For the past few days he has started squatting in strange places instead of his litter box. One time, in fact, he was sitting, trying to tinkle (the word *urinate* offended Harvey's sense of decency) in one of my open clothes drawers. Now...I'm so scared, Eggie, he just lies on his...uh, my chair. He won't eat; he just lies there looking awful."

"You've said enough, Harvey. Bring him over at once; he's probably blocked," Edgar said.

"Blocked? What do you mean? Is that bad?"

"It could be if we don't see him promptly. It means he has stones, calcium deposits, lodged in his penis. They are blocking the flow of urine," Edgar explained.

"Oh," came the voice over the telephone. "Well, what can we do about the stones in his...uh...you know, his *pencil*?"

Pencil...now that was a new one. Many clients out of embarrassment called the penis by different words learned during their elementary years: "piddler," "doo-doo," "thing," "private," "pickle," but today we'd learned a new term for it, *pencil*.

"I can try to dislodge the plug manually, but if he's prone to stones, he'll probably need a urethrostomy eventually. For now, bring him up here, and I'll catheterize him. We must expel the urine."

Soon, a white compact sedan rolled up the driveway, a backwash of dust spilling over it. Harvey emerged stiffly and reached into the bucket seat beside him. Out came the yellow bundle which he cradled lovingly. Harvey's face was somber.

"Let's see him, Harvey," I said, opening my arms for the bundle. But he wouldn't let Beauty go; he was really worried. Edgar took him gently from his arms.

After an initial examination, Edgar declared, "We have caught the problem just in time—his condition is stable, but he needs immediate attention to expel the toxic urine. No doubt the kidneys are beginning to shut down and are poisoning his entire system."

After only a few injections and manual manipulation, which this time Harvey didn't want to watch, Beauty came unblocked, shooting out a lovely stream of urine. Only another veterinarian can appreciate such a beautiful sight because urinary blockage can be a life-threatening situation, bringing death in a matter of days or even hours.

"Okay, Harvey, he's all right now, but cases like this usually recur. You might decide to have a urethrostomy done on him eventually. It's a bit expensive, but well worth it. At least you'd know this wouldn't happen again."

Harvey hitched the tranquilized yellow bundle onto his other hip. "Now, uh, understand, Eggie, expense is no problem, absolutely no problem. Lucinda and I want only the best for our Beauty," he said, pulling the blanket flap down over the dozing cat. "But, about the operation, now; is it safe? Will it hurt him? I don't want to see him hurt." He cleared his throat.

"It won't hurt him: I'll guarantee that. He won't even know what's happening; he'll be under anesthesia. What will hurt him more, though, is not getting the operation done if he really needs it. Should he have another of these attacks, it could kill him in a few days if it should go unnoticed."

"Yes, oh, yes, I understand. Go ahead, keep going; tell me more about it. What is actually done?" He hoisted the yellow bundle and resituated it in his arms. Harvey was so anxious and fidgety when it came to Beauty.

"Essentially," Edgar said nonchalantly, "we cut off his penis."

Harvey choked, and the sunny bundle popped into the air. Edgar could have explained it a bit better than that, I thought. Harvey looked as though a hand grenade had gone off in his stomach.

Stuttering and fumbling, Harvey said, "Cut off...cut off his...*pencil*?"

I gave Edgar a dirty look. Then he realized his mistake. Edgar knew that the operation was safe and painless, but Harvey knew nothing of the sort. All he had heard was, "cut...penis."

One could only imagine Harvey's nightmare of the event: surgeons in white gowns and masks perched like vultures, carving knives poised for the slice, the slash, hovering over poor, defenseless Beauty, lying with his pencil exposed, a sacrifice upon the altar, a gift to the god of pencilectomies.

I gave Edgar another dirty look.

"Well," Edgar said apologetically, "Harvey, it's okay. What we do is cut a section out of the urethra to enlarge the tubal opening so that the stones can get out; they can't become lodged in the small opening of the penis anymore." Harvey shuddered at the word. "It's really not as bad as it sounds, and a surgical team usually does the work, at least in the practice I'll recommend. Should you decide to have it done, I will be glad to assist in the operation, even though I really don't do much small animal surgery these days. In fact, I would be honored to hold Beauty's paw when he goes under the knife."

"Yes, yes," spluttered Harvey. "I would appreciate that so much, I certainly would."

"And I'll help, too," I said. During a few small animal operations I had assisted Edgar as the sponge girl, the prep person, the anesthesia assistant, and the general "gofer," providing suture material, bandages, antiseptic powder, etc.

My introduction to the operating room had come when Edgar spayed my parents' Newfoundland dog at his first job with the multi-vet practice.

Harvey began shaking his head. "All right, all right, Eggie, I don't want to take any chances. Make an appointment for Beauty, and we'll bring him down for the operation. I want to do what's best for him, and if he'll eventually need this operation, then we'll do it, right away...won't we Beauty?" Beauty wriggled in his yellow blanket, an affirmative response.

"We'll let him get over this episode and do the urethrostomy in a few weeks," Edgar said.

As Harvey set his yellow bundle carefully on his car's front seat, he said, "Beauty and I trust you, Eggie; we know you'll do what's best for the Beaut."

"Don't worry, Harvey, we'll take care of your Beaut," Edgar called after the retreating car.

20

Animal Facts and Fiction

While Edgar served his animal clients, I was teaching high school, and I took many of our animal stories to school with me. My students appreciated a few minutes away from the books and the opportunity for us to get to know each other on a different level.

"Honestly," I said to my first period English class as the fog drifted past the window one morning. The tenth graders were in their usual early morning stupor. "Timmy was out on the town last night," I said, throwing my hands into the air.

Sixty drowsy eyes turned toward me. Ah-ha, they thought, a teacher with a problem—interesting.

"Who's Timmy?" one asked, stifling a yawn.

"Oh, my cat. I'm telling you, he's crazy!" I exclaimed, turning to sharpen a pencil.

"Why?" another student asked. The whole class was perking up a bit.

"Oh, it's nothing really." I changed the subject, "We really should get into this grammar lesson right away this morning; we still have a lot to do on adverbs." A groan rose from the class.

"Well, maybe it'd be better to get it off my chest and tell you guys; it's just that it's so maddening." I stared out the window at the rain coming in torrents, but out of the corner of my eye I could see I was getting to them.

"Yeah, go ahead. Get it off your chest," a student offered. "Tell us about the cat already."

Gearing up, I walked right up to the kids in the front row. "Well, last night he bugged and bugged me to let him go to the mall. He felt he absolutely couldn't live through the night without getting a new cassette for his tape deck."

"What!" I heard one kid say in a tone of voice like, "Who're you trying to kid?"

"Yeah, can you imagine—a lousy tape by the Kinks! I told him I'd give him a kink in a minute if he didn't stop bothering me. But he kept whining about the darn cassette."

"Oh, boy," one turned to another, his eyes rolling. "She's off the deep end this time."

"I'm telling you the cat is nuts!" I paced deep in thought. The entire class was attentive now. It certainly wasn't our lesson on adverbs, but this just might get their attention. "After all," I said, "it was the prin-ciple of the thing; he was grounded, and he knew it. But he still had the nerve to ask me to go out, and on a school night yet."

"Wow—spaced out," another voice muttered from the back of the room.

"Sure. He's grounded," a girl with bib overalls teased. "What did he do to get grounded?" she said, egging me on some more.

"Made a mess!" I shouted, looking up at the ceiling in rage. I loved acting. Putting my all into it, I shook a pointed finger in the air, "He was roller skating in the basement!"

"Roller skating! A cat!"

"Yes, well," I admitted, "I said he could since it was too cold for him to skate in the garage."

"Oh, WOW!" came a voice from the back of the room. Eyes were beginning to pop now.

"Yes, he was roller skating in the basement, which, understand, I didn't mind, but…."

"But what?" Amos blurted.

"Well, that wasn't good enough. He had to really 'get into it,' you know. He had to drag his tape deck downstairs so that he had music to skate by." Amos shook his head in appreciation of Timmy's need to skate to music. "Then, on top of that, he decided to drag his strobe light down there, too, and his lava lamp. He's really into 'cool,' you know."

"What! Tape deck, strobe light, lava lamp—a CAT?"

"Yes," I said with a serious look. "I did tell you Timmy was a cat, didn't I?"

"Yeah, sure," another student said. He turned to a friend, "Just let her ramble. Go on: get it off your chest, Mrs. B," he told me in a soothing voice. Nobody, I took notice, was sleeping now.

"Well, he stayed down there for three hours. Imagine! Edgar and I were trying to read the Sunday paper, but who can read with all that music blaring and pounding up through the floor? You know how it is—your parents get annoyed when you do it, no doubt," I admonished.

"Yeah, we know how it is," one admitted in all honesty. His look was no longer incredulous.

I continued, "So, finally, I marched right down into that basement; after all, it is our house you know, not his, and—GADS! You should've seen him!"

"Why? What was he doing?" Jennifer blurted.

Another student interrupted, "I can't believe this!"

I said, "There he was boogying around the basement to 'It's Been a Hard Day's Night.' Can you imagine! He got into my old Beatles' albums and the turntable I had stored there. You should've seen him—his roller skates made a hell of a racket on the concrete. I couldn't believe it! There was my cat racing around the basement in slow motion under the strobe light, and the record player was screaming its heart out. It was just too much!" I cried.

"This is just too much," said another. Then another kid asked, "Then what did you do?"

"I did the only thing I could. I took the needle off the record, shut off the strobe light and lava lamp, and turned on all the lights. I said, 'That's enough! We've had it, Timmy!'"

I faked a look of complete horror and continued, "Then I saw them, all over the basement!" I paused, my eyes big as soup dishes.

"What?... What did you see?" Mark demanded.

I shook my head as if to clear a horrible memory, "Big scratches. Big ruts where his skates had dug into the concrete, especially in the corners. It was awful—there were big, ugly gouges all over the place, just like a car makes laying rubber."

"Oh, no, all over your basement?" one girl sympathized. "How will you ever get rid of them?"

"I don't know. Probably have to have a mason fix them. But Timmy's grounded for a good long while. Oh, he makes me so mad sometimes." I sighed and shook my head. "Well, anyway, I'm glad I got that off my chest. We better start working here."

"I don't believe this," said John, a guy with shoulder-length hair and a headband.

"Yeah, I didn't either when I got down to the basement," I agreed. He gave me a curious look. "Now, open to page seventy-four," I said, "and we'll finish adverbs."

21

In Search of a Needle

We were quickly finding out that in the veterinary profession each day offers new perceptions, new possibilities, new personalities—those of both people and pets. Some horse owners cater to their horse's every need. As you might guess, this kind of client may become a source of major irritation to the already harried veterinarian. The worrywart will not hesitate to call at one in the morning with the announcement that his horse has been lame for the past two weeks. Then he adds insult to injury continuing with, "When I got home from the party, he seemed much worse, Doc." Edgar tolerates this type very well, but if the owner could hear me grousing and growling in the background, he might think we harbored a cougar.

Yet for all that, the doting animal parent has good intentions. When we leave a barn, it's good to know the animal will receive conscientious nursing care from its owners and that, with proper nutrition and exercise, it will probably make a full recovery. Best of all, these owners tend their animals faithfully through their geriatric years until their demise.

For example, one of our friends has a twenty-five-year-old horse plagued by bouts of arthritis, ringbone and general apathy caused by old age. We know that old Red will stay on the farm, keeping the pigs company and taking Mary out for an occasional walk through the fields.

Red is an equine member of their family, and he will eventually die comfortably on the farm.

But some people overprotect their animals and are, at times, oblivious that they do. Some with good intentions try home remedies on cuts and scratches that only aggravate the injury, while others overfeed grain and then need the vet to cure a bellyache or recommend a diet. As part of his professional services, Edgar teaches children and their parents that too much kindness and generosity can sometimes be harmful.

We are friends with one such doting family, the Sigleys, whose life centers around Misty, their daughter's pony. Trudy's Shetland has better medical care than some show thoroughbreds; he receives first class accommodations and gourmet food daily. He is allowed in the house and always attends family picnics and holidays, including Christmas, when he is invited into the house (to the delight of all the relatives) for his grain ration. Misty is always immaculately groomed, and his stall is probably as clean as my bathroom. He is the king of the castle.

Many times, on our way home from a call, Edgar swings into the Sigley driveway, remembering that Mrs. Sigley had wanted Misty's teeth checked or a bump examined. Mrs. Sigley stands, arms across her chest, muttering over and over, "What would we do if anything ever happened to Trudy's pony? We all love him so much." On average, Edgar checked Misty once every three weeks—a lot for a healthy pony. But no one, especially Edgar, wanted anything to happen to him.

The little girl fussed over her pony more than some girls doted over their dolls. She once tied blue bows in his mane and tail and painted his hooves with children's nail polish. The end of Misty will devastate Trudy, and that, in turn, will hurt the entire family—and us.

Likewise, for some horse fanciers, taking care of Flicka occupies them around the clock. Should she start the sniffles, the vet will be called the next day. For the next two weeks she will enjoy her convalescence in a cozy straw bed, sporting the latest in horsey fashion: an Irish plaid woolen blanket, matching hood with peeper holes and woolen leg warmers. Her master devotedly becomes her slave, taking her temperature three times daily and carting flakes of hay and fresh buckets of water throughout the night.

To such a horse lover's stable, we were once summoned to check a lame foot. It was freezing outside, and we had battled a bad snowstorm to get there. Slipping and sliding, the back end of the truck swerved around on the ice-covered road. I could envision our pickup, with its 1300-pound veterinary hospital in the back, going into a tailspin and all the drawers opening up, spilling pills and bottles along the road. I had visions of the refrigerator compartment popping open and the bandage compartment flipping its lid, trailing strings of cotton and vet wrap behind us in the snow. Finally, carefully, we pulled up to the front door of the stable.

We hopped a small drift forming in front of the barn door. Snow swirled behind us as we stepped inside. Whisking the dry flakes from our coats, we stamped our boots in the dark musty stable. There in the twilight of the chilly barn stood the owner, Mr. Scott. At sight of us, he flitted like a phantom to the horse's stall and carefully coaxed the horse into the open barn. Then he formally introduced the animal to us, "Baby, dear, this is Doctor Balliet and his wife. They are going to fix your hurt leg." Baby peeked at us from under her insulated red hood and blanket, a kind of horsey snowmobile suit. The horse was normal size but, with the blanket enveloping her like a thick second skin, she looked as big as a draft horse.

The owner bit his lip and got right down to business. No coffee and donuts at this place, I thought, shivering. "Good to see ya, Doc, but I wish I didn't have to—I don't know what happened to her. Yesterday she was just fine. But I let her out to pasture this morning, and when I brought her back in, she just didn't seem to want to walk right," Mr. Scott grounced (that's Pennsylvania Dutch for "complained"). He was a slight man of about sixty, standing with slumped shoulders and wearing only a nylon windbreaker. He had on no gloves and wore skinny black socks under black dress shoes soiled with sawdust and dirt smudges. He looked cold in contrast to his horse who looked stifled in the overstuffed playsuit.

"Okay, let's see where the problem is," said Edgar. He bent over, lifting the horse's back foot. Mr. Scott held Baby by the halter, cooing into her ears, "It's okay, Baby, everything will be okay in a few minutes."

Testing for pain, Edgar pressed the pastern area above the hoof; it was normal. Baby turned her hooded head and eyed us through her peeper holes. Around her eyes skin wrinkles formed that indicated she felt anxious.

I patted Baby on the side of her neck. "It'll be okay now. Don't worry." She eyed me with suspicion.

"I believe the problem is in the hoof, but I'll do a nerve block just to be sure," explained Edgar thoughtfully.

"What does that do?" questioned Mr. Scott. His face hung blood-hound-like, crinkly and droopy with worry.

"It's no big deal, really. I'm going to anesthetize the two main nerves running down the leg into the hoof. We'll wait five minutes, and then, if she doesn't limp when she walks, that means the problem is in the hoof. If she continues to limp, we know the problem is somewhere else in the leg. Then we simply diagnose and treat the leg wherever the problem is."

"Will it hurt much?" Mr. Scott winced. He shifted from one dusty foot to another. He must have been freezing in that thin windbreaker and his office shoes.

"Many times, they do feel something like a pin prick as the needle is inserted. But she doesn't seem too jumpy; she'll be all right, won't you, Baby?" Baby didn't say anything; she just shifted her weight. "Don't worry," Edgar whispered under his breath as he took the needle from its pouch, "we won't hurt you." The material around the peeper holes buckled and folded.

This was like trying to read someone's expression under a surgical mask. All you can interpret are the eyes peering over the top. It made for dangerous business when dealing with a horse. One can be given fair warning of being kicked or bitten by a horse by reading the body signals it sends out: laid-back ears, a twitching flank, skin that is nervous to the touch, a tense look on the face and the skin around the face, a stiff poll (the top where the head and neck meet). Here, we didn't know what kind of signals Baby was sending out underneath her blanket.

Suddenly, Mr. Scott said, "I can't stand needles. I can't watch." The sawdust billowed in a nervous cloud as he stamped his feet; he swallowed with difficulty, but he still hung on to the lead rope.

Mr. Scott's hands were turning a scaly scarlet hue with the biting cold, and he crouched alongside his horse with both feet together like a tin soldier, trying to preserve what little heat he had. I pitied him in his frigid condition, and my teeth chattered in empathy.

"Okay, then, you just keep his front end busy while I work on his back end," Edgar directed.

This situation was not ideal for targeting a thing as tiny as a nerve on a horse's leg. Since the horse was all bulked up with blankets, she was difficult to work around. Worse, however, was the lighting. Outside it was pitch black, and it wasn't much better inside. The bulb hanging overhead must have been forty watts, certainly not bright enough for painstaking work.

"I don't see how you can see anything," I said, squinting.

"You're right. I've got to have more light. Go out and get the flashlight under my seat," Edgar said.

I ran to the truck.

In another ten minutes the horse, now brightly lit, was prepped for the procedure. Arms loaded with a bottle of lidocaine (an anesthetic), the cumbersome flashlight, two syringes and two needles, I stood ready to assist.

"Now, do you have the two needles and the syringes of lidocaine ready?" Edgar asked. "I'm going to hit one nerve at a time. Just be ready to hand me the juice after I stick the needle in," he added.

As Mr. Scott cooed candied words into Baby's ear, Edgar, crouching behind the horse, lifted and stretched the animal's hind leg out, supporting it between his knees.

"Now shine the light here," he indicated, pointing to a spot on the leg.

Moving directly behind the horse, I shuffled my armload of stuff and tried to shine the flashlight on the right spot. While Edgar gripped the leg between his knees, I bent over, shining the light onto the animal's ankle.

"Good, that's great. Now give me a needle and be ready with the syringe," he ordered. "How are you doing up there, Mr. Scott?" Edgar called. "How's Baby doing?"

"Oh, fine, just fine. She's as calm as an old dog," Mr. Scott assured. He shot me a reassuring smile.

"Good, good. That's what we want to hear. Here goes the first needle. Just keep that light steady, Gay," reminded Edgar, "and watch yourself—just in case."

CRASH! In less than a second our world had turned upside down. There was a loud clash of water pails, and I found myself on my back amid old horse buckets, worn-out tires and used horse shoes. Before I realized what had happened, Edgar was crawling out of my lap. "Are you all right? Are you all right?" he yelled, grabbing my shoulders.

I blinked, shaking the fog from my head. "Yes, I'm okay, what about you? What happened?" We both gripped each other like Ike and Mike, blurting the same questions, giving the same answers: "You-okay-yes-I'm-okay. What-about-you? You-okay-yes-I'm-okay."

I stared up at my husband and the horse. The grain barrel lay over on its side, a victim of the accident, its contents on the floor. A stack of buckets had crashed down and lay scattered around in a half moon. Horse brushes, horseshoes, buckets of farrier nails, whips, crops and pitchforks all decorated this corner of the barn, all haphazardly strung around like pickup sticks. The place resembled the aftermath of a barroom brawl. But even more incredible was Mr. Scott, who was panting a string of apologies.

"It's okay, Mr. Scott." Edgar reassured him. "We're just fine— just fine. Just as long as no one is hurt, everything is fine. Don't worry: these things happen. Horses are very unpredictable animals."

But Mr. Scott's apologies were not aimed at us. He hadn't heard a word Edgar said. His face was up against Baby's, and he was stroking her capped forehead with his hand. He ignored Edgar's assurances, cradling Baby's head in his arms, cooing, "Sorry—I'm so sorry, Baby. That must have hurt just terribly, didn't it? So sorry, my Baby."

As Edgar helped me up, we retrieved the flashlight that had rolled next to a set mousetrap, the bottle of lidocaine, miraculously unbroken, and the syringe. But we found only one of the needles.

"Where's the other needle?" Edgar questioned, searching the barn floor. We looked, our noses to the darkened floor, in vain. Mr. Scott was still consoling Baby. The missing needle was gone, hopelessly swallowed up in the mass of junk that littered the corner.

I said, "I don't know. It must be here some...." And with that, as I glanced up at him, I saw the lost needle—sticking out of Edgar's scalp.

"My God!" I wheezed, staring at Edgar, eyes popping, mouth gaping. I covered my face with my hands.

"What's wrong? What are you staring at?" shouted Edgar, bug-eyed.

"The needle! The needle! Don't you feel it? It's sticking right out of your head!" The needle dangled in Edgar's hair, its white base pointing skyward.

Finally, he yanked it from his scalp. By luck it had only penetrated about an eighth of an inch. "I can't believe it," he giggled, amusing disbelief on his face as he twirled the needle wonderingly in his fingers. "I couldn't feel it because of the anesthetic in it. Wow, that's never happened before."

Baby stood, seemingly unperturbed in the corner of the barn. Whether from emotional relief or release, suddenly we both burst out laughing. Trying to catch our breath, we heard Mr. Scott's predictable reaction, "Poor girl, poor Baby, how that must have hurt."

Edgar proceeded to prepare another needle. While Mr. Scott soothed and distracted Baby, Edgar blocked out the nerves in the foot to check for lameness. No sooner had Edgar given Baby the two shots than the horse went sound. Certain now, that the problem was in the hoof, Edgar diagnosed Baby with a bruised sole and prescribed corrective shoeing and analgesics.

22

Beauty Goes to Hollywood

Some weeks later, Harvey brought Beauty in for his surgery. The surgery team consisted of Edgar; Doctor Adamson (a small animal surgical specialist); Rick, an assistant; and me.

We are proud of the professionalism of our veterinary surgical room. Most people have no concept of the degree of expertise and the kind of technical surgical procedures used on animals today. Surgery on equines can encompass tumor removal, bowel and stomach surgery, orthopedic surgeries and numerous others. Fewer operations are done on cows, sheep and goats, but cows generally go "under the knife" for repair of a displaced abomasum or stomach. Every operation on an animal abides by the same medical standards and proficiencies as those performed on humans. The operating room is no less sterile, the doctors no less trained or competent, no less caring. The expertise is equal to that necessitated by humans, and, in some cases, it is even more exacting. To be sure, Harvey would only entrust Beaut to the best, and I was sure Edgar was.

This day Beauty shed his yellow, fuzzy blanket for a hospital-green surgical drape. After the surgical assistant, Rick, clipped Beauty's hind end and soaped and scrubbed it down to a slick shine, the anesthetized cat was cantilevered onto a special tilting surgical table that offered a singular, bird's-eye view of the operating site. Beauty's, in Harvey-speak, "button-hole" stared silently from beneath the sea green, sterile drape.

Throughout the hour-long procedure, Rick monitored Beauty's vital signs and heart rate. A urethrostomy is quite a meticulous operation because the organ is so tiny and the attached tube to be resected no thicker than a piece of yarn. This could rival human eye surgery for its precision. The doctor demonstrated surgical handiwork at its finest as he resected the fragile tissues, stitching together a new plumbing system for Beauty. It was fascinating how the doctors could decipher one piece of tissue from another, cutting and discarding pieces here and there and carefully preserving and attaching other ones at different places.

All was precision, organization and expertise, accomplished even amidst conversation of hot sausages and where to get the best onion rings in Allentown. Moments like this proved that nothing was quite so impressive as the talent of a surgeon.

The operation completed, we took Beauty, bleary-eyed and a bit sore, to the intensive care unit. Specially heated and with monitoring devices for the critically ill or those coming out of anesthesia, this ICU paid testament to veterinary medical efficiency. Every recovery cage had a video camera which projected images of the patients to the hospital's nursing staff. One dog rested in his cage as the EKG hooked to him recorded his heart's every bleep and blip.

Beauty had come through the surgery fine. A day later Harvey picked Beauty up, as normal as every other cat in the block, only minus one part. Later Harvey joked that "Beauty had had the lead taken out of his pencil."

The telephone jangled in the living room a few days later.

"Gay...Gay...it's Harvey here," he shouted into the phone. Something was wrong.

"What's the matter, Harvey? Is something wrong with Beauty?"

"Yes, as a matter of fact, there is. Why, Gay, for the past three days...uh...uh...he hasn't had a...."

Oh, boy, I thought; Beauty's constipated. This time I wasn't going to help facilitate the conversation. Harvey would just have to learn to say the words that grossed him out.

"Yes, Harvey," I said, "go on."

Harvey stuttered, "He hasn't...uh...boomered yet. Not in over three days."

"I see," I said, smiling.

"Yes, and he's looking a bit depressed. He won't eat, just lies around and sulks."

"You could try giving him an enema, Harvey," I suggested. "That might be all he needs. They're just like people. Sometimes they need a little help getting things going again."

"An enema?" He sounded flustered. "I should give him an enema?"

"Yes, do you have a Fleet enema at home?"

"No, no, never had one, never *had* to have one." I heard him swallow hard. A red glow seemed to flow out of my phone's earpiece. Harvey probably wondered why his cat couldn't have "clean" things wrong with him like colds, stiff joints or dermatitis. At least those things he could talk about. His voice was pleading, "Do you think Eggie would do it for me? I really don't know how I would do such a thing."

"Okay, Harvey, bring him up in a half-hour, and Edgar'll take care of him."

"Thanks so much. I'll be right there."

Of course, Harvey refused to watch the administration of the enema. It offended his sense of decency, too, as it offended Beauty's. He had a right to be concerned about Beauty, for the cat was depressed and lethargic. Edgar palpated his gut area and, saying it felt like an over-stuffed beanbag, he gave the enema.

Harvey had prepared for the event, in any case. In the back seat of the white compact car sat Beauty's cat box, ready just in case the enema started to work in the ten minutes before they made it home.

Fifteen minutes after Edgar and I had waved good-bye to Harvey and Beauty, the phone rang. It was Harvey.

"Oh, Gay, I'm so happy. Beauty doodled in the car on the way home...uh...I mean in the litter box in the car. And it was wonderful!"

"It was wonderful?"

"Yes, it was great!" Harvey continued, evidently hoping I'd ask for details on the episode. I didn't but was in for a blow-by-blow description of the miraculous event anyway. Drums rolled in the background as Harvey whispered feverishly, "Oh, oh, wait! Beaut's scratching in his litter box right now." The drumroll continued, and then I heard an imaginary cymbal crash. There was a long pause and then Harvey said, "Well, he did it again—isn't that wonderful!"

"Yes, yes, Harvey; you must be very proud. I hope Beauty is feeling better now. I'm glad to hear he's going to the bathroom."

But Harvey wanted to tell more.

I took the bait, "How was it?"

"Absolutely normal!" he yelled. "It's fantastic!"

Fantastic! Hardly a description of a cat's manure.

"Yes, he pooped in the car on the way home." It was déjà vu all over again, but I let him purge himself. "Ah, boy, did he go. I'm telling you, he went all over the place." I began to burp thinking what it must have smelled like in that compact car. "I'm so pleased, and do you know, Beauty looks so much more relieved now, that he has, you know...." I tapped my fingers on the desk. "Uh…boomed. Tell Eggie thanks from me and the Beaut."

"That's just great, Harvey. I'm happy for you and Beauty. Now everything should be all right for him. I'll tell Edgar everything came out all right." I couldn't help the pun.

The next phone call from Harvey came a few weeks before their scheduled trip to California to visit their daughter. He needed an appointment for a health certificate for Beauty because they were taking the cat along with them.

"You're taking Beauty to California with you?" Edgar asked in disbelief.

Harvey was all enthusiasm, even though Edgar tried to discourage him, saying, "Well, really, there *really* are some good animal boarding places in the area. I could recommend a few for you."

There was a long pause. Putting Beauty in a kennel for a couple of weeks was out of the question. "Okay, okay," Edgar relented. "I'll make out a health certificate for him. But I really don't think a cat needs a health certificate to cross into California." Another long pause. "All right, if you insist. I'll make one out for you. Bring Beauty up, and I'll take a quick look at him. There's probably nothing wrong, but, just to be sure, I'll look him over anyway."

Again there was a pause.

"What did you say? A tranquilizer for Beauty? For the plane ride? Yes, I see, just in case," Edgar repeated. "Sure, Harvey, I'll give him a few pills for his, uh…fear of flying." I smiled at Edgar, and as he said goodbye to Harvey, he winked at me.

In an hour Harvey was driving his little sedan up the driveway, dust billowing behind his car. Edgar had the health certificate all filled out and officially signed, and Beauty's flight tranquilizers were in a neat paper pouch.

Harvey hopped out of the car, this time with no yellow blanket in his arms. His booming voice scared our cats back into the barn. "Hello Eggie, Gay. How are both of you today?" he yelled, the brisk wind whipping his gray hair into a lather around his head.

"Fine, fine," I said. "How's Beaut, Harvey? I hear he's going to be visiting Hollywood pretty soon. You better make sure he doesn't fool around with any of those actress kitties. He is quite a Don Juan, you know."

"Hee-hee," Harvey giggled, his gray hair still lifting and parting to the whims of the breeze. "Yeah, don't worry; we'll keep an eye on old Beauty out there. But he can't get into too much trouble—remember he doesn't have his pencil anymore." He snickered. "But, seriously, I certainly wouldn't want him to get accustomed to that crazy California scene: twenty-four-hour partying, midnight surfing, souped-up cars and fast women. He just might decide to stay out there, and Mommy and Daddy wouldn't like that, now would we?" He said this into the car where from behind the windshield peered two cat eyes, wondering cat eyes, curious and mischievous.

"You know we went to the airport yesterday," Harvey said.

"You and Lucinda? To pick up your plane tickets?" I volunteered a guess.

"No, Beauty and I went…uh,…for a trial run."

Edgar and I looked warily at each other. "A trial run?" we said in unison.

"Yes, I want to make sure Beauty feels comfortable and safe, so I put him in his little carrier and walked him around the airport."

I couldn't believe it. "You walked him around the airport?" I asked, my mouth dropping.

"That's right, in his little carrier, you know. I took him right inside the airport, past the ticket desks where I introduced him to one of the ticket girls, past the luggage conveyor belts, on the escalators—just all over the airport—even in the jetport lounge area where, I must admit,

I had a trial run martini myself." Harvey looked proudly at Beauty, who had scrambled up the back of the driver's seat; he perched on the head-rest, watching Ben, one of our cats, chasing a leaf.

Harvey continued with pride, "He was so well-behaved. And I made particularly sure that he heard a few jets taking off and landing. He really didn't seem bothered too much by the engine noises; he just sat in his carrier like a good boy. Of course, I'll take the tranquilizers, just in case," he said. "But he really did act brave and grown up, didn't we, Beaut? You were a real Boy Scout."

Weeks passed, and I had forgotten completely about Harvey's and Beauty's trip to California until one afternoon a jet flew overhead while we were delivering a calf at a neighboring dairy farm.

That's when I thought about Beauty and his first plane ride—Beauty, black glasses in place, relaxing in a cushy chair in the first class section with an appetizer of fresh milk and a plate of stewed killies before him. Stretched out in the plane seat listening to "California Dreamin'" playing on his Walkman earphones, he was a picture—lightly tossing the fishes into his mouth, with Harvey and Lucinda sitting proudly beside him.

Part II

Tales of Experience

Tyger, Tyger burning bright,
In the forests of the night.

William Blake
The Tyger

23

Into the Forest Primeval

The Siberian snow tiger yawned again in my left ear. My facial hairs were tickled to attention while the loose hair around my face fluttered under the cat's hot, humid breath. Slowly, very slowly, I turned toward the huge patterned face as whiskers gently brushed my cheek. I looked into Reba's right nostril, and a large tongue parted the lips, lashed to each side and disappeared back into the mouth. I was so close that the tiger's features were fuzzy. The wild predator who had only seconds ago met me and my husband had decided to be friendly and forego a human lunch in favor of a giant can of Whiskas cat food. I smiled with the thrill of being inches from the feline lips, whiskers and patent leather nose.

Reba sighed again in my ear, and I backed an arm's length away. Sitting on a wooden perch, Reba turned her striking face toward me, and I immediately averted my eyes so as not to challenge her authority. Jungle cats consider a stare a threat. I certainly didn't want to irritate this animal. Likewise, when Edgar entered the pen, he took off his baseball cap. Reba didn't like caps or hats of any kind. That sort of thing could transform a tranquil tiger into an angry beast in a matter of moments.

The coffee-table-sized cat sat on her haunches watching us—her owner, me and Edgar—waist-high on her shelf. With my head and eyes in a submissive posture, I reached out slowly with my left hand. Speaking in mellow, subdued tones, I touched her shoulder, careful not to relay any message of hesitancy or fear. I stroked her fur, so carpet-thick—not soft—but deep of pile and texture, and shiny.

"Reba was donated to our center immediately after she was born. She weighed a pound and was so close to death that we had to feed her through a tube," her owner, Grace, said. "Do you know that there are only three hundred Siberian tigers in the wild and only five hundred remaining in captivity? The black market sells every single part of the tiger, even the blood, for aphrodisiacs. A tiger this size would bring in sixty-five thousand dollars."

"She's exquisite," I told Grace.

The short dark-haired woman smiled proudly. "Yes, she's quite a character, too. When she's in a good mood, she plays with the workers and me as though we are her toys. She'll stand up on her hind feet, wrap her front paws around our waists and walk along behind us. In fact, she'll sneak up behind us if we are working on her swimming pool and push us right in. And she still wants to be carried around because she was used to that as a baby, but she doesn't realize that she's too heavy to be held anymore. That doesn't stop her from asking us, though. She's also very nurturing. She helped raise the cougar kittens born here. She carried them around in her mouth and protected them as if she were their mother.

"Nevertheless, I have to be careful when I want to enter her pen. We have to assess her mood whenever we want to interact with her. We don't just walk in, unannounced, so to speak. Some days she doesn't feel like having people fussing with her. Then we know to stay away. All she has to do is take a swipe at one of us with those paws, and she can easily knock us to the ground."

"No doubt," I said, turning to Grace. "I wouldn't want to face such a huge cat in a bad mood."

"Re-ow-ow-ow-oow, Re-ow-ow-oow," Reba growled. The roar filled the air as if resonating inside a fifty-gallon drum.

Then I heard a choking intake of breath. It was Edgar. There he stood with both of Reba's front feet on his shoulders. He was catatonic, and so was his smile. The big cat grinned, licked her lips and slid her tongue along the top of his head. A portion of his hair flipped up and remained stiffened as with styling gel. Dwarfed by the size of the animal, he hunched down under the weight of the cat. He looked a bit nervous.

For his sake I hoped Reba was still in a good mood.

"Okay, big girl. Stop brutalizing our veterinarian. You're scaring the life out of him." Grace took Reba by her collar and backed her off Edgar's shoulders. The tiger let out a tinny roar of protest and immediately sat back obediently on her stoop. "Can you see any cataracts, Ed?" Grace asked. "She was actually blind as a kitten. I had taken her to a human doctor, and he said she'd be blind forever, that she had cataracts, and they would never go away."

Edgar turned and looked Reba in the face trying to detect the cloudy culprits that could block light and sight. Immediately, Reba thrust her head forward. Instinctively, Edgar looked away, having momentarily forgotten not to challenge her with a stare.

"It's a bit hard to examine the eyes of an animal who takes offense at my looking at her," he chuckled. Then Reba looked away at a worker cleaning the aisleway. In that split second Edgar was able to get a good look at her eyes. "They look clear to me—no signs of cloudiness or anything that would indicate a cataract. I never heard of an animal outgrowing them, but I suppose it's possible. I've been watching her since we got here, and she certainly seems to follow people's movements; she noticed my staring at her right away. We'll keep checking her at intervals, but for now there doesn't seem to be a problem."

Reba licked the remains of cat food from Grace's hand, and her owner rubbed the giant feline's head. Soon the cat lay on her stoop, mesmerized by the constant stroking of her face. "She's my baby," cooed Grace. "She's a wonderful animal."

Edgar and I quietly left the pen so that we wouldn't disturb Reba in her meditative state. We ended up back in the hallway where we had first entered the wildlife center about an hour before.

Hours earlier, we had driven to Pocono Lakes to check the tiger's eyes and the eyes of a coatimundi, and to administer a TB test to one of the monkeys. The leaves were at their peak of fall color, so the seemingly endless ride became a cinematic wonder. In another few weeks, the crimsons, pinks and brilliant oranges would all be reduced to a dull dried brown in anticipation of the heavy Pocono winter.

After we had pulled up to the Genesis Wildlife Education and Exotic Center, we were escorted along a woodsy path toward the animal houses. Grace and several workers greeted us at the door where immediately my breath caught the pungent odor of wild animals. The place was immaculate, yet the scent of the wild was strong all the same.

First, we entered the primate center. To the left were rows of spacious pens that housed the Old World monkeys: the African guenons and the Asian macaques. The resident of the first pen on the left was Timmy, a rhesus monkey like the kind used in laboratories. Grace explained that he had been brought to them in a guinea pig cage after being rescued by an animal rights group. He had survived a rough life thus far, having been kept by five different people, some of them neglectful, in the last ten years. It had taken Grace another five years to renew his trust of humans, for he had been badly treated by his previous owners.

Timmy's major problem was psychological. The meanness of humans had turned him into an aggressive individual toward anyone other than his friend and owner, Grace. One of the first times a worker tried to clean his pen, Timmy had reached out, grabbed him by the shirt and hauled him to the ground, pinning the man there even though he was behind the fence. The monkey was several times smaller than a human, yet he was a real powerhouse.

As Grace pointed out the long-tailed macaques from Malaysia, I turned away, oblivious of Timmy. Suddenly, he reached out and grabbed a pencil from my shirt pocket. It lodged outside the cage, so I immediately snatched it back. But I was hardly a match for the wily, nimble-fingered monkey. His tiny, thin fingers grasped the pencil with no intention of letting go. And before I could stop him, he pushed his nose through the fence and bit off the eraser. "Hey," I said. "Cut it out! You shouldn't eat that!" I twisted the instrument from him and placed it, battered, back in my pocket. Timmy squealed, rattling the diamond wire fencing back and forth.

"Well, guess we ought to see about this TB test. How about it, Grace?" Edgar said. "I think Timmy might be a little more than offended if we try to catch him in a net."

"Oh, no, that definitely would not be good. He'll revert to the nasty thing he was before I got him. Please don't do that."

"Okay, then we need to tranquilize him, so that none of us, including him, gets hurt doing this. I need to inject the tuberculin into his eyelid. Then, in three days, I'll come back up here and look in his eye for any swelling. If his eye doesn't swell, then the test was negative. First, though, we need to give him a little sleepy juice." Edgar headed for his truck to draw up the ketamine and Valium cocktail that would put Timmy into a stupor for a few minutes, just long enough to administer the tuberculin test. In a few minutes Edgar was beside Timmy's pen, ready with the first injection.

I could see that Timmy was growing suspicious. *What were these strange people doing beside his pen—only his pen? Weren't they interested in the other monkeys in the room?* he must have thought. Suddenly he ran to the back of the cage, crawled on his stoop, and began picking his nails, all the while surveying us and pondering our intentions.

Edgar kept the injection hidden. Monkeys were quite intelligent. If Timmy saw the needle, he would know it was for him and go positively ballistic. Grace opened the cage. Timmy hovered in the corner, eyeing us. She said, "Come on, you big baby. Come to Mommy. We're going to put you in la-la land for awhile. You be a brave boy and come to Mama."

With that, Timmy hopped down from his perch and sat at Grace's feet. He peered anxiously at her and held out his arms for her to pick him up. Grace bent over, lifted him up and cradled him, speaking soft words in his ear.

A hush came over the room. Timmy looked intensely at us as she cooed in his ear. She whispered, "Timmy's a big, brave boy, isn't he? I want you to be good when you meet Dr. Balliet, Timmy." Then in the same subdued voice she told Edgar to enter the pen.

Edgar turned his back, readied the tranquilizer, then faced the pen and went in. Timmy scrunched his head up under Grace's chin for protection, but she assured him everything was going to be all right.

"Hi, Tim ol' boy," Edgar said. Timmy pulled his head from under Grace's chin and looked suspiciously at Edgar. Edgar patted Timmy on the shoulder with his free hand and held a conversation with the monkey.

"What do you say, Timmy? Busy day today? Have you gotten any new toys lately? I see you have a stuffed animal there—looks like a monkey, just like you." He continued to stroke Timmy's shoulder. "In just a few minutes you can go play with it again—none the worse for wear."

Timmy relaxed and lay his head against Grace's collar bone. Edgar continued to stroke his shoulder with his left hand, and Timmy closed his eyes. His lips relaxed into a semblance of a contented smile. At the same time, Edgar removed the injection cap with his teeth and plunged the needle into the thick of the monkey's thigh, injecting the solution simultaneously.

Timmy's eyes flew open like sprung window shades, his head swiveled on ball bearings, and he let out an ear-splitting screech. In a matter of split seconds, I could see the monkey turn from Grace and lunge at Edgar's head, grabbing a shock of hair. Grace hung onto the animal, but Timmy was still free to use his hands and face in the attack.

Instinctively, Edgar stood still, but the monkey hung on, his mouth agape. Grace worked frantically to loosen the monkey's fingers, but they were locked onto a clump of Edgar's hair. Edgar stood rigid, his face toward the floor, his scalp a prisoner of the monkey's clutch. It was a bizarre Victorian tableau, of sorts, with all the action stopped momentarily; Grace clung to the monkey, the monkey clung to Edgar, Edgar clung to life. Though his initial instinct was to pull away from the clutching paw, Edgar, who looked rather nervous with good reason, managed to keep his head and hair by not panicking and keeping very still while he waited for the chemicals to immobilize the animal. I, too, was just as speechless and motionless, waiting for the next move.

We didn't have long to wait. Within minutes, as the drugs took effect, the monkey relaxed and loosened his grip on Edgar.

Edgar sneaked out from under his limp hand. Soon, the monkey went as soft as a bag of laundry. Grace could feel his limpness, too, and supported his head on her shoulder.

Though the monkey's eyes were open the whole time Edgar injected the tuberculin, Timmy couldn't retaliate. Grace held him, and then, after it was over, placed the monkey on a towel in a corner of his pen.

"Almost had to call Hair Club for Men, didn't we, Doc?" Grace laughed as they left the pen. Edgar put the caps back on the needles and dropped them into his shirt pocket.

"Yeah, that was pretty close, but I figured he'd go under in a few minutes. So I was just biding my time until the drug took effect." I caught his eye and winked. Edgar winked back and continued his confident speech. "I'm glad we don't have to do any of the other monkeys today, though. My head can't take any more punishment."

We left Timmy to his recovery. Next to him resided the long-tailed macaques: Spice Ann and Mario, son of Chad and Isabela. Quite a bit smaller than Timmy, Mario looked as if he were wearing a topknot on his head. He had a pixie look and was definitely Grace's favorite.

"Okay, just one," she said. With that Mario reached out through the wire fence and pulled on Grace's ponytail. She winced for a second and then turned around. Immediately, the monkey eyed the piece of hair he had taken and then put it into his mouth. "He's flossing his teeth," she said.

"What?" I giggled. "You're kidding!"

"Looks like both of us are losing hair today," Edgar laughed.

"Oh, no," she said with all seriousness. "I know for a fact he's flossing his teeth. He does this everyday—he grabs a piece of my hair and cleans his teeth. Don't you, boy?" she cooed. "You're my boyfriend, aren't you?" He sat on the concrete floor and repeatedly pushed the invisible hair up between his teeth and then pulled it out again. Indeed, he *was* flossing his teeth. After several minutes he let go of the hair and jumped back onto the side of his cage. His lips screwed up into a wide grin, and he grabbed Grace's index finger which he immediately put into his mouth.

"Easy there, Buster. Don't eat my finger." Mario curled himself around the bars of the cage, trying to pull Grace into the cage with him—right through the wire fencing. All of a sudden Grace began to yell, "Izzy, get him! Izzy! Izzy!"

I looked in the direction of Grace's yells, and there in the next cage sat two adult monkeys. At the side of the cage a baby monkey clung precariously. The baby wasn't at all sure-footed, hanging onto the fence first with one hand, then loosing its grip and quickly switching to the other hand. It was beginning to weaken, and if someone didn't do something fast, it could fall to the concrete floor.

"Izzy! Izzy, get your baby NOW!" Grace yelled.

One of the monkeys reached over to the baby, grabbed it around the midsection, and plucked it off the side of the cage. The baby's mother tucked it underneath her and looked out at us as if for approval.

"Good girl, Izzy. If you can't take care of your baby, then I'll just come in there and take her myself." With a look of remorse, Izzy lowered her eyes and clutched her baby to her.

We came to the end of the monkey pens, turned to the right and stopped at the brown ruff lemurs, Lola and Lorenzo, and their black-faced lemur friend, Lil. Lemurs, Grace said, were from Madagascar; and the black-faced was the most endangered of the species. Once they had our attention, the female leaped from her perch onto the side of the cage to be close and personal. They had comparatively long thick fur with long, substantial, prehensile tails. They sported huge, bulgy eyes— like clear chocolate marbles—that gazed intelligently down a long, pointy nose.

Lola grunted, clinging to the fence to get closer to us. With that, Lorenzo let out another grunt and leaped onto the fence alongside Lola. Lil, however, sat staring curiously from her little perch. I stroked the underside of Lola's belly and brushed Lorenzo's tiny nose as it protruded through the fence. Then, moments later as we moved toward the next pen, Lola and Lorenzo flew back through the air to their safe perch alongside Lil.

The next pen looked strangely vacant, but it wasn't. Actually, two bush babies named George and Barbara Bush resided there, and they were trying to sleep amid all the commotion. They lay, curled in a ball in a hollowed-out log resting on a shelf. "Bush babies are nocturnal creatures, and if they are disturbed, they can become irritable," said Grace. So, out of respect, Edgar and I tiptoed quietly to the last pen.

A short while later, Edgar and I were standing side by side admiring Jerry, a New World Capuchin monkey. He, along with the lemurs and bush babies, was from South and Central America. Little did we know while we were standing admiring Jerry, who was playing with one of his plastic toys, that above us, standing on a rail sizing up the entertainment, was a bizarre animal called a binturong.

I gasped as a soft-fleshed foot reached for my shoulder, and a hairy body lowered its weight onto my left shoulder. Though I couldn't really see the creature that had climbed aboard my back, I noticed Grace smiling, so I didn't panic. I stayed still as the animal, which I guess must have weighed between thirty and forty pounds, wrapped its hairy body along the back of my neck. A wild smell permeated the air. What I hadn't realized was that I supported only half the animal. The rest of it was standing on Edgar's shoulders. In fact, it had used Edgar as a bridge to get to me. I took a deep breath, reached my hand up alongside my back and felt the coarse, stiff hairs of the bear cat.

Then I looked sideways at Edgar. The creature straddled both of us: two front feet on my farthest shoulder, one foot on my shoulder nearest to Edgar, the other back foot on Edgar's near shoulder, and the long prehensile tail wrapped tightly around his neck. "Oh, my God," I whispered. "She has you by the neck."

"Yeah," Edgar coughed as the tail clenched tighter around his throat. "She's really hanging on. Guess she's afraid she might fall." He giggled, and then Grace offered help.

"Right there is Sweet Emily's cage. Why don't the two of you just walk together side by side, just like you are, right into her cage. She'll jump off you then, you'll see."

So, very gingerly, Edgar and I walked in tandem, the binturong riding our shoulders, her anaconda tail wrapped firmly around Edgar's neck, into the walk-in cage. Once inside, I felt a push, and Sweet Emily leaped overhead and landed with a thump on her shelf. Once freed of our burden, we could finally see the animal who had mistaken us for a couple of trees.

In comparison to her body, Emily's head looked relatively small. Like so many of these animals which really belonged to the mongoose family, her fur was incredibly thick, like a bear's, and long. Her talented tail, the diameter of which was the size of a cantaloupe where it attached to her body, was capable of suspending the body from a tree limb or, in our case, from a human throat. Tiny, tufted ears framed a face having clear, round dark eyes set beneath a rather protruding brow bridge. Her nose was pointy and set off by long white whiskers.

Indeed, her disposition was slow and sweet. Her days she usually spent crawling across the top of the monkey cages where she inspected each one's inhabitants. Then when she tired, she climbed back into her own cage and fell asleep.

After Sweet Emily had returned to her pen, we stopped back to see Jerry, a typical organ-grinder monkey. Having survived living in several zoos, Grace said he had made a remarkable comeback. They discovered him in a zoo with a chain around his neck. He had taken years to tame since his mishandling and for some time had tantrums and incidents of aggression and biting. He was much better now and had learned to trust people.

Jerry stuck his fingers out of the diamond wire fence, and I gently touched the diminutive fingers, his nails, and the soft padding beneath the fingers. They were so delicate, so fragile, so humanlike, and I couldn't imagine that people could mistreat such an animal. He looked me in the face—a face characteristic of us all, with miniature eyelids, fuzzy eyebrows and tiny lips. The face wrinkled into a smile, the mouth screwed itself up into a mischievous grin, and then suddenly the monkey let go my fingers and sprung back to his perch. We continued to look at each other, as if at a mirror.

We said goodbye to the monkeys and entered the next room where Reba the Siberian tiger and a host of other animals lived. After checking Reba, we went on to see Choco and Prunella, the coatimundis from South America. They were easygoing sorts, being the South American relative of our raccoon. Edgar got as close as they would allow to inspect a cloudy eye on Choco. Indeed, something was wrong with the coatimundi's eye.

"Let's try some antibiotics for awhile. We'll start with Baytril first. If that doesn't work, we'll switch to something else. Just put it in her food as you have in the past." In the cage next to the coatimundis lived a gennet cat or African civet, also related to Sweet Emily and of the mongoose family. Being nocturnal, she was curled up, half asleep, in a miniature snug sack. At Grace's whispered suggestion, we peeked quietly into the sack to admire its beautiful ringed tail. She was sleepy and was known to attack with the speed of a Concorde if suddenly disturbed.

Before we met the last animal, Grace led us to the upstairs loft where a variety of birds and rodents lived. The flying fox bats from Australia and the Egyptian fruit bats were just hanging around taking in an upside down view of the world. They were curious animals, always wanting to be a part of the action—the cleaning of the cages, the feeding, the training sessions. Who would ever believe bats had any kind of social tendencies? But they hung together in a mass, the many eyes following in synchronization as we moved back and forth before them.

In the background a crow screamed unmercifully. When Grace reached through the cage and stroked him, he became subdued, but when she stopped, he immediately began to bounce on his perch and demand more rubbing. "I take him with me to schools and other places." Soon, a rainforest bird called a turocco privileged us with his song—primitive, mellow and tropical. Next to the turocco was a chestnut severe macaw, who shouted "Hel-lo" to the ringing tones of a recuperating blue jay that had learned to mimic a telephone. "Ri-I-ing, Ri-I-ing, Ri-I-ing, Ri-I-ing," rang the blue jay. Chester answered, "Hel-lo! Hel-lo! Hel-lo! Hel-lo!"

"Thanks for getting the phone, Chester," Grace said, and then she took us over to another cage. There slept three sugar gliders—flying squirrels. She also kept a few flying mice. Also recovering in several cages were a mallard duck, a bald robin, a few starlings, bunnies and others who were destined to be released once they were healthy.

"Fascinating," I said. Edgar was glued to the side of the bat cage, returning the stares of the hanging fellows. In a few minutes we climbed down the steps to check the cougars: Kiki, Katie and her five-month old cub, Baby.

Grace entered the pen first and, after having assessed the moods of the mountain lions, motioned us to follow. Leaves had begun to flutter into the outside pen, totally enclosed with heavy duty wire fencing all around and even over the whole top. Katie, the mother, sat surveying the property from atop a tree stump while her mate, Kiki, lounged nearby on a large rock. Little Baby, the cub, gnawed on a deer rib cage inside an Igloo house. We could hardly see him, so enveloped was he in blankets and the carcass.

Grace led us to Katie, who was the friendliest and most approachable of the three. She nodded to me, so I reached out and rubbed Katie behind an ear. The German shepherd-sized cat pointed her face to the sky and pursed her lips, relishing the attention. Then the purring started. It was a giant sound compared to the little "br-rr-rr-ing" of my own house cats.

"Yes, cougars are the only wild cats that can purr. Katie here is a sweetheart. She and her mate and cub get along fine with Reba, too. They are great buddies. In the wild you would never see a cougar associating with a tiger.

"You know," Grace added with a laugh, pointing to the plastic swimming pool in the center of the pen, "cougars hate getting wet. But when Reba's in a playful mood, she'll see the cougars getting a drink from her swimming pool and will push them right in like she does with us and then she jumps in the pool right after them. Boy, do they get mad."

Katie, a lovely creature of a bronze shininess with distinct black markings in the shape of an "M" on her face, was purring at full power as I stroked her forehead. Her head was perfectly round and as big as a grapefruit. Her deep, yellow eyes were rimmed with kohl. Baby was the image of her, and from his little Igloo he chewed noisily on his lunch.

The last animal Edgar was to check was the two-toed sloth; so we left the cougar pen and went back inside. We had seen sloths in Costa Rica during a recent trip, but, of course, they were too far up in the trees to get a good look. Here, Peekaboo clung to a tree limb right before our eyes. Above her hung a cluster of fresh grapes tacked to a branch, and her task for the next three hours would be to eat those grapes, one at a time. For sure, it would take her several hours to finish the treat since her velocity was about minus Mach seven.

Looking like a plumped-up blonde wig, Peekaboo hung beneath the grapes, slowly approaching one, sizing it up with her black nose, and finally reaching her lips up and around it. Then she sucked it off the vine. Her face was tiny and round, with eyes similar to the lemurs, though not quite as large.

Grace said, "It takes her days to move from one end of the five-foot-long pen to the other." Everything about her was slow; she was incapable of fast movement even if provoked or scared. All she could do was react at a rock's pace. I wondered why, what kind of chemistry could slow down a being such as a sloth. What, exactly, made them so lethargic? Then I wondered if its bodily functions were equally anti-accelerated.

"Yes," Grace said. "A sloth goes to the bathroom only two times a week because their digestive system is so slow." While she explained

Peekaboo's mosslike pace, I watched the sloth reach for a second grape. In five minutes she took it into her mouth, and in another two minutes the jaws came together, and the grape disappeared.

Peekaboo's reverse-warp speed was having an eerie effect on us. Edgar and I had become mesmerized by the "slo-mo" Peekaboo, and when we said good-bye, we spoke in subdued voices and backed slowly and deliberately away from her pen. Once free of Peekaboo's tranquilizing effects, we checked Timmy. He had recovered from the tranquilizer nicely and was sitting on a tree limb with his stuffed animal. He didn't look as though he was holding a grudge.

After we said goodbye to Grace and began the return drive home, we realized the day had left us strangely refreshed. The world of the primordial—the animal world—can energize one as no other can. It moves us away from the need for manufactured entertainment like trips to the movies or malls. Here we were able to bond with the tiger, the binturong and the sloth and share their special realm, a realm that humans can only observe from afar in the modern world.

Human "progress" has set us apart from the natural world, from the primitive habitat from which we long ago originated. Most people feel uncomfortable around wild and strange animals, preferring the company of a pet cat or dog that is more accepting of our civilized attitudes. As for those who have alienated themselves from animals altogether in favor of computers, television and other marks of materialism, a valuable part of themselves has been destroyed. They have lost their affinity for that final remaining strain, that yearning toward the natural, the instinctive, the primal.

Indeed, our visit with wild things had renewed our ties with nature herself.

24

Tucker's
First Clinic

A tiny building lay in a small hole scooped from the side of a granite cliff. The rock walls loomed like a Roman amphitheater and dwarfed the little clinic, a concrete block box no larger than fifteen feet by fifteen feet. It was a house built for a Lilliputian: the one every five-year-old draws with his first red crayon: a square with a steep roof; one center door flanked on either side by a little window.

"Well, what do you think?" Edgar said, easing his truck over the rutted parking area.

"What is it?" I asked, mouth agape.

"This is our friend Tucker's new small animal clinic. I thought we might get some ideas for our own. How do you like it?"

It was certainly not small animal hospital ideal. No bushes or flowers decorated the outside of the little box, nor was there any kind of porch. Only one pock-marked cement step served as the welcome mat. The gravel parking lot licked right up to the shack's very edges making it stick out like a sore toe.

"This is Tucker's small animal hospital?" I said hesitantly, letting myself down from the truck. The whole place looked abandoned. It was so stark and alone beneath a canopy of solid rock.

A pigeon flew to the roof. He ruffled his feathers and settled comfortably on the peak. The air was still, but, then, caves were seldom windy. Edgar stepped onto the front step and pulled open the storm door; I waited behind him.

"Tucker's here. There's his truck parked out back," Edgar said, pushing the inside door. It wouldn't budge. "The knob turns, but it won't budge," he said, and he heaved his body against it.

I elbowed myself alongside Edgar, and together we rammed the door. It moved an inch and stuck again. We heaved into it, and it moved another inch.

"What's going on here?" I gasped, backing up for another attack.

"Here, let me do it; you'll hurt yourself." Edgar flew at the door, and it gave way, slamming against the inside wall. I grabbed at the swinging door but missed, hitting my knee on the door.

"Glad you dropped in. How do you guys like my new place?" a voice behind us said. We both turned to see Tucker. I mustered a smile, but felt the stark concrete walls closing in around us.

"Well? Come on. What do you think?" Tucker asked, his eyes wide with pride. I looked at the stained, leaky walls and then at Edgar chewing his index finger, obviously contemplating a profound remark. An honest compliment was hard-coming, but one of us had to say something.

Tucker looked affectionately around.

I said, "Hey, it's a start, Tuck. You'll be able to make a nice go of it here, and after you fix it up a bit and maybe throw on an addition or two, it'll do just fine for a small animal practice."

How can someone tell a friend her baby is anything less than beautiful? Can she be truthful and remark how its proboscis looks just like its father's when all through high school everyone called dear ol' dad Nozzle Nose? Tucker's was, indeed, a homely baby. A bowed-out wall divided the Quonset hut simply, unpretentiously into two rooms.

His mustache drooped. He said, "Well, actually, I have fixed the place up quite a bit already." I swallowed hard, smiled again and shook my head in appreciation of the less than obvious fact.

He continued, "I had linoleum laid a few weeks ago. Unfortunately, the roof was leaking pretty bad for some time; and I guess the underlayment was still wet and caused the new linoleum to buckle after it dried." Edgar and I glanced at the rippled floor; its undulating waves made me dizzy, and I shifted my glance to the cement walls as a wave of nausea washed over me. The door gaping open behind us was caught on a hill of warped floor. Edgar gave it a swift push, knocking it off its perch, and it crashed onto its latch.

"Yep," Tucker said, twirling the end of his mustache, "there's a bit more to fix up, but I believe it'll work out pretty nice for me here."

He continued, "This room is where I examine and treat the animals. I've turned it into a combination waiting and examination room—plus, it's my treatment area."

It seemed like a lot to put into a seven-foot-square area. If he had more than one client and animal in the waiting-examining-treatment room, the place would be stuffed full. Then we stepped into the other room. Tucker was gearing himself up for his favorite subject: surgery.

A stainless steel table was tucked into the corner. Tucker continued, "Yes, this is the surgical bay; I put them under, do the surgeries, then wake them up here." I leaned on it, surveying the area. Suddenly the thing buckled, and Tucker lunged to steady it. I smiled weakly, regaining my balance.

"Have to fix that, too," Tucker chuckled, rearranging the table legs to straddle the ripples on the floor.

I looked under the table for the problem. Could it be a shortened leg, the bad floor, a drain hole?

Two frightened yellow eyes stared at me from under the table.

"There's a cat under the table!" I cried. I crouched to where a tiger cat was leashed to a table leg. It peered from around a side of it.

"Kitty, what're you doing down there?" I said. It came out and nuzzled against me.

"I'm going to spay her in a few minutes, and I don't have any cages yet, so I have to tie her to the surgical table."

"What is your next project for this place?" Edgar questioned, fiddling with the doorknob to a single closet. Edgar still hadn't commented on Tucker's new hospital.

"Next thing is to get some hot running water in here," Tucker said with a smile.

"Gad," I exclaimed, careful not to tip the surgical table, "How can you function without hot water?"

"Well, that part is rather easy. It's having no water at all that becomes a problem every once in a while."

"You have no water at all?" Edgar asked incredulously.

"Nope. Hey, I got this place for a couple grand, so I couldn't expect much. I have to carry buckets of water from home every day. That gets to be a drag, but like I say, it's only for a while, until I install the plumbing."

"Do you have a well on the property?" I asked.

"No, actually," he said. He had a faraway look. "I have to get to that, too, one of these days."

I contemplated the water stains on the ceiling, patterned in dark prehistoric dinosaurs.

Edgar had been lurking around the closet door like a dog at a fox hole. "Tucker, what's in this closet?" he asked. "I swear I hear scratching."

"Open it and see."

When Edgar opened the door, a bulbous, glistening object thrust through the crack. It was a nose, and attached to it was a dog. Wedging itself between the door and the jamb, the nose pushed determinedly ahead, revealing a Saint Bernard that weighed over one hundred pounds.

"Brandy, meet Dr. and Mrs. Balliet," Tucker said, patting the dog affectionately as he introduced him. Brandy inspected us with a nudge of his slippery nose. I reached down to pet him, too.

"I'm afraid to ask what he was doing in the closet," Edgar said.

"Did a castration on him this morning; his owners will be picking him up soon. Just before you got here I had to leave, so I put him in the closet until I got back."

We didn't have to wait very long for another surprise. Huddled in the corner next to the surgery table stood a dilapidated refrigerator that had once upon a time served some little grandmother. Tucker was quick to point out this new, old acquisition—another pride and joy. His mustache crawled up around his face in a broad smile as he told us about the fantastic deal he made on the appliance.

"Mrs. Mahoney said she'd sell it to me for ten dollars for getting it out of her house. Imagine that," Tucker marveled, "ten dollars for a refrigerator. Ya can't beat it."

"Hell, that's a great deal, Tuck. I paid fifty bucks for my old fridge, and I had to put a new seal on it, too." I could see Edgar's curiosity as, very carefully, he pulled the handle gently for an inspection.

Edgar gave the door a yank. I gasped. A giant liver in a clear, plastic bag oozed over the top shelf, teetering at the edge. Suddenly it slipped over the side. Edgar lunged after it, kneading it with flattened palms back into place.

Tucker shrugged. "Had a cow die unexpectedly on me yesterday so I did a 'post' on it—nothing substantial really. But I'm sending some specimens in for histology. I just can't figure out what she died from."

Edgar closed the refrigerator door as part of a lung threatened to lodge in the opening.

"Here, let me close it. There's a trick to it, sort of," Tucker laughed, and with that he pushed the wad in, shutting the door so quickly that he could've taken his own hand off in the process.

"Well, so what do you think of the place?" Tucker said, his eyes sparkling.

Edgar looked around, rubbing his forehead, musing, pondering the question for such a long time that I thought Tucker would burst.

Tucker shifted nervously, cracking a ripple in the linoleum floor. "Why, yes," Edgar said shaking his head, staring at the bare walls, "I think it's just great for your first hospital. You'll have to fix up quite a bit yet...."

"Yes, yes, of course, I know that," Tucker yelped, nodding.

"But it'll be fine in no time at all," Edgar smiled, surveying the tiny room, its unbalanced surgical table and its refrigerator full of guts.

To me, the whole place seemed too overwhelming. I liked and respected Tucker: he was dedicated, hardworking and very intelligent. He loved veterinary medicine. Yet the probability of turning this dry shack into even a meagerly functional animal hospital seemed as

unlikely as the probability of the anthill in our backyard becoming a
new Everest. But I couldn't dampen his enthusiasm.

"I think it looks pretty good, too, Tucker," I said hesitantly, trying
to mitigate my doubts. I was hopeful, too. "In time you'll get it fixed up
the way you want it, and maybe even add on to it," I reiterated the idea,
imagining so many animals stuffed in cabinets and closets throughout
the small house.

We turned to leave, and Tucker followed us the three steps to the
door, a ray of sun shining through the window. I grabbed the doorknob
and yanked it, pulling and scraping the door across the floor.

As we stepped onto the gravel lot, Edgar remembered something. "By the way, Tuck, I'd like to borrow your lead gloves. I need
them to x-ray a foal's leg tomorrow."

"Sure, they're in a box on the front seat of my truck," he pointed.
I climbed into our truck and waited while Edgar went for them.

Suddenly, there was a startled yelp. It was Edgar. I had never
heard Edgar shriek before—it was surreal: men don't usually scream.
What could have happened?

I jumped from the truck as he stood rigidly bent over Tucker's
truck seat. "What's the matter?" I yelled.

"Look! Look!" he pointed, gesticulating at the box. "I just
reached into the box for the gloves, without looking, and felt something
furry. Look, it's a dead cat, just lying in the x-ray box. It damned near
scared me to death."

There lay an orange, tiger-striped tomcat at peace with himself
and the box in which he rested.

A voice interrupted, "Yeah, a lady wanted me to do a post-
mortem on her cat so I picked it up at her house for her. There are the
gloves you wanted, right underneath it."

Edgar gently lifted the cat and slid the gloves from under it. "I
certainly didn't expect to find a dead cat in your x-ray box, Tucker.
Shook me up a bit, I'll admit."

Tucker's mustache arched in a knowing smile. We walked back
to our truck.

"So you really think it'll take off, huh?" Tucker asked, facing his
building, his pride and joy.

"Fix it up a bit more, and it'll serve you well," Edgar nodded.

As Tucker contemplated his animal hospital, I couldn't help thinking about the problems he would have to surmount here in the coming months. Yet, though there were many obstacles, I also knew that the future lay not within the shell of the building nor the concrete walls or linoleum but within the doctor himself.

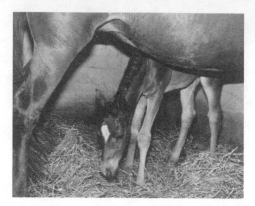

Only hours old, Fancy stands on unsteady legs next to her Mom, Merry.

Gay on Fancy after a riding lesson with her instructor, Gale Remington.

Gay and Fancy winning their place ribbon at a horse show.

Edgar and Fax in the showring.

Jim Bob, the horse with the wily tongue, greets Gay.

Tucker Jones proudly shows off his new clinic.

The Topman twins with a deer at feeding time.

Dan checks on a buffalo herd at the Temple LeHigh Game Preserve.

Gay's father hugs Daphne,
the family's Newfoundland.

Leon Murphy with one of his
metal creations, a copper and
brass sculpture of a ship.

Leon Murphy with his pet
turkeys, Hekyll and Jekyll.

Jim Kindred hammers a horseshoe
on an anvil in his mobile farrier
shop.

Edgar and Gay spend time with their favorite storytelling farrier, Jim Kindred, while Ivy Mae the pig looks on.

Gay and one of her divine swine friends, Lowell.

Edgar and Gay enjoy the company of Reba, a Siberian snow tiger.

25

The Cat-Bird

Edgar helped out two days a week at a veterinary clinic doing routine examinations of cats and dogs. It was not a job he preferred, cooped up in a tiny concrete cubicle, but it was a job that gave us extra money. So, on a Friday night from six to nine o'clock, he saw various species of felines, canines and birds, or as I called them, "airlines."

I played receptionist, and one day a middle-aged couple walked into the examining room carting a cloth-covered, two-foot-wide container.

"Hello, Mr. and Mrs. Rosen, what do you have there?" I asked.

"It's an African gray," the husband said, lifting the cloth and exposing a large gray parrot. The bird looked from side to side and tilted his head up and sideways as I peered in at him through the bars. We stared at each other for perhaps a minute: I was fascinated by the different tones of gray feathers and the red markings around his head; and he, as curious about me as I him, swung his head around and stared intently at my earrings.

"He's really handsome," I said half to Mr. Rosen and half to the bird himself. "Does he do any tricks or say anything?"

"Well, about the only thing he does is imitate our Siamese cat," Mr. Rosen confessed with embarrassment. "He meows. It's because my wife and I are never home during the day, and the only thing he hears is the cat talking all morning and afternoon. Watch, I'll make him imitate the cat," he said, and with that Mr. Rosen began mewing and meowing, his face pressed against the cage. Within a short time, the bird, its beak opening wide, emitted a long, thin cry, imitating the loud, babylike noises of a Siamese cat. He strutted up and down on his perch, hamming it up for everyone. Soon cat cries were ringing out like machine-gun fire, and after a few minutes, tiring of the game, the parrot slowed his pace, firing a meow only every so often.

"Gads, he certainly does make a racket," said Edgar coming into the room. "What's his name?"

"Dudley, Doc," Mr. Rosen looked sheepish. "My wife named him." He gave her a cursory glance. "We are taking a cruise on our yacht," he said in a businesslike manner, "and I want his feathers clipped so he can't fly. We're planning to let him loose aboard the boat, and we don't want him flying the sloop," he laughed. "He cost a grand."

"Wow! Okay, but it's really a shame to cut them; they're so long and beautiful. I'll only take off what's absolutely necessary—just tip off the flight feathers. Now how shall we catch him?" Edgar eyed Dudley.

Apparently Mr. Rosen had everything worked out as he had earlier choreographed the procedure. "First, I'll reach in the cage with this glove on." His wife handed him a huge welding glove. "And then I'll simply grab him and bring him out. While I hang onto his body, you cut the feathers."

"Okay, sounds good," Edgar said, reaching for the clippers.

Mr. Rosen slipped on the glove, and immediately Dudley backed up against his cage, squawking, his beak agape, his claws clattering along the wooden perch. Evidently, this was not the first time he had seen that menacing glove. Mr. Rosen opened the cage door with one hand and reached in with the gloved one. With a sudden shriek, Dudley hopped, panic-stricken, to the farthest side of the cage—away from the awesome hand—beak wide open, bony feet clinging to the cage. He reminded me, for an instant, of Faye Ray with her back flattened against the wall of the Empire State Building.

"Hey, hey, it's okay, Dud," Mr. Rosen soothed, his face against the cage. Dudley squawked a deeper warning. Then there was a moment of silence before the strike.

The terrible mitt seized Dudley, and simultaneously the bird sent up a raucous cawing and screaming that made us all flinch. Then, in self-defense, he clamped his beak in a succession of firmly-planted bites, right into the glove. He could not cut through the heavy material; nevertheless, he put that throttle down with every intention of having a finger for lunch.

His voice shaking under the bird's savage attack, Mr. Rosen tried consoling Dudley, "Ho, Duds, we're not going to hurt you. You'll be all right. Daddy's not going to hurt you." But Dudley knew he was lying. He let go, his tiny head spinning around, and targeted a new area on the glove. Then he stretched his black patent leather beak into a snapping turtle threat.

Once caught, the mitt pulled Dudley through the tiny cage door which he instinctively clutched onto with his strong feet. But the bird wouldn't fit through; it was like trying to pull an opened umbrella backwards through a small door. Prying off the claws one at a time with his other hand, Mr. Rosen, with Edgar's help, forced the bird from his safe house.

Quickly, Edgar clipped away the ends of the delicate flight feathers. Although the procedure was painless, spitting and cursing in bird language, Dudley fought Mr. Rosen's grip to the bitter end, trying to find a target.

"I think that's enough. At least, according to the books, it's supposed to be. And I certainly don't care to take too many feathers off because he'll look funny," Edgar remarked after the job was finished and Dudley was inside his cage.

"All right, Doc, if you say so. I just hope he doesn't fly away," Mr. Rosen said.

"I've never done this before, I'll admit," Edgar repeated, "but the book says this should be adequate. You were a good boy, Dudley," Dudley brooded on his perch, and Mr. Rosen slipped the cover over the cage. Dudley was starting to settle down.

As we bade *bon voyage* to Mr. and Mrs. Rosen and Dudley, the bird's voice trailed down the hallway and out the door—in a Siamese's farewell song.

A month later Mr. Rosen's name was on the evening's appointment list. "Oh, boy," I said, "maybe he's bringing Dudley in for something. I hope Dudley is all right." A few minutes later Mr. Rosen and the covered cage were ushered into the exam room.

Mr. Rosen said, "Hi, Doc. Hi, Mrs. Doc. Guess what? It didn't work. We put Dudley on the boat, opened the cage, and he promptly flew overboard and out to sea."

"Oh, no!" I gasped. Edgar rolled his eyes.

"Yes, he attempted a mad escape to a neighboring boat—actually gave it quite an effort—but, well, we had been feeding him a bit too much before the trip. He could still fly, somewhat, but he just couldn't keep his fat little body up in the air. He landed *smack* in the drink: had to scoop the poor sucker out with a fishing net. He was the only fish I caught the entire trip." Mr. Rosen laughed again, "Needless to say, he spent the rest of the trip on deck in his cage."

"I'm glad he's okay. Sorry that happened; I hoped clipping only his flight feathers would work, but apparently he needs more cut," Edgar replied.

So poor Dudley was wrenched from his cage again, squawking and cursing. This time, however, the job was more thorough. Afterwards, Dudley perched in the back of his cage, embarrassed. No longer the sleek, dignified relative of the American eagle, he looked more like a humble farm chicken.

26

The Guy
with the Boat...

The next morning, I stirred the creamer round and round in my coffee and watched the white swirls melt away. A starling landed beyond our breakfast window on the birdfeeder, which swayed under its weight. Then the starling snatched a sunflower seed and vaulted into the air. The cats were battling over an empty tuna fish can I had left in the garbage overnight, and the horses in the pasture were barely visible in the morning mist.

Edgar sipped his coffee, the steam rising from the cup, then he recalled yesterday's experience. "I turned onto Two-forty-eight and right there near Ackerman's Ice Cream Stand, right next to the road where the shoulder cuts in—remember where we pulled off the road last year on the way to Beltzville Reservoir to check the radiator in your car—right there it was. I couldn't believe it.

"What was it?" I asked.

"A boat!" he exclaimed. He sank his teeth into the end of a jelly donut and slurped the jam leaking from the other end.

"Well," I said. Unfinished chores that I had been neglecting obsessed me: editing another chapter for my second book, shampooing the living room rug, riding two horses for the show on Sunday. What could be so exciting about someone stopping to check his boat by the side of the road?

Edgar looked annoyed. "A boat!" he repeated. I shrugged una-mused. "A boat! Not a canoe, rowboat or fiberglass lake boat—this was a *real* boat: a big, old-fashioned, wooden, twenty-two-foot, ocean-going fishing vessel! It was lying on its belly in the dirt by the side of the road—in Lehighton, Pennsylvania."

"What?" I said. "On the ground? A boat?"

"That's what I said." My chores could wait now. He continued, "I couldn't believe my eyes. I wondered why the traffic was all backed up. In fact, I was really mad because I was already late to geld that colt up at Snyder's."

I nodded and gulped my coffee.

"The traffic was crawling along, and I saw some kind of distur-bance up ahead at the pull-over. I just can't get over it—a huge boat sit-ting in the gravel—on the frame of a trailer. The trailer's wheels were gone! I don't know what the hell happened, but as I was passing, I saw a man standing beside the boat just staring at it—sort of glum, you know, and rubbing his head.

"Nobody was stopping to help this poor guy. Everyone just stared and kept on going. So I pulled over. You should've seen the car he was using to pull that huge rig—an old beat-up Chrysler Brougham. It was more rust than it was car."

"Then what happened?"

"Well, I asked him if he could use some help."

"And?"

"He just stood there scratching his bald head, staring at the boat sunk to its axles in the dirt. 'Jesus Christ...Jesus Christ,' was all he kept saying, like he was in a trance and couldn't believe it. Poor guy. I mean—what the hell does a person do when the wheels blow off his trailer, and his boat is sitting high and dry on its belly beside a four-lane highway?"

"I'd cry," I offered.

"Well, it was so pitiful, yet I could hardly keep from laughing."

"Laughing?" I admonished.

"Yeah, the whole thing was surreal. Like those cartoons we used to see as kids: this boat would be sailing along, and then someone would unleash the dam. Then suddenly the boat sat, stranded, on a hill of dirt.

Plus, the guy was a real character himself. You would've died if you had seen him.

"He finally convinced himself that the trailer had actually broken, and then he seemed to notice me for the first time. 'Howdy,' he said so calmly, 'got a little problem here.' And then he smiled. You should've seen him. Big man, about fifty-five years old with about a two-week growth of beard, and he was sweating like mad—so bad that he had to blow the drops off the end of his nose as he talked. Over his pot belly he was wearing a white T-shirt, and he had on bright, kelly green shorts, like pedal pushers. And you should've seen the shirt. It had every kind of grease spot and tomato stain on it you'd ever imagine. To top it off, he had on these skinny, worn-shiny white socks that were slipping down into the backs of his shoes—old black wingtips, no less. I mean—no sneakers or sandals or anything—black wingtips—at the height of summer, in ninety-five-degree weather."

I held my hand over my mouth and giggled. What a pitifully humorous sight it must have been!

"Then he walked over to his car with his head down like he was thinking real hard. There were other people in the old Chrysler: a woman—his wife, I guess—and a daughter who looked about nineteen."

"What were they doing?" I asked.

"Nothing that I could tell. But they must've been hot in there They said hello. They were both attractive, and the daughter was an exact replica of her mother. But both of them looked very annoyed." Edgar cleared his throat so that he could imitate the wife's high, nagging voice. "His wife said, 'Ralph, what are you doing back there? Come on, let's go. I thought you were only going to check the boat?'

"Ralph was his name, poor guy. But I still could hardly keep from laughing. Can you imagine," Edgar roared, nearly bent over in hysterics, "he said to his wife, 'We ain't goin' nowhere, Annie—less my name's Noah.' He was incredible; he just smiled at her. He said, 'Annie, the wheels fell right off the trailer; I don't know what happened.' He said it so nonchalantly, as if it had happened to him a hundred times before. I could hardly stand it!"

Edgar cleared his throat again and in Ralph's wife's voice said, "'Oh, Ralph. *Now* what did you do? Doesn't anything ever go right?

Every damn time we take this boat out something like this happens,'
she said. It reminded me of a scene right out of Walter Mitty. Then she
got on the poor guy's back to sell the boat: 'It is nothing but an alba-
tross, anyway. You didn't hurt yourself, did you?' she said to him.

"Next thing I heard the daughter. She chimes in, 'I knew that
would happen, Daddy—broke the axles, didn't you? Remember when
you were pushing the boat the other day, and I told you the tires were
bending. I bet you were pushing the boat again, weren't you—to
straighten it out on the trailer. And the wheels bowed, and blew off, just
like I knew they would, huh? Well, you can't say I didn't warn you. I
told you so,' she said. I pitied him, but he didn't seem to mind the bad-
gering at all. And he answers, 'You'll have this in a small town with a
McDonald's and a post office.' The daughter and wife just rolled their
eyes and shook their heads.

"Then his wife saw his shirt, and I guess, because I was there,
she was embarrassed because it was so dirty. She got on his case again,"
and then Edgar assumed his high voice again, "'Oh, Ralph, just look at
your shirt. Why, I just washed that yesterday. Can't you keep it clean for
one day?' She winked at me and made a *tsking* sound and said to me,
'Honestly, he's so oblivious.' But Ralph just scratched his head. Then
his wife smiled. She said, 'Come on, Ralphie. Let's get someone here to
help us with the boat. Then we'll go home, and I'll make you spaghetti
for dinner.'

"Ralph smiled and looked at me. 'Ya like spaghetti? Want to
come home with us and have spaghetti?' I damn near howled right in
front of him. Imagine—his boat's sitting in the dirt by the side of the
road, and he's inviting me to a spaghetti dinner.

"I turned down the invitation but offered to call a gas station
from my truck phone. Afterwards we talked for a while. He's a real
interesting guy. You'd like him—seems he built that boat himself.
Actually, it's the third one he's built. He just sends away for the plans,
orders all the wood and fiberglass and builds it in his garage. He is a
physics teacher who took early retirement. Said he just wanted to test
out the new motor at Beltzville Lake before he took it to the shore. Said
he used to do a lot of scuba diving off Jersey and then got interested in
boating. Now he takes friends and his family fishing, mostly for flounder, bluefish and mackerel."

"Oh, boy," I commented, "I love bluefish."

"Hell of an interesting guy. Seems real intelligent, once I got him talking. What really impressed me was that he did some diving with the guy written up in *National Geographic*, the one who discovered the sunken treasure ship, the *Atocha*."

"Hey, that is pretty neat. Well, then what happened with the boat?" I asked.

"When I left, a wrecking crew had arrived and was setting up their gear. When I passed that spot on the way back, the boat was gone. Ralph was probably at home eating his spaghetti."

A few weeks later during small animal appointments, I ushered in a middle-aged man carrying a cockatiel in a cage. His wife trotted amiably behind as the door to the examining room closed. No sooner had Edgar greeted the couple than he rushed back into the pharmacy where I was counting out pills.

Worm pills rolled out of their bottle and all over the counter as Edgar suddenly grabbed me by the shoulders. "Those people in room two—that's them—the guy with the boat! What's his name—now what's his name?" he said, pounding his forehead. "Ralph! That's it! That's the guy—you remember my telling you about the fisherman?"

"Gee, I can't wait to meet him," I said, trying to share his excitement. Edgar ran back to examining room two but stopped just before the door; He straightened his stethoscope around his neck, swallowed a lump in his throat and set his hand on the doorknob. You'd think he was about to meet his all-time hero, Alan Alda. Finally, he stepped into the room.

I scooped all the worm pills into their bottle and followed Edgar inside.

Ralph's wife was a neat looking woman with slightly graying hair worn in the "wedge" cut. She wore a rose-colored pantsuit, the jacket of which she held casually over her arm. Standing in the far corner, she was small and thin and deferred the place of honor, beside the examining table, to her husband.

Her husband was her exact opposite. He was a walking advertisement for leisurely lifestyle, *haute cuisine* and grunge. He was living proof of what happens to a person who refuses sunscreen because his face and wide forehead—I couldn't tell where the forehead ended and where the bald scalp started—were a scaly red: lobster red from a bad case of sunburn. Yet as I surveyed the entire length of the man from his head to his feet, the red patches eventually lightened to pink on his arms and chest and then turned into moon-white on his legs: like an upside-down thermometer.

Sitting askew over his scaly scalp was a baseball cap with the words, "Harvey's Bait Shop—Barnegat, New Jersey." A picture of a worm crawled along the bottom of the words as creative underlining. The yellow of the cap contrasted to the navy blue T-shirt covering his broad middle. The shirt said, "America—Love It or Leave It." The T-shirt gave way to a pair of darker navy blue shorts that he had hoisted up and over his belly, making him look short-waisted, like the McCoys's Grandpappy Amos.

And there, completing his outfit, were the white socks, thread-bare with the elastic shot, crumpled down and scrunched under the heel area of his black Thom McAn dress shoes.

"You're the guy helped me with my boat?" Ralph said.

"Yeah, that's right. And you're Ralph." Edgar smiled.

"Yep. Say, that spaghetti was good. Ya shoulda joined us."

Edgar laughed. "How did you make out that day—getting the boat home?"

Ralph nodded to his wife. "I hitched Annie to the trailer, and she pulled it home for me," he said with a straight face.

"Oh, yeah?" Edgar laughed.

"Yeah, took her about seven hours, but she pulls like hell. She put some pretty good ruts in the road, though. She was beat afterwards, but she still made me spaghetti."

Annie rolled her eyes, and Edgar put his hand to his mouth. Then he introduced me to Annie and Ralph.

"I brought you my oven-stuffer roaster," Ralph said setting the cage atop the exam table.

A gray cockatiel with a yellow cap and peach cheeks gazed unperturbed through the bars.

"I see," said Edgar bending down to look at the cockatiel, who scooted sideways on his perch. "What's his name?"

"Ronnie," Ralph offered. "Reagan's his last name."

I giggled, and Annie rolled her eyes. Suddenly, Ralph started to cough, hacking violently into his hand. "'Scuse me," he apologized, "can't throw this damn cold."

Annie opened her purse and handed him a lozenge. "Here, Ralph." He took it obediently, and she closed her purse with a snap.

"I told him to see a doctor about that cough, but no—he knows better. Too chicken to go, that's what it is. He's afraid. Can you imagine: a big brute like him afraid to go to the doctor?" She pursed her lips.

"I'm not afraid, Annie. I'm here, aren't I?" he said. "Doc here can treat an old dog, right? All he has to do is give me some dog pills, and I'll be wagging my tail again."

She gazed at the ceiling in resignation. "Yes, that's right, but then I'll have to put up with your barking at night."

"RO-O-O-OOF! RO-O-O-OOF!" Ralph barked, and then he screwed his lips up around his gums and began sniffing the air until he found a target in Annie's neck. He tickled her with his nose, and she let out a shriek that embarrassed her immediately. He laughed, and she wiped her neck with her suit top.

"Honestly," she scolded. "You're incorrigible."

Edgar winked at me.

"Down to business, Doc. Ronnie here, we think, has a cold. Anyway, he's been sneezin' and coughin' for about the past three weeks." Ralph's face knitted with concern. "He's eatin' fine and seems to be normal in every other respect, except for the coughin' and sneezin'."

Edgar turned the cage toward him and looked in at the bird. Ronnie eyed him with suspicion. "Been eating okay, you say? Hasn't had any change in any of his other habits? What about his behavior? Has he been as lively as he always is, or does he just sit in his cage and mope?"

Annie offered his case history. "Well, he has still been saying, 'Pretty bird.' And he has been doing his wolf whistle. In fact, just last night he gave us part of Beethoven's Fifth Symphony."

"His Fifth Symphony!" I choked.

"Well, only the first part, really," she corrected.

"Wow, he must be very talented," I remarked.

Ralph chimed in, "Oh, yes, he's quite a *birduoso*." Annie rolled her eyes.

At this point, watching her, I tended to doubt some pet owners' relative sanity. According to some owners, there is real animal talent out there going to waste. Mr. Fox's water spaniel can water-ski—on one ski, no less; Sally Longfield's Siamese cat sings along with the piano—she takes the alto part; Professor Latimus's Irish wolfhound can read, and Dr. Latimus is quick to point out his pet's preference for Shakespeare over the editorial page; Mrs. Sander's beagle, Sandy, watches television and, said Mrs. Sander, "She understands every word. She even howls when her soap opera characters cry."

"I'll be right back," Edgar said. "I need a better stethoscope." He headed to the pharmacy.

Ralph blew out another loud, raspy cough. He covered his mouth as his lungs strained almost to exploding. Next he gave a little gasp, then a wheeze. As Ralph's coughing episode continued, the coughs came in fits and starts. Then there was silence. Again I heard a kind of tiny, tinny hiccup.

"Okay, let's listen to his air sacs," Edgar said, coming back into the room. "What will he do if I handle him?"

"Ever give a shark a body massage?" Ralph replied.

"Ah, come on, he can't be that bad," Edgar joked. "He's such a cute guy." Edgar sized up the bird.

"Pretty bird," Ronnie chirped. We all laughed.

"That's right, you're a pretty bird," Edgar said as he approached the open cage door with a hand towel. Quickly he flung the towel over the bird. There was a struggle underneath the cloth, then just as quickly Edgar grasped Ronnie behind the back and pulled him from the cage. The moment was tense. Afterward, surprisingly, all became quiet; the towel had a subduing effect.

Then Edgar lifted the corner of the towel that covered Ronnie's head. Like lightning the bird's head swiveled around 360 degrees— shades of the Exorcist—and planted a bite on Edgar's knuckle.

"Yeow!" Edgar shrieked, but he hung on, flipping the towel back over Ronnie's head. There was Ronnie's beak mark—not unlike the mark of Zorro—only in the shape of a V.

"Damn," Edgar fumed, "looks like a can opener got hold of me."

"Maybe he thought you were a can of beans," Ralph offered gently. Annie was upset, not for the bird but for the vet. She was embarrassed her pet would harm anyone. Then Ralph scolded Ronnie who was oblivious under the towel.

"That's all right: you warned me," Edgar said. "Guess I'll have to examine him through the towel. I'm certainly not going to let go, or I'll never get him again."

Edgar put the stethoscope to Ronnie's lungs and listened for quite a while. Then he released the bird back to its cage where Ronnie straightened his feathers. In a few minutes he was sitting calmly on his perch as if nothing had ever happened.

"I don't know, Ralph. He seems sound as far as I can tell. His lungs and air sacs sound fine, and his nares have no discharge or anything. There doesn't appear to be anything wrong with him."

With that Ralph started to cough again, and we all became silent waiting for the spell to end. Then I heard it again, and this time so did Edgar. A tinny gasping sounded, and then a round of delicate sneezing echoed from the bird cage.

Edgar looked at me, and we both looked at the bird. Ronnie was coughing or, rather, making coughing noises. Then there was silence, and the bird paced up and down on his perch, his wings out at his side. He had a look of concentration on his face.

Edgar motioned to Ralph, "I'd like to do one more test on Ronnie. Could you just cough one more time?"

Ralph looked puzzled but complied, treating us to another round of hacking and spasms. And then the steely hiccups came again, and we could all hear and see Ronnie's solo as he imitated Ralph's coughs in miniature.

"There! That's his cough! That's why we brought old Perdue here—for a lousy cold that he's fakin'?" Ralph smiled sheepishly, and Annie rolled her eyes again. Edgar and I laughed.

"Jesus Christ… Jesus Christ," Ralph repeated, and he scratched his bald head. "I don't believe this." He coughed.

Ronnie coughed again.

Ralph jerked his head and threatened the bird, "Cut that out or

I'll make a fish lure out of you." Ronnie just stared with his bright button eyes.

"Well, that was an easy case to cure," Edgar commented. "Wouldn't mind more like that." He handed the bird cage to Ralph.

"Sorry about that," Ralph said. "We really thought he was sick." Annie shook her head and refolded her suit top over her arm.

We said goodbye, and as Annie, Ralph and Ronnie walked out the door, the bird whistled a tune that was a miniature Army mail call. "That's right," I heard Ralph scold Ronnie, "you're off to boot camp after that stunt." But afterwards, as their footsteps became distant, we heard the sounds of laughter; we couldn't tell from whom it came—man or beast.

27

"Dr. Gay Balliet"

Who would argue that a veterinarian's animals get the best medical care in the world? After all, when his or her cat looks depressed and lies curled in a ball, the owner-veterinarian has only to skip into the house for a shot of penicillin and a few pills to perk up kitty. And when his or her horse gets the slightest cold or runny nose, the vet quickly responds with his armory of drugs. Who would argue?

I would. Our animals always seem to be the last treated. It wasn't that Edgar didn't care about them. No one could have cared more, but Edgar was so busy tending everyone else's animals that our own were often ignored. When the horses were due for their worm medicine, there was the same old answer, "Tomorrow, maybe. Tomorrow I'll do it. I have umpteen calls to make. I just don't have time tonight." This year, the horses all walked around with their tail hairs scrunched up from rubbing their backsides against trees, fence rails and stall doors. I nagged: Edgar promised. Three months later Edgar finally took time off from his calls to deworm them.

One day our horse Nicholas was sick. A violent cough reverberated in the barn: Nicholas sounded wheezy and a pus ball clung to the end of his muzzle. "Please. Would you look at Nick?" I begged. "He might have a bad cold. He could get pneumonia. Maybe you should put him on antibiotics."

"Oh, yeah," Edgar mused, "I did hear him coughing the other day. Don't worry. It's nothing much, a slight cold. It'll go away by itself. If it gets any worse, then I'll put him on antibiotics," he added, his mind elsewhere.

"Well, why don't you do something about it now?" I demanded.

"He'll get over it himself." Then he walked into his den, ignoring my tirade.

And, in fact, Nicholas did get over it, but my hurt feelings simmered. Recently one of the outside cats couldn't keep any of her supper down. I informed Edgar.

"Just hair balls. She'll be all right in a few days."

For the next three days she was sick, depositing every meal back on the grass shortly after she had eaten. Finally, late one night, I scooped her into my arms and took her into the living room. Standing before my weary husband, I demanded he pay attention. "Look, this hair ball theory of yours is the pits. This cat is sick, *sick* do you hear! She has not been able to keep any food in her for four days...*four days*, and she's *very* thin! You must examine her now and do something about whatever it is that's wrong with her—before she dies!"

"My, she does look a bit peaked," he admitted, looking guilty. "Let's see her." The animal winced as he deftly felt her belly. "Abdomen seems a bit tense. Not dehydrated yet, but there is definitely something worse here than a hair ball. She might have an impaction. We'll run a blood sample, too, to see if there's any infection."

And so he went to work on her. In a matter of a day she was drinking chicken broth, and in three more days she was running and playing again. She had had an infection and a daily regimen of penicillin resolved the problem.

Considering our situation at home and Edgar's day and night practice, I began to wonder what help I could depend on when Merry, our brood mare, foaled. Would my husband be there at the moment of birth, ready to help with any problems? Or would I find myself alone at the event?

Merry was three weeks late this time. For two weeks I had been checking her for signs of impending birth. Shifting her weight back and forth, Merry regarded me with disgust as I bounded once again into the pasture, anticipating a change in her udder. But time and again as I felt up between her legs for her swollen udder, there was not much difference, no tell-tale waxing on the ends of the teats, a prelude to dripping milk and impending labor. There was only a slightly larger udder, and, from all indications, she could foal anywhere from the next day until another two weeks. I was anxious with thoughts of a foal grown too large to pass into this real world without complications, imagining a diseased or stillborn foal, sometimes the cause of a late birth.

During her pregnancy, Edgar did check her routinely, kept her shots up to date, and monitored her gestation. Periodically, Edgar also checked her udder. But for two weeks after her due date, she offered us no indication of *when* the big event would happen. She was planning this, no doubt, as a total surprise. Would he be available during the actual birth? I kept asking myself, and my worry grew.

On Friday, April 3, I ran out to the pasture as usual to check Merry's udder. At this point, she was three weeks late. She had carried a foal for almost a full year instead of the normal eleven months. This day her udder was different. Not only was it much larger than it had been, but now there were small, clear, waxlike blobs hanging from the teats; she was waxing. That meant she would foal in six to forty-eight hours. Well, that was lucky. The only time Edgar would be unavailable in the next forty-eight hours were the two hours tonight he had to spend doing small animal appointments in the Allentown clinic. And that was only a half-hour drive away. The probability was good that he would be able to attend the foaling.

At five o'clock I led the horses in from the pasture to feed and bed them down. Before Edgar left for his appointments, I showed him the wax that had formed on the ends of Merry's teats.

"Yes, sirree," he cried. "Looks like she might foal late tonight or tomorrow sometime."

"Finally." I sighed. "I don't know how much more waiting I can take."

Walking to the house, we discussed how convenient that she should foal over a weekend. "That way you'll be home for sure," I quipped. "If she has any problems, you'll be here to help. But you know," I said, pausing before the door, "you better give me some iodine just in case, on a long shot, she has it while you're gone."

The foal's umbilical cord must be drenched with iodine that prevents a fatal disease called joint-ill. Many foals die simply because the owner neglects to dip the umbilical cord in iodine, thereby allowing bacteria to pass through it and irreversibly infect all the joints.

"Oh, she won't have it tonight. Remember, I said six to forty-eight hours after beginning to wax. At best, she'll have it late tonight," he said.

"Well, okay, if you say so." Then I turned but stopped short, "No, let me have the iodine just in case." He turned to the truck, looking somewhat sheepish, and gave me the bottle.

"Now," I said, "just in case it does come while you're away. What do I do?"

"It won't," he interrupted, setting his chin stubbornly as if his words were prophetic. "I'll be home in time."

"I don't care," I said. "Just tell me what I should do in case she does have it."

"If she should start going into contractions, call me right away. I'll cancel all my appointments and come right home."

"Promise?"

"Yes, I promise. If you call and say she's actually starting to push, I'll come right home." He walked away, looking guilty again.

"Phew," I sighed, leaning against a wall and twirling a strand of hair. "Then you promise to be here?" I yelled after him.

"Yes, I promise," he called. "But you'll see; she won't have it then, probably not even tonight."

"Well, if she has it…. Just in case, what should I do?"

"First, make sure it's coming out properly, like in a diving position," he said. Then he continued in a detached monotone, "If it is, when the head is out far enough, open the sac around the muzzle so it can breathe. Make sure there's no fluid or mucus around the nose. That's it," he said, raising both arms as if he just explained something as simple as extruding spaghetti from a pasta machine. "You know all that stuff anyway. I don't have to tell you what to do."

"Okay," I repeated, "then if something happens, you will come right home?"

"Yes, yes, yes, but it won't; so don't worry," he replied. Then he hopped into the truck and left me with my bottle of iodine.

Sometimes I need him, and he's not there. I get furious when it's really something important because while everyone else's husband seems to be around to help out, I'm usually fending for myself. Of course, I've learned valuable lessons in independence through it all, and he doesn't do it on purpose. He's just busy doctoring the animals. But it would have been nice to have some help assembling the gas grill, setting the fence posts, nailing all the rails along the lower pasture and unloading a full hay wagon before a thunderstorm broke. One time, I almost met my sticky demise when he left me for an emergency in the middle of fiberglassing the inside of our homemade wooden hot tub. Racing against the hardening of the resin, I nearly plastered myself to the inside of the tub, like an insect caught in amber.

So it was no wonder I doubted his promise. That evening, even the six o'clock news could not wipe out imaginary horrors of Merry's foaling. I kept picturing images of a waxing udder and of Edgar's short speech on what to do if *it should happen*. News of the assassination attempt on President Reagan passed nearly unnoticed as did the uprisings of Polish workers. The only thing that mattered to me was Merry and her three-week-late foal.

It would do no good to stay out in the barn and watch for signs because mares are notorious for withholding giving birth in front of anyone. In 95 percent of the cases, if an owner decides to play midwife, even sleeping overnight in the barn, the mare will hold back delivery until the owner's quick dash to the bathroom.

Nevertheless, at six-thirty I sneaked out to the barn and quietly peeked in at Merry standing beside her food bunk, her back legs shifting uncomfortably. She was not eating her hay which was highly unusual for her. Again, I checked her udder, nearly falling on my backside as the teats freely dripped milk. Fifteen minutes is all any mare needs to give birth, the process being surprisingly quick. Any labor lasting beyond fifteen minutes can endanger both the life of the foal and the mother. I broke out in a cold sweat. "Don't tell me you're going to have it soon?" I said, rubbing my hands. I chewed my nails. "Edgar won't be home until nine o'clock. You just can't have it without his being here," I tried to convince her and myself. As if understanding, soon Merry began munching her hay and stopped kicking at her belly—all signs of discomfort disappearing. I breathed a sigh of relief, realizing she was okay at least for now.

I stood watching for some time. Her condition didn't change. She just eyed me casually. After a half hour elapsed, I decided to take my bath and get ready for bed, figuring that afterward I could check her, uninterrupted for the rest of the evening.

But a tub bath, a luxury for me most times, did not calm my apprehension about our mare. All I could do was sit in the bubbly hot water, tense as a stick. With the steam billowing around me, I could only think of Merry out in the barn ready to burst at the seams. And, of course, I worried that she would do just that before Edgar got home.

At last I crawled, light-headed, from the water. Drying off, I donned my purple flannel nightgown which came almost to my ankles, brushed my teeth and slipped on my cozy moccasin slippers. I was all ready for bed, and it was only 8:15.

Time to check the mare again—since I hadn't for approximately forty-five minutes. I ran downstairs, scattering the cats. Then, slipping on a pair of rubber mucker boots, I strolled into the night.

The evening's lovely gentle breezes whipped the ruffles of my nightie into a flutter around my legs. It was a warm breeze, and the scent of spring was in the air. But as I enjoyed the darkening woods around me, there was coming from the direction of the barn a strange rustling sound. It was the sound of straw being churned round and round, like ocean waves spilling onto a beach.

"What's that?" I cried, then jumped into a gallop. Through the barn door to the side of Merry's stall, I flew. The horse was thrashing in the straw.

"Oh, no!" I groaned as the rotund animal, heavy with foal, tossed and tumbled on the floor. "She's going to foal! Very soon, too! What should I do?" I yelled at a passing cat.

But then, as if by magic, the mare rose to her feet, shook the straw off like a dog, and casually began to nibble hay. She didn't fool me, however. Realizing that she was probably trying to fake me out, I decided to do the same to her.

Turning off the lights, I said as usual to the horses, "Good night," and tromped out the door. Then I tiptoed quietly back to peek through a crack in the barn door. The outline of the mare standing in a corner was barely visible.

Minutes passed, and I stared at her while the breezes played with the ruffled hem of my nightie. Once again the horses all became quiet. Suddenly there was a thud. I peeked through the crack. The mare had dropped to the ground like a rock. My feet went heavy in my mucker boots; my skin prickled.

"This is it!" I thought panic-stricken.

My feet raced me away from the barn—purple nightie streaking through the dark woods to the telephone hanging just inside the garage. My fingers sprinted over the buttons: "Hello, this is Gay Balliet. I must speak to Dr. Balliet. It's an emergency!"

"Just a minute," the receptionist said so calmly I could have choked her.

"Yeah, Gay. What's up?" Edgar answered in a cool voice.

"She's going to have it right now! And I'm all alone!" I blurted. "She keeps dropping down in her stall. She's restless, kicking at her belly; she's dripping milk. I know she's going to have it. You must come home! Please!"

"Now calm down. As long as Merry doesn't stay down, she's not having it. She's not going into contractions, is she?" he asked, calmly.

"No, I don't think so," I choked. "But I know she's going to have it any minute, and if you don't come home, I'll just die. I'm scared. You promised, remember?" When I became upset, I sounded like a twelve-year-old.

"I know, I know, but I'm in the middle of some emergencies. I'll be done in less than an hour. Then I'll be home. Besides, you said she's not even down yet. If she goes down and starts pushing, then give me another call," he said in that same annoyingly calm voice.

Mine was agitated. "Well, I'll check her again. But you promise you'll come home if I call and say she's pushing?" I asked, twisting a corner of my nightie around my fidgety fingers.

"Yes, I promise. If she starts pushing, I'll come right home. I have to go now."

"All right. You promise?"

"I promise," he said. "Goodbye." Then he hung up, and again I was alone in the dark woods, in the gently blowing breeze.

Back to the barn I sprinted, gritting my teeth, nightie sucked against my body. But peering through the crack this time, instead of seeing the mare's shadow shifting silently by her feed bin, there was nothing visible at all. My gaze dropped to the stall floor where she lay prostrate on the ground. She was huffing and puffing fiercely.

Spinning around, I flicked on the barn lights and then had my long-awaited answer. She was starting her contractions. Now she did not even rise when I ran in horror to her stall. She just lay there, nostrils flared, huffing and snorting.

"No, this can't be!" I screeched, hands gripping the side of the stall as my eyes popped at the heaving form before me. And back I raced, nightie twisted around my legs, to the phone. This time I blurted at the receptionist, "Tell Dr. Balliet she's pushing!"

Anything could have dissuaded me from returning to that barn. My fear of being alone and facing a problem foaling was more than I could handle. It was then that I discovered I was one of those people who falls apart in an emergency. My body broke into a cold sweat, tufts of cotton bloomed in my mouth, and all my joints seemed to separate from their sockets. For only a second I thought—going back to when I was a little girl of seven—who should I call if I were in trouble? "Mommy and Daddy!" I yelled. I ran to the telephone.

"You must come over! I'm all alone, and Merry's going to have her foal any minute. You must come; hurry!" I yelled to my perplexed mother.

Slamming down the receiver, I raced back to the barn, aglow with lights. I panted, staring bug-eyed at my mare flat out on her side. A low grunt rose from the stall floor. I gripped the wooden stall wall, clenched it almost until my fingers dug right into the wood.

Suddenly, one tiny white hoof, still enclosed in the amniotic sac, appeared like a shot, from Merry's backside.

Instantly a change overcame me—a thorough transformation of my demeanor. At sight of that diminutive hoof, I suddenly became a brave person. The adrenaline in my blood, instead of reducing me to a weeping, blithering mess, transformed me into an obstetrician.

Not even considering that Merry could have the foal normally and by herself, I flew into the stall. Edgar's advice resounded in my brain, "Break the sac around the foal's nose and wipe away any fluid so that it can breathe."

Soon the foal's head began to emerge alongside a front leg, and then, with another great heave from Merry, the entire head popped out. A huge gush of water and other fluids flushed into my mucker boots. The sac still covered the nose. "Oh, no, it'll suffocate!" my brain screamed. I tore open the sac, feeling for the first time the tiny, furry muzzle I had imagined so many times. Then my fingers quickly snatched the mucus and fluids away from the nostrils. But they weren't moving, they weren't taking in any air! The nostrils were still, and for the briefest second the thought hit me that the foal might be dead.

On Merry's next contraction, I grabbed the slippery legs still encased in the sac and pulled. Half the foal was outside now, but the hips and hind legs had yet to arrive. Within less than a minute, however, Merry gave another heave, and with that the foal and the rest of the fluids splashed out onto the straw bed, the foal sliding against my bare legs and the hem of my purple obstetrical gown.

I remembered Edgar had once said to always let the umbilical cord alone, to leave it attached to the foal so that it could get all the blood still coursing around in the placenta. The foal lay spread in a heap before me; and now that it had arrived, the nostrils began to quiver. It was alive.

Stripping the placenta from the body, over its hips and legs, I rubbed the foal, trying to stimulate it because I had read somewhere to do that. Then its head moved, and the whole body followed in a grand awakening.

Suddenly, I felt tremendous elation, accomplishment and contentment. It was all over: the foal had arrived alive with no problems, and Doctor Gay Balliet had assisted in the delivery—all by herself. It was terrific. The foal was one of the biggest, most beautiful foals I'd ever seen. But most important, it was alive and breathing well.

I grabbed the iodine bottle, lifting the foal's back legs to expose the umbilical cord still attached to the mother and doused the area with the germ-killing iodine. We had a boy!

Merry, recovering from the birth, still lay in the straw, taking deep, satisfying draughts of air. Then she raised her head and nickered.

Then I stood back in the far corner of the stall just observing the new family. The foal lay wet and shuddering behind his mother, and every now and then he raised a trembling head, peering out from those blinking, questioning eyes. Soon Merry rolled onto her breast bone and scrambled in the straw to her newborn. After a preliminary sniff test, she began licking her baby all over. The foal grunted and squeaked, moving in rhythm under the mother's strong tongue.

It wasn't until much later that I noticed my own condition. There I stood in my flannel nightie. It was not too terribly dirty, but my hands were covered with sticky fluid and blood and looked awful. So, too, did my mucker boots; they shined with amniotic water mixed with straw and dirt. Straw stuck to my ankles as did particles of sawdust and manure. I was a mess, but I didn't care.

Presently a car came up the driveway. My parents ran to the barn as I gestured with bloodied hands that everything was in perfect order.

"Thank goodness you're here," I gasped. "I need some moral support. I just delivered our foal. Come on. Have a look at him," I said proudly, leading the way to the stall.

"My goodness," my mother said, "isn't he cute? You mean you delivered him all by yourself?" I nodded. "Oh, that's right," she continued, "Edgar is doing appointments tonight. Oh, you poor thing. You must've been half crazy here by yourself."

"A redhead, very nice color," my father said as he leaned, smiling, over the stall. "Boy, he's quite big, isn't he? He's all right?"

"Yes, I think so. His membranes look good, and his color is quite good," I remarked. "I called Edgar but I don't know when he's coming home. He's still doing appointments. But it's all right; everyone's in good health, and at least you came. I've had a rough night."

Merry looked at me as if to say, *Who had it rough*? Then she continued licking the foal, the two of them contented and peaceful.

We all watched in silence. Then Merry rose on shaky legs, and the cord broke. She continued to lick the colt's face with long, sweeping licks.

"That's funny. He's not Merry's color or the father's. He's chestnut," I said.

I decided to call him Merry's Shadowfax, Fax for short.

"He has such a tiny mane. It must be only an inch long, and his tail is so cute, too, with little white strands, like frosted hair," my mother said. "Look at his legs—they're so long."

"Yes, he's one of the biggest newborn foals I've seen," I commented.

For perhaps an hour, my parents and I, in the light of the barn, enjoyed watching the foal and mother becoming acquainted, laughing and commenting as the foal made its first awkward attempts to stand. The front legs crossed in front, folded under, and then the hind legs followed suit, depositing the animal in a bundle on the floor only inches from where it had started. Because of its unusually large size he had trouble navigating his legs, and the first trip to the mother's udder was a difficult challenge.

Slowly, I approached so as not to alarm Merry and offered a stabilizing hand to the foal, whose attempts at standing seemed hopeless. First placing his long legs out in front of him, then gathering his hind ones up underneath him, I wrapped my arms around his belly. He and I tried, he pushing and me pulling, but his weight was too much. Back down in the straw he landed with me nearly on top of him. We tried many times, but he was just too heavy. He would either have to gather his own strength with time or Edgar would have to help him when he came home.

"Here comes Edgar," my mother said as the thin headlight beams appeared down our driveway.

"It's a boy!" I cheered as he ran into the barn.

"You did it by yourself?" he marveled. "I can't believe you did it by yourself. He's huge! We'll check him out right away," he said walking briskly to his truck for his stethoscope. "You did a great job. Oh, yeah, Merry, so did you."

I just smiled.

28

A Buffalo Calf

The Gaelic crimson and gold shades of fall had replaced the summer's lush greenery. Edgar was working hard and so was I, taking care of our own animals and teaching my students. I rode Fancy and Nicholas until the first snowflakes fell. Then the scene changed so quickly. I wasn't fully prepared for the first blizzard to ricochet through the land.

Edgar and I were about to come to the aid of a pregnant buffalo in one of the area's wildlife preserves.

I marveled as a snowflake slid down my back. Stamping my feet, I hollowed out an insulated, snowy hole to stand in as another ice ball sought out the bare skin peeking out between my coat collar and scarf.

I had forgotten to tuck my scarf underneath my coat collar, leaving two centimeters of my neck naked and exposed. Each flake sizzled there as I struggled to reposition my frost-covered scarf.

There, I waited in a snowbank in the middle of a glacial buffalo range, clutching heavy obstetrical equipment and a bucket of antiseptic. Bracing against a blast of frigid air, I shivered in the knee-deep drift as the wind howled.

My puffed eyelids closed against the blizzard. Despite the difficulty, I resolved not to abandon the weighty OB instruments in a snowdrift for escape to the warm truck. I could not retreat, tail between my legs, because my husband endured the elements, too. There was an obligation to remain—a sharing of the elements and our commitment to heal on this buffalo range.

A few yards away Edgar lay, struggling to pull a buffalo calf from its tranquilized mother. With each tug on the obstetrical ropes, he slipped a little further toward the ice-covered creek while his red hands hurried against the stinging cold.

"Be careful, Hon," I called. "You're awfully close to the creek." He repositioned himself and resumed work with no reply. At times like this I felt useless; I was no help here. What else could I possibly offer except my company and moral support? Only Edgar was responsible for saving the mother buffalo and her child. My only support was that I was there if he needed me.

There was no warning about this kind of trial by ice by the women at the auxiliary tea a year ago which now swirled through my frozen thoughts. They all were so toasty on that past December afternoon, munching coconut delights, sipping herbal tea, and chatting around Mrs. Witter's chandelier-lit dining table about the upcoming bazaar.

The drone of conversation had mesmerized me as had Mrs. Witter's Siamese cat who was asleep, breathing rhythmically, on a brocaded chair. It was the kind of cozy scene portrayed in Jane Austen's *Sense and Sensibility*, a favorite book of mine.

But now the wind had built a snowy fortress around my legs, and again I tried to find Edgar and the buffalo through the blinding squall.

I clung to a bucket of Betadine antiseptic solution, my hand molded into an icy clutch around the bucket's metal handle. I squinted through the snowflakes that cut like glass shards to see if Edgar and his assistants had made any headway extracting the calf. Inching toward the men and buffalo, I dragged the winch, chains, hooks and bucket, now heavy with great chunks of ice and snow. Fighting my way forward, I was still about twenty-five feet from the action.

Edgar was rearranging himself in the snow to gain a better foothold while he manipulated the buffalo calf back down inside its mother. The last thing he wanted to do was a fetotomy—removing a fetus from its mother with a scalpel, piece by piece. Instead he had to push the calf back inside and reposition its limbs to the correct position. But it seemed as though Edgar was fighting a losing battle, for he had been jockeying the poor calf for over a half-hour, and the tranquilizer was wearing thin. The buffalo was beginning to fight back, and her hoofs menaced the air. Alarmed by the bison's increasing alertness, the men sat on her great square head and tied her legs together with ropes.

What made matters even more difficult, besides the intense cold and driving snowfall, was the position in which the buffalo had fallen in a tranquilized stupor. In her futile efforts to flee, she had fallen to the edge of a frozen stream. Edgar could hardly examine the cow because as he pushed inside her, he lost his footing on the slippery ice.

Shuffling still closer, my breath freezing to my lips, I saw Edgar give a sudden, great heave, and the calf slipped out of sight and back into the mother. Now he could reposition it and help it out.

The preserve's helpers tightened the ropes around the mother's hocks, but her hoofs slit the air like gypsy knives; I was afraid Edgar, working so closely to her hind end, might become a target. She was awakening quickly; speed was imperative.

Once Edgar had arranged the calf's legs in their proper diving position, he would call for the winch and chains. So, I lifted my snowy bucket with its cold antiseptic and gathered the OB chains and winch, ready to run.

A few minutes later the call came. "Okay, Gay, hurry!" he yelled, his face a mottled red. His right arm was lost inside the buffalo as he labored to keep the calf positioned correctly.

"Hurry up! Give me the winch and chains, and put the bucket here, right in back of me," he shouted.

I leaped forward. Finally, I had my chance to help.

Little did I realize, however, that under my feet lay a nasty ice patch. Lurching forward with the heavy chains and winch in one hand and with the bucket of water in the other, I flipped off that patch of ice like a rocket from a launching pad.

One leg stretched to twice its length as it whisked from under me like an elusive skateboard. And that leg pulled behind it the other leg. It all happened in a kind of slow motion, my body parts falling like dominoes. I did a classical pirouette into the air that ended in a body slam onto the ground. The imprint was no snow angel as the snow spurted out in a puffy halo large enough to resemble a meteor hit.

It happened so suddenly that I never heard myself yell, but I heard the chains clanging and a horrible slosh from my bucket as both articles accompanied me into space. Upon impact, a wide ribbon of water laced around my legs, freezing on contact to my pants. I tried to sit up, first righting the bucket, and then regathering the chains and hooks, their links filled with snow. But I felt like a turtle trapped on her back in thick layers of clothes and stiff boots. I could not bend at all.

I rocked back and forth, trying to maneuver my weight into a more manageable position, but encased by layers upon layers of insulated underwear, sweaters and a coat covered with snow and ice, I floundered helplessly on the ground.

Edgar, unaware of my predicament, shouted, "Come on, Gay, hurry. This buffalo is almost out of the anesthesia; I need that stuff right now!"

From the corner of my eye, I saw the buffalo twisting and straining to rise.

"I'm trying, I'm trying!" I grunted. At last, in one desperate heave, I flipped over and pushed myself to a kneeling position. Then, as a baby trying to stand, I backed up into an upright position.

Grabbing the winch and chains, I abandoned the bucket, useless now without water. "I lost the antiseptic water; you'll have to do without it!" I said, shuffling to the edge of the creek.

"Okay, but give me the chains! Hurry." Then he looked at one of the assistants. "Here, Dan. Set up the winch around that tree and. . . ." And so the team went into action. Dan, the manager of the preserve, sprinted to the tree, setting up the equipment while I stood by with my clothing anchored by snow.

Relieved that my job was done and seeing that, as Edgar cranked, the calf began to emerge from the mother, I began to make my way back to the truck. Arms at right angles to my body, I trudged through the high snow. The truck sat at the end of the buffalo path about a quarter mile away. Clinging onto nearby trees and stopping to catch my breath, I slogged through the snowdrifts.

Then Edgar's muffled voice sounded somewhere far behind me. The howling wind drowned out the words, so I carefully turned 180 degrees in the direction of the yell. Through the driving snow, it was hard to discern a dark hulk approaching. But the mother buffalo was awake and on the move, coming straight for me. Edgar's garbled yell came again, "You're on the buffalo path! Get off!"

Two flinty eyes stared out of a hairy boxhead as she chugged steadily closer, each step fast, deliberate and robot-like. She was solid as a Sherman tank. Paralyzed by a fear of falling and being trampled, I managed to emit a high-pitched whine. And then as the animal bore down on me, I closed my eyes and leaped, bullfrog fashion, down a steep embankment.

Submerged chest-deep in a snowdrift, I opened my eyes just in time to see the buffalo charging. I braced for the hit, but it didn't come. She had at the last moment turned onto another trail. But why? Then the answer became apparent.

Yelling and flailing his arms, Dan was running behind the cow, becoming a wild beast himself. His ululating banshee call echoed through the valley and chased the buffalo back to the herd. He was a Tarzan who saved my hide. Through the blizzard the buffalo retreated out of sight.

"It's all right, Gay," Dan yelled, picking me out of the drift

"You saved me," I panted, dusting the clumps of snow from my jacket. "She was coming straight towards me." The wind howled, whipping snowy tornadoes in the air.

Dan, blowing into his fists, said, "That's because you were blocking her path back to the herd. You were in her way. You have to move fast out here."

"Thanks for saving my wife, Dan," Edgar laughed as he reached us. "I wouldn't have wanted her to be steamrollered by a buffalo." He was such a comic.

Packing up their equipment, the other two men climbed into their four-wheel drive truck and pulled away. Edgar, Dan and I trudged to our truck. The wind blew us as if hurrying the aliens out a back door.

Back at the preserve's headquarters, we drank coffee around a metal card table. I cupped my thawing fingers over the mug and let the steam warm my face before taking a sip.

I watched the chunks of snow begin to melt and slip down the side of my boot as the old, rusty kerosene heater belched.

"I'm glad they'll be okay now, Doc," Dan said, emptying the coffee urn into his cup. "It would have been a shame if they...."

For the second time that day my mind turned to Mrs. Witter's tea party under the crystal chandelier: "We must plan a bazaar and introduce Gay to everyone." Dr. Forner's wife sipped her tea daintily.

"It would be better to have it in the fall, don't you think?" her friend replied, and the fire crackled warmly.

"Don't you, Gay?" Edgar said.

"Huh? What?" I looked at my tin coffee mug containing the grounds of my last drink. "What?"

"I said, don't you feel good about today? Those animals would surely have died." He paused; he was becoming philosophical again, but I liked him that way sometimes. "I mean, even in all the cold and under the most absurd conditions, in the end, don't you feel good about the whole thing—you know, not only saving a life but bringing a new one in?" He mused, turning his coffee mug around in his hands.

My own thoughts sped backwards to the cozy fireplace and crystal chandelier. I heard one of the women complaining, "The bazaar—in the fall? Really, I don't think so. Sarah, pass the croissants, please."

Then in my mind the primitive plains appeared where we had struggled under nearly impossible conditions. I thought, amused, my icy fall could enlighten Baryshnikov on new ballet techniques and wondered if my claim to fame would be as a human snowball; and, lastly, of my aspiration toward martyrdom at the hands of a wild beast. Then I thought of that cow and her baby, healthy enough now to roam the preserve's plains with the rest of the herd.

I shook my head, casting away all thoughts of tea in china cups, crystal chandeliers and bazaars and gulped the bitter remains in my mug. "Yes, it does feel good. Really good," I agreed.

29

If at First You Don't Succeed...

Fancy and I were preparing for another horse show. I wanted to make a respectable showing. At least I wanted not to fall off this time. So, we practiced until exhaustion set in.

Beads of sweat sprouted like tiny seedlings. First one salty bead then another popped out on my forehead, and as I signaled Fancy into the canter, I felt the droplets pooling into one large dribble down the side of my nose. It clung to my upper lip, then, finally losing its grip, burst in the air into a thousand droplets.

"Sit back!" my trainer, Gale, ordered. "That's why you always fall off! Now *sit back*, do you hear me? Get her collected; she's too strung out: *Don't you feel it*? Pull her together. Let her come up in front." Gale yelled, her eyes glued to our every move.

As I rode, my ponytail swished sickeningly against my sweaty neck; it felt awful—heavy and gummy. I was really tired and losing my ambition and concentration in this boiling, humid weather. Fancy, too, had lathered up a greasy foam between her hind legs, and sweat balls popped out and rolled down her neck in streams.

But Gale stood military-like in the center of the ring, giving orders that took no more of her strength than to move her lips. Her ponytail arched out behind her head; it did not flop like a wet dish rag. To the contrary—it hung crisply with an authoritative air.

Of course, she didn't sweat. Her petite face retained that television, peachy cream complexion. Gale turned slowly, ordering instructions as Fancy and I plummeted around the ring. I could feel the color in my cheeks rising to the edges of my skin, and it wasn't the color of peaches. Blotches of feverish red beets blossomed on my face. I was ripe for the picking. My eyes, inflamed with the heat, burned like shriveled light bulbs in my head.

"Okay, stop and park her out; you're through," Gale called striding toward the barn.

I swallowed the boll of cotton going to seed in my throat and slid off the saddle. My knees gave out, and I nearly collapsed when I hit the ground. "Rough time, huh, Fancy," I said, patting her. Her eyes strained, nostrils pumping, and steam rose from her body. I could have warmed hot dog buns on her back. "I know, I'm beat, too," I told her. I ran the stirrups up their leathers, gathered the reins into a bundle, and we trudged back to the barn.

As I untacked Fancy, Gale analyzed the lesson. "It really wasn't that bad; you did pretty well. Just remember to sit back; sit back. You must keep your weight off her front end.

"Make sure you cool her out real good today. She had quite a workout—fifteen minutes hand-walking, then rinse her down with a body wash."

I bade her a feeble goodbye.

She called over her shoulder, "Good luck on Saturday. You'll do fine. See you next week." Then she backed her car around and sped down the driveway, her ponytail waving in the breeze.

I hit the ground. The audience groaned. "No...it can't be! Not again! I'll never get through a horse show without falling off and making an idiot of myself," I thought as I lay on the ground. But this time the ground was too soft, too soft—something was wrong. I rolled over to shake the dust off my coattails and rolled right into Edgar. I was in bed, a pillow gripped around my head.

"Ow," he blurted, his hand cupping his face, "You hit me in the nose. What's the matter?"

"Oh, my God!" I said, propping myself on an elbow. "I dreamt I was at the show, and I fell off again. It was awful; everybody was laughing. I felt like such a jerk." My heart was still pounding.

He put his arm over me and closed his eyes. "It's all right." He patted me. "You're not at the show yet. Just go back to sleep. It's only four-thirty in the morning. Wait until we get up at six, then you can worry again." He rolled over on his side and fell back to sleep.

And, of course, the world's worst worrywart would do just that. Whenever there was a problem I'd pace the floor, picking mercilessly at my cuticles until I worked out a resolution. And if there could be no solutions, I'd still fuss and fume. Edgar always would say, "What're you worrying for? It won't do any good anyway. What will be will be, and no amount of stewing is going to change it." But I was no fatalist. When a plaguing situation righted itself, it was because I had worried it right.

So, this was the big day. I fidgeted between the bed covers, my fingers to my mouth. So many things had to be done: give Fancy her bath, braid her forelock and mane in ribbons, ready the tack, have my saddle suit, gloves, hat and shoes ready, and pack the cooler. I jumped from the bed and headed for the bathroom, opening a window; the woods were silent except for an owl's eerie hoot, and a couple of cats lay sleeping on the patio.

In the heavy mist, I headed for the barn and flicked on the lights. Fancy snorted, jumping from her sawdust bed and blinked her eyes against the stinging light. But she didn't seem to resent my early intrusion, probably in anticipation of an early breakfast.

By 6:00 A.M., the trailer was loaded, and Fancy was ready to go. Edgar, sleep still in his eyes, stumbled downstairs, "What in the world are you doing? How long have you been up?" he blinked, rubbing away the eye sand.

"Since four-thirty," I said, smearing the mustard on a ham sandwich. "Edgar," I said, "do you think I'll fall off again today?"

He sighed, exasperated. "No. No, I keep telling you that you won't fall off. You'll do just fine. Now what did I tell you about that damned worrying of yours? It only makes you miserable, and it doesn't help anything." He rolled his eyes and poured himself a cup of coffee. He sat at the table, and a cat jumped on his lap.

"I can't help it; I'm scared. I just *can't, can't* fall off again," I said, wringing my hands.

He struggled to put on his shoes while the cat clung to his lap.

"You won't, I'm telling you. You'll do all right." He paused. "You're beginning to blither, ya know."

"All I want to do is just complete the class on top of Fancy. I'm not asking to place, just stay on, that's all. And I know I'm blithering and whining; I'm nervous." The sandwich lay mummified in its plastic wrap, mustard leaking from its edges. "Guess I ruined our lunch," I said, shaking my head.

We arrived at the show grounds early in order to practice and take the edge off Fancy. She would probably be hyper in this new environment with its noisy crowds, strange horses and surroundings. Experience proved I'd have to tire her out so that she wouldn't misbehave. That was part of my problem at the first show; she was feeling too good—too spunky—and that precipitated her spooking and my dive into the dust. So after we unloaded her, I saddled up.

People scurried antlike around the show grounds. Grooms carted bucketsful of water; mothers led children to the snack area; little girls in their saddle suits paraded by with their horses; and, of course, there were the many horses and riders going to the showring for a class or to the practice ring for a workout. There were many different sights and sounds for a young horse like Fancy to feel anxious about. This was not Fancy's old stomping grounds with its familiar scenes: Louise the cat, sitting on her favorite rock; the sparrows fluttering about the horses' legs as they grazed, stirring up tasty bugs; the beat-up bathtub, their drinking trough, lying in a shady corner.

Hoisting myself into the saddle, we went to the practice ring and once again I felt the tension mounting beneath me. I called to Edgar to hurry, "Please stick around until we see that she'll behave." I bit my lip and rearranged my weight. If she spooked, I had to be in perfect balance with her in order to stay in the saddle.

"Okay," he called, "I'm right behind you. I'll be there in a minute."

Edgar was so good to me, giving up his day off to take me to the show. And he waited on me, fetching the brushes, going back to the trailer for a towel, safety pins, etc. He made the whole task much more bearable. Yet, I always had a sinking feeling that he did it out of pity, and that made me feel even more insecure and miserable.

Most people go to horse shows mainly for fun. We've seen many of Edgar's clients having tailgate picnics at their horse trailer. In fact, we've "crashed" a few of them, too, joining in on the fun and food. While the show is in session and riders are waiting their turn for their class to show, they may even take a leisurely trail ride around the show grounds. Many first and second place winners proudly display their blue and red ribbons on the windows of their trucks, each in competition with the other. These people seem to have fun at the horse shows. And yet I wasn't having any fun at all. This was a task, a challenge to be conquered. Should I succeed in the end, I would feel great, no doubt, but it still would not have been fun. Well, I thought, maybe the fun part would come as I paid my dues in the form of years in the show circuit.

The lack of fun was evident when Fancy and I first entered the practice ring going clockwise at a walk. I sensed something ominous. A light current issued from somewhere under the saddle and manifested itself in the seat of my pants. It was the surge of spirit, of brute strength, and it was coming from my horse like a kind of electrical charge. In a matter of minutes, this manifested itself more definitively, becoming stronger and ever more tangible. It was an indescribable feeling—a climate of tension that rose invisibly, like steam—a tingling sensation.

Another horse trotted past. Suddenly, the vague ominous stirrings burst into reality as Fancy squealed and leaped into the air. Hers was a burst of wild, of freedom, of playfulness. Fancy was having fun. She plunged back to earth, all four feet hitting the ground at once, and then the eruption began in earnest. I gritted my teeth and clamped my legs.

Then, a small peachy voice chirped in my ear, *Sit back and balance yourself; don't lean forward. You won't stay on by holding tight with your legs. You must be in balance with your horse and have her under you.* My guardian angel had Gale's voice.

A scream rose in my throat as Fancy skipped in the air again, and I wanted to yell at the little voice, "But I'm going to fall off! Look at the lunatic I'm riding!"

But the angel ignored me. Fancy was feeling good. It seemed as though she had just discovered herself, her strength, her wild spirit. Her front legs pumped nearly to her chin while her back legs propelled her over the ground like an antelope. I struggled to maintain my balance. In minutes, my shirttail ripped from my pants, but I could only let it dangle there for fear of taking my hands off the reins and losing everything.

The other riders steered their horses in a wide berth around us, and my cheeks reddened. That loose-jointed feeling surged through me once more, "It's all right, girl. Settle down. Don't be upset," I begged, but she ignored me and sprang again into the air.

I felt as though I were captaining my ship through a hurricane. On the first wave Fancy dropped me then flipped me puckishly into the air. I landed back in the saddle, and then another wave scooped me up again. But for all our tossing, my boat hadn't sailed far. We pranced nearly in place, Fancy hopping and high-stepping like a Lippizaner. All I could do was ride out the stormy seas without diving over the deck. All the other riders had left me to flounder alone at my battle station.

As we jerked and bumped along the rail, Edgar watched. "My God!" I wheezed, working the reins. "What is wrong with this animal? She's gone absolutely crazy. What should I do?" Fancy sprayed gravel against his legs. "I can't show this horse. She's a wreck. I'm going to fall off!" I yelled. "If she's like this in the practice ring, she'll completely flip out in the showring."

We reeled around the far side, Fancy grunting and snorting; my ship's boiler threatened to blow at any minute.

We came around again, "I'm getting off! She's a mess. We'll just have to go home, and I'll have to forget about ever showing her." I would just have to be satisfied with riding the hills and pastures and forget about blue ribbons and silver trophies. The showring, I decided, was for the birds.

Then Edgar said, "Don't give up. Don't let her work you like that. She thinks she has your number. So, fool her. Work her until she's ready to drop. That prancing isn't tiring her out; work her at the canter until she's too tired to give you a rough time. Maybe she won't think it's so much fun to act this way. Don't worry; you won't hurt her. You have her so well-conditioned that her stamina is endless. She's so physically fit that no amount of walking her around this ring is going to settle her down. But cantering will take some of the wind out of her sails."

"But, what if I fall off?"

"You won't; just sit back. She wants to go, right? Then let her go, and go, and go until she doesn't want to go anymore."

My face was red hot, but I was too scared to sweat. The morning was warm, and those stringy sun rays meant an even hotter afternoon. I urged Fancy into a canter. One time, two times, three times, we flew around the ring, the gravel hitting the fence rails as her feet pounded the ground.

Foam flew from her mouth, sticking to my jeans, and her breathing was becoming thicker and deeper. We pitched again and again around that ring, and little by little her stride began to slow and smooth out, and her hopping flattened. The tension was ebbing beneath me. She was tiring. Had she finally given up?

After an hour of work, her gaits were as smooth as if she were on ice skates, and she was listening to my verbal commands. Her ears were alert for instructions. She was a tractable and agreeable cruise vessel now that the fire had cooled.

I, too, had exerted myself to exhaustion as every muscle had sought balance aboard the horse. Every breath seared my throat, and my T-shirt clung, soaked with sweat, to my back. A side-sticker menaced my abdomen.

"That's enough. I don't think she'll give you any more trouble now. She's beat," Edgar called. "Maybe next time she'll think twice before giving you a hard time at a show."

Nodding, I slid off her back. I patted her lovingly on the rump, and we walked back to the trailer where I sponged her down. In a half-hour our class would begin.

Exhaustion does have its merits. It's similar to being drunk. When a person is wasted either way, nothing matters. The body surrenders, and "Who cares?" becomes the creed. Dressed in my pressed, dark green saddle suit with matching black shoes, gloves, and derby, a kind of careless oblivion overcame me, and I raised my water glass to toast my upcoming success or failure—I really didn't care.

"Class twenty-four, Owner to Ride, enter the ring, please. We are looking for numbers 15, 64, 28, 135...," the announcer's voice droned. Any breed could enter, but the rider had to be the horse's owner, and that alone qualified me to enter my walking horse in competition with trotting breeds.

"Don't forget your number. It's one hundred thirty-five," Edgar said. I repeated it.

The other horses began entering the ring. There were twelve of them, a pretty large class. I chewed the cuticle of my index finger, hoping that Fancy would not go berserk with all the crowding and side-stepping that was likely to occur. A numb sensation drizzled down my throat and into my toes, draining my courage. Suddenly, I didn't want to go into that showring. Instead I'd have rather ridden Fancy in the other direction, toward home, through the shopping mall parking lot and over and across the interstate highway. At this point anything seemed better than making an ass out of myself again.

"Go on, get going," Edgar prodded, slapping my fingers from my mouth. "You'll do fine. Sit back, remember everything Gale told you, and concentrate on finishing the class. Stay on this time."

A river of horses washed me into the ring. They trotted past in a counterclockwise direction around the ring. Their strategy was to trot proudly into the ring in order to catch the judge's eye. Like the last show, the riders used the exhibitor's trick: enter the ring at a trot to stand out from the crowd.

While the other riders vied for the judge's attention, smiling coyly or trotting dramatically past, I attempted to fade into the background, slinking amongst the other riders like a ghost. I merely wanted to complete the class on top of the horse, not draw attention to myself by wiping up the ring with my body.

So I rode Fancy quietly, dutifully around the ring to the calls of the announcer. After the canter, he called out "Walk," and we obeyed unobtrusively, Fancy nodding her head in walking horse fashion, moving surely and rhythmically. We were molded into the group, doing our thing while every other horse did his or hers. Fancy had had all the "bugs" worked out of her, and it seemed to have worked; she was tired of going around in circles. She had no intention of giving me a hard time. Besides, the sun, as predicted earlier, began to broil, and the heavy humid air sank into our backs, slowing us even more.

Fancy dripped sweat, but we had done our best. Fancy had behaved herself because she was too tired to do anything else, and I had stayed aboard my mount, blending in perfectly. I was cotton-mouthed and grimy-faced from the dusty ring but happy with my wallflower appeal. We had done it at last: made it through a class without a mishap.

All I had left to do was make it through the lineup: park Fancy out, back her, then move back in place and park out again. That was easy; Fancy was at her best when she wasn't moving at all. I noted the irony in that thought as we stood still as moss. We parked out at the end of the line, the farthest from the exit gate. It would take a while for the judge to get to us since he had to see the horses back individually.

"Miss, back your horse, please," the judge repeated. Fancy backed easily, came forward, and parked out again. She did so willingly, ending in a superb park out with her legs stretched like a hobbyhorse.

"Thank you," the judge said, and I smiled, nodding. He went to the next horse. A hand was waving from the rail. I squinted; Edgar gave me the "okay" signal, and I smiled back.

Then the judge stepped back in front of our lineup, gave the ringmaster the tally sheet, and walked from the ring. My mind was still adrift when the announcer's voice broke the static.

"First place goes to number...." The voice trailed off in my mind. This was just a formality now, waiting for the winners to take their ribbons. I barely listened, for I would certainly not be included in the winner's circle. But I was content. Besides, my real prize was staying in the saddle. The first place winner stood two places below me in the line, and when her number was called, she trotted her black gelding forward to claim her ribbon.

Second place claimed her ribbon, and the announcer continued his winning list: "Third prize goes to number one hundred thirty-five, Gay's Merry Shadow, owned and ridden by Gay Balliet."

One-thirty-five, I thought. That's nice, too. It was very nice that there were such good riders and horses here. Suddenly my mind hissed, *What? Number one hundred thirty-five? One hundred thirty-five! Is that me?* I sat blankly, looking up and down the line of horses to see why third prize didn't claim her ribbon; but when I looked straight ahead, Edgar was waving his arms in a frenzy. I was 135!

The announcer repeated, "Third prize, number one hundred thirty-five, Gay's Merry Shadow, owned and ridden by Gay Balliet. Claim your ribbon, please," the voice urged.

I will always remember my exit from the gate. At first realization my mouth went completely slack, hanging open like a puppet's mouth. Then in a daze, I urged Fancy forward. I was a zombie with a Mona Lisa smile as I walked her past the other horses in the ring. I neither heard Edgar nor our horsey friends hooting and clapping on the sidelines, nor did I feel the crowd watching me, the third place winner, as I weakly, gratefully, gripped my yellow ribbon.

Suddenly the idea hit me, and a warm, full feeling enveloped me. My eyes became small as my cheeks pushed up over my cheek bones in a wide grin. For a split second I was annoyed with myself, for my smile caused a chain reaction in my face which closed my eyes and made me momentarily blind.

Glowing, Fancy and I left the ring. I couldn't believe it; not only did I stay on my horse, but I also managed to win third prize.

And, of course, it was not merely *having* the ribbon I'd been denied as a child that intrigued me, it was what that ribbon represented: months of hard work, grinding myself and my horse during each practice session most every day. It meant someone actually thought I was an equestrienne—adept at riding a horse; they judged me to have skill and talent on horseback.

What was more remarkable was that I had actually won in a sporting event, I, the one sixth-grader whom the gym teacher declared a "physical wreck." The one high schooler who crouched in the corner when the volleyball came at her. The one who, in her college gym class, begged to play the goalie position so that she wouldn't have to run.

I was always the one nobody wanted on their team: the jinx, the slow poke, the klutz. Whenever the gym teacher made us pick teams, I'd be one of the last kids picked, standing in the middle of the gym, ankles crossed and hands clasped in embarrassment—me and the fat girl, the ones everybody knew couldn't get out of their own way.

But here I was, a yellow ribbon in hand, and, conclusively, an athlete, of sorts. It seemed I was discovering myself for the first time, as if, in a way, I had been newly reborn. This yellow ribbon magically snuffed out any misgivings about my physical self, for I had done it, even if I'd never do it again. Fancy and I were an athletic team this day.

Back at the horse trailer I jumped into Edgar's arms. Friends congratulated us, and Mrs. Derhammer pinned the silky, pleated ribbon to Fancy's halter. The Sigleys came past with Misty in tow, and they gave us the thumbs up.

"I knew you'd get something," Edgar said, helping me off with my coat. My smile was relaxing, and my cheeks receded—I could see again. "That judge was watching you pretty closely. You and Fancy did a great job."

I hugged Edgar again and wiped the foam off Fancy. "You're such a good girl," I said. She stabbed her muzzle into her hay bag, and the ribbon flicked in the air.

"My first ribbon, Eggie," I crooned, calling him by his pet name. "You did it, you know," I said, trying to be mysterious.

"What do you mean, I did it?" he asked.

"You and Gale did it for me: her constant discipline and your support and confidence. I couldn't have done anything without you. I love you."

He wiped my forehead with his hand. "What do you call this?" he asked, holding out his hand.

"What do you mean?"

"What's on my hand?"

I saw the wet slick glistening. "What? Do you mean the sweat?" I said in disgust.

"Yep, it's yours. In fact, I'm surprised we see no blood along with it. You and Fancy did it together—the two of you plus a lot of hard work. I'm really proud of you, Hon."

"Thanks," I said, and Fancy nudged me. "Yep," I said, "we did it, me and," I hugged Fancy around the neck, "my showboat."

30

The Topman Twins

A call came in a few weeks later for Edgar to check two of the exotics at the Topman farm. Along with being dairy farmers, the owners also raised deer as pets. So, we set out promptly for the countryside just outside the town of Bath.

Edgar eased the truck down the long gravel driveway flanked on either side by two perfectly manicured stretches of lawn. The driveway opened up into a great parking lot surrounded by a large stone farmhouse, dairy barn and milk parlor, a heavy equipment building and pastures—an idyllic Pennsylvania Dutch farm. The cows grazed in the pasture to our right, lying contentedly as only cows lie—flat out like flounders. They didn't seem to mind our truck bumping past on our way to the barn.

Shutting off the engine, Edgar hopped to the ground and walked through the swinging metal doors to the milk parlor. A duck waddled to my side of the truck and quacked its way around to the back, beak to the ground in search of cracked corn or wheat that might have spilled from a grain wagon.

The Topman boys, Arthur and Victor, emerged together with Edgar from the cow barn. Each was a carbon copy of the other, for they were identical twins. Both were well-proportioned and muscular, conditioned by the twenty or so years of hard work on their dairy farm.

These men showed evidence of having thrown and stacked tons of hay bales in their lifetime.

Their fair-skinned faces, one an exact replica of the other, looked thoughtfully out from under heads of thick, naturally curly, strawberry blond hair. They shared the serene and simple look of choir boys.

The Topman twins were down-to-earth, honest, friendly people. In fact, the whole family was. They were hard-working folks who ran the dairy farm as a family operation. They worked ten hours a day, seven days a week, yet their energy never seemed to wane. And their temperaments were much like the animals they served, bovine calm and imperturbable.

"How're ya dere," one said, leaning into the truck cab. The other stood beside him.

"Okay, how about you, Arthur?" I asked smiling.

"Chust fine myself. I'm Wictor, though, not Arthur," Victor smiled sheepishly, not wanting to sound offended.

"Sorry. I'll be able to tell you guys apart some day," I assured him.

"Yeah vell, even our mother gets us confused sometimes; course she's not gettin' any younger, naw," Victor said.

Arthur laughed and nodded. Then Victor laughed and nodded.

"This job could be interesting, guys," Edgar said. He reached into the back of the truck and retrieved his otoscope (for checking ears) and ear mite solution. "Are you sure you want to do it?"

"What are you going to do?" I asked, leaning over.

Arthur offered an explanation in his songlike Pennsylvania Dutch accent, "One of the deers hass ear mites, we think." Arthur looked for approval from Victor, and Victor nodded. These guys not only looked alike but thought alike, too. He continued, "Yeah, she's been shakin' her head and scratchin' at her ears wit her back leks." He scratched his head as if in sympathy with the itchy animal. Victor dug a finger in his ear, too, and grimaced.

The Topmans kept the small deer herd in a high-wire pen. They enjoyed the animals as pets, talking to them through the fence and throwing goodies in for them to eat. They once told me, "We chust stand and vatch them; they are so pretty, ya know."

"Have you ever had to catch her before to give her vaccinations or to deworm her?" Edgar asked, hopping back into the truck beside me.

"No," they replied in unison, shaking their heads simultaneously.

Arthur signaled Victor to speak. "We nefer haf hadt to do nothin' with her till naw."

"She could be a problem, ya know," Edgar cautioned. They looked at each other. "You say she is friendly enough and used to people, though?" Edgar tugged on the brim of his cap and pondered the situation.

"Yah, she's dat," Arthur said. "But I chust bet she von't like dis."

"No, she von't like it much at all," Victor added.

"Sure you guys can handle her?" Edgar bit his lip. "An excited deer can be pretty dangerous. I don't want anybody getting hurt. Ear mites won't kill her, you know." He looked at the twins seriously.

Arthur and Victor looked at each other in silent debate.

Victor said this time, "What do ya think, Art?"

"I don't know. What do ya think, Wic?"

"I think we shuldt do it, before it gets worse. Besides, you cudt gif her a shot den too, huh Doc?"

Edgar slid from the truck and reached into his drug case, "Sure, I could do that."

Arthur agreed, "Okay, I'm vit you, Wictor. Let's do it oncet naw."

"Climb in here with Gay and me, and we'll go down to the pen," Edgar offered, hoisting himself up behind the wheel.

"Sure...sure," Arthur said, nodding.

"Sure...sure," Victor agreed.

They climbed in the truck beside me.

Edgar started the truck, and soon we were heading down the gravel path past the aluminum equipment shed. The four of us sat side by side in the cab. I studied the brothers. From their knee-high, black rubber boots to their hay-strewn muddy jeans and cut-off flannel shirts these men were virtually without difference. Each was a replication of the other in their appearances, the way they sat and the way they talked. Their mannerisms and expressions were identical. It was uncanny and a bit disconcerting to be sitting beside what seemed like a set of clones.

Pulling up alongside a small building which was, in actuality, a chicken coop, Edgar stopped the truck. A threatening bang sounded from within the coop.

Here was an animal that had been closed up in pitch blackness for twenty-four hours with hardly room enough to move. She was furious, and she wanted OUT!

"Is this where the deer is?" Edgar asked apprehensively. He cracked his knuckles and bit his lip.

The twins started talking at once, each one drowning out the other's conversation. When it became apparent that they were getting nowhere fast, Victor stopped, then Arthur, and with a glance the two made a secret pact to reorganize the discussion.

Arthur took the floor. "Vee coaxed her into dis coop last night. She didn't seem to like it too much, though."

"No, she didn't," echoed Victor. "She came after us a little bit, but we got awt right avay."

"You're sure you want to go through with this?" Edgar asked after another kick racked the depths of the chicken shack.

"Yah. Yah," Arthur and Victor said, nodding together. Their golden curls gyrated in unison. They eyed each other in confidence. "Vee'll take a chance, naw."

Arthur told Edgar the plan. "Wictor and I will go in and pin 'er up against one of da walls. Vhen ve're ready, vee'll call. Den ya can come in and check 'er awt."

Victor instructed, rubbing his strong hands together, "Yah, ya chust keep the door closdt behind us vhen vee go in. Doan't open it, no matta vhat, unless vee say it's okay."

Arthur nodded, "Yep...unless we say 'okay'."

Now the Topman boys were known in the community for their brute strength; but with that ominous banging reverberating from the chicken coop, I wondered whether even they could restrain an angry deer.

I clasped my hands and bit my lip as the deer shifted in the coop. "Just be careful. Don't get killed over a bunch of ear mites," I joked.

"Vee voan't," Arthur and Victor said simultaneously.

Edgar, Arthur and Victor approached the back of the chicken shack, tiptoeing softly to the wooden door. Edgar kicked the latch loose and cracked it open. A loud thud rang out. Quickly, Edgar slammed the door and looked at the boys for an indication to terminate the exam. Instead they nodded to go ahead as planned.

Again, Edgar creaked open the door. This time, strangely enough, there was no sound. We all looked anxiously at each other, and Arthur and Victor nodded again to keep going.

Then, with caution and deliberation Edgar opened the door

wider, bracing for a possible attack. There was no sound. Arthur raised his hand to wait while Victor peered cautiously through the foot-wide opening into the dark, cavernous coop.

When Arthur signaled, Edgar quickly slung the door wide open, and the two men ran inside. The door slammed shut behind them. I clenched my fists and winced, expecting an explosion.

Nothing. There was no noise, no ruckus, nothing at all. For a second we relaxed. Edgar was a statue frozen against the chicken coop door, his full weight against it. He looked scared stiff, not only for himself, but for the men penned inside with a wild animal.

The silence did not last for long.

A blast from a hoof resounded within, and then a simultaneous yell from the twins. Then the coop began to shake in earnest. The thuds and cracks to the wood sounded to an awful crescendo, and the little coop buckled with each blast and body slam from the deer. Amazingly, the Topmans weren't yelling for Edgar to unleash the door.

"UH!" came a grunt from the shack. A second later there was a low thud, like a body hitting the wall. The chicken coop shivered again. "Hold her naw, damn it!" a voice erupted from within.

"Vait oncet!" the other yelled.

"Hold her!" the other hollered.

"I'm tryin!" said the other.

Another loud groan resounded, and the door which Edgar body-pressed snapped open an inch beneath his hold. Edgar lay his weight into the door and repositioned his feet, his face set. If he let the deer escape, it'd run away. That wouldn't do; it was, after all, a pet.

"Awch, my foot naw! Grap her in the front; I'll get the hindt endt!" one of the twins yelled. The entire coop was in motion, and the awful grunts and groans of man and animal wracked the air.

"Geez, my handt! Watch awt!" screamed the other.

Then as suddenly as it had started, the coop became silent. Dead silent. A weak voice said, "Okay, Doc, we got her. Ya can come in naw…quietly…if ya don't mind."

Edgar took the otoscope and ear mite solution from me, and, opening the latch, tiptoed in. There was a momentary scuffling, but that died away as quickly as it had come. Soon Edgar reappeared, unharmed. Shortly afterward the twins followed, but what a sight they were.

They were wet with sweat, their happy blond curls matted and droopy. Their shirts had come untucked from the pants and a few buttons dangled by their threads.

Arthur held his hands out and examined his torn-up fingers. He tested each one for broken bones, sucking on the bloody scratches while Victor bent down and slid his jeans up his left leg to look at a lump already growing there.

"Cheesus, that was awful, naw," Victor said, shaking his head.

"My whole body aches," Arthur interjected, rubbing his shoulder and testing his neck for soreness. "She sure iss powerful naw."

"At least we got the ear mites," Edgar kidded as they rubbed their sores. "She does have quite a case of them. When I shined the light in her ears, I could see the black gunk in them. They're pretty bad."

"Yah, it vass vorth it, to get ridt of the buggers," Arthur said, spitting on a bloody cut on his hand.

"Yah, it vass," Victor agreed.

Edgar winked at me as he pulled the ear mite bottle from his pocket. "Here you go, guys," he held out the medicine.

"What's diss for?" Arthur asked.

"This is tomorrow's dose." Edgar read from the bottle's label: "Four drops in each ear to be administered twice daily or as needed." He stressed the word "daily." The air was silent. "Yep, that ought to get rid of them then. Maybe even three times a day would be better still," Edgar said, staring at the directions on the bottle.

Arthur and Victor wore pained expressions. There was silence for a few more seconds.

"Sure, Doc, sure. If you think it's best, vee'll do it naw," the men agreed with resigned expressions.

Edgar's smile grew into a laugh. "God, no. I'm only kidding! Just treat her one more time tomorrow, and the mites will be gone. We don't need you guys getting pulverized."

Arthur and Victor began to smile. Then they, too, started to laugh. And each time they looked at each other, they laughed harder, mirror images of each other.

31

Excitement at the Allentown Fair

Earlier in the day Edgar had telephoned. "Come along on this one," he kept insisting.

"For what? To see what?" I asked, curious.

"I have to check some of those circus tigers and a camel at the Allentown Fair," he finally replied.

"Tigers? Well, you know how interesting I think they are, especially after meeting Reba. And a camel up close is something I'd like to see. Count me in."

Now I was waiting expectantly. It was an enticing invitation to see the behind-the-scene circus world, its animals, and its people—those odd gypsies who roam from state to state and fair to fair, living day by day, tending their animals and practicing their perilous stunts. It was an opportunity too good to miss. But I was somewhat worried about Edgar stepping into a cage with tigers who might be very different from Reba's calm temperament.

We had learned that every day is a challenge for the large animal veterinarian. Sometimes the excitement and the peril involved with examining and treating the spirited horses, wild zoo animals, exotic birds and others just becomes too real, too imminent. It can be a risky business. One time, Edgar had to treat an Angus bull that outweighed a three-quarter-ton pickup truck. The farmer who owned it had only a thin rope with which to tie the monstrous animal to a post. With a quick turn of its head, the bull had snapped the rope like an old rubber band and pinned Edgar to the wall like an insect in a bug collection. And how many times a week did he catch a scared horse because its owner was afraid of being hurt by his own animal? This tiger exam, too, conjured all kinds of exotic dangers.

The Allentown Fair is the Lehigh Valley's largest, longest running, end-of-the-summer festival, stretching over approximately seventy-five acres and enticing people from near and far. There are various mechanical rides and foods of all ethnic variety such as Mexican tacos and Greek gyros to Pennsylvania Dutch dishes like funnel cake and sausage sandwiches. Among our favorites are the curly French fries and Yocco's hot dogs with that special chili sauce. We love to walk the fairgrounds amidst the crowd armed with delicacies like baked potatoes with various toppings such as cheddar cheese, sour cream and chives, bacon bits, and deep-fried veggies: mushrooms, cauliflower, broccoli, onions and zucchini. All is delectable even if high in cholesterol.

At the fair, the competition among the 4-H groups boasts Pennsylvania's proud specimens of roosters, pigs, cow herds, sheep and other animals. In a three-city-block-long building, local granges display their crafts: homemade quilts, dresses, canned foods and samples of fresh home-grown vegetables. All this, plus more, attracts thousands of people to the fair each year.

Today, we drove to the gate entrance where the guard ushered us through like VIP's. To the happy sounds of a distant steam calliope and to the smells of various kinds of fatty delights, Edgar and I sauntered past the concession stands and games of chance, making our way to the circus area and the wild animals.

We wound around the tractor trailers that transported the various animals to and from the circus, and in the air there lingered the faint odor of the wild. In a grassy clearing, Edgar and I stood entranced before the circus world, alive with animals and people rushing antlike through their daily chores.

The circus workers bustled, carrying feed and buckets of water for the animals. The helpers matched exactly the images I had already pictured: young, tough-looking men wearing earrings and gingham bandannas. But one thing was absent from all the hullabaloo. I had expected these circus helpers to be full of fun and to be carefree, living and working as they were away from the life of convention and the social demands of society. I thought they should be performing their chores laughing and joking. On the contrary, their arms loaded with slices of hay and grain buckets, their heads bent to the ground and shoulders weighted down, the men trudged almost grudgingly about their tasks; they did not joke or even chat in passing. Each one seemed set upon completing his job, be it feeding the elephants or grooming the horses.

The elephants stood chained by the ankles in the midst of a thick blanket of straw. All in a row, five of them rocked and swayed, their gray scaly trunks sniffing and feeling periscope-like as they searched for friendly, food-bearing humans. Approaching these huge beasts, we thought their strength awesome, certainly capable of snapping those weak chains from the ground. Yet despite their massive power, they seemed such docile creatures.

It might have been their continual rocking that created this innocuous impression I had of them. The swaying had a calming effect. Back and forth their bodies rolled; giant feet lifted then sank back to the ground; cracked leathery trunks rose, searched the air, then fell back to the ground, and then the animals began their gentle movement once again. All this was somehow soothing. They were like hypnotists with their swinging pendulum-like trunks, beckoning an onlooker into a trance.

As I stood mesmerized by the elephants' size and motion, Edgar wandered off to find the tigers' owner so that he could examine them. A circus helper wearing a beret gestured toward a silver trailer, and Edgar walked toward it. While he was gone, I decided to explore the rest of the circus compound myself. Passing a tent where long-haired young men curried the show horses, I walked around the end of a tractor trailer and stopped dead as I came face to face with eight tigers. They were in small barred wagons, one tiger to a wagon, exactly as they are pictured on boxes of animal crackers.

I was instantly transfixed. As when I stood near Reba, I felt the exquisite, otherworldly aura that surrounds these huge, majestic beasts.

There is a presence, and once again I felt the strange, almost supernatural power. A tiger has a certain air of command, a kind of magic having nothing to do with its strength or its ability to kill its prey. It harbors the primeval spirit that humans lost centuries ago. That lost connection to the wild unknown is what held me spellbound. I felt a magical attraction to that mysterious primitive essence that lies repressed within us.

Very still once again, as I had been with Reba, I stood, perhaps two feet away from one of the provocative striped cats as it paced in its mobile barred wagon. With every turn in the cage, the wagon rocked on its wheels and was soon set in perpetual motion by the tiger's incessant pacing.

I was a statue. Bright gold tiger eyes held me as he moved front to back and back to front, setting his barred wagon to rocking. Every so often, he broke stride by raising his big face, rolling back his lips, and showing his finger-length incisor teeth. Then he roared. The air flowed from his mouth on the red carpet of his tongue, his warm, moist, ho-hum breath hitting me squarely in the face.

In a low voice, the same voice I use with my kitties at home, I cooed, "Hello, handsome. Do you have a busy day today? Are you going to put on a fine show tonight? I think you are the most beautiful cat here, and you know I recently met a Siberian snow lady you might find entrancing."

He answered with a noncommittal flick of his tail and continued pacing.

Minutes passed as I bonded with the tiger a mere foot from his cage. Our conversation was largely one-sided, but I had only to imagine his part of the intimate discussion. Spellbound by his tremendous power and size, I barely noticed the change in his behavior. He eyed me curiously—for a reason of which only he was aware. His bold stare was no longer simple observation on his part but an inspection. Each time he drew near he stopped, cocked his head, an intensity seeping into his eyes. There was no fear or equivocality in those feline eyes, just a deep concern, a personal interest, in a human specimen.

He shambled back to the other end of his cage, never taking his eyes off me. I began to feel a little uncomfortable. But what could he do, caged in an iron-barred wagon? There was nothing to fear of this animal, only everything by which to be beguiled. Nevertheless, instinctively I backed away and to the left when suddenly I heard a *pop*. At that moment something like a pea or pellet flew out from under his tail and whizzed past me as I jumped sideways. I cannot say for sure, but I guessed he liked me, and, claiming his territory as all cats do, marked this odd, female statue as a dog marks a tree for his very own.

The tiger sashayed around his wagon, a lusty leer in his eye. Then I backed away, thanking him for his flattering hospitality.

I wandered back to the elephants since Edgar was still nowhere around. The goliaths still swayed from side to side, trunks feeling the air. They were calm, serene. Considering their size, only a fool would provoke them to violence, but here, at home in the grassy field, they seemed almost harmless.

In a moment, Edgar, accompanied by a slight, middle-aged woman and a teenaged girl, came from the silver trailer as I reached out to touch an elephant's inquiring trunk. The young girl carried a box in her hands, and as she opened it, the woman commented, "I see you like the elephants. Why don't you help Elise feed them a couple of donuts while your husband and I look at the tigers?"

This woman and her daughter, both dressed in faded blue jeans and cut-off tops, looked no different from any other mother and daughter, except for the thin, red streaks on the older woman's hands and neck. Later she told us they were scars from tiger attacks, from some of which she had barely escaped with her life. She explained that each tiger was an individual, and that one, in particular, had a mean temperament. It was this one that had attacked her during a show.

"But," I stammered at Edgar, unable to control my uneasiness, "how are you going to examine that one?"

"I'll make sure he's not foaming at the mouth or visibly sick," Edgar reassured me.

While Edgar and the mother went to check the tigers, I had my first lesson in hand-feeding an elephant. Elise offered a soft jelly donut and instructed me to hold it out to one of the beckoning trunks so that the elephant could wrap its trunk around the tasty morsel. All right— this ought to be a snap. The elephants had smelled the goodies in the box, and five trunks began waving madly in the breeze, only inches away from my face. So, I stretched my hand out to one of the trunks.

Well, I did try. But, for some reason, when I pushed the donut into the tip of the trunk, it fell to the ground with a *plop*. I was puzzled. Weren't elephants' trunks supposed to be as supple and dexterous as a human's fingers? What was wrong with this big klutz that he couldn't even hang onto a donut?

After the cruller had rolled to the ground for the fourth time, gathering particles of sawdust and straw, Elise offered advice as I again tried stuffing it into the tip of the trunk. "Don't put the donut up his nose. Here, hold it out like this," she demonstrated, "and he'll wrap his trunk *around* it."

I held out the donut on the palm of my hand, and to my surprise, a thick, flexible hose of a trunk eased up to the powdery object, sniffled the goodie, then curled its nozzle right around it. The elephant picked it off my palm as gracefully as a colonial gentleman taking a candy from a lady's hand. "Oh," I said, embarrassed, "then I was shoving it right up his poor nose. No wonder he didn't take it."

She offered no comment, no reaction to my naivete, nor did she smile at my blunder but only dug in the box for another treat. As we fed the remaining donuts to the other elephants, I broke the silence, asking Elise questions about what she did in the circus, when and where she went to school, and if there were other girls her age traveling with the circus. She answered me politely but seemed a bit reticent talking with a stranger who was an alien to her world.

She seemed much more grown up than other kids her age. What kind of life could a circus offer a young girl? Where was the security of a permanent home life when every two weeks the silver trailer moved out onto the lone, open highway? Where were other girls she could gossip with about school activities and sweethearts? Where were the football games and dances a school offered? Conversely, the circus life, filled with wondrous animals and exciting shows in which she already participated, offered a taste of show business. And, in addition, this kind of life offered an independence, a feeling of being grown up that regular school kids only develop well after graduation, if then. Still, there was a lot of sacrifices that the crowd never saw when jolly performers paraded their stunts and acts in the ring.

As Elise, with her serious face, and I fed the remaining donuts to the elephants, the sound of the calliope echoed from one of the circus tents; someone was practicing a tune for tonight's performance. But it was a somber tune. As I took one more glance around the grounds, I wondered if, tonight, the clown's happy face might be hiding a deeper, underlying despair.

In a few moments, Edgar appeared from the silver trailer. He motioned me to follow him. We hurried past the elephants, then past the horse tent and then to a couple of make-shift wooden stalls where various heights of four camels stood munching quietly on hay.

A bandanna-wearing fellow strolled over and said with a grim look, "You the vet?"

"Yes, I am. Where is my patient, and what seems to be the problem?" Edgar said, glancing down each of the four open-ended stalls that housed the camels.

"Here's the girl you want to see." He pointed to the camel resting comfortable in the last stall. A yellowish discharge drooled from her back end.

"Oh, I see it," Edgar said, interested. He stepped to the side of the stall, being careful not to move directly in back of the camel. A camel could kick a person into the middle of next week if it got irritated. But this one looked sedate. She was obviously quite old and stood with one back leg cocked in a resting stance. As Edgar moved in alongside her, she turned her head nonchalantly, munching hay, only vaguely concerned about the stranger at her side.

"Should we tell you to put her feet in the stirrups?" I chirped with a laugh.

Edgar set to work with a chuckle. "Quite a discharge we've got here. When did you notice this? Is she pregnant, or could she be?"

And then I saw it happen. My yell came too late. When Edgar's fingers made contact with the animal's private parts, I saw her head whip around and her mouth open to the diameter of a cantaloupe. In a microsecond she had Edgar by the buttocks.

My shriek was nothing compared to Edgar's. It was a yell that sounded nothing like a grown man's. It was more a cartoon character's wail—a high, banshee-like scream.

Just as quickly as the attack happened, it stopped. In the excitement, Edgar had dropped the tail and released the vulva, and likewise the camel let go of him.

My hands flew to my mouth as I gasped. I looked at Edgar waiting for an explosion of pain. Instead, he simply wiped the sweat from his brow and limped casually from the camel's stall.

"She bites," the bandanna-wearing man said.

"Is that right?" Edgar said. He turned to look back at the animal munching hay quietly, and it was then that I noticed a huge wet spot on his jeans over his right buttock. The wet mark was the size of a plate and hung with several strands of saliva. It wasn't blood, just spit mixed with bits of chewed hay.

Seeing that he was all right, I stifled a giggle. But Edgar wasn't smiling. I knew he was all right physically. But I also knew what was really hurting him more than anything was his pride because of the unearthly shriek he let escape him. I had been shocked, too. It was so uncharacteristic of my stoic husband.

Then again, so was a camel almost biting off one's buttocks.

Edgar prescribed a course of antibiotics for the camel, and we walked back to the truck. Gently, very gently, he lowered himself onto the seat, and then he started the engine.

32

The Endless Day

Every morning we open the window and let in the beauty outside. The birds flit busily collecting morning bugs, and usually an awakening cat stretches on the patio. The horses are already stirring, with Fancy and Fax peeking through their barn windows. And the woodsy, morning odors have a moist freshness that lends a crisp scent to the air. Every morning is a new beginning, even though the day which lies ahead may be a seemingly endless one.

One Saturday morning, Brian, our puddle-colored, long-haired cat, lay straddled on a cherry log. As I watched him from the window, he reminded me of a surfer riding out the waves, only these were the verdant waves of May apples, raspberry vines and chickweed.

"Hi, Bri," I called. "Looks like you had a rough night." His fur was all ruffled and burr-ridden, and his knitted brow and droopy eyes bespoke a night of tomcatting and carousing, playing the part of Mr. King Kat Kool. It inspired me to poetry:

Junkyard Cat
King Kat Kool, prowlin' city,
yellow lantern, ivory knives
pierce,

slice,
the Saturday night,
the neon glimmer.

Stud cat, all in black
lookin' like a Cadillac
g-l-i-d-i-n'
s-l-i-d-i-n'
down the
middle
of the
sidewalk
searchin' for Miss Calico,
Queen of the condominium.

He takes her breath away—
Her soft foot pads perform
a coquette's sashay
against the lamppost—
a witness.

Stud cat—42nd Avenue King,
illumined—sinewy silhouette
under the lamplight
flicker.

Now woo that green-eyed sweetheart
curling round and round—
enticing.
How do you charm a lady?

Stud cat—King Kat Kool,
Rev up,
Psych up that bold bravado,
that irresistible song.

> Send those sensuous pleas airward
> like sizzling rockets
> on the
> Fourth of July!

"Well, I certainly hope it was worth it, Bri," I laughed, and he looked up at me with combined detachment and irritation.

Turning from the window, I bumped into Robert, mashing his paw beneath my foot. A high-pitched, "Ree-e-e-e-ow-ow!" split the air, and I jumped, stubbing my big toe on a cabinet.

"Yee-ee-ow-ow!" I yelled, gripping the bathroom sink and cursing. Robert gazed, unperturbed, at me.

Then I heard Edgar. Bleary-eyed, he shuffled into the bathroom. Robert trotted over to him, snaking around and through his skinny legs. "Hi, Robert," he grunted.

As I splashed water into my face, he complained, "Can't sleep around this place. What's all the racket about? First, I hear a cat scream bloody murder; then you do."

I explained our accident as Robert snake-danced. Robert always had a bizarre fascination with Edgar's legs. The cat never bothered with mine, but every morning the gray tabby did a dance around my husband. Lately, in fact, Robert had even added a spurious lick: in and out, around and through, *lap* went the tongue…in and out, around and through, *lap* went the tongue.

"Crazy cat," Edgar burbled through a face full of suds. Robert continued his serpentine gyrations when suddenly there was a loud scream. "He bit me! He bit me right in the leg!" Edgar yelled. "You'll find yourself out in the cold this winter, if you don't watch it, Robert!" Edgar rubbed his leg.

So began the morning of the day of all days. By six-thirty, the five horses were debugged with various fly repellents and loosed into the pasture. The nineteen cats lay on hay bales in the barn or under bushes relaxing after their fish breakfast, and Diane, our newly-adopted Irish wolfhound, lay with a full belly in her spot in the garage, tucked up between the garage wall and the grill of my car.

After Edgar left to begin his calls, I began the long-ignored chore of weeding the garden. I macheteed a path to the vegetable garden, and tackling the chickweed and crabgrass with a hoe, hacked and plucked the rebel forces from my suffocating vegetable plants. Two cats, Lance and Arthur, watched the battle of the green fog. After much time and effort I conquered the bushveld, and at the end of my toil, had six, thirty-foot rows of onions, peas, tomatoes and cabbage plants lined up like soldiers.

Afterwards I resembled a slimy dirt ball, sweat and ground co-mingling on my skin. Numerous mosquito bites peeked through the grime, and my jeans felt like soggy diapers. I walked from the tidy garden, bowlegged and with arms outstretched, as if I were plagued with prickly heat. Then I headed to the swing for a little relaxation.

Soon my nagging conscience spoke, *You really* must *ride Fancy today to prepare for the show this weekend. She and you need the practice.* I groaned. Not even bothering to argue with my conscience, I hoisted myself from the swing and strode toward the barn.

Taking a deep breath, I threw the barn door open and stepped into the pasture. "Fancy... Fan-n-n-n-see-ee-eee-cc-ee," I called in my sweetest, most melodious voice. "Where are you-u-u-u-u?"'

Her ears perked up like antennae, and then I saw the chagrin etched across her muzzle as if she had eaten a lemon. She obviously dreaded a workout, and, of course, I couldn't blame her. Her expression said, *Go away. I don't want to lug you around. It's too hot!*

Fancy's eyes closed to tiny slits. Her head lowered, and her mouth drooped as if caught in an overwhelming weakness. Certainly, she thought, I would not ride her today, no...certainly not in her weak and febrile condition. But there was nothing wrong with her; she was a big strapping girl, an equine as fit as Jane Fonda. But then her lip drooped lower and her feet shifted uncomfortably in the dust. How could I possibly saddle up and ride this sorry, debilitated animal?

In contrast there was her round belly, born from lazy afternoons gorging in the pasture, and her shining, muscled rear end. She always had bright, curious eyes that now, all of a sudden, had become sickly and pathetic. The decision was made: "Fancy, we are having our workout, whether you like it or not."

So, for the next hour, we practiced: riding figure eights in the ring, circling to the left then the right, cutting diagonals and practicing leads.

Horseback riding is not merely sitting in a saddle as immobile as a sack of wheat. Actually, the sport has yoga as its basis and depends on an awareness of the body's muscles and bone alignment. The stomach muscles, hamstrings, muscles in the feet and calves, shoulder blades, head and hands, and thigh and gluteal muscles must all work harmoniously in order to achieve good balance. The mastery of equitation demands the highest kind of concentration and physical ability, and it takes years to learn.

While on horseback, a person should feel every muscle straining toward its right position. The tendons in my ankles stretch down and twist the foot inward while the calf muscles tense and relax to give direction and drive to the horse's hind end. The abdominal muscles are tucked in to align the spine over the horse's center of gravity, and the thigh muscles are constantly adjusting their pressure. Too, one's arms and hands must "feel" the delicate shifts and changes through the reins from the horse's neck, head and mouth, and they must adjust for the correct response. In fact, a person riding correctly and according to the rules of a balanced seat uses most every muscle in her body—seeking that "oneness" between horse and rider.

That is why, after an hour of practice, my body was raising the tattered flag. I was almost completely done in. Four hours in the jungle and one in the cavalry were wearing this soldier thin. Surrender was imminent.

Finally, I had to muck out and sweep the barn. The pitchfork dragged behind me like a prisoner's ball and chain while flies buzzed from the stall floor as I plunged the fork into the manure and lobbed it into the wheelbarrow. After the five stalls were clean, I swept the hallway and loaded the dirt and hay onto the wheelbarrow and onto the manure pile.

Again, the swing beckoned me. Then as if it were a beguiling vampire, it lured me into its arms. As I floated dreamily, drifting back and forth, the birds whistled contentedly, except for a crow raucously complaining about one of the cats. A tractor pulled itself throatily through a nearby field, and a lone diesel truck whined, shifting gears, up a hill.

On the swing, my steamy skin cooled luxuriously as my eyes twitched in a preliminary to sleep. A fly zoomed past, its airy backwash on my cheek, before the voice of my conscience began to nag: *You should, you know. You haven't been there for three days; you're avoiding it. If you don't go today, you won't go tomorrow or any other day.* The voice died away, and as I dropped off to sleep, it pierced like a shot, *Come on, get up! It'll be good for you. Get it over with, and you won't have to go again for another day.*

"All right, all right," I moaned, "I'll go already."

In a half-hour I was dragging through the doors of the health club. I stopped just inside. I really didn't feel like exercising. Backing out the door and away from the torture chamber, I felt an insistent tapping, not unlike Poe's raven; it was my conscience. So I walked inside, presented my membership card and went to my first piece of equipment—the bicycle.

Beside me on another bike, an enormous woman pumped, stubby chin jutting in determination, chubby fingers gripping the handlebars in a speeding frenzy. Her wheel spun faster than mine, so I quickened my pace; I would have no trouble keeping up with this human steam engine beside me.

The sweat poured from her face as she pedaled with a vengeance. Furiously, she rode, her fleshy hips rocking rhythmically on the spindly seat, her wide shoulders bent over the handlebars. Faster I pumped in what, in my imagination, would be a race to the finish.

For the third time this day, sweat burst from my pores. A stream flowed down the back of my black leotard, pooling at my waistline as I strained forward. For fifteen minutes we pedaled, and our bikes rattled toward the finish line. As my knees raced, I shot my competitor a sideways glance; but she wouldn't meet my eyes. There was no question that my wheel was spinning faster than hers, but she evidenced no intimidation. Instead, she watched my wheel from the corner of her eye and met the challenge, driving her feet even harder into the pedals. She had to know she would be the loser, that I was winning by virtue of my faster spinning wheel.

Suddenly, the big woman stopped pedaling, and the bike's front wheel slowed to a stop. Then she climbed heavily from the seat, scowling in my direction. I pedaled even faster than before, hurtling into the wind, sweat droplets streaming down my face; I would not only pedal faster but longer, too. I watched as the big woman strapped herself to the thigh machine; the apparatus squeaked and strained with every squeeze of her meaty legs. But I was pleased: she had obviously retreated from the "victor of the velodrome."

Then as I pedaled leisurely, a very pretty, small thing flitted to the big woman's bicycle. She smiled politely, positioned her tiny bottom on the seat and placed her painted fingers delicately upon the handlebars. A petite grunt sounded, and the little, pointy knees began to move above the pedals.

"God, I can hardly move this thing!" she exclaimed. "What can be wrong with this bike?" She looked down at the resistance dial. "Oh, no wonder," she said cutely, "the setting is on five. No wonder I could hardly pedal."

My eyes shot to her bike's gauge. "Five?" I gasped, leaning over the dial on my bike. "Don't tell me the person before you was riding at number five?" My eyes bugged as I read my own dial. "One-and-a-half?" I shrieked. "My resistance is only one-and-a-half?"

"Oh my, I don't see how anyone could pedal for any length of time at number five," she said.

"Yeah, neither do I," I muttered. "I've always done my rides at the one-and-a-half resistance point. I thought nearly everyone did."

"Yes, well, I guess if I ever want to get out of this place, I better start working, right?" she giggled thinly.

I snickered, "Yep, guess so." But I was mortified; the big woman had beat me—she was pressing twenty pound weights to my measly five.

I climbed from my bike, and the pretty little bird beside me reached down to adjust her pressure dial. Surely, she'll set hers at one or below, I thought. But my self-esteem suffered a final blow as she snapped the dial to two and began to pedal furiously.

Dejected, I switched to my next machine. When I absolutely could not do another shoulder press, leg extension, abdomen tuck or hip flex, I dragged myself to the locker room and retired to the steam bath.

I loved the Turkish steam bath. Into the foggy chamber I stumbled, groping for a seat on the hot, slimy tile. A pair of legs appeared out of the mist and attached to them was the torso of an older woman. Curling into a ball on the highest shelf where the steam was the hottest, I breathed slowly, evenly, sucking in the moisture until an eerie inner pressure began to rise beneath my skin.

I inspected the pores of my forearm. Just when I had thought the last ounce of sweat had been drained from me, more drops exploded. The water rushed from my skin, and at once I felt an overwhelming dizziness. Then it came again—the feeling that I relish yet dread: that weak, crushing sensation that, if I weren't careful, would send me crashing to the floor in a dead faint. Seconds later I emerged rubber legged into the cool hallway and staggered to the shower.

Strangely revived by the steambath, I dressed and headed home. My skin tingled, and my body had that satiated, washed-out feeling brought on by hard work and exercise. Finally my conscience was at ease: my daily chores were finished, and I could vegetate freely until dinner.

At home, the swing again beckoned. Although the desire to sleep had nearly overcome me earlier, it seemed to have left now as I lay stretched out in the warm breeze. I was tired but not sleepy. So I relaxed and stared complacently over the pasture and woods, taking small, chewy bites out of an unripe pear.

Presently, a familiar rumble sounded up the driveway. Good— four o'clock in the afternoon, and Edgar was done with his calls. He'd have some time to relax before dinner. I waved as the dust cloud rolled over me. He cut off the engine and stuck his head out the truck, "Looks like you've had a tough day." He was being sarcastic. He stepped out, slamming the truck door.

"Come on," I said, patting the seat beside me. "Sit down here, Hon, and swing with me."

He plopped beside me. The odor of cow hit me, and as I took his hand, I noticed the callouses; it was not a soft hand. His pants bore smudges of blood and manure, and dust had settled permanently in the threads of his trousers.

"Rough day, huh?" I confirmed the expression on his face.

"Sure was. I saw a lot of animals today, that's for sure. I'm beat, and I just want to relax a little before I see about any phone calls."

I couldn't expect empathy for my exhausting day. After all, how could weeding, riding a horse, mucking out and working out at the health club compete with wallowing in pig and cow dirt? I felt as though I had been an indentured sailor for the day, but Edgar would, no doubt, think I'd been on a Princess Cruise.

As I started to speak, his beeper burst into song. A singular feeling of dread creeps over us when the beeper goes off, for it usually foretells an emergency. It has a jarring noise that has conditioned us like Pavlov's dogs. At the sound of the buzzer, our heart rates increase, the blood pressure rises, and the hair on our heads stands at attention. The sound of the beeper signifies acute interruption—interruption of routine work such as loading hay into the barn; interruption of sleep at three o'clock in the morning or a rare nap in the middle of the afternoon; interruption of bodily functions; interruption of leisure time, such as opening Christmas presents at Grandma's house and taking a walk through the woods; interruption of our sex life.

For us, the sound of the beeper is a thing to be dreaded but not resisted, for behind its insistence is an emergency: a horse with colic, milk fever in a cow, a laceration of some kind, or some other catastrophe. And behind every emergency lies the need to heal or to save a life.

"Well, guess I better see about that, Gayzie," he said, squeezing my hand. I knew what that squeeze meant—this day is not done yet, Honey. I stayed on the swing while Edgar went inside to make the call. Moments later he emerged from the house. "Want to go along? There's a horse that can't stand right. The people say he seems to have lost his equilibrium. It's down around Emmaus."

"Sure, I'll keep you company. We'll be back by six-thirty, don't you think? I'd like to eat at the Gourmet Chalet if it's all right with you?"

"Yeah, call from the truck, but make the reservations for seven-thirty, just in case. Come on, let's go."

The quickest way to get to Emmaus is to use the four-lane highways: Route 22 and Route 309. Before we get to the highways, however, we have to travel through a few small towns where the usual bevy of cement trucks slows traffic. Once beyond the small towns of Northampton and Cementon, we could make good time along Routes 22 and 309, skirting Allentown. Even during rush hour, it would take us forty-five minutes to get to Emmaus.

Thirty minutes later, while speeding down Route 22, a clicking sound began from somewhere beneath the floor on the passenger's side.

"You hear that?" Edgar said, leaning toward the sound.

"Sounds like something's loose. Started a couple of minutes ago, didn't it?" I said.

"Who knows! Something's always going wrong with this truck. Wonder what it is this time. I'll check it at the farm." But the noise grew menacingly louder, drowning out Sheena Easton on the radio.

"Sure doesn't sound healthy," I said, biting my lip. We headed onto Route 309, and Edgar's face darkened as the knocking grew more vicious.

"Think we ought to stop somewhere?"

"Nah," he scoffed, "it'll be all right. Probably something minor that's loose. After all, the truck's still going, isn't it? We'll be all right."

Finally, we pulled into the driveway, scattering the ducks and guinea hens, and scaring the cats that had been dozing on the porch.

Jumping from the truck, Edgar hit the hood, and it flew open, exposing the metal guts. He poked around, wiggling the radiator hose, jostling the air filter—jiggling any part that might be the culprit.

Meanwhile, convinced the loose item was on the passenger side, I inspected the undercarriage on hands and knees, looking for something dragging.

"Ah, here it is," Edgar confirmed proudly, lifting up and down a loose sheet of metal. "See," he said, letting it drop again and again. "This is it. It even sounds like the same noise."

I didn't think it did.

"No big deal," he said. "I'll have it fixed one of these days."

"Yeah, sure you will. Just like you fixed that one lug that came off a wheel. How many weeks have you been going with only four lugs holding that wheel, instead of five?"

"Oh," he said sheepishly, slamming the hood closed, "only about four weeks now. Don't worry, Curly'll fix it sometime."

"Sure," I said.

"We really need to take a look at this horse already. They said he'd be in a little box stall off the main barn. There," he said pointing to a small white building, "that looks like it."

As we started to walk toward the box stall, I heard a cry of pain. I gaped at Edgar, who had fallen to his knees beside the right front truck wheel.

"Damn," he moaned. "Look at this wheel!"

I looked and swallowed hard.

"We're lucky nothing happened."

All four lugs that had held the front wheel to the shaft had nearly twisted off. The screws hung by their last threads, and all that held the wheel on was the steel shaft which had almost been ground through by the weight of the truck. We had almost lost a wheel.

"And to think we were going sixty miles an hour on Routes Twenty-two and Three-oh-nine," I gasped. How easily that wheel could have slipped off the shaft, plunging the truck's entire right side right onto the highway, bringing us to a screeching halt in the breakneck, bumper-to-bumper traffic. And who knows what we could have plowed into or what could have plowed into us.

"Well, guess what?" Edgar said sheepishly. "I can't drive that sucker another two feet. We're stuck here. I'll see about this horse, then we'll have to arrange something so we can get the truck fixed." He headed toward the barn and looked back at his truck. "Guess I'll have to give Curly a call. Maybe he can help us out here since he lives only a few towns away."

Curly is a good friend; he also owns a gas station. Since Curly owns horses, Edgar and Curly trade veterinary calls for work on his truck. The system works out well for both.

When the medical truck is under the weather, the clouds build over us, too. Not only does its incapacity hinder our plans, but it also drags Edgar into one of his blackest moods. This is the only time when Edgar "gives up the ship." I'm always amazed at how he surmounts all kinds of fiascos: lightning hitting the well and severing our water supply, a flooded basement, no electricity from time to time, and a delayed pharmaceutical shipment. All these things he bears with a stiff lip, but when the vehicle breaks down, his world turns black.

Edgar trudged from the crippled truck with his shoulders hanging, his head magnetized to the ground, his feet dragging. He was not the husband I knew; but my marriage vows and our joint commitment to healing obligated me to stick tight during sickness, health and vehicular breakdowns.

I followed him into the barn. A black cat came through the door and regarded us with interest. Then she meowed and curled herself back outside.

Edgar examined the gelding. He found only a small scratch on the left hip and under it, a swelling the size of a half dollar. Then he led the animal outside to the gravel driveway, spinning him, backing him and trotting him forward, trying to elicit the dizziness for which we were called.

"Well?" I said, already knowing the verdict.

"Here," he said, giving me the end of the lead rope. "Take him back to his stall; he's not lame, not dizzy, nothing. All he has is that lump on his hip. Now it does look fresh, like it happened maybe an hour or so ago, and it could be that he was 'ouchy' on it for awhile. He probably got kicked or banged into something. But there's nothing else wrong with him. He's clinically sound."

"Great," I said. "Here we are called out on this emergency that's not an emergency, and now we have our own real emergency—on a Saturday night, too. No garage will be open for repairs this late."

Edgar's shoulders sagged lower than ever at the reminder. He walked slowly over to the tilted wheel, contemplated it and kicked the tire. For a moment the desperation turned to anger, but as he walked to the farmhouse to call Curly, his shoulders sank again.

A few minutes later Edgar appeared. No one was home. He walked to a neighbor's to use their phone. When he came back, he seemed in better spirits. "Curly's home and he'll arrange for a tow truck." Curly would call his buddy to open his auto parts shop so that we could buy new lugs.

"Lucky thing Curly was home, or I don't know what we'd do," Edgar said, putting his arm around my shoulder. "Curly's a lifesaver."

For forty-five minutes, we waited. I sat on an old tire, watching busy ants carry their eggs across the gravel. Six o'clock came, and we still had no ride. Edgar had paced the barnyard for the umpteenth time, examining the horse again and again. Somehow I believe he would've felt better had there been something slightly wrong with the animal. At least our own misery would not have been in vain. And we could kiss our dinner reservations goodbye.

Just then, the tow truck rumbled into the driveway and lurched to a stop. A short, stocky man, greasy with the lubricants of his trade, nodded silently and, seeing the crippled vehicle, backed up to our truck's front grill. He and Edgar exchanged words with much gesticulation and pointing. Then the wrecker man set the wheels of rescue in motion: wrapping chains around our truck's undercarriage, manipulating a bunch of lines and devices and finally, hoisting it into the air.

I looked inside the tow truck. A young heavy but pretty woman had accompanied the man to this emergency much as I had accompanied my husband on this call. *That was quite nice of her to keep him company on a Saturday evening, but where were we going to sit?* We couldn't ride in our truck hanging eerily in the air, and their truck didn't have an extended cab. They were big people, and there was clearly not enough room for all of us in the front seat of the truck.

When the man nodded for us to climb in, I whispered to Edgar through gritted teeth, "Where are we supposed to sit? There's no room."

"Don't worry about it. We'll fit in somehow," he assured me. "I'll just be glad to get to Curly's garage."

The large blonde woman shot us a sterile glance, apparently not the slightest bit worried about where we would all sit. She turned, looking straight ahead as we approached; and when Edgar opened the door, she reluctantly moved over next to her husband. She seemed annoyed at the inconvenience.

As we climbed into the truck, I gave her one of my unthreatening looks with my mouth and eyes twisted into a wince of subjugation. Surely I was no threat; indeed, this was her truck, her seat. I only wanted to borrow a section of it temporarily.

Strangely, I felt like a lioness in another lioness' territory, an interloper into her part of the jungle. And, oddly, I felt less secure, less boisterous than usual, less aggressive on someone else's property. Must be animal instinct, I thought uneasily. But Edgar probably felt none of that. He probably didn't feel the cold irritation radiating from that woman.

Her name was Liz; her left thigh rested on her husband's lap, and she held his two-way radio. We were packed tight as licorice twists. This was the closest I'd ever been to a stranger's ear, and I hoped she didn't mind my breathing into it. In fact, we were so packed inside the truck that a strand of my hair lifted and fell to Edgar's every inhalation and exhalation. His left leg served as a settee for my right buttock.

To ease the awkwardness I asked Liz about her part in this expedition. "I bet you guys are glad the day is almost over. Did you have many jobs today?"

Liz jiggled the two-way in her lap, and then a sound much like Woody Woodpecker's laugh erupted from her. "YE-A-A-A-AH!" Her voice vibrated deafeningly.

"This is a pretty good-sized engine you have in this truck," said Edgar, gripping the edge of his seat as we flew over a bump.

"YE-A-A-A-AH!" shrieked Liz. The word reverberated, ricocheted off the metal ceiling, and escaped out the window. My ears were ringing.

"Looks like both of our guys are on call," I remarked.

"YE-A-A-A-AH!" she riveted. She was beginning to warm up to us, and now she seemed pleasant enough, but that voice! It could crack glass.

We could not get to Curly's soon enough.

"Do you go along with your husband on a lot of his calls?" Edgar asked, diverting the attention away.

"YE-A-A-A-A-AH!" she machine-gunned.

"Have you been in the towing business for a while now?"

Why couldn't he ask her a question requiring a negative answer, I wondered.

"YE-A-A-A-A-AH!" she blasted. I turned to Edgar, mashing my nose against his. My tolerance was wearing onion-skin thin.

Finally, we pulled into Curly's parking lot where Liz's husband silently lowered and unhooked our truck. We thanked the couple for their trouble, and they made out a bill that made ours for the non-emergency horse call look anemic. Crawling from my seat, I said goodbye.

Within minutes, Curly drove into the station. He, Edgar and an assistant repaired the truck wheel to the latest hit song, "Man Eater." They worked, hammering, welding and blow-torching the offending wheel off the shaft.

At ten o'clock that night, Edgar and I finally rolled into the driveway where our nineteen cats, five horses and one dog vociferously demanded their dinners. We gobbled our take-out steak sandwiches to the eleven o'clock news and headed up the "woody mountain" to bed.

Edgar's voice rose out of the dark beside me, "Some day, wasn't it?"

"YE-A-A-A-AH!" I buried my face in the pillow.

33

A Dog in Cat's Clothing

The next day, I had a few more chores to accomplish around the house: doing laundry, cleaning the bathroom and sweeping cobwebs out of the barn loft. I had finished them all and was about to start mowing the lawn, when the phone rang.

"Gay," a broken female voice sounded urgent over the phone. "Is Edgar around? I'm at the stable, and I have an emergency here. Please…is he there?"

It was a voice I didn't recognize at first, for its crackly, panicked quality was so uncharacteristic. Then I realized it was my riding instructor, Gale. She was usually unperturbable. Something must be very wrong.

"My God, what's wrong, Gale? Yes, Edgar is right here.… We'll be over in ten minutes."

I signaled my husband. "Gale has an emergency." We were out of the house in seconds.

When we arrived at Gale's, a crowd of teenage girls had gathered in a quiet semi-circle in a corner of the barn. All activity at the riding stable had come to a standstill. No one was riding in the indoor arena, nor had anyone fed the horses, and they were restless. It was, after all, five o'clock, an hour past their feeding time, and the place was usually a blur of activity then. Except for the Doberman puppies whining in their cardboard box, silence prevailed.

As we got out of the truck and ran over, a girl looked up from the frightened group huddled together. They all looked somber. Gale stood in the midst, holding a bundle. She placed it in Edgar's arms.

"It's PJ. A horse stepped on him. I think he may have broken his leg," Gale explained. "Is there anything you can do?"

PJ, short for Puss Junior, was one of the offspring of Puss Senior. He was an exceptionally handsome orange domestic shorthair about two months old and was one of a litter of three kittens that had won everyone's heart. The young girls, between lessons and grooming the horses, played and fussed with them every day. Puss Senior's kittens stole the show, and Gale found herself as enamored by them as by any of her horses.

But her favorite, the one she'd become instantly attached to, was PJ, the chubby orange upstart who made a habit of curling in her lap during lunch.

PJ was afraid of nothing. Consequently, many times he found himself in a precarious position between a horse's back legs. At such times, everybody kept still until someone quickly scooped him out of the danger zone. Then he'd trot off after the person who saved him. He was always underfoot, trailing after his human friends. His littermates looked upon him as a guide and followed him among the straw bales and into the stallion's stall. Unfortunately, this time his fearlessness had led him to a near disaster beneath a horse's hoof.

Edgar unfolded the flannel rag. Puss Junior meowed, his eyes bright and intense, but he didn't struggle as Edgar palpated the hurt leg. Suddenly PJ squealed. "It's definitely broken," Edgar said. Careful not to hurt him, Edgar examined PJ while the kitten looked on with interest. In a few seconds PJ was purring. "His purrer is fine, it seems. And I think, other than the leg, the rest of him is all right, too."

"Do what you can, will you, Edgar? PJ's a favorite around here. I've never had a kitten like him."

"That may be easier said than done. He is awfully small, you know. The bone is too small to pin, so I'd have to cast it. Kittens usually don't do very well with casts because they're so active. Usually, they get it off before the bone has healed."

Gale looked worried, "Please.... Try it anyway. We've got to give him a chance." In the background the young girls huddled, listening to the prognosis.

"Okay, PJ, I'll do my best," Edgar promised. PJ mewed, his voice muffled in the old cloth as Edgar took him to his truck.

Edgar moved slowly, deliberately, and we molded the plasterlike material around the hind leg, watching all the time for any signs of internal distress. Edgar sometimes worked on his clients' small animals on the tailgate of our truck. Actually, people seemed to prefer this to an office visit; they could have their animal treated right at home and not have it stay overnight.

"I think the bones are aligned pretty well. If he can keep himself quiet and doesn't lose that cast, then he might have a good chance at recovery. If that doesn't work, then we might have to amputate." I shivered and Gale crossed her arms, shutting out the thought. "Of course, amputation is a last resort." Edgar nodded.

For the next six weeks, PJ would have to be sequestered with two of Gale's favorite dogs: Molly, an Australian shepherd, and Tiki, a miniature poodle. Molly and Tiki were house dogs that had been with Gale since she was ten, and they preferred the warmth and comfort of the barn's tackroom to the outdoors. Molly and Tiki, however, didn't realize that their preference for the tackroom made them the perfect baby-sitters for PJ.

That first evening, PJ, temporarily renamed Pegleg, thumped through the Dutch doors and into the tackroom. The old dogs stared at the kitten who promptly made himself at home in their nest of old T-shirts. What began as a sacrifice for the dogs turned out to be a blessing for them and PJ, for PJ's friendliness quickly grew on them and they became two doting mothers. They made much ado about their charge, licking his fur, cuddling him and entertaining him.

Molly and Tiki doted on PJ day and night for the full six-week convalescence. When Gale let the dogs outside to run, PJ mewed and paced the tackroom so that Gale worried that his cast might break. And when the two dogs came back to their waif, the dogs and kitten nuzzled each other as if they'd been separated for weeks.

For six weeks, the two dogs and PJ kept each other company in the tackroom. They slept together, played together, ate and communicated together.

One day the Dutch door to the tackroom hung open. Edgar and I had come to take Coggins tests on the horses. Molly sat in the aisle snapping at a fly, but I saw no trace of Tiki so I looked into her cozy bed. There she lay with PJ curled asleep inside her thigh. Tiki wagged her tail when she saw me, and that woke PJ who blinked and mewed through a wide yawn. Tiki sniffed PJ, nudged him, and shifted onto her back, her paws in the air as though she wanted me to rub her belly. PJ rose stiffly, dragging his cast behind him, and stretched. I rubbed Tiki's belly and at the same time stroked PJ's head, but the purr that had been PJ's trademark was silent. Instead, PJ thumped his tail. As I slicked back the fur on his forehead, his tail beat more violently. Then suddenly PJ crashed onto his back, his paws in the air, his lips parted, begging me to rub his belly.

"That PJ is something else, isn't he?" a voice said from over the Dutch door. It was Gale. "He doesn't know he's a cat anymore, I swear; he acts more and more like a dog every day."

I rubbed their bellies. "Well, this certainly is strange behavior for a cat. Cats usually don't like their bellies scratched." PJ rolled and pawed the air.

"That's nothing. Once that cast comes off, I don't know whether PJ will ever act like a normal cat again. PJ was always very vocal, but now he's ridiculous," she laughed. "You know the way I talk to my dogs, and they sort of talk back. They sound like they're mumbling and draw it out as long as I keep talking to them. Well, PJ does it, too. Now, watch."

Gale slid through the Dutch door and bent down beside me. Tiki immediately rolled onto her chest and sat upright; PJ did the same, mirroring the dog's smile. "Just listen."

Gale started to question the three comrades about their night— whether they watched the "Tonight Show" or the news; when they finally got to bed; what they would like for breakfast; and if they would like to meet the Easter Bunny tomorrow. Soon Tiki began to talk, burbling answers in a long, drawn-out whine, her muzzle pointed. Then Gale began to discuss international affairs and the fighting in Beirut, and whether Tiki had any thoughts on the matter of Star Wars or Reaganomics. Tiki grumbled and gurgled replies, but soon there was a higher, thinner voice joining in. It was PJ. Just as intense on the subject of Kadaffi's terrorists and the Queen of England's latest extravaganza, PJ set up a mewling and meowing quite unbecoming a cat, but similar to Tiki's. Gale continued with the local news and the plans to build a sewage dump in our backyard to which Tiki and PJ exploded in a harmonious crescendo. It was incredible.

"There," she exclaimed, as the pair became silent. "Does that prove it, or doesn't it? PJ thinks he's a dog, there's no two ways about it." She reached for a treat and gave it to Tiki, who perched on her haunches, paws in the air. PJ immediately assumed the same stance. "See," Gale said, "and I didn't deliberately teach him to do that. PJ saw Tiki do it, and he started doing it, too."

"Wow," I said, "this is a case for the animal behaviorists. Sort of a Romulus and Remus story, isn't it?" I smiled.

"Sure is," Gale said thoughtfully. "Guess Edgar is going to remove PJ's cast today, too. Maybe once he associates with other cats, he'll start acting normal again."

But PJ would no longer be a normal cat. His constant company with Tiki made him a canine feline. Occasionally, he ambled up to one of his littermates, but they didn't impress him. He thumped his tail when he was happy, bared his gums when threatened, and continued to grumble in Tiki language. He never attempted to jump on anything, content to stay glued to the floor. Whereas the other cats climbed into the loft, PJ stood at the bottom rung of the ladder gazing up, quite sure he was incapable of reaching any height above his own head. He even developed a funny sashay to his walk rather than the springy gait of a cat. He was a dog in cat's clothing.

PJ was quite a character. One time, he crawled into a visitor's car for a comfortable place to sleep. The woman drove home that evening, parked her car on one of Allentown's busiest downtown streets, and went to her apartment. The next morning she drove to work. There at the Lone Star Cement Company she heard a voice from the back seat. There lay PJ curled in a ball. The woman had to chauffeur PJ back to the barn and arrived back at work an hour late.

Like a dog, PJ came when he was called. Bounding across the field, leaping through the thistles and fescue grass, we recognized the orange blur that was PJ coming for supper. PJ also accompanied Gale to the mailbox, walking side by side with Tiki and Molly. And when Tiki was busy elsewhere, PJ strolled down the road with Gale—a strong, mature cat.

PJ overcame his first disaster with no problem, thanks to Tiki's diligent care. But as Gale stopped her car in our driveway one day, I knew something was wrong again. And I knew it had to do with PJ.

Gale paled as she related PJ's misfortune. She had been cleaning some tack late one afternoon when PJ walked into the tackroom. He had been mangled by something the likes of a Sherman tank. He mewled to her with great sad eyes and hobbled to Tiki's bed. His back leg was broken, the right shoulder dislocated, and his jaw dangled by a thread. A great string of saliva drooled at his feet as he struggled across the floor.

"I knew it was Edgar's weekend off, so I got him to Dr. Tucker Jones's office as fast as I could. He didn't give much hope for him. He told me it would be a couple of hundred dollars to fix him up, and that he still might not be able to eat right or walk right again. But I had to do something. After all, it's no ordinary cat we're talking about here. It's PJ. I couldn't have asked for a better job on him, and he took excellent care of him. PJ is back home in his nest beside Tiki. Of course, I have to hand-feed him every few hours. But if PJ gets better, it'll be worth it. If something happens to PJ, we'll all be a mess."

I made my first hospital visit to PJ the end of that week. I brought him some soft cat food which I shoveled with my fingers into his poor wired mouth. But he was hungry and expressed his appreciation, mewling through his dinner, his pink tongue licking my meat-smeared fingers with healthy savagery. He was terribly beat-up, flinching when I accidentally touched him on a sore spot. He lay in his ragged nest with his back leg stretched out behind him.

Weeks passed and along with my weekly riding lesson, Gale gave me an up-to-date account of PJ's condition. He was getting the best of care; all Gale's students offered to nurse PJ back to health, each one taking a certain feeding and entertaining him so that he wouldn't be bored all day. Gale gave riding lessons to an audience of PJ, Tiki and Molly nestled in a corner of the arena. As the rider trotted past, his eyes followed, and there, too, his feedings took place. He probably had more to eat now than he had when he was healthy. And when Tiki was running outside with Molly, she periodically came inside to check on PJ. PJ was on the mend again, and the barn settled into its routine once more.

At times I am grateful for my myopic view of the world. I wouldn't want to be omniscient, experiencing—feeling—all the hurt and hunger, seeing the lab animals suffer and the pain of every grandfather's death. Better off blind to life's daily miseries, I am grateful I didn't have to be there when PJ died.

He died characteristically. He dragged his body in through the Dutch doors and folded himself heavily in Tiki's bed. Someone had heard a quiet mewling in the tackroom but hadn't really thought much about it. It was a busy day at the barn; a horse show had everyone in a rush. Saddles and bridles were hustled into the horse trailer; horses were readied, blanketed and wrapped with leg wraps for the ride to the show. Everyone was hurrying, and the barn became silent as the trailer pulled out of the parking lot.

Surely no one knew that PJ had eaten rat poison. And no one had noticed PJ lying motionless in his nest of rags. Nobody heard PJ's quiet mewling from within the tackroom—nobody except Tiki.

When they came back from the show, they saw Tiki in her nest, panting, and PJ lay curled beside her. His expression was painless in his death. Tiki nuzzled her possession, but PJ did not respond.

34

Macho Man

The world reeled past in a flutter of colors: June colors—shades of green dotted by daisy-white and dabs of yellow. We rode our truck parallel to a lazy creek that trickled into a valley with a meadow. We rolled through pasture land and gradually climbed through a woods full of blooming mountain laurel and wild rhododendron.

The lush Pennsylvania countryside is wild and romantic, especially in the Poconos with its hidden lakes and clean, meandering streams. And now, it suddenly unfolded in a wild verdant lather around us: forests, dense and junglelike, opened up into small sea green clearings that, just as suddenly, closed up again against the woodland. In contrast, the Dutch farmsteads with their cow herds and acres of crops are tame and classical in their orderliness: here all is flat, sectioned into fields of soybeans, corn, wheat, barley and oats. The classical landscape is equally appealing in its orderliness and tidiness.

Just as appealing as Pennsylvania's countenance is her personality of changing seasons. Just when the summer heat brings the grasslands and trees to their most verdant, autumn begins its reign, marshaling in cooler weather and changing the color scheme to magenta, rust, gold and sienna. Even winter I welcome in its gruffness: its cold violence and power, a thrilling climax to the year. To me, Nature is an inquisitive child romping among the seasons, pretending rage in the ice storms, sullenness in the summer heat, sadness in the fall showers and tranquility in the spring skies.

I awoke from my daydream as we parked beside a stone bank barn. Tucked into a hillside, it was an older barn of fieldstone and oak rafters. It was cool like a cave.

Three young people were looking down over a stone wall toward the creek. I saw a horse, probably our patient, standing in the barn.

A woman with a long mahogany braid said, "Hi, you Dr. Balliet?"

"Sure am," Edgar said, smiling. "Is your name Kate Crawfield?"

"Yep, that's me." She beamed. Bright blue eyes glistened from her porcelain complexion. "And this is my friend, Kelly," she introduced, and a peppy, redhead stepped beside her.

"Hi, I'm Gay, but not really," I piped. The two girls giggled, and Edgar rolled his eyes.

"Now what can I do for you, Kate?" Edgar said, climbing from the truck. A young man who had been standing with the girls still had his back to us, a leg propped on the stone wall. He stared, brooding at the creek and pasture.

Kate began, "Well, it's my horse, Harry. Yesterday, Kelly noticed blood coming out when he'd...." She stopped, looking uncomfortable. Now here was another one who didn't want to say the word "urinate."

She stuttered and began again but could not get the word out, so Edgar helped her. He said, "urinate." He said it so matter-of-factly that it startled her.

"Yes, yes, that's right!" she blurted, feigning forgetfulness. Apparently the spell was broken now, for she had no further trouble explaining Harry's condition. "Yes, every time he goes there's blood at the end of it...when it's done comin' out, ya know. Also, there's this pink thing sticking down from his thing; it's like a scab or something, and it's bloody, too. Anyway, Kelly's horse doesn't have it."

"Kelly, what's your horse's name?" Edgar asked, shaking his thermometer and walking over to Harry.

"Miss Piggy," she giggled. I choked back a laugh; her horse was a female. No wonder Miss Piggy didn't have that pink thing Harry had. Edgar winked. I wondered how Edgar would fair at sex education.

"We're going to check his temperature first to see if he has anything brewing. It could be if he had blood trailing his urine, then he might have cystitis." Edgar contemplated the case, thinking of differentials.

Edgar inserted the thermometer into Harry's rectum. It didn't bother Harry any, but the young women eyed each other as if they had both been shown the centerfold from *Playgirl*.

Edgar reached up inside Harry's sheath. A horse will suck his penis up inside his body when the vet tries to clean it off—for, like an old attic trunk, it becomes dirty and musty with time. But Harry let Edgar examine it without any qualms. "Good boy," said Edgar, "not many horses are so agreeable."

Kate giggled, hiding her face. "Oh, Harry," she squeaked, "I can't believe you." Kelly snickered, too.

The girls glanced at me and their smiles faded, but I smiled, too, to show them I found Harry amusing also. They grinned even broader.

These two innocents were somehow refreshing. Sometimes at some of the larger horse ranches, the clients act as if they know more than the doctor does; sometimes they know quite a bit, in fact; but they never know more about what is medically wrong with their animal than Edgar does. And if they think they're smarter than Edgar, then they're certain geniuses when they compare themselves to me. To them, Dr. Balliet's "assistant" is virtually invisible.

After fishing inside Harry's sheath, Edgar pointed out the pink projection. "Is this the scab you saw?" he asked Kate.

"Yeah, that's it," Kate said, squinting at the organ. She didn't want to get too close to it.

"That's perfectly normal," he said. "That's his urethra, and it's fine."

"Oh," Kate said and smiled.

"You could clean it sometime—the penis I mean; it seems to be quite dirty. See?"

"Yeah, yeah, I see," she said, backing away.

I kept from laughing by concentrating on the pitchfork propped in a corner. Then I turned and saw the young man leaning over the Dutch door, his blond hair sculpted neatly across his forehead. His T-shirt touted the rock group Black Sabbath in black evil-looking letters, and he propped his foot on the Dutch door.

"Hi," I said.

"What's up, Man?" he returned, staring straight past me.

As I watched him, I could not help thinking that the "macho" man represents a strange phenomenon in American society, a phenomenon

that deems all that is tender, sincere and caring in the male species—
gauche. He usually frequents singles bars, nightclubs and other loud "in"
gathering places. He calls his car *rod* and spends most of his day *working
out*, the equivalent of flexing in front of a mirror at a health club. His
vocabulary consists of a few grunts and commonly used linking verbs
joined with the pronoun *I* and the adjectives *tough* and *cool*. The nouns
he routinely uses to refer to his girlfriend are *chick*, *hag* or *old lady*. Nearly
every conversation begins with, "Yo, Man," regardless of the sex of the
person spoken to. He generally dislikes animals and those actions humans
display toward them: cuddling, petting, stroking and cooing loving words
in their ears. If they do tolerate animals at all, they usually prefer dogs,
specifically pit bulls, Dobermans and dogs perceived as attack dogs. They
certainly despise cats because of their feminine, independent nature and
will not own any animal that they feel they cannot dominate.

I, however, have discovered that the macho man is nothing more
than a human shell: women serve only as tools or objects for him. Should
he stumble into marriage, he will avoid wearing his wedding band for fear
of looking like a sissy. If he does mistakenly marry, he will seek martyrdom in the "trapped husband" syndrome and will seldom pass by an
opportunity to flirt, to the acute annoyance of his female partner.

I don't like this kind of person. His hot car bores me; his bursting
muscles nauseate me; and his playboy image sends me into hysterics. But
his overall opinion of women and other less aggressive men as valueless
is what really revolts me. But his is an act—performed purely for show.
His mask of superiority hides an interior that is seriously lacking in self-
esteem and self-respect. He would be one to be pitied except for his fault
of compensating by being abusive and tough with other people.

Perhaps the "macho" man's origin is a mystery, like that of the
insect, but I look forward to his demise. Unfortunately, it was obvious
that today we were experiencing one of these creatures before it had
reached extinction.

Edgar removed the thermometer and said, "Ninety-nine-point-
five. It looks good. So, if he had cystitis, he must be pretty well over it by
now. Did he eat all right today?" Edgar asked.

Our male friend interrupted, "Ha! He eats good all the time. If I'd
get half the care he gets, I'd be a friggin' king." He snorted, looking away.

Kate said, "Dr. Balliet, this is my friend, Mike."

"Hi, Mike," Edgar said.

"Hey, it's cool. See, I told ya, Kate, we didn't need to call the vet out. I figured Harry'd get over it without any medicine. I'm tellin' ya, these damn ol' nags can take care of themselves," Mike said, still mesmerized by the pasture beyond the stone wall.

Edgar bristled. "I really think he might've had a touch of cystitis, but there's no need putting him on any antibiotics unless it's absolutely necessary. Just keep an eye on him; if he stops eating and you notice the blood again, give me a call. Otherwise, I don't think there's anything here to worry about. Did you want me to check anything else while I'm here?"

Kate asked, "What does this *Codgekins* test do that I hear so much about?"

Despite her inexperience with horses, her intentions were good: she had called the vet for all the right reasons. I could appreciate this pet owner more than the know-it-all who experiments with home remedies and who calls the vet only when it's too late.

"The Coggins test is simply a test for a contagious deadly disease known as EIA—equine infectious anemia. If you plan to show or board Harry with other horses, you should have one taken."

"Okay, and give him any shots he should have, plus dewormer," said Kate.

Edgar went to the truck for the vacutainer needle and tube, the injection and dewormer paste. Squeezing through the Dutch door, Edgar struggled past Mike who made no attempt to move and continued to stare over the pasture as if this veterinary business was wholly boring.

"Who's going to hold him while I take the blood test? I need to hit a vein," Edgar asked, looking for volunteers. Harry stood with his eyes nearly closed.

"Here, I'll do it," Mike volunteered, yawning and sidling into the barn. He pulled his T-shirt down over his pants and strutted over to Harry, snapping a lead shank through his halter and over his nose. He jerked the chain lead a couple of times, and Harry flinched.

"Mike, don't do that. Harry didn't even do anything, and you're beating him already. You can catch more bees with honey, remember," Kate said.

Harry's eyes were wide. "Don't tell me how to handle this horse, Kate," Mike warned.

Edgar stabbed the vein. With that, Harry reared, his front legs pawing the air. He almost knocked Edgar over.

"Whoa there, Harry," Edgar said, patting him on the neck. Harry's eyes were white and big as dinner plates. "Come on, we're not going to hurt you—just stick you a bit. It's nothing more than a nasty fly bite." Edgar hadn't expected such a reaction, especially after the horse let him handle his sheath. Mike hadn't helped by getting tough right away.

I looked over at Kate and Kelly; Kate chewed her nails, and Kelly shifted nervously.

"Ready, Mike," Edgar said.

Mike yanked the chain, and Harry threw his head. "I'm ready—won't let this stupid horse knock me around. I'll teach him who's boss."

Edgar tried again, but this time Harry went completely berserk, side-stepping and pinning Edgar against the wall. Most horses hardly notice when Edgar takes a blood sample—he's so quick—but Harry was upset.

Unfortunately, Mike, who had created the situation, was of little help. After the first incident, he was scared. He had been holding the lead rope from four feet away. Anyone knows you can't restrain a horse from that far away.

Kate knew Mike was afraid and offered to hold the animal.

"No!" he yelled, his eyes intense. "I have him under control here. Just stay away! What's wrong with this goddamned horse anyway? He's a complete asshole." Mike was red-faced.

"He just doesn't like needles, that's all," Kate said, her fingers flying back to her mouth. "But he's good for everything else."

"Yes, he certainly let me examine his sheath with no fuss. A lot of horses don't tolerate that well. But he is really needle-shy. Well, let's try again," Edgar said.

Before we had a chance to discourage him, Mike cracked the lead chain over Harry's nose. The horse hit the rafters. I winced. He was scaring the animal even before Edgar gave the injection. And hyping him up only made the situation more dangerous. I began to worry yet couldn't offer assistance, for Mike surely would have been offended.

They tried again. This time at the first sign of trouble, Mike let go of the rope, leaving Edgar to battle it out himself. As Edgar sank the needle home, Harry went into orbit, knocking Edgar into the wall. I could have wrung Mike's neck for abandoning him like that. Quickly, Edgar composed himself, but he had not appreciated Mike's cowardice. Had there been a person at Harry's head to soothe and reassure him, to hold him tighter, he might not have panicked. They had to try again.

Mike braced himself, his jaw set, and held onto the rope—again, from three feet away. Edgar saw the slack rope, and he was not willing to risk another pounding.

"Christ, give me that rope. You have to hold his *head*," he said, demonstrating. "You're not doing me any good holding him from so far away." Mike backed away. With one hand, Edgar steadied Harry and with the other held the needle. The tube for the blood he kept ready in his shirt pocket.

Quickly Edgar jabbed the vein and at the same time spun Harry in a circle around him while the blood drained into the tube. "It'll all be over shortly, Harry," Edgar reassured him as they went round and round in the hallway. Then Edgar slipped the needle from Harry's vein.

"It sure is strange his reacting that way to a lousy needle, but some horses are like that," Edgar said. Harry stood sleepy-eyed in the hallway. "Do you want to hold him while I give the flu injection now, Kate?" Edgar said.

"Yeah, okay," Kate said. She held the horse by his halter. Mike wouldn't move, unwilling to give up his position to Kate and thus admit defeat. While I watched from outside the half door and Kelly watched from another stall, Mike stood in the midst of the action.

"Now remember to spin him around us in a circle, Kate," Edgar reminded her. "That way he can't kick any of us, and I should be able to inject him while he's circling us," Edgar said.

When the needle struck home, there was a great brown blur in the hallway. That was Harry. Somewhere nestled in the vortex were Kate and Edgar. They were safe as long as Harry was to their outside and as long as the maelstrom did not cave in.

But Mike had been standing to the outside of the circle. This time when Harry exploded, a flash burst past me. In one giant leap, Mike had cleared the half door and seconds later stood beside me, struggling to look casual.

Finally, Edgar and Kate managed to vaccinate and deworm the horse. And no one had been hurt.

"We did it, Kate. Good job," Edgar complimented her. She giggled self-consciously. Edgar added, "He's difficult when it comes to injections;

otherwise, he's a good horse to work with." The injection over with, Harry stood nearly asleep.

Mike, propped safely beside me, was clearly angry. From behind the Dutch door, he blew out his chest and said, "That horse is an ASS-HOLE—a complete ASSHOLE. You should've gotten rid of him when I told you to months ago. I'll kill 'im when I get ahold of 'im again. He's no damn good; I'm telling ya—no good. And I'll teach him who's boss."

Then Mike turned to me, "Can you imagine? She paid a grand for that sonofabitch of a horse. She's crazy." Then he glared at Kate, "And I tell ya, I'm gonna beat the shit out of 'im when I get ahold of 'im again."

I wanted to call him a "sis," a "louse," and a "big, stupid bastard," but the look in Edgar's eyes warned me to keep my mouth shut.

However, Kate said it all for me, more subtly, but succinctly. "Oh, Mike, don't be so silly. He's not gonna know what you're mad at tomorrow or any other day. Besides, he doesn't do it to be mean; he's just scared. And you ain't gonna kill him next time you get a hold of him cause from now on, I'm gonna handle him. He's my horse, and I can make him listen to me."

Mike smirked. It hadn't looked good for a girl to control a thou-sand-pound animal when he couldn't. "Well, I wouldn't feed him tonight anyway," Mike fumed.

"That's silly, too, Mike, and you know it. He's not gonna remember nothin' that happened today; you'd just be torturin' the animal," she said.

Edgar and I smiled as we headed to the truck. This macho man was tamed first by a supposedly dumb animal, then, very rationally, chewed out by a woman. What justice! Mike sat on the stone wall and stared into the pasture. His tough guy image met an untimely demise here, in this barnyard this afternoon; his machismo came tumbling down. He might just as well have been standing in front of us stark naked, for underneath his cloak of superiority, he was as vulnerable and human as the rest of us.

Mike tried one last time, "Well, I just don't...."

"Look, Mike," Kate scolded, "I don't want to hear anymore. I can handle the horse, and I *will* handle the horse."

Edgar started the engine.

Kate waved and called, "Thanks, Dr. Balliet, for looking at Harry."

We both smiled; but Mike in a last ditch effort to save face, turned around and said, "Damn horse has got to go, Man." Then he turned to his stone wall.

Part III

Touched By
All Creatures

*...every thing that lives,
Lives not alone, nor for itself.*

William Blake
The Book of Thel

35

Hawk Mountain Sanctuary

Southeastern Pennsylvania would turn into a tropical rain forest if the humid summers were to continue, I began to think. Breathing became difficult and was like inhaling pure mist instead of air. People everywhere moved sluggishly, barely finishing household and farm chores only to fall exhausted into the nearest chair. Any normal activity seemed impossible in such weather. We relished thoughts of the dead of winter, so far away.

One muggy day, after another torrential rainstorm, we were called to dehorn some baby goats at a gentleman's farm along the base of Hawk Mountain. Hawk Mountain, as the name implies, is a bird and wildlife sanctuary where people from all parts of Pennsylvania and New Jersey come in October and November to watch the hawks ride the air currents above the mountain.

Long before Edgar and I were first married, we had taken many day trips to Hawk Mountain about an hour's drive away and hiked the rocky paths through the woods. In those days, we had little money, and it was a relatively inexpensive trip which brought us back to the natural world we both loved. I remember finding a large rocky outcropping over the cliffs. The two of us would sit for an hour or so spellbound by the primal wilderness spread out beneath us. Humans were meant to live like this, we often thought, close to nature in an unspoiled setting rather than the city or some bull-dozed suburban development. What a shame that many people have lost touch with the world from which they have originated, trading it, instead, for shopping malls, movie theaters, computers and virtual reality. Many have lost a part of themselves, a good part of themselves, in the artificial world they have helped create and sustain. At times, I feel myself being pulled, lured by objects and total "worlds" that money can buy. At times I lose, becoming overwhelmed by a fancy fad or gizmo, but later I think about the relatively minuscule value of the object against what is really important to me and our world: nature and all things natural. In places like Hawk Mountain, Edgar and I can reidentify and solidify ourselves and our lifestyle.

Now we were going there again. I took a deep breath of the out door air in anticipation of refreshment. We drove toward the base of Hawk Mountain, windows open, in search of Earl, the goat farmer who had called us. The old macadam road was overrun with dense foliage and groves of pine and ash trees. There was silence here to listen to, for it was devoid of any traffic except us. We stopped at one house to inquire if it was the correct place, but it wasn't. We pulled to the side to get our bearings, and within seconds great clouds of mist curled eerily in through the windows and enveloped the truck as if we were headed toward some other world. We had to turn on the headlights, yet it was only mid-afternoon. The air was moist and warm and filled with the scent of forest molds and pine trees. We half-expected to see the wolfman burst through the underbrush. It was a little scary, but it had an exotic, primeval lure for us, too.

Up ahead, a shack loomed out of the fog as the sun struggled to filter through the trees. Suddenly, a man emerged from the mist, his tall muscled body clad in a T-shirt and jeans. His rugged, stern face seemed incongruous next to his long ponytail and pierced ears.

"You the vet?" he said as we pulled up alongside. Edgar nodded. We climbed out of the truck. "I'm Earl Quinn. The goats are up in that shed in the woods," he said motioning us up a grassy hill. "Watch your step there. With all the rain we've been having, this place is a swamp. In fact, right now we have a stream running right under our house."

As we mucked our way to the barn, dehorning equipment in hand, the water sloshed up and over our sneakers, no matter how carefully we stepped. The strange call of some junglelike bird was penetrated by the sucking rhythm of our shoes pulling out of the wet grass.

The black and white goat kids, huddled in a corner of a rundown shed, had to be caught singly and carried out to the dehorning area. Each goat, weighing only about twenty pounds, stubby legs flailing, was brought, bleating, into the area outside the shack. The dehorning process was finished shortly with Edgar snapping off the horn buds of each baby goat.

After the dehorning, Earl offered to show us his property. "My goal is to establish a public game preserve at the base of Hawk Mountain. I only have a few wild animals and birds, but I intend to slowly build the preserve either by breeding or buying animals from other zoos or preserves.

"I'm really fascinated with wild animals; I believe that in time I can build this place into a very special animal sanctuary. In fact, a rare species of pheasant is being delivered sometime this week. He's a handsome bird all right," he said.

"It sounds like a terrific idea," I said, "but you do have a long way to go." The rickety wire pens leaned precariously and yielded to the rain-soaked ground. It would take thousands and thousands of dollars to realize his dream.

"Yeah," Earl said, "but Doc will have a lot of different animals to take care of then, I'll tell you. My buddy Pete helps me out with the animals; he loves them." A little man peeped from around a corner of an outbuilding. He reminded me of that other farmhand whom I came to know, Jakey. Pete waved, grinning, and I waved back. "Yes, Pete's my right hand man, aren't you, Pete?" Pete laughed gleefully and came out to stand beside us. He was mud-encrusted from head to toe. "He and I set up this place together. We're gonna make it big some day, won't we, kid." Earl slapped Pete on the back, and Pete giggled with delight.

Pete lunged playfully after Earl and assumed a boxing stance, giggling, "Yes, sir, sonofabitch. We're gonna do it real soon, and I get to tend the rabbits."

Earl and Pete led us on a walk through the genesis of their game preserve. While we plodded through the marshland, we saw Earl's remarkable wild animals of which he was so justifiably proud. Wild birds accompanied us around the grounds, cackling and cooing in the mist. Earl already had a number of exotic pheasants and chickens. Some were iridescent, some gold and red: beautiful jewel colors glittering in the sunshine. Some sported combs on their heads; some had rainbow-tinted beaks; others had luxurious, sweeping tails. Their avian sounds became muffled in the fog; the atmosphere was otherworldly.

Soon Earl showed us his most prized possession, a three-foot-tall sun bear named Zen wearing a white bib of fur across his chest. His home was a makeshift wire pen; nevertheless, Zen looked happy.

Earl sent Pete for a piece of butter bread which Pete brought back in the pocket of his mammoth overalls. Earl waved the piece of bread in front of the bear. Zen stood up on his back legs, front legs clawing the air above his head and turned four deliberate little circles. Then he bleated, demanding his reward. Earl stuffed the bread through the wires, and Zen, with a shrill squawk, clasped the bread between his paws, first licking it clean of the butter, then gobbling it down in one lump.

"He's gorgeous," I marveled.

"Seems in pretty good health," Edgar said.

"He's happy, all right," Earl agreed. The bear twirled around once more, like a ballerina. We laughed.

We said good-bye to Zen, and then Earl and Pete took us to see more penned birds: species of golden pheasants and various multicolored birds. Behind these pens were more species of duck than I ever was aware existed. They scolded us loudly as we passed by.

Shortly, we came to a group of stacked cages: foxes, raccoons, skunks, and possums in animal apartments, one atop the other. The fox looked suspiciously at us over a sharp, straight-whiskered nose. It would have been nice to pet and hold him, but he was wild and would probably bite.

Finally, we visited the deer pen which extended into the nearby woods a few hundred yards. The ten-foot-high wire fencing was necessary to prevent the white tail and fallow deer from jumping out. The relatively tame spotted deer, waving their white tails, slowly approached, looking for goodies. Then a buck gingerly sidled up to sniff our fingers. He enjoyed having his face rubbed.

"I'd like to expand my deer herd," Earl said, rubbing one black wet nose as it poked between the box wire fence. "I don't see how people can hunt these beautiful animals," he said. We agreed, and Edgar scratched the deer on the side of his neck as it rubbed against the fence.

The tour over, we walked with Earl and Pete toward the truck, passing the pond where Earl kept the black swans. "We promise we'll be the first people to visit your wildlife sanctuary when it opens," I said. We waved to the sun bear, took one last look at the newly-dehorned goats, said good-bye to Pete and Earl, who was beaming at having shown us his zoological dream, and started the truck. We left the two standing in the mist-enshrouded road.

Earl Quinn's dream of a wildlife preserve might never be realized, but we could see that the animals and humans loved life here, so simple and basic—so honest and uncorrupt. Earl, unlike many in the chaotic modern world, owned himself, did the things he really wanted to do, kept company with animals and nature and the kind of people that provided him with contentment. For that he won my wholehearted admiration.

36

A Web of Mingled Yarn

Why does a person empathize with one group or individual yet block himself off from another's pain? Why does a family man, appalled by abortion advocates, shrug his shoulders apathetically at the slaughter conditions of cattle and horses? Why do some protest those mistreating a puppy yet are complacent toward the cruelty inflicted by hunters and trappers?

Once a fellow teacher refused to sign my petition to save the harp seals. He said he wouldn't sign it because he couldn't feel sorry for the seals when there were people starving in Afghanistan. Couldn't he feel for both groups? Why such single-mindedness? Does it take too much time, too much energy to feel compassion for non-human creatures that suffer, too? Shouldn't we feel touched by all creatures?

We could all benefit from Shakespeare's and Melville's advice: we must enable ourselves to weave the web of mingled yarn, appreciate the grayness—the duality—inherent in life. We need to temper, distribute our feelings and efforts—not race blindly after a single, isolated cause.

This rightness of philosophy was brought home to us on a farm near New Tripoli.

"She was only a cow." At least that's what many people would tell us afterwards—just one number in the dairy herd, nameless...born simply to produce milk, that's all. But Edgar and I had treated that cow with a dedication and diligence others reserve primarily for humans; our concern reflected our love for all living things. Nonetheless, she died, another victim of man's cruelty to animals.

It started when the telephone rang insistently one icy February morning. It was an emergency: "I have a cow down with milk fever. Would you come out? I can't afford to lose another one from my herd." The farmer's voice was hurried, gruff.

"Certainly," Edgar said. "How long has she been down?"

"She was down already last night. Thought maybe she'd get up on her own and I wouldn't have to spend money for the vet. But she didn't get up. One of my best milkers, too...gives eighty pounds of milk."

"All right, I'll be there in half an hour," Edgar said. He asked if I'd go along to help.

"Sure," I said, glad to make his job easier.

I hurried my feeding chores. It was an unbearably frigid day. The wind, heavy and deadly cold, swept over the trees and barn. Our horses shivered in their straw-lined barn stalls, ice crystals forming around their nostrils—each moist breath frozen. But outside the barn the minus-zero cold was practically intolerable.

Although I stayed outside only a short time, in minutes the hoary blasts had given my face a mild brush burn. I even had second thoughts about assisting Edgar with this emergency but knew if he had help, he could finish the job faster.

Donning thermal underwear, down-stuffed coats and woolen scarves, we set out to the farm. The truck rebelled at being pulled from its comfy garage; the motor pulled hard. And after thirty minutes the heat from the engine was just beginning to penetrate our insulated boots and gloves.

This job should not take long. We simply had to administer an intravenous calcium solution, and within minutes the cow would get up and walk happily away. Before we knew it, we'd be back in the truck heading for home.

"This is awful. I have to keep scraping the frost from the windows, it's so cold out there," Edgar said, rubbing his gloved hand back and forth over the inside of the windshield, icy flakes falling onto the dashboard and around the steering wheel. "All the moisture we're breathing out is freezing to the windows." Some time passed as we rattled stiffly down the ice-pitted road.

"Well, here we are," he said, finally peering through his peephole in the frosted window. "I'll have to ask the farmer for hot water to warm up the bottle of calcium; we can't give it to her this cold."

Edgar jumped out and grabbed a bucket from the truck as a man appeared, walking briskly from the house. He was tall and rail-thin and so heavily bundled in clothes, with the flaps of his hat pulled so low over his ears, that the only feature visible on him was his nose. Edgar went to fetch the hot water. A rap on the window startled me, and I read Edgar's lips through a hole scratched on the window. "The cow's in back of the barn in the pasture. Get the IV tube and needles from the back. I already have the calcium heating in the bucket."

I climbed from the truck, "Out in the pasture? In this cold?" I gasped, twisting my woolen scarf tightly around my neck and running to get the equipment. After arranging a tray with the tube and needles soaking in antiseptic solution, I followed Edgar's icy footprints over a barbed wire fence and into the pasture.

About fifty yards away, facing away from us, a cow lay on the frozen ground. She was on her breast bone, unable to move, staring blankly beyond the pasture toward the wood's edge. The blasts of wind pelted her unmercifully.

Balancing the supplies on the tray, I ran to Edgar, who'd already listened to her heartbeat and checked her overall condition. Edgar stood quietly, his attention on the cow.

"My God!" I said, setting down the tray. "A healthy animal can hardly survive out here in this hell, let alone one that's sick. Why doesn't the farmer pull her into the barn somehow, or cover her, or at least put a few straw bales around her?"

"I don't know," Edgar said, attaching the IV needle and tube to the steaming calcium bottle. "It's really awful out here—it must be a twenty-five-mile-per-hour wind. You'd think he'd try to make her as comfortable as he could, anyway. The more she stays here in this cold, the less chance she'll have of ever standing up. She'll get even stiffer. Here, hold the bottle while I try raising a vein." And he stepped gingerly over the cow's neck, the needle poised on a vein. Except for a single glance at us, she didn't move at all.

As the fluid dribbled slowly into the animal, Edgar listened to her heartbeat. She was huge, her sides bulging, heavy with a calf that weighed her down like a boulder. It's no wonder she couldn't stand up, I thought, swallowing hard. I patted her sides with my free hand. Her furry hide felt crackly under my hand, it was so covered with frozen dirt and ice. She gazed without expression, but somehow she understood we were there to help. I continued to rub her ears as the fluid drained into her.

"There," Edgar said after a few minutes. Returning his equipment and empty IV bottle to the tray, he assured the cow, "That should do it, old girl. We'll try to help you up in a few minutes, then you can join the rest of the ladies in the barn."

But after fifteen minutes she still didn't stand up, her legs still not strong enough to lift her heavy body, stiff and numb after twelve hours of lying on them in the frightful cold.

Edgar took the electric prod to her hide a few times, but without any result. She groaned as the shock riveted her body. She rocked in place, trying to rise, but her legs could not support her. Edgar never liked using the electric prod, but if she got up, it would've been well worth the brief shocks. After three prods she lay panting, a distressed look on her face. "Please, let's not use that thing on her again. She just can't get up....She can't," I said.

"You're right, it's doing no good, and I don't want to hurt her. All I want is to see her get up and walk away. She must need more calcium. I'll be right back with another bottle," he shouted as he plunged up the pasture to the truck.

"I'm sorry," I said to the cow. "We're doing it for your own good." I patted her neck once again; it was stiff with ice. So I stood in front of her trying to break the bitter wind's brutal attack on this solitary, vulnerable creature. Unbuttoning my coat and placing it over a patch of her back, I gave her what little warmth and protection I had. Her ears flicked back and forth.

Most of the Dutch farmers Edgar and I had come to know and appreciate felt a special bond with their animals, whether pets or economic entities of the barnyard. Up until butchering time, most livestock farmers saw to the comfort and contentment of their herds, realizing that a well cared for pig or dairy cow yields more meat and produces more milk. A healthy, happy animal is easier to bring to market and makes one's livelihood easier. The farmers we knew would have provided their cow some kind of shelter, somehow. This Amish man obviously didn't regard the cow as a living being. He just didn't give a damn.

Edgar came back and put the new calcium bottle in the rapidly cooling water bucket. I was angry as I pulled my coattails further around the cow's frozen backside. "Where is this farmer? What's he doing for this cow? Doesn't he care about her at all? Doesn't he have any pity for the poor thing?" I yelled, hoping the farmer could hear me as he sat snugly in his house.

"To him this is just another member of his dairy herd. You know that," Edgar said, starting the drip on the second calcium bottle. "It's not right, but that's the way it is sometimes on a farm. The animal is purely a commodity."

I turned abruptly to rub the cow's back, tears stinging my eyes. Edgar said, "I'll tell him to put some bales around her for tonight if she still doesn't get up. That'll break some of this wind. If he doesn't, this cold is going to kill her. She'll have to have water, too."

I pulled my coat farther around the cow, my knees touching her frozen spine. I bent over her, stroking the stiff wrinkles of her neck and the back of her head. She didn't protest or complain; she merely looked blankly ahead. I apologized for the treatment she'd been given by that farmer. I was ashamed of a fellow human being.

When we pulled away from the barn, I scraped away the glaze from the inside of my side window. The frozen cow lay in the same position as we'd first found her—facing toward the woods as if contemplating her bleak future.

The next day Edgar was called back; the cow still had not gotten up. Edgar said the farmer sounded irritated over the phone, mentioned something about all these vet trips costing so much.

She was still in the same position in the pasture. There were no hay bales around her, nor any buckets of water. I was amazed she had survived the night. Then, as Edgar pulled the truck into the farmer's driveway, I saw it: the green, rusty bicycle—Jakey's bicycle.

"Look, doesn't that bike over there belong to Jakey the farmhand?"

Edgar looked. "Sure does. Jakey must be here helping out with the milking. I can't believe he rides his bike in this freezing weather."

"Hmm," I muttered, blowing steam into my cupped hands. Jakey was a wonder.

"Anyway, let's see what's happening with the old girl."

Again Edgar administered calcium, but this time he found it difficult to even locate the vein, the cow was so dehydrated. She was an oasis in a desert; no living thing could battle such a hostile environment. She lay bare against the elements, an island unto herself.

The wind whipped and hurled itself upon us and the cow. The animal's condition had worsened. She seemed to have shrunk down lower into the ground. But to me, the worst part of it all was that no one seemed to care, except us—not the farmer, busy with his own problems, not his wife or half-grown kids. The cow was alone and dying—not complaining, not fretting about the unfairness in man's world, not wishing her tragedy upon someone or something else. She was merely waiting for the end.

I thought about the injustice of it all and our uselessness in this situation. The farmer had ignored our suggestion to protect the cow with straw bales—too much trouble—not worth it, perhaps. Yet what more could Edgar and I do? We didn't own her. We could not force him to do something or humiliate him into it. We were powerless because this was "only" a barnyard animal to him. The cow could only suffer her life away in silence.

Edgar, however, was not prepared to give up. "I took a blood sample this time," he said as we returned to the truck. "It's possible that she's lacking potassium, besides the calcium. That, then, would solve her problem unless she has a paralyzed nerve or even a broken leg. If that's the case, then I'm afraid we can't help her. But I've a hunch she could be low in potassium."

It was then that I noticed Jakey, the leprechaun, peeking at us from behind the corner of the milking parlor. We had known each other many years by now and I waved, but he didn't wave back, and he wasn't grinning as he had been working at Herman Zettlemoyer's farm. His face was surprisingly serious.

As we traveled along the highway, I again saw the field and the cow's back to us—turned away from the human race that condemned her. She had been born simply to serve people by producing milk. Every day for her had been the same, being led into a stanchion and yielding her milk. She had served her owner, provided him with a livelihood, yet this was her reward—to be left dying in the cold. She would be left to a miserable death because she was now economically useless. The last image I remember as the sun set over the woods was the pathetic scruff of hair between her ears, disheveled and dirty with ice, flipping from side to side in the wind. I shook the dismal images from my mind and the tears from my eyes as we sped toward home.

The next afternoon the blood results came in and showed a low potassium level. Edgar called a nearby chemical company for the needed drug, potassium phosphate. By dusk we arrived back at the farm with the potassium diluted in the IV solution.

There, propped up beside the milk parlor, stood Jakey's rusty, green bicycle.

"My God, look!" Edgar followed my gaze to the down cow in the pasture.

"I'll be damned," Edgar said, pulling the truck to a halt.

"Good ol' Jakey!" I said.

The cow lay in the same place as we had left her the day before. But now she lay surrounded by straw bales stacked two high. Around her was draped a heavy canvas cloth, and all that showed of the cow were her ears sticking above the straw bales. In front of her was a mountain of alfalfa hay and a pan of grain. As we hurried from the truck, she looked more content as she munched hay. I noticed the canvas around her, tucked neatly in and around her belly. I was touched. I looked at Edgar who shook his head with a smile. "Jakey. Jakey did this," he said.

The cow licked her nose and continued eating.

Presently, a trundling bundle of a man came out of the milking parlor, bucket of water sloshing from side to side. It was Jakey, and he nodded a quick sheepish smile from under his heavy woolen cap. He set the bucket of water in front of the cow, and she sucked in great draughts of it.

"Okay-dokey, Betsy, here water for you. Feel better now?" Jakey said to the cow. I wiped the tears from my face with my mittened hand. "I be here all night—sleep in milk house—warm there." Jakey looked up at us and smiled. "Betsy okay now."

"You're a good man, Jakey," Edgar said. I saw the glassy look in my husband's eyes at the appreciation of something so fragile. "Just let me in there to give her her medicine, Jakey," he said. In a few minutes the potassium had drained into the cow.

The next day was bleak and the sky turgid. But the wind had died down at last. Edgar and I drove swiftly to the farm to check on our patient. She was still there, a forlorn bundle in the pasture. Jakey was standing next to her, comforting her, perhaps, or just keeping her company. But when we pulled up to the barn, the farmer walked vehemently up to the truck. Before we even had a chance to see the cow, he gave us his verdict.

"I called the butcher. He's coming in an hour. I've already spent too much money on this cow; she'll never get up. At least I can sell her for her meat."

My guts twisted.

Edgar retorted, "But she's due to calve in a few days. Even if you don't want to wait, I could put her to sleep after we take the calf out. The calf is still alive. You could get money for a live calf." Edgar's eyes shifted to me. But I couldn't look at him. All I could do was look down at the animal stranded in the pasture. I swallowed hard. I hated the farmer.

"If I ship her, like this, before she calves, she'll weigh more. I can get more money for the extra pounds. Besides, calves aren't bringing much money on the market now anyway." The farmer scuffed his toe at the icy ground.

I felt nothing but revulsion. I wanted to kill him or at least make him suffer as he made his cow suffer. I wanted to attack him verbally, too—the least I could do—but Edgar was already giving me the eye that warned me to keep quiet. We climbed, disenchanted, into the truck and started for home.

Edgar said, "It's a terrible situation, I know. I can't do much about it, but if there's one consolation, it lies in the fact that Jakey is caring for her until the very end. That little guy is incredible; I'll bet he watched over her all night long."

I sniffed away the tears. "I know he's a good soul, but the cow…?"

"Sometimes things don't work out the way they should. Don't worry, she'll be happy until the end with Jakey. He'll keep her comfortable until the butcher comes." He stopped.

And as we pulled away from the farm, we saw Jakey rearranging and adjusting the canvas cloth around the cow.

In the course of our veterinary practice, while meeting a variety of wondrous characters animal and human, I've discovered that "web of mingled yarn," that concept of life about which Shakespeare wrote. He felt, as Herman Melville conveyed in *Moby Dick*, that a healthy philosophy of life should embrace a mixture of feelings and attitudes, the gray areas between black and white. This grayness enriches us as people, for if we perceive life as a mingling of yarns, a harmonizing of polar ideas, then we have learned to accept, in some ways, all beliefs.

Yet so many people align themselves to only one thread, closing their minds to the other fibers that make up the tapestry of life.

Society must hold that farmer, any farmer or person deriving a living from animals in any way, accountable for the reasonable comfort of his animals, be they cows, pigs, chickens or any zoo or circus animal. Ultimately we are all responsible, however indirectly, for the plight of these animals. We all are responsible for an animal's suffering at the hands of the livestock dealer and zookeeper, for we create the "public demand." We demand the mink stoles; we demand the veal parmigiana; we demand lower prices on the meat and dairy products. We demand that animals entertain us; therefore, we should be accountable for any neglect of these animals.

Yet because it is a barnyard animal or a resident of a zoo, many turn a disinterested eye. Their interests are limited to humans and maybe the domestic pet. Don't we cringe at a person's maltreatment of his dog? Don't we call the Humane Shelter when we know of a horse being beaten or starved?

What about the farmer who neglects his animals so that he can save pennies? What about the veal farmer who raises a calf in a wooden crate, without benefit of sunlight, without allowing it to set foot and play in a pasture until the end of its short life? A veal calf is kept in an anemic state so that the meat is pretty, tender and pale. Then, in a few months when the calf's spine hits the top of the crate—like a ripe peach on a tree it's ready for the picking, for the killing. And what about the crowded shipping conditions of animals en route to the slaughterhouse where many are trampled in the melee and arrive dead at the packing plants? What about the cruel living conditions of turkeys given one square foot of living space until butchering time? If we are all to benefit in the end from these innocent beasts, then the least we can do is see them to the slaughterhouse in comfort and dignity. By our very intelligence and understanding of the "mingled yarn" we must be concerned about the animals as much as we are about our own kind.

Thinking back on the pathetic situation of the down cow, I determined that Jakey, a man of compassion, lived a life fashioned after the "mingled yarn": he loved and cared for the animals as well as the farmers and neighbors around him. He had a dual appreciation of all life, human and non-human.

37

Swine So Divine

Edgar and my comrades dot the countryside around our home like Easter eggs anticipating the hunt. Around the corner of the house stalks Milton, the cat; lounging on hay bales in the barn loft rest a variety of felines, all different colors and shapes, all with human names like Robin, Annie, Marcus, Elaine, Kramer and George. The horses are literally "outstanding in their field," knee-deep in the lush pasture. Living along with us in the house are also several cats and several saltwater fish.

Across the street at our other farm live another unlikely animal family known for their cantankerous and oftentimes sweet personalities: Scotty, a Scotch Highland steer; Benji, a miniature burro; Sophie, a mammoth jenny or a large donkey and her daughter Thumbelina; Larry the llama and his sidekick, Al, the alpaca. Theirs is a multicultural world where only minor quarrels break out and are quickly resolved.

I'm sure my need to live life amid a slew of animal companions is hardly unique. Surely every five-year-old who has ever begged his or her parents for a puppy, cat or horse probably retains, as an adult, a similar enthusiasm for most fuzzy and feathered friends. For many of us, our animals become our idealized friends, loyal and honest, never judging, never criticizing.

Of all the friends we have in our menagerie, I would have never guessed that the one species of animal I could relate to especially well, the one breed that was most like myself and therefore the most intriguing, would be—well—the pig.

Swine are divine. I find myself endeared to the sounds of their contented grunts; I share their love of popcorn, peanuts and taco chips. I, too, am fond of curling up in a soft blanket for a nap, and I like being stroked behind the ears by a loving companion. The porker will always hold a very special place in my heart, for he is a character more of the human variety than the animal kind. This attraction to pigs may sound strange, to some, but to those that know and understand pigs, my unbounding affection is entirely rational.

Our three pig friends: Lowell, my first-born; Lucille, a refugee expelled from her Allentown home; and Ivy Mae, a beautiful silver-backed pinto baby I brought home six months ago, fill our days with amusement. In particular, on rainy or snowy days, Lowell helps me cook. He licks out the brownie bowls and cleans up any scraps I may have dropped on the floor. Lucille has found a new position being a nanny for Ivy Mae. She shares a pen with Ivy and coaches her daily on the attributes of good and decent pig behavior such as climbing on sofas, hunting acorns and taking long walks along the woods' edge. Ivy Mae, though very young, is actually the most cosmopolitan of the three pigs. She has accompanied us to the grocery store, though she waits quietly in the back of the Jeep. She goes for walks with us in town, entertains at family reunions and attends various other "pignics" such as graduation parties. She is a gregarious girl and my best friend.

Unless you own one, it is difficult to appreciate the unique charms of a pet pig.

Webster's Collegiate Dictionary defines a pig as "a wild or domestic swine; PORK; one [a person] that resembles a pig, i.e. an unkempt person; an immoral woman; a police officer." None of these definitions, however, explains what a pig truly is. To me, a pig is an animal that is more human than some humans.

A person wise to the ways of piggery must know that a pig, though it may physically resemble that which is regarded as a "swine," is certainly not swinelike in the traditional sense. While it does have four stubby legs that strain to support the tublike belly filled with fat and happiness, while its nose does resemble a receptacle for an electric plug and while it sounds much like an animal of the barnyard, a pig is not simply a breed of livestock with bad manners and body odor.

On the contrary, a pig is more sweet smelling and cleaner than many people. Humans are supposed to be hygienic creatures; however, most everyone knows a pig-person who is far more slovenly than a pig-pig. A pig-pig prides him or herself on cleanliness and wouldn't be caught dead with crumbs on his face. Yet observe the pig-person with his goodie box. The pig-person stuffs his or her mug with Cheez-Its, Combos and beer while sprawled in a Snug Snack before the TV. He or she is the same one who dribbles spaghetti and clam sauce down his shirt and wipes up the droppings with a garlic stick. He or she is the same one who emerges from the local Chuckie Cheese with a greasy shirt and a bellyful of gas. Who is the real "pig?" I ask.

On the other hand, the animal that has unwittingly acquired the epithet of "pig" is more deservedly called by a human name, such as "Lowell." For a pig is very like what a human should be and deserves a human name.

My pet pig, Lowell, for example, is a neatnik. He never defecates in his pen, preferring to relieve himself far away from his tidy abode. And when he does, he turns his back in modesty. In addition, he arranges his bed each night before he goes to sleep—pushing, prodding and poking the straw into sleepy submission. Then he tunnels underneath and falls asleep.

My human-pigs communicate with me as no other person ever has. They sense when I am upset and snuggle against me. And when I am past comforting, they whine in tandem to my agonizing sobs. For example, Lucille snorts with zest and gusto when I discover something hilarious and roar out loud. When she wants a treat, she makes her desires known, chortling and chuckling, dancing like a ballerina, and gently nudging me in the leg with her snout. Likewise, she admonishes me with a high, shrieking voice if I forget her orange juice in the morning. And she scolds me like a grandma if I neglect to offer a pillow when she visits in the house.

Again, sometimes my pigs are so humanlike they scare me. Their intelligence, for example, is unnerving. Just the other day, I heard a knock on the back door. I wondered who could be there. I finished my chore when the knock sounded again—louder, more insistent.

"Who is it?" I yelled.

And then I heard it—the chuckle, the bellow through the nose, the insistent "fru-u-ump," "fru-u-ump," "froo-oo-oom." And then came the knock again.

And, like Poe, I called, "Who is that knocking on my chamber door?"

I opened the door. There stood Lowell, his front feet perched on the stoop, his face intense, demanding.

I gasped, amazed that the animal had figured out that the break in the wall that constituted a human door was actually, to him, a gate to the human barn. And how did he know to knock? Did he know what the action of "knocking" was? Had he seen other visitors rap at our door and then enter? With both the door and my mouth wide open, Lowell promptly walked into the house, ignoring me, the catatonic human, frozen with awe.

Besides being intelligent, my pigs are also more appreciative of the arts than most people. For instance, Lowell loves music—particularly Gloria Estefan. Whenever he hears her voice crooning "Everlasting Love," he falls over on his side in a dead, adoring faint. For minutes, he lies on the ground with my stereo headphones in his ears as he soaks up the sounds like a dried-up sponge sopping up water.

Truly, pigs are exceptional associates. And for someone who enjoys good food as much as I do, a pet pig is a talented consort, a veritable, versed restaurateur. For sure, there is no eating alone when one is surrounded by pigs. And if a person dislikes sharing any food, the pig will soon correct that miserly behavior with a lesson in generous comportment. They will eat almost anything, but they will not wolf down a wad of edibles as one might think, but instead carefully taste the first bite to see how delectable it might be. With the verdict out, the pig will stand and muse upon the treat. Then, having decided that nothing else in the world tastes quite so good, the animal insists on more. Then starts the vocalizing. Like a wind-up toy, the demand for more begins, "Whree-ee-ee, whree-ee-ee, whree-ee-ee!"

This insistence, this persistence, I find attractive because I recognize it in my own demeanor, and I can appreciate anyone, man or beast, who pursues an object of desire with a vehemence spurred by self-satisfaction. That trait, in itself, allows me to view myself with more objectivity and understanding. I am not quite so hard on myself and my gourmet wallowings knowing that *appetite* is a natural tendency and call to action. To Ivy Mae, Lowell, and Lucille go my "thank you" for sanctioning a sense of self-satisfaction and self-determination.

In fact, Lowell, Lucille and Ivy Mae are three fastidious, gregarious, vainglorious creatures. To my mind they may, in fact, be more human than us all.

38

The Decent Soul

Within the eastern Pennsylvania countryside, dairy farms adjoin each other, and one farmer's wooden fence may turn into another farmer's electric fence just as the cows change from wide-eyed brown Swiss to black and white Holsteins. Some farms are neat as a pin while others are littered with broken-down equipment and odds and ends for future flea markets, all of it lying askew in the barnyard and front yard.

Whatever their farm setting, our clients come in all shapes and sizes, with many different personalities and idiosyncrasies. To this day, the one we admire most is the Decent Soul.

He or she is dignified, generous, hardworking and the most grateful of clients. He or she is poor materially but rich ethically. The Decent Soul's accomplishments come from long hard work and diligence. This rugged individualist has a dignity and force that allows him or her to love other humans and animals as well as himself.

On one farm lived the Hefflers who were rather typical Pennsylvania Dutch farmers. Their simple home did not attempt to impress anyone. Shacks that sheltered goats, turkeys, tractors, dogs, corn cobs and pigs dotted the property. A mess of old tires, farm equipment rusty with age, weathered, broken gates and discarded milk jugs loaded up the area between the house and sheds. And everywhere, *everywhere*, were cats, geese, hens with chicks behind, dogs, and flies—millions of them.

The Hefflers' home, surrounded by a wrought iron fence brownish-red with rust, resembled a ramshackle Cape Cod: there were no shades or curtains, and pieces of wood loosened precariously from the outside walls. No grass adorned this yard, only a rickety doghouse with an old dog panting inside.

Pulling off an old concrete highway onto the Hefflers' dirt road, we parted a sea of white geese and ducks—perhaps three hundred of them blocking the lane. As we drove through the cackling crowd, obviously disrupted from their afternoon stroll, we came to a stop in front of the unadorned house.

Clyde Heffler walked painfully from the barn, handkerchief in his rough, blemished hand. The farmer, in his seventies and stooped from all the years of early morning milking chores, appeared in overalls three sizes too large. A wizened face and single-toothed grin reflected much physical hardship but a content heart. He doffed his soft, floppy hat when he saw us.

A soft-spoken Dutchman of few words, Mr. Heffler straightened up and said in heavily accented English, "Hello-a, Doc. Hot day, ain't it? Undt dese flies are really badt dis year." He wiped his handkerchief over his brow.

"Hello, Clyde, how are you these days?" Edgar said, pulling some tubing and a stainless steel pump from the back of the truck. "So you've got one with mastitis? Other than that, how's everything going?"

"O-o-oh, awl right, I guess. Can't complain. Last veek da compressor vent in da milk parlor, but dat's fixed naw. Lost a cow, ya remember ole Missy, too-a last veek. She was a good milka, too-a. O-o-oh, vell, vhat can ya do-a? Say, naw, Miriam vanted ya ta look at Goldie, von of our cats." The Hefflers had approximately twenty-five cats, most of them free to scamper in and out of the house at will. "Goldie iss loosing her hair-a in great bik patches, and she's gettin' so skinny too-a."

At that moment, Goldie sauntered over as if she knew we were speaking about her. She curled lovingly around Clyde's pants leg, leaving great tufts of fur clinging to his cuffs.

Clyde picked her up, and she purred, cradling herself in his arms. He stroked her gently with his rough, waxy hands. Then Edgar motioned me to look over at the barn's edge. There, propped up against a battered corncrib, stood a green, rusty bicycle. It was Jakey's, the farmhand.

"Say, Clyde," Edgar remarked, "where's Jakey today?"

"Oh, hee's in havin' a sandwich before we start the milkin'. Acshally, hee's probably feedin' the cats his lunch rather than eatin' it hisself. Ve're going' to start irrigatin' the corn dis afternoon, so vhile Jakey does the milkin', I can see about the vaterin' too-a."

"Jakey's a pretty good help for you, isn't he?"

"Yop. Yop, and he's a nice fella even if he ain't too-a bright. I voodn't do vitout him, and neither vudt da cows." Again, I glanced over at the green, dilapidated bicycle. Jakey was a wonder.

"Well, let's check out Melba's mastitis," Edgar said.

"Okay-a. Chust follow me," Clyde said, shuffling over to a small shingled shack next to the barn.

As we walked inside Melba's pen, Clyde said, "Vhen I knew ya were comin', I separated ol' Melba from da rest off da girls-a. She doessn't like to be away-a from da others, naw, so I chust haff her chained here-a until ya're done."

Melba stood in a small box stall. She was tied to a corner post by a lightweight chain, the kind I might have used to harness a Welsh terrier. Dairy cows, however, weren't usually a discipline problem. They were calm, tranquil animals that had long ago given the word "bovine" its soothing reputation.

Edgar sauntered up to Melba, affectionately patted her flank and lay his equipment in the straw beside her. Then he crouched down to examine her ailing udder. Indeed, it looked swollen and sore to me; in fact, it glowed a red angry color. Melba turned her head, an expression of pain in her large liquid eyes.

"Okay, now-a, Melba," Clyde soothed, stroking her head. Melba seemed a little anxious being the subject of this small crowd's attention. When Edgar touched the side of her udder, she danced off to the side, switching her tail. Then, as he tried again, she scooted into him, pushing him away. For the next few minutes, she hitched sideways, back and forth, back and forth, a thousand-pound pendulum pivoting at the end of a skimpy metal chain.

Edgar grabbed the tube of mastitis ointment from his equipment pack and, managing to hold Melba still, pushed the plunger until he could see the medicine at the end of the insertion tip. He crouched down again at Melba's side as Clyde clutched the flimsy chain. Cows didn't relish having a needlelike object inserted into a teat, and I bit my lower lip as Edgar pushed the tube up one inflamed teat.

Suddenly, Clyde yelled, "Who-o-o-a! Who-o-o-a, Melba!" I saw the five-foot chain rip through Clyde's hands as Melba struggled against him. With the cow leaning in the opposite direction, the dog chain strained for all it was worth, which was about nothing. Then it snapped like a piece of string licorice. When it let go, so did Melba's weight. She plummeted backwards, her back feet scuffling in a panic to regain balance. But it was too late. Her hind hoofs tangled, and she fell like a dead weight onto her side and pinned Edgar helplessly against the side of the stall.

For what seemed like minutes, but was in reality only seconds, half of Edgar lay beneath Melba. But not a peep did he make. The mastitis tube clenched in his fist dangled from his hand as he lay propped against the stall wall like an abandoned puppet. Then, almost as quickly as she had fallen, Melba untwisted her legs and rocked herself to an upright position. I gasped as Edgar stood up, dusted himself off and calmly contemplated the mastitis ointment in his hand as if being pinned under a cow was an everyday occurrence.

Whether for his cow or Edgar, Clyde's face registered apprehension. "Ya okay-a, Doc? That must of hurt her-a a leetle bit. Otherwise, she wouldn't have done that. Melba's always so good."

"Yeah, guess so, Clyde. But that mastitis has to be treated, or Melba could lose her whole udder. Let's move her to a stanchion. Then she can't back over us," Edgar said quietly. Inwardly, I was more than concerned but kept silent.

Melba didn't like the treatment in the stanchion either, but she couldn't very well refuse with her head contained between two thick metal bars. Finally, the treatment was over. Then Clyde led Melba through the barnyard where she could join the rest of the herd. Afterwards, Edgar and Clyde went to treat a retained placenta while I played with the cats.

As Edgar and Clyde returned, Mrs. Heffler appeared at the truck. A short, stout woman in her late sixties or early seventies, she stood solidly on her two legs, thin white anklets turned over at the cuff. Smudged green sneakers with racing stripes adorned her feet. As she talked with us, she continually smoothed her cream-colored dress with small pink flowers. She stored a crumpled tissue between the two top buttons.

Her round and wrinkled face was pixielike. Her sparkling eyes shone from under a psychedelic, cloth golf hat. A rampage of hair—gray and stick straight—stuck out in all directions from under her hat. Her bright eyes were matched by her mouth whose wide smile bragged a single tooth, just like her husband's. She greeted us in her high-pitched voice, "Vy, hello-a, Docta. How've ya been? Haf ya bin bissy deese days-a? Are-en't da buks badt, naw, dis time off year-a? Vy, I vant ya ta chek my piks, too-a. Da von seems ta be a leetle beet seeck. She doan't eat, naw." She stopped to catch her breath. "Andt ya must check Goldie awt too-a." She smiled grandly and sprinted toward the pig barn, so off we went to check out the pigs.

As we were packing away the equipment, Mrs. Heffler dropped a large cantaloupe onto the truck seat. We thanked her, but she embarrassedly cut us off with a shake of her hand, her eyes on the ground. "It's nawthin', really. Chust enchoy it, naw-a, and thanks for lookin' at Goldie for me-a," she said with satisfaction.

On our way home that evening I thought about that good family. Long before it ever became a social issue, Mrs. Heffler knew what it was like to be a real feminist. Growing up beside farming men, she had always pulled her weight with the milking and slaughtering chores. She would have never expected doors opened for her. She was liberated, yet she didn't know it, or maybe she did. She worked, lived, and reacted as an equal to her husband.

To some people, Mrs. Heffler might be considered an unlucky woman, but it would take some convincing to make her and me believe that. She is a life force, dignified because of her determination and durability. Working from dawn until dusk, reaping the benefits of the good earth upon which she raises fruits and vegetables, she has little time for television or shopping sprees. She and her husband—and Jakey the farmhand, too—are true heroes. They have grit and spirit. And it is through the efforts and kindness of Decent Souls like them that our world gains its strength.

39

Timmy's Last Adventure

To me, animals are human—mini-persons who are only handicapped by the fact that they don't speak our language. But I've always maintained that one does not have to communicate verbally with an animal to understand it and become part of its culture.

We can interpret their feelings as they are manifested in their eyes and in their posture. For instance, I can feel they appreciate me if their skin does not crinkle and shrink away when I go to pet them and if they sidle up against me.

The position and movement of the tail on a dog or cat can communicate standoffishness, fiendishness, suspicion, friendliness or submission. I communicate with my horses by blowing lightly in their nostrils, and they do the same to me, letting me know everything's okay. And my pig: well, let's say we have a very special relationship. He and I talk on every subject, and we understand each other perfectly.

Certainly some animals, like people, communicate more effectively than others. A few barn cats let me know by the expression on their faces and their lowered tails that they'd really prefer being let alone. If I don't take the hint and continue to pet them or hold them, I can feel the rigidity welling up inside them. There are times, in all my playfulness, that I'll turn to pet one of our animals, and depending on its mood, it may give me a cold shoulder. It'll simply face away from me. They deserve the right to be grumpy occasionally, as we all do.

Timmy, our cat whose adventures, make-believe and real, I shared with my students, always liked people. He came into our lives as an abandoned three-week-old kitten, and Edgar and I showered him with all creature comforts. We saved him from death two times—when we first found him at three weeks of age under a neighbor's picnic table, eyes encrusted with pus and mucus seeping from his tiny nose, and again when urinary crystals blocked his urethra, demanding immediate surgery. Both my husband and I came to love this cat as a unique individual.

He was a loud, very vocal feline, meowing a deep-throated greeting whenever we came home. He demanded attention with meows that punctuated the air when he was dissatisfied with something or wanted his dinner. And he came yowling to us when we called him.

We loved him for his unquenchable need to please us and make us laugh. Many times, Edgar would pick him up to entertain our friends and demonstrate our cat turned machine gun. Timmy became limp in Edgar's arms, his long, thin black body stretching out to some two-and-a-half feet. Then Edgar, assuming a military stance, held him straight alongside his own body, one hand clutching Timmy around the neck, and the other around the feet, as a soldier at attention with a gun. Then he lifted him into the air, still stretched out, and pointing his head toward our friend, took aim and fired, jerking the cat in a gun's kick-back. Edgar made gun noises with every shot fired from our gun/cat. Putting Timmy back on the floor, trick accomplished, Edgar gave him a lusty pat on the back, and Timmy raised a loud meow for a repeat performance, his slinky body rolling through Edgar's legs.

Daytime always found Timmy curled up in a corner of the sofa taking a siesta until one of us came home from work. Then he'd rouse himself and follow us around the house, asking what we did all day, and if he could have a snack. During the summer, he played outside with the barn cats, probably playing army with them since he was so good at being a machine gun.

Timmy really liked us; he did not simply tolerate his owners, but played and darted at us from behind chairs and corners, hunching his back and fluffing his tail in a mock-fury posture. Then he'd run back to the sofa like hellfire, nails digging into the hardwood floor.

At night, he liked to curl into a little ball next to Edgar, and with a contented meow, begin sucking the skin on his arm. Abandoned by his mother before weaning, he developed the habit of sucking not only Edgar but his own fur as a pacifier.

We found Timmy dead at the end of our woods one day. Something had killed him, a fox possibly, or maybe a wild dog, or maybe a hunter thinking he was a wild creature. We don't know. We asked the same old questions: What did it? Why did it have to be Timmy? Why did we let him outside? Why did he have to wander so far away from the house?

Underneath the green chapel of the woods that would be forever Timmy's peace, we stared and clutched each other through our tears, for our precious friend was gone. We buried him by the large glacial rock on which he had played sentry while scouting the woods—this rock, so unyielding, so immutable and so immortal as his memories for us would be.

40

Edgar Makes the Show Ring

Even though our lives through the years have been thoroughly engrossed with animals—horses in particular—Edgar continually refused my plea to show his horse, Fax, alongside Fancy and me. He preferred a casual ride through the woods instead of the heat of competition. He just could not tolerate the preparation and anxiety that clouded horse showing. So, for a long time, I tried my best to ignore the constant urge to badger Edgar about the thrill of competition, instead going along with him on relaxing trail rides around our property. On Saturday afternoons we often rode through the brush, spooking rabbits and pheasants from their hideaways. Our horses, Fancy and Fax, felt freer, happier on the trail, pointing their muzzles into the wind and stepping gracefully around the pine trees. They seemed more relaxed there as they carried us through the woods of ash and oak. We had our own Pocono setting and listened to locusts purring on tree trunks as we rode through the brush.

One day, I could restrain myself no more. I broke my fairly short-lived silence and asked Edgar if he'd like to show Fax. He told me he could never find time for all the preparation: days, weeks of perfecting every gait, turn and head position of the horse, plus every position of the rider, too; washing and polishing the animal to a shine the day before the show; tediously braiding the ribbons; readying the dressing room with food for horses and humans; trailering the animal, practicing and showing him and when it was all over, trailering him back from the show. "Too damned much trouble," he said. Nope, he was content just to watch me show.

I knew there was another reason he didn't like horse showing. He virtually became my vassal for the day. And worst of all, he never won a ribbon or received any congratulations for his trouble. He merely chauffeured me and Fancy, then got water for Fancy, brushed her and put her tack on while I dressed. Then, before we entered the showring, he straightened my pants' cuffs, fetched my derby and gloves and dusted off my shoes. Despite his wishes to be elsewhere, he became my groom.

In the beginning, the pampering was enjoyable, but after a while a creeping guilt began to take hold of me. While I rode happily away with my ribbon, Edgar trailed, uncomplaining behind, preparing to untack my horse.

I didn't force him into this servitude, to be sure. He was a generous soul. But the more shows we went to, the worse I began to feel. Oh, I thanked him, but that seemed hardly enough. People praised me and patted Fancy for a fine showing, but nobody ever told Edgar he did a good job dusting off my shoes or lugging the water bucket.

Finally, a few months later, during the lunch break at a show, I fell exhausted into a lawn chair and plucked a dried beef sandwich and soda from the cooler. I had almost eaten the whole thing when I realized Edgar was missing. I found him at the back of the trailer dutifully serving the horses water. I felt guiltier than ever. My horse shows were taking his time, his effort, *our* weekends, and he never complained.

When he put the empty bucket on the ground and sank into a lawn chair beside me, I volunteered a remedy. "I can't stand to see you waiting on me like this," I said with my hands clenched as Edgar laid my neatly dusted shoes at my feet.

"It's okay. I really don't mind, as long as you're happy." That made me feel worse. "Why? What's your suggestion anyway?" he asked.

"You won't like it."

He frowned. "Try me…."

"Well, I think we could both have a good time at these shows if you would show Fax in a few classes." I bit my lip as Edgar rolled his eyes and grimaced.

"Now, just listen to me," I said. "Instead of your playing show mom to me all the time, you could be out there winning your own glory."

"Phs-s-s-st!" he spat. "I don't need any glory. I'm fine just watching you win."

"Now hear me out, Edgar. I'll do all the preparation on Fax before the show: washing, braiding, getting your clothes ready. But you have to *show* him."

He shook his head. "No, I don't want to."

"You're being silly. Fax has had all the training Fancy ever had. Even though he's two years younger than Fancy and is not quite as set in his gaits as Fancy is, even you have to admit he's a good looking show prospect. He's actually even smoother at the running walk than Fancy is. We're wasting him just riding him once a week through the woods. Wouldn't you like to be able to show him alongside our clients and friends?" I paused to let that point sink in. "He's a great animal, perhaps even better than Fancy. Be proud and tell the world he's great and he's yours!" I was bordering on melodrama so I reeled in a little of my enthusiasm. "Really, Eggie, I think you'd make an admirable showing."

"No," he said.

This called for a different approach. "Can you imagine what everybody would say when they saw their vet out there riding a horse? They'd say, 'Geez, never thought you could do anything else with a horse other than doctor it!' Or, 'God, look at Doc. He sits his horse like a champ! The Doc's got a damned good lookin' horse there.'"

Edgar smiled placatively and said, "I don't care what anybody thinks of me as a rider, and I don't really care if they like Fax or not." This battle was tough, but I kept my biggest cannonball for last.

"Aw-w-w-w, wouldn't it be better if we could both show at the same time?"

"Phs-s-s-st, who cares?" he said with a flick of his hand.

"It would be so much more fun to do it together—you, me, Fancy and Fax."

"Nope, I don't think so," he said, unimpressed by the whole thing.

"I thought so," I said with a grin.

"Thought so, what?" he asked. He poked a fingernail between two teeth.

"Well, I can see your point. I can imagine how you'd feel," I mused, staring at the sky.

"About what?" he said, brows knitted.

"Competing against me. I guess it wouldn't look too great—your wife beating you in the showring," I said, lowering my eyes. I peeked a look at him.

His face was reddening. His eyebrow jerked. He smirked, "Ha! How do you know you'd beat me and Fax?" He drew a big circle in the dirt with his toe.

I knew I had his attention. I played on it. "Well, I really can't say for sure, except that I have been doing rather well this year. It's entirely probable that with all Fancy's and my practice, lessons and show experience, we'd be your biggest competitor. Of course, I really can't say for sure, but I probably would place ahead of you." I pulled one boot onto my foot. The discussion was closed.

"Heh heh," he chuckled. He thought for a moment, drawing the circle bigger, and then his toe and foot came through the middle of it, destroying the design.

"Okay, just to prove a point, I'll do it. Order my show duds. We'll need to be spiffed up for the show at Walnut Crest in two weeks." His chin jutted. "I'd *love* to beat you in the showring!"

Good. His competitive spirit had risen to the occasion. Actually I had several motives for wanting my husband in the showring. I wanted him to show Fax, because he had yet to feel the satisfaction of winning a ribbon; he'd enjoy it as most people did. And he'd enjoy sharing a ray of the limelight, not lying behind the scenes waiting on the "princess and her steed." More than anything, this was a chance for the two of us to share an experience I loved, to be able to set aside the working world and have a mutual pastime. I knew he would come to like the sport; we could like it together.

For Edgar's debut, a friend tailored a navy blue, pinstriped saddle suit just for him, and we bought complementary jodhpur boots and a straw hat. Fax even got a new bridle.

We arrived at the show grounds early so that Edgar and Fax could practice. After a half-hour's work, he came back to the trailer and hopped off.

"How'd he go?" I asked as I brushed Fancy for her model class. "What I saw looked pretty good."

"Pretty well," he said, patting Fax. "His gaits are really smooth, and he hardly seems excited at all. I guess I'll go down to the officials' stand and register us." He untacked Fax and tied him beside Fancy.

"Are you nervous?" I asked.

"Nah, what's there to be nervous about?" He strolled away.

Edgar entered himself in the All-Day Plantation Pleasure class, a two-gaited class for beginning horses and riders. Fax was only three years old, and his canter wasn't polished yet. Fortunately, I would not be in his class, for Fancy and I had mastered the canter. I could watch him from the sidelines.

We entered Fancy in the Model class, the first class of the day. When Edgar came back to the trailer, I was already dressed and had Fancy tacked. I pecked Edgar's cheek for good luck and began to lead Fancy to the ring, a short distance from our trailer.

"Now, when you hear your class being called, get yourself into your outfit. Don't forget your tie and remember to put your number on the back of your suit coat," I called.

"Yes, Dear," Edgar winked. "Break a leg."

The Model class took long, about thirty minutes, but Fancy placed third out of ten horses. The wait was tiring, and the sun was beginning to sear in earnest. It was brewing for a hot, humid day.

Fancy and I trudged up the hill. Suddenly, we heard a horse screaming. For some reason, it sounded like Fax. I became immediately concerned and, tying Fancy to a tree, I rushed back down the hill and found Edgar and Fax.

"What's wrong?" I called out.

Edgar flailed his arm at Fax. "He became a raving lunatic when you took Fancy away. He went absolutely crazy on me! He ripped the lead rope right out of my hands! Didn't you hear him screaming for her?"

"Yeah, that's why we came back."

"He acts as though she's his mother." Edgar wiped the sweat from his forehead. I followed alongside as Edgar tried to walk Fax around to calm him down. But Fax was still agitated, and suddenly, he broke loose again.

With us in hot pursuit, Fax started to run toward the showring. Finally, Edgar caught up with him and grabbed him around the neck. But the contest wasn't over. Fax wouldn't stop. He dragged Edgar around the grounds. In desperation, Edgar finally grabbed the horse and pinched his nose to shut off his air supply.

Fax became motionless.

Now Edgar was as upset as the horse had been and began explaining his actions to me. "Well, I didn't know what else to do with him! I couldn't do anything but try to stop him; he wouldn't listen."

Slowly, we walked back to the trailer. Edgar hooked Fax to a stronger rope.

"That could've been a disaster," I moaned. "Funny, I didn't hear him calling to Fancy while I was in the ring." I looked at my husband. Sweat poured down Edgar's face. "You poor thing," I said.

"What the hell is wrong with Fax?" Edgar's face colored cardinal, and the sweat rolled down his face and neck. He was a wreck.

"Well, don't dwell on it. You'll miss your class if you don't hurry. What's the matter?" I said. I looked him over and started. "My God! You're still in your jeans! You've got to get into your outfit! Do you realize your class is in only fifteen minutes?" In that time, he would have to put on a suit, a shirt and tie, boots and hat; tack up Fax; get on the horse and get him to the ring. He'd never make it in fifteen minutes.

With a discouraged look, he stepped into the dressing room, and I could hear him banging around inside as I tacked up his horse. Just as I buckled Fax's bridle, Edgar stepped from the dressing room. I was stunned. He looked so dapper in his formal riding habit, so regal, so English. Astride Fax, a big, 16.2 chestnut, the women watching would be entranced.

I straightened his number on his back, fixed his coat collar and pulled down the stirrups on the saddle. He was all set to go.

"How do I look?" Edgar asked.

I smiled at him. "I'd like to ravage you," I said. "But there's no time. Hurry up, get on. You only have five more minutes until show time."

He looked down at his trousers. "These pants seem kind of tight at the calves. Do they look all right?"

"You look wonderful. Your horse is ready. Now get on; be cool and calm; do your best in that ring. Remember, this is Fax's first class, so don't expect miracles. Just try to keep him under control, and do the right gaits at the right times. Break a leg, Hon."

He kissed me and put a foot into the stirrup. "God, these pants are tight. Are they supposed to be this tight?" He vaulted into the saddle.

Suddenly there was a horrendous R-I-I-I-P!

Edgar's expression was one of absolute horror. "I did it now! I ripped open my crotch!" he gasped, looking down.

There it was—a huge, four-inch-in-diameter, gaping hole. His underwear shone out like a flashlight beam. It was a white island in a sea of blue.

Edgar's face was purple. With only five minutes before his class, he teetered on the brink of frenzy. There was no defense against a hole. One could not talk it away, beat it into submission, report it to any authorities or the like. It was an uncompromising hole, and it would have to be met on its own terms.

And I was not much help. I didn't know whether to laugh or cry, the whole situation was so incredible. Unable to stop giggling, I apologized for my amusement and my ballooning red face. It would've been much better if I could've cried instead.

"Hurry, don't just stand there!" he shouted, his face like a red beet. "Hurry and get me some safety pins!"

"You're not really going into that showring with your pants open like that?" I asked horrified, my hand clasping my mouth.

"I certainly am. I didn't drag Fax all the way down here for nothing. I'm going in that ring no matter what's hanging out!" he vowed, lips pursed.

The comment conjured up a scene that made even me blush, and I hunted for safety pins, weakened by laughs I could no longer control. We pinned his pants shut, but it was no good. The pins stuck out, and so did his Fruit of the Loom.

Then I had an idea.

"Here! Let me try something! I'll pin your coat below your last button. That should hide everything!" And it did. Pinning the front coattails together concealed all the white. A person would have to look awfully close to see anything now.

"Now, hurry, get down there and show your horse," I called as Edgar urged Fax into a run.

I ran behind and arrived just in time to see Edgar and Fax make the first lap at the flat walk. There were five other horses in the ring with them. To me, Edgar and Fax looked great, as if nothing had ever happened. My dear husband faked placidity extremely well. No one would know that he was wearing "avant-garde" riding pants specially designed with a comfort air hole. Fax high-stepped along the ring, passing most every horse and rider on the inside. He moved so well, and Edgar looked so dignified on him.

The last gait was called, and then the riders lined their horses facing the ringmaster. Fax backed perfectly and parked out as if he'd done it a hundred times. I felt really proud of them both. Then the judge's sheet went to the official's booth.

Silence filled the air. I crossed my fingers while we waited. Finally, the announcer read the winners. When he called Edgar's number for second place, the crowd roared. All Edgar's clients, including the Derhammers and Sigleys, were clapping and hooting with a vengeance. And I raised a victory fist. As Edgar and Fax exited the ring with their red ribbon, everyone was clapping. Edgar flashed me a look of pleasure.

Outside the ring, Edgar was congratulated by our friends and clients, and I thought again how grand he looked in his outfit.

"Yee-hah!" a cowboy shouted.

"Look at Doc! Don't we look spiffy, there," Willy Tinner yelled. "Made a good show there, Doc. Glad to see you *on* a horse for a change." Willy's family, all six of them, surrounded Fax, patting his flank and talking to him. They obviously thought it neat seeing their veterinarian on horseback.

"Almost didn't recognize ya, Ed," Victor Topman said, leading his little girl, Amelia, around the field on her pony. "Lookin' right smart. Got a pretty good lookin' animal there, too."

Edgar's cheeks were glowing. He was as proud as an Olympic medal winner. I was proud of him, too. I knew how wonderful it felt, regardless of age or circumstances, to win a ribbon on horseback. I knew he was falling in love for the second time in his life. And I had won a prize, too. I had found a horse-showing partner.

41

Animal Treasures

Because we literally live with animals each day, it's easy for us to understand how people come to love and depend on their animals in ways that no human can offer.

Blackie was such a treasure to his owner. He was a small terrier, his black hair grizzled gray with age. He was brought to the clinic in an old cardboard box lined with worn kitchen towels. That night the box left with the owner but without Blackie.

Hours earlier, the telephone had rung in the small animal clinic, and our receptionist put her hand over the receiver and said, "Dr. Balliet, Mrs. Hoch is on the line and says her dog is paralyzed. She'd like to speak to a doctor."

"Okay, put her through," Edgar said.

"Hello, Mrs. Hoch," Edgar said. "What's wrong with your dog?"

Mrs. Hoch's voice, between gasps, repeated the problem, "Oh, Doctor Balliet, it's Blackie. I think he's dying. He's not moving at all. He just lies there...and looks at us...he won't move. He...."

Edgar's eyes narrowed, and he interrupted, "Did you try to get him up or see if he could stand at all?"

"Yes, but he seems so weak, and he just flops right over on his side. Then he lies there panting and gasping...."

"All right, now, try to calm down. I'm going to ask you to lift his lips and check the color of his gums. I'll stay on the phone while you do that. Now go ahead," Edgar instructed.

Shortly she came back on and said, "Doctor, they're sort of bluish and pale looking. His eyes look funny, too," she worried. Her voice shook. "You must help him. I think he's dying!"

"Yes, bring him in right away. I'll see you here at the office in about fifteen minutes."

"All right," she cried, and as he hung up the receiver, her sobs died away.

Pulling into the clinic's lot, we noticed an old Chevy, its olive green paint flaked over large patches of rust. We unlocked the door to the hospital and brought the office to life, flicking on the lights, opening inner doors, and turning on the soothing sounds of the inter-office stereo system.

Presently, a woman in her sixties, dressed in a worn overcoat made of a kind of wool curled tightly in little balls, entered the waiting room carrying an ominous cardboard box. We went into the examining room, and I softly closed the door behind us. I tried to make light conversation with the woman, hoping in some way to ease her anxiety, but she really couldn't have cared less about my silly analysis of the weather. The woman carefully opened the flaps of the box and peered inside. Then her blue-veined, sinewy hand reached quietly into the box and began stroking her pet.

She didn't say a thing; just patted her dog. The woman's whole body and soul were directed onto her pet's declining condition. She hovered over the box on the examining table staring, transfixed, before it. Her face was etched with worry. I didn't know what to say.

As we waited for Edgar, I studied the woman. She seemed a stolid edifice formed purely from emotions—distress, confusion, pity, love and desperation—all incapable of being breached by any outside influence. This woman had become so empathic to her dog's distress that she was beyond this world's reality. She was like a surreal wall: impenetrable, unyielding in adversity's grip. She was so attuned to her dog's struggle with death that it left her motionless and unhearing before that cardboard box.

The silence broke; Edgar entered through the examining room's sliding doors. "How is Blackie doing, Mrs. Hoch?" he gently asked, retrieving his stethoscope from his pocket.

Startled, she looked up, and the words burst from her mouth in a prelude to tears, "He is just so weak and limp, Doctor. I really don't know what's wrong. One minute he...he was playing on the sofa, and the next he...he was just lying there on the floor gasping and panting. I couldn't get him to stand up again. He's just so weak...weak...weak," she repeated, slipping back behind her wall and stroking her pet lying in the depths of the cardboard box. I turned away.

As if in a trance, she recalled the day before. "Just yesterday he was fine. He even chewed up a sock, and we had him out in the back-yard all afternoon. He's such a good dog...such a good dog...such a good dog." She petted Blackie.

"How old is he, Mrs. Hoch? I've forgotten," Edgar asked as he reached into the box and lifted out the limp animal.

"He's thirteen years old this year," she muttered, touching Blackie's side as Edgar laid him on the table.

Blackie, a miniature terrier, blinked at us, looking first at Edgar and then at his owner. It was true. The dog was so weak he could only lie still on the table—able to move no more than his eyes.

"Well," Edgar swallowed hard, "he's lived a good life so far. Thirteen years is a long time for any dog. When they get this old, we must brace ourselves for these kinds of problems." As he slid his stetho-scope up and down Blackie's rib cage, he continued, "Some dogs never even see age thirteen. Others get arthritis, cancer and cardiac problems. All you can tell yourself is that he has lived a good life; at this stage he really is living on borrowed time. It's hard to face the death of a pet, but we all must do it some time."

"But he's such a good dog. He just ca–ca–can't die. Oh, please, won't you help him somehow?" Mrs. Hoch pleaded.

Then I noticed her fingernails. Although her nails were short, they were painted with a clear polish containing differently colored, glit-tery pieces. Nail polish is a luxury women wear in happier, celebratory times: the sparkling nails were a paradox to her misery.

Edgar tried to console the woman. "Of course, I will try to do everything for Blackie I can, but right now his heart is beating irregularly." Edgar listened again to the dog's chest. "It is possible, considering his weakness, that he might have had a stroke. We'll have to keep him overnight, run some tests and examine him more thoroughly." He was not prepared for her sudden, unexpected reaction.

"No!" she screamed. I cringed. She cupped the little limp animal in her arms, crying, "No, you can't keep him overnight!"

"It's all right," Edgar said swallowing hard. "He hasn't left us yet, Mrs. Hoch. We might be able to save him, but he must stay at the hospital if we're to give him the best care we can. You must realize that, at this point anyway, the prognosis is not good, considering his age and present condition." She continued to sob. Edgar said, grasping at straws now, "There is a chance. There is always a chance he'll recover."

How glad I was not to have to tell the poor woman her companion would probably not live through the night. There is such a responsibility in relating the news of death. It must be said with the right choice of words, with understanding and caring. The doctor has the responsibility to sound the death knell, to lay the facts out straight to the owner, not giving any false hopes or promises. However, if not done with compassion, the results can be psychologically devastating.

Edgar found such disclosures very difficult. His own stoic Dutch nature made dealing with distraught clients even more troublesome.

Likewise, I'm glad I don't have to come up with condolences that are well-meant but never make the grieving person feel any better: "He's lived a good life"; "He *is* thirteen years old—you must expect something like this to happen"; "We all must die." There's never any consolation that can soothe the bite of Death. I always feel that my own inane platitudes only make matters worse.

Suddenly, the woman in the moth-eaten wool coat picked up her ailing pet, and cradling him to her face, she sobbed uncontrollably. She was hysterical, and I didn't know what to do. So I said nothing. Edgar promptly pulled the animal from her arms telling Mrs. Hoch he'd call her in the morning.

"I'll take the very best care of him that I can," he promised, and with that he whisked Blackie to a back room for a complete physical work-up. I patted her shoulder and followed Edgar to the examining room, as the woman left, a wall of misery.

We both stooped over the dog as he lay panting on the examination table. Edgar lowered his stethoscope to Blackie's heart. "His heartbeat is incredibly irregular. He's had a rough day. Watch him so he doesn't fall off the table; I have to run over to the pharmacy for some special medication. I only hope we can help." Edgar hurried down the hallway.

Alone with the ailing animal, I smoothed the ruffled hair on Blackie's head as his eyes questioned me. He did not seem to be in any pain, but he had that strained, staring look of a critically ill patient. Besides having a physical problem, he probably was also afraid of this strange room, the table he lay on, and the strange person hovering over him. So I talked to him, hoping, somehow, to lift his spirits, quipping about his having a pleasant vacation here at the hospital, about his receiving excellent care and about our staff's superior ability to perform miracles.

Then I picked up Edgar's stethoscope and, pulling the ends into my ears, pressed the disk to Blackie's chest area. "Lub, dub, dub, lub...dub...dub, dub, dub.... His heart continued its uncertain rhythm. For perhaps five minutes I listened to his heart, and then, becoming almost mesmerized by the beating sounds thudding dully in my ears, I slipped into a kind of daydream.

Suddenly I awakened. To my horror there was no heartbeat coming from the stethoscope. Blackie's eyes were open wide, and his mouth opened every few seconds as if gasping for breath.

"Oh, no!" I yelled. "He's agonal! Edgar!" I screamed, using the medical term for the signal which is a death knell. "Come quick! Blackie's dying! His heart has stopped beating, and he's agonal!"

Edgar, who had just come back, raced down the hall and into the exam room. He grabbed the stethoscope from my ears and put the disk to the animal's heart. With a half-closed fist he pounded the dog's rib cage to try to start the heart beating again. Again and again he pumped Blackie's chest, but still there was no response. And all the while Blackie's mouth stretched open in that agonal gasping toward death.

As he frantically worked to revive Blackie, I filled a syringe with one cc of the adrenaline Edgar had just gotten, the wonder drug and only possible hope for this dog. But as Edgar injected it into his vein, Blackie became still. He was dead.

"That's it," Edgar said quietly, the syringe now loose in his hand. "I must call Mrs. Hoch right away." I didn't say anything but stared down at the lifeless form before me, petting the body gently. Edgar dialed the telephone, then came a pause, then a stammered, "Hello, this is Dr. Balliet, Mrs. Hoch. I'm very sorry, but Blackie just died. We tried everything to save him, but his heart just gave out." Edgar paused. "He seemed like a real nice pup, but he did live a long life, much longer than others, in fact." He hesitated, searching for the right words. "What matters is the quality of his life with you, not the quantity. Just remember him the way he was. I'm sorry I couldn't help. Goodbye, Mrs. Hoch." He hung up the receiver but sat rigidly at the desk, his hands together. Silently, we left the office and took the long ride home.

About four weeks later on a Thursday night, I was surprised to see Mrs. Hoch's name on the appointment list. Hopping happily after her on the end of a chain, a German shepherd puppy marched; he was saucy. Mrs. Hoch greeted Edgar with a smile. "Thank you for your help with Blackie," she said with a grateful look. "I know you did what you could. I did think about what you told me—about remembering Blackie for all the happy times we had. Well, I still think of him every day, but a few days ago our family decided it was time to adopt a puppy from the humane shelter. Isn't he cute?" she said, lifting the dog onto the table. His furry skin hung and rolled back and forth as he scooted around on the examining table, laughing and panting into Edgar's face.

"He sure is handsome, Mrs. Hoch. He looks like a healthy, energetic fellow. Well, now you can start a new life with this little guy. I think eventually you'll like him as much as you did Blackie."

"Blackie will always have a special place in my heart, but Sammy is our new dog now, and we all really like him. I want you to check him all out and give him shots for viruses," she insisted. With that, Sammy planted his firm little bottom on the table and stuck out a pink tongue, seemingly grinning at his new owner.

42

Daphne's Message

Although Blackie's owner had made a good adjustment to his demise, sometimes the only way I can quiet the sad memories of animal patients like Blackie who have died is to recall the more humorous moments of the past, such as the one that involved my parents and their dog.

My mother always liked the name Daphne, so it wasn't surprising that my parents called their new dog Daphne when Edgar brought the Newfoundland pup home. At six months old she was as big as a newborn calf. Her thick black fur, roly-poly figure and lumbering walk characterized her more as a member of the bear family than a dog.

Because of her visage, Daphne's initiation into the neighborhood created pandemonium among the residents. One afternoon, when Daphne had escaped her dog pen, the elderly ladies in town feared a grizzly had wandered in from the Blue Mountains. As she loped down the sidewalk, chasing groups of boys into the treetops and sending mothers and young children dashing into their homes, the streets of our village became suddenly empty. Daphne never meant to scare or harm anyone; she just wanted to play.

But her size was intimidating. Even as a puppy she was huge, with a round skull and a wide, laughing mouth. She had a sidewalk-dragging tongue and feet the size of pot holders. My parents didn't take her for a walk—she took them—dragging my mother down the railroad tracks, hot on the scent of a juicy groundhog. And when she needed pet items, my parents always had to search for extra extra large sizes, for a Newfoundland blossomed to an ample 125 pounds or more. Her food dish was a Tupperware dishpan, her rawhide bones were copies of a brontosaurus shinbone, her leash was a horse's lead rope, and her collar was a heavy duty leather, mail-order catalogue specialty item. Her bathtub was a young child's first swimming pool with Mickey Mouse's portrait on the bottom. And we bought her a horse bucket for a water dish.

Yet even with her tremendous size, her personality was gentle and friendly. She loved to play hide and seek and catch roly-poly things like herself. As a youngster, she was always happy-go-lucky, until she met up with my grandmother's sadistic Pomeranian.

Kokee was his name. He was a fifteen-pound, fifteen-year-old tyrant, a canine Napoleon demanding allegiance of all other animals and people, too. With his fluffy chest thrown out and tail curled firmly over his saggy back, he strutted around our two-acre property guarding against any intruders. He was king of the patch, and his authority even extended over my parents who could not step outside without Kokee demanding a piece of cheese or meat for safe passage. He was my grandmother's only son-dog, and he was spoiled rotten.

Every day, Kokee swaggered around the yard to the tune of "King of the Road," flushing bunnies from their nests and preventing chipmunks from collecting their nuts—nothing could live in peace with him around. Yet my grandmother commended the little Caesar for a job well done. He was a nasty thing and a snob.

When Daphne rolled onto our two-acre patch, the little dictator bristled. Even though my parents and grandmother introduced them, the little grizzled Pom sneered at the new laughing pup. To Daphne's offer of friendship, Kokee grimaced and brandished his yellow-stained teeth. But as with all true generals, he did not reveal his plan of attack until one day in particular.

Daphne had been roaming the yard, searching for tasty sticks, when suddenly we heard her yelp. Kokee promenaded by with victory sweet in his mouth—a patch of Daphne's velvet fur. Taking the attack personally, Daphne, with sad eyes, slunk under the honeysuckle bush. My father scolded Kokee with a good shake and pried Daphne's fur from his mouth. Kokee spun and snapped, and I could've told him my father wouldn't tolerate that.

While Daphne was growing up, she endured Kokee's increasing crabbedness. Every time Kokee patrolled near Daphne's pen, Daphne crouched in her house, lying still until he was past. And she seldom ventured from the front yard for fear of meeting up with him.

That first year, Daphne was relegated to peasant status under the emperor's rule. She suffered his scorn and abuse, and even her attempts at peaceful coexistence he viewed with malice. When Daphne wandered too close, he bared his teeth. Daphne bore her load without complaint and retreated many times with a new tell-tale bald spot on her back.

My parents and I only partially realized the torture Daphne was undergoing during the reign of terror. And though my father urged her to fight back, Daphne would not defend herself.

As Daphne grew older, she became smarter. Whenever Kokee lurched toward her, she knew to withdraw quickly before he could grab hold. And one time after Kokee made another unwarranted attack, she showed her gums and growled—initially, not too certain she actually could carry out her threat, but at least confident that she was allowed to defend herself.

One day, while Gramma lay asleep on the lounge on her sun porch with *The Price Is Right* blaring on the television, the Pomeranian was to lose his first battle.

My father and Daphne were playing fetch. Kokee straddled his grassy hill and watched with apparent unconcern. For the twentieth time, the stick sailed across the yard. Daphne rolled after it, nearly tripping over her tongue, then she lapped it into her mouth. Suddenly, Kokee dashed down the hill, spitting and gurgling. With one quick lunge, he leaped at Daphne's heels and bit down.

A howl penetrated the air, and Daphne spun around, growling. Her hackles rose, and she stood over the little tyrant, threatening revenge. Kokee sat back on his haunches, startled into silence.

And that was as far as the altercation went: Kokee retreated up the lawn to his porch. My father chuckled, "Good girl, Daphne. It's about time you put that little bastard in his place."

So began the turn of events in the lives of these two canines. For one who had been maltreated, youth and sinew gradually overshadowed seniority. For one who had ruled with an iron paw, an era was drawing to a close.

In another six months, Daphne had grown to the size of a steamer chest. One hundred and sixty pounds of muscle and bone frolicked through the yard after many a stick. She became so big and strong that my parents had increasing difficulty taking her for a walk, and they dreaded meeting a rabbit or other creature that could provoke Daphne into a dead run, for it took the two of them to hold her back.

One day, my father, a carpenter, physicist and boat builder, was puttering over a new invention in the garage. The garage was his second home. On special days my mother brought donuts for him, and on this day he invited Daphne into the garage to share the goodies. Chewing the good donuts, she lay watching the busy highway, her legs stretched out before her, her big face laughing and smiling at the passersby.

My grandmother was on a seaside vacation with her senior citizen group, so my parents were babysitting Kokee. He was plainly bored for the second day in a row and probably irritated that he hadn't had any of Gramma's jelly bread in two days. He strode from his grassy knoll and headed for the garage.

With his tail curled over his back, he headed directly for the box of donuts. Just as he sank his teeth into an eclair, Daphne lunged. Within seconds she had enveloped Kokee like a bat enveloping an insect.

"My God!" my father told us over the phone that night after the accident, "all I heard was this high thin wail, muffled because Daphne was smothering him. I didn't see any white of Kokee, just Daphne's black fur, and then I heard, 'YIPP!' and then silence.

"Oh, God!" he groaned over the telephone, "I thought she killed him. I tried to pull her away, but she held on, and I couldn't pry her loose—she's too strong. Finally, she let go. I thought I'd die. Kokee was unconscious—not that I really cared, for all the aggravation he caused Daphne—but Gramma would've had a fit had anything happened to that dog. So I shook him and pumped on his heart a little like they do in the movies. Then he started to breathe. Ask Edgar if he'd check him over before Gramma gets home tomorrow."

The next day, Edgar examined the puncture on Kokee's side. "That's a pretty good gash," he said. "I'll sew it up, and she'll never know the difference except for the square inch of shaved skin."

When Gramma came home, she found Kokee asleep on his chair; and as she expected, he only greeted her with a vague snarl. No doubt she told him about her grand experience at the shore, the twenty dollars she won on the slot machines, and the eloquent men she flirted with. But, of course, such experiences were of no interest to Kokee.

A few days later, Gramma visited and remarked to us, her eyebrows knitted, "I just don't know what to think about Kokee." She patted Daphne on her smiling head as the dog handed her a paw.

"Oh, yeah?" my father said nonchalantly, glancing over his newspaper. "What's the matter with the old guy?"

"Ever since I've been back, he hasn't been right. He just mopes around all day. Acts kind of stiff, almost."

"Huh, that's strange, isn't it?" he said. Daphne glanced in the other direction.

"Yeah, but I think I fixed him. I told him if he wasn't any better by the end of the day, I'd fix him up good."

"Fix him up?" my father echoed. Daphne raised her head.

"Uh-huh. I did it a few minutes ago."

"How's that?"

"I gave him nineteen tablespoons of castor oil and a soapy enema. I figure he's just constipated, that's all. That'll perk him up."

"Yeah, sure will," my father said with a smirk.

"And he's getting another dose tonight, too," Gramma added.

My father cracked a smile, and Daphne lay contentedly on the carpet. Whoever said "revenge was sweet" sure knew what he was talking about.

43

A Human Jewel

Surely this was the dwelling of some mafia gangster or other villain, I thought as we drove in. Beginning at the entrance, the long driveway was lined with stolen traffic signs and warnings to "All Who Entered" in a setting that resembled something out of the paranormal. The atmosphere made me feel anxious, but Edgar persevered. A colicky horse needed our care, he said, and we had to attend. As our four-wheel drive truck idled at the bottom of the slope, which seemed to resemble the base of Mount Everest, I had my doubts whether we'd make the summit without a tank of oxygen. I could tell by Edgar's manner he also felt a little anxious.

"Do you think we'll make it?" Edgar said, staring up the long and rocky road that would lead to the colicky animal at the top of the mountain.

"Not without a Sherpa," I scoffed. "Can you imagine this place in winter? Looks like a road to nowhere. It goes straight up the side of the mountain."

"I just hope the truck doesn't get stuck," Edgar said.

Edgar shook his head, forced a smile and pointed to something sticking from a clump of ragweed. "There's another one of those friendly signs," he said. It was a black and white cartoon.

"What's it say?" I asked, squinting. "Drive up closer."

The sign came into view. The cartoon was of a hunter in caricature.

He hung from a noose, and a rifle dangled from his hand. His choked tongue protruded from his mouth. The inscription read, "Conservation at any price." I looked at Edgar; he looked at me. Then he put the truck in gear, and we began the ascent.

The road was lined with more stolen road signs. The next one we came upon was at the first bend in the road: "Enter at Your Own Risk." Further along, a speed limit sign, "Ten Miles Per Hour." The trees formed a canopy that made the rocky path dark and murky in the coming dusk, like Transylvania.

"What kind of place is this?" I asked. "What did you say the guy's name is?" The motor whined as we chugged up the incline. As we rounded another bend, a new sign came in to view: "Alcoholic Beverages Prohibited. Park Closes at Midnight."

"Leon Murphy," Edgar said as he squinted at his direction sheet. "This sure is a strange place, kind of eerie, isn't it?"

"I'd say that was an understatement. What does this one say?" I peered at a homemade notice nailed to an oak tree. It read, "Caution, Animals at Play."

The truck churned around another bend, and through the thicket I could make out a house set amidst pine trees. We skirted a large rock and rattled past a stolen stoplight propped on a pedestal. "Wow," I remarked, "looks like this guy got his money's worth from the Department of Transportation. He could start his own interstate with all the stuff he stole. Ya know, I really don't know if I want to help you with this call."

We were obviously in the vicinity of an eccentric or a kleptomaniac. Ought we be party to such outlaws capable of purloining traffic signs and bold enough to tear a stoplight from its post without regard for unwary motorists? It probably wasn't safe to associate even for ten minutes with someone like this—one who offered no hesitation to hanging one of our own kind. Would Leon Murphy tolerate the likes of us, a teacher and a doctor, meek and law-abiding members of society? No way, I thought; a pussy was not safe in a land where hunters ran for their lives.

"I want to go home," I demanded. "I don't like it here."

"Don't be ridiculous," Edgar chided. "You're letting your imagination work overtime again. True, this guy may be a little strange; but he's evidently got a sick animal, and that's what we've come to see. In a few minutes we'll be out of here and probably none the worse for it."

The wheels of the truck ground to a stop at a white frame house. Parked nearby was a camper, and a rusty car slumped before the garage doors. A crimson fire hydrant stuck from the ground, and behind it I saw movement in the approaching dusk. "Look!"

Edgar saw it the same time I did. A buck with huge antlers stood eyeing us. Edgar shut off the engine, and the big animal blinked, then turned and marched along the side of his wire pen. Behind the deer pen was a barn, and through the trees from a distance I made out the form of a woman with a horse. Suddenly, a rough looking man appeared.

My fingers went to my mouth, but Edgar hopped from the truck. "Leon Murphy? Edgar Balliet. Got a problem with a horse?"

The man took a swig of beer and tapped his chest for a pack of cigarettes. He took them from his shirt pocket, jiggled one loose and snapped it into his mouth. Reaching to his back pants pocket, he retrieved a lighter and flicked a flame to the cigarette. He sucked on it and puffed a cloud of smoke into Edgar's face. "Yep, sure do. Got colic. Wife's walking him so he don't roll. Take a look at him." He slurped at the edge of the Stroh's can and led the way to the barn.

Reluctantly, I followed, grabbing the stethoscope. We followed a path past the buck and into the ramshackle barn. We stepped out into the pasture where a sway-backed, skinny strawberry roan pouted at the end of a lead rope. Leon's wife smiled as we came into the pasture.

"Shirley, tell him what happened," Leon said, swallowing another mouthful. He pulled on his cigarette and puffed a cloud into the air.

"Well," she began, "I was laid up for two weeks and couldn't get up here very much. Leon was working double shifts, so we let the horse out to pasture to take care of himself; but he must've gotten into some bad weed." She pointed to a brushy area of the pasture. It did, indeed, look as though a horse had dined on ragweed, for that was the only vegetation visible. The rest of the pasture was dust and supported nothing edible.

Edgar administered an injection to make the animal feel comfortable before he did a rectal and tubed him with mineral oil. "Let's give him a few minutes to feel a little better," Edgar said. "This guy's pretty old, isn't he?"

"Close to thirty years," Leon said. "Had him since he was a pup." The horse stood quietly at the end of the lead, and within minutes his eyes lost that inward, pained stare. He looked around with interest. "Yep, won a lot of prizes with this old guy in his time. He was born here, and like me, he'll die here. He's a good ol' buddy. Name's Pal."

Well, the guy couldn't be all bad. Anybody who'd support an old worn-out horse and care for him as a geriatric was okay in my book.

"Yeah. We've got him on hay now."

Edgar did a rectal exam to check for a blockage. I steadied Pal by his rope, whispering that he needn't be alarmed. But he was so mild-mannered, he didn't need any calming. Edgar felt no blockage in his intestines but did elicit a pain response when he twitched the mesenteric artery. "Uh-oh, he probably has worms. We'll get him through this episode, and then he's got to be dewormed. I hate to give him Ivermectin if he has a heavy burden. Using that on an old horse like this could do him in. But this medicine should be a milder dewormer for him. In fact, we'll deworm him twice with this. That'll fix him."

"That's my fault. With all the work I've been doing lately, I've neglected old Pal. He should've been dewormed months ago," Leon admitted.

"What's your line of work?" Edgar asked.

"Metalwork," Leon said. He gulped his beer as Edgar slipped the rectal sleeve off his arm. "Want a beer?" he asked.

"No, thanks," Edgar said. "We're stopping for dinner after this."

A foghorn wailed from the direction of the barn. I looked, and two peacocks paraded curiously around a wire enclosure.

"That was a peacock?" I said. "You have peacocks?"

"Yeah, Mutt and Jeff," Shirley replied. "They're our watchdogs."

She saw my surprise. "Yeah, that's right. Actually, they're better than watchdogs. If anybody strange comes around, they carry on something fierce. Leon, show them your menagerie, why don't you."

To the left of the horse barn were more wire pens surrounded by pine trees and brush, and through the gray dusk one could see all kinds of exotic birds with jewel-like colors. Leon explained, "See those two on the upper branch?" Two beautiful birds with royal blue breast feathers and a blue crown, black-and-white wing feathers and a red mask were perched in an upper branch of a pine tree. They chortled to us. "Those are silver pheasants."

Another brilliantly plumed bird strutted from behind a bush and pecked slowly about the enclosure. Its almost three-foot, peppered white tail lifted gracefully as it walked. "That's a Lady Amherst pheasant," Leon said. "There's another one on a nest," he pointed. "Oh, yeah, that's Hekyll. The other one is Jekyll."

"Over there is George, a Reeve's pheasant." The bird turned its head. It was gold, brown, white and black and sported a two-and-a-half foot sweeping tail. "And here is my favorite: a golden pheasant. I've got a few chickens, too. Cluck, here," he said pointing to one sheltering a chick beneath its wing, "is the sole survivor of a dog attack. I used to have about forty chickens running loose around here, but a pack of wild dogs got them all. Cluck is the only one left. She's replenishing the supply with a new brood."

As we headed back down the path, Leon indicated the wild turkey pen; but because it was almost completely dark outside, I could only make out dark profiles roosting in the pine branches. Then, we passed Max, the buck, who was a European fallow deer. He kept his spots year round.

"Neat place you have here," Edgar said.

"Yep, I enjoy these guys. Watching them relaxes me after a day's work," he said. We trudged down the rocky path to the truck, and Edgar reached inside and handed him two boxes of deworming medicine for Pal.

Crickets were strumming tunes with their wings, and the air was moist with the coming night. A light shone from the basement door, and I could see Leon's metalworking tools shining on his workbench. "Probably he makes wrought iron benches or does repair work or something," mumbled Edgar. As he gave Leon directions for the dewormer and what to look for as signs of improvement in Pal's condition, I wandered past the rusty car and peered in through the basement door.

A flash of light reflecting off chrome drew me closer, and forgetting my manners, I walked through the door. Here was a find the likes of any sunken treasure. I was transfixed before the masterpieces. Leon was no ordinary metal worker: he was an artist.

On the walls and floor of his workshop were the fruits of his labor. Formed of copper, brass, chrome, bronze, steel, silver solder and a metal he would later tell me was everdor were three-dimensional sculptures. They ranged from the simplest star burst to scenes of graceful trees with flying geese. But my breath caught at the miniature seaport with a tavern and dry goods shanty, a loading dock with two vessels moored in the water, seagulls perched on pilings and a metal flag of the United States. Here was a Grandma Moses working with metal. It was a feast for the eye. There was so much to look at, from the ladder dipping dockside, to the burned-in letters at the boat's bow naming it the *Narwhal*. There was even a miniature lobster trap and an old-fashioned gasoline pump with handle and nozzle.

"This is my shop," Leon said as he and Edgar came through the door.

"Gay, what are you doing in here?" Edgar said embarrassed.

"Oh, it's all right...entirely all right. It's only my workshop," Leon said.

"Look at these beautiful scenes, Edgar. I've never seen anything so painstaking and gorgeous as these. We've seen metalwork at craft shows, but nothing compared to this," I said. "This is real art."

Edgar looked around. "This really is something, Leon. Do you design these all yourself?"

He nodded. "Of course, it takes me about two months to complete a scene like *Mystic Seaport*. Here, let me show you another room with the stuff."

We wound around through a dark corridor and into a playroom that doubled as a storage room. Metalwork scenes lay all over the floor. A blacksmithing scene of the old days was caught in miniature with a horse and carriage, hitching post and livery stable done in minute detail. In another corner was a gristmill with a waterwheel, it had metal stones for grinding the grain to flour and beyond the stream and tiny metal bridge lay a pond with a rowboat.

The work was that of a meticulous craftsman, an undiscovered sculptor of life. My initial reactions toward this place had been half right. The man was a bit odd—eccentric would not be wrong—but with his love for animals and his ability to recreate the world out of metal, he was a human jewel.

A part of Leon now graces my parents' living room wall—sailing ships in a bay. And soon we will own a veterinarian hospital scene, and whatever horse our artist puts there, I will name Pal, just for Leon.

44

Tales from
the Twilight Forge

Just like Edgar, our farrier meets up with all kinds of characters. Jim Kindred always has stories to share when he comes to shoe our horses. For this reason Edgar and I anticipate his arrival with great enthusiasm. This is a chance to share another's world, to see another side of the working life so that we can put ours into the proper perspective. Just like ours, Jim's stories are sometimes bizarre, sad, thought-provoking, but they are always entertaining. While the smell of hot metal from horseshoes cooking on the forge permeates the barn, Edgar and I sit on hay bales sipping iced tea and listening to Jim's recent tales of *The Twilight Forge*.

It's true that on days when the farrier comes we virtually stage a quilting party as Edgar and Jim take turns spinning yarns. Occasionally, it turns into a competition as to who has the best story. The contest is usually close and the winner determined by who can get me laughing or crying the hardest. While Edgar imitates the whiny Mr. Harvet, who swears that tobacco juice has kept his twenty-year-old horse worm-free all these years, Jim counters with an equally amusing story.

He, too, has his share of irritating clients, like the lady who ordered rubber shoes from a mail-order catalogue. Mrs. Rockwell saw them advertised in a horse magazine alongside a miracle aloe vera curing salve; and she was certain this was an upcoming, space-age horseshoe. It was supposed to soften road concussion and provide four-wheel drive traction for the animal in snow and ice. Jim warned her the product wouldn't work, but she insisted he put them on her horse. A week later Jim happened to be at the barn where Mrs. Rockwell boarded her horse. Jim said he was shoeing a horse when he heard another being led out to pasture by the farm manager. Instead of the usual "clippity-clop," "clip-pity-clop" of a steel-shod horse, he heard a kind of "smushity-smush," "smushity-smush." When he looked up, Mrs. Rockwell's horse was walking by with the new rubber trail shoes, and what a sight it was, said Jim. The horse looked as though it were wearing snowshoes; after only a few days of wear the rubber had compressed, smooshing out around the edges. The mare was literally wearing pancakes; and what was left of the shoes was dragging behind each foot—frayed strings of rubbery threads.

Of course, each of the men has his own stories about clients who cannot control their horses. Edgar has the incredible Ms. Wilkes, who would swear on a Bible that her horse Sally has a wonderful personality. Yet when Edgar goes to float Sally's teeth, he usually ends up with bicuspid marks on his shoulder.

And Jim is never at a lack for tales of man-eating equines and their doting owners. These stories are usually amusing, but we'll never forget the one about the time Jim narrowly escaped being crushed by a horse. Two days before he came to our place, he had tried to shoe a rank mare no other farrier would go near. The minute he picked up her hind leg, the horse buckled and sat on him. Only by a second's grace did he manage to scramble away—right before the animal did a banana split over where he had been standing.

Every day Jim survives ten-hour stints supporting thousand-pound animals on his back. Blacksmithing is particularly strenuous, and only the strongest make it a career. Usually the art attracts shorter guys: all that bending seems easier on a smaller-statured person. Although Jim is tall, about six-feet-two, he doesn't seem to have too many back problems. I saw him only one time with a back brace.

More wearing than the strain upon the spine is that induced by the annoying horse owner who decides to groom his horse while Jim's working on its feet. While he works on a back leg, dirt and horse dander the size of dimes float and finally settle along his neck, itching him like particles from a wool sweater. He calls this being "haired."

Being "haired," as Jim calls it, must be much like being slimed—a nasty treatment. In the spring all the unblanketed horses shed profusely. And much as some people can't resist picking a scab that's ready to fall off, some owners can't resist picking out tufts of loose hair from their horses. The most opportune time to do it, of course, is when the farrier has the horse tied and is trimming its hoofs. Jim has offered to make these owners fur coats with all the "fallout" he accumulates on his back. But in the summer, he says, he actually grows to appreciate the prickly hair sticking to his neck and down his pants because it gives him extra insulation against the heat. And he especially likes the clump of hairs in his coffee as he's shoeing: it gives him a little extra protein.

Jim must also deal with the client who considers his animal a horse-child. While he's bent over tacking a shoe to a foot, he endures mommy's scoldings, her wet kisses to a muzzle, her hugs around her horse-child's neck and her feeding goodies. And, he says, there is no limit as to what a client will feed his horse. While he's struggling to balance a shoe on a rear leg, its owner is serving a gourmet dinner at the front end. He's had clients feed them everything from watermelon candy to a full course meal, including sauerkraut dogs, and chocolate-coated pretzels.

When Jim comes to our place to shoe, he meets another kind of client. I personify my animals and relate, as I do with my students at school, the narratives and my conversations with and about them. He seems to enjoy my describing the problems my teenage horse, Fancy, is having with the other jealous fillies at school. "Competition among peers is so intense," I say, "and the other girls are so catty." Jim says he understands perfectly, but that I should just give her a chance, and she'll grow out of that stage.

Then when he shoes Shadowfax, we discuss Fax's obsession with football rather than showing; and the fact that when he does agree to horse shows, all he does is watch the cute fillies instead of concentrating on what he's doing in the showring.

One day when Jim dropped by, I was in my best storytelling form, and Jim played along like the master storyteller he is.

"Hi, Jim," I called, walking into the barn. "How're you doing?"

"Fine, fine, and yourself?"

"I'm fine," I said. "But Fancy is driving me crazy."

"What's wrong, Gay?"

"Every time you come, Fancy and I always end up arguing the night before."

Jim caught the glint in my eye. "Oh, yeah, why do you suppose that is?"

"She always wants something different, can never be satisfied with just having her feet trimmed and her old shoes reset. My mother says she's the same way I was when I was young—always bugged and bugged for alligator shoes. Never could get what was practical—had to have alligator shoes and a matching alligator purse."

"Kids will be kids," Jim shook his head. "Now what does Fancy want? Maybe I can accommodate her today."

"She wants Smurf stickers on her hoofs. Says it's all the rage at the shows these days, and she doesn't want to look 'out of it.'"

Jim smiled and went to his truck to set up his forge.

I followed Jim, continuing my tale, "She really is too self-conscious about fashion, but I think I finally convinced her that her friends would like her just as much without those silly stickers. I told her she could put rainbow stickers on her hoofs when she's just hanging around the pasture but not for a show. Finally she agreed but insisted on Papa Smurf stickers or, can you imagine, Betty Boop. That's when I really put my foot down."

Jim played along. "Yeah, I can see your point. Besides, did you tell her that if her friends didn't like her without those stickers, they probably weren't true friends anyway?" He looked thoughtful. Even I could hardly keep a straight face at that remark. Then he reached into his van and pulled out his farrier's box. He added a few more coals to his pot-bellied stove and blew air from the bellows to start the embers burning. Soon the coals burst into flame, and smoke began to accumulate in the belly of the stove.

This blacksmith carried his own forge with him. You could never miss him on the road either, with that stovepipe protruding from the roof of his van. Next, he pulled out a waist-high metal stand upon which he set a small anvil. He stirred the fire around in the stove, flicked a fan switch, and shortly the smoke and fire were gone, leaving a pretty orange glow. Now that the coals were ready, he would remove Fancy's old shoes, trim down her hoofs, check her angles and fit her to a shoe her size.

I took another look inside his van as he went to the barn to tackle Fancy's first foot. There, like wallpaper covering the inside of his van, hung scores of shoes of every shape and size: regular keg shoes for standard shoeing, jumper shoes with toe grabs, shoes with trailers for corrective shoeing, heavier shoes for saddlebreds or walking horses.

I went back to the barn to check on the farrier's progress. Jim had taken off Fancy's last shoe; but when he straightened up, she had the end of his T-shirt in her mouth. She promptly let go when he rapped her lightly on the nose.

"Edgar will be here shortly. I told him you were coming so he shortened his afternoon. He didn't want to miss you."

"Good," Jim said, taking the nippers from his farrier box. "I've got a story to tell him."

Jim was such a nice, easygoing guy. What a perfect personality for a horseshoer: the quiet, slow-moving kind. The animals seemed to sense his inner tranquillity, and even the most spirited horses turned to pudding in Jim's hands; they sensed his imperturbability. When we had to have corrective trimming done on our three-month-old foal, he held her tiny hoof so still, so firmly, yet so harmlessly, that she wasn't scared. She stood like a brave little girl.

"There he is!" Jim said, smiling. Edgar walked into the barn carrying glasses of iced tea.

"Hey, Jim, how's it going?" Edgar plunked himself down beside me on a hay bale and tweaked me in the ribs. I winced and wished he'd do it again.

"Okay. Yourself?"

"Fine," said Edgar, swiping a passing cat into his lap.

"I see you're working pretty hard these days. Saw you going down Route One Hundred the other day for something," said Jim, fitting a shoe to Fancy's front foot. So the easy conversation flowed.

We followed Jim to his van and watched as he poked metal around in the fire. He lifted Fancy's new shoes and turned them around, burying them deeper into the coals to distribute the heat.

Then, walking back into the barn with a hot shoe in the tongs, he picked up her foot and pressed the shoe to the bottom of her hoof. It sizzled, and an acrid smell along with a giant smoke cloud billowed up from Fancy's foot. She wasn't bothered at all by it, but the fog was so thick and black that I could hardly see Jim through it.

"Hey, Ed," said Jim, stepping out of the smokey curtain like a magician. "Did you hear about the Hobird at North Sixty Ranch?"

"What? Hobird?" questioned Edgar. He had never heard of any bird by that name. "What are you talking about?"

"You mean you haven't heard about the discovery of a rare bird that has claimed an area of the ranch for its nesting site?"

"You're kidding? A rare bird?" I raised my eyebrows.

"Yes. Hey, I'm not kidding. This kind of bird is almost extinct in the United States," Jim marveled.

"The *Hobird*?" Edgar asked, rotating his tea glass thoughtfully. "Boy, I've never heard of it before."

"What does it look like?" Edgar asked. He was trying to recall his eighth grade "Bird Project." Every eighth grader's mother must've bought him or her a copy of *A Field Guide to Birds of North America* which he or she took along everywhere: to the movies and to the toilet. He continued, "I don't recall ever hearing about that type of bird."

"Well, it's dark tan and has a long beak. The legs are real thin and long. Oh... and I forgot. It's about as tall as, uh...me."

"You!" I blurted. "Six-feet tall? Get out!"

"Yeah, I'm not kidding," Jim said with assurance, as he tacked the shoes onto Fancy's feet.

"God, I've never seen a bird that big," I said, eyes like saucers. "Where is it at North Sixty Ranch? I want to see it!"

Edgar always said one of my major faults was my gullibility. I guess I trust people too much.

That is why I marched to the superintendent's office one day to see why all the other teachers except me received a Christmas bonus. Luckily, the principal caught me moments before I stomped into the administrative office; he told me there was no such thing as a Christmas bonus for a teacher. I had been tricked by my fellow teachers.

And that is why I went into hysterics one day in the faculty room at a teacher who had a gas problem. I thought it absolutely *gauche* that anyone, much less a professional, would blatantly fart every two minutes for a fifty-minute period. Oh, how he moaned that he had had too much to drink, plus too many spring onions the night before, and how sorry he was, but he just couldn't, *couldn't* keep that gas penned up inside him. Meanwhile with every loud effluvium, I cried out in embarrassment and incredulity. Only at the end of the period did he show me the mechanical farting device. The other teachers went absolutely berserk as he demonstrated for me again, and I thought I'd hernia-ize myself, I laughed so hard.

One would think I would learn my lesson.

This time Edgar stepped in, "Now wait a minute, Jim. A Hobird your size, with tan skin, long thin legs and a long nose? Who are you talking about?"

Jim smiled, but he didn't break character. I was a little disappointed, realizing there actually might not be a six-foot-tall rare bird called a Hobird.

Jim evaded Edgar's question, "I heard it while I was shoeing at North Sixty one day."

"Yeah, sure Jim. Who is it?"

"Like I said: I heard it while I was shoeing." Then he took on a theatrical stance. "I had noticed that someone took a horse out of the end stall—to work with it, I guess. Anyway, soon I heard a terrible scuffling and clattering of hoofs. Then...." He cupped his ear and leaned as though listening in the direction of the noise.

"Then...?" I prompted.

"Then it started, softly at first, then a bit louder until it hit a fortissimo." He raised his hands like a conductor. Then the hands came crashing down, and he boomed, "'Ho!... Ho! Ho!...' It was only one word, 'Ho!' Then," said Jim, "I heard more scrambling, and the voice sounded again, 'Ho! Ho! Ho!...'"

Edgar began to laugh, holding his belly. "Oh, no, Jim, I know now who the Hobird is: Willy Tinner." Then, Edgar gruffly imitated the voice, "Ho-o-o-o! Ho-o-o-oo-o-o, Sheika! Ho! Ho! HO! HO! Sheika, HO!"

"What are you guys talking about?" I said.

Jim chuckled and eyed Edgar.

"One of the boarders at North Sixty," Edgar said, "is Willy Tinner; he has a thoroughbred yearling filly named Sheika. Willy turned Sheika into a spoiled brat; she does anything she damned well wants to in this world, including bullying Willy, but he refuses to use any kind of restraint on her: no twitch, no chain under the chin or across the nose, no physical discipline whatsoever. He simply and *continually* yells, 'HO!' at her, hoping that she'll have mercy and will stop behaving like a lunatic. The trouble is, like a bad kid who knows she'll never be paddled, she's got Willy's number. She ignores his yelling, which is more whining and nagging than anything else; she probably just considers him another pesky fly. Whenever she gets the chance, she tears him to shreds."

Jim shook his head. "It's true; Willy's the Hobird. It's really a shame; that horse is downright mean to him." Jim was still smiling.

Edgar continued, "What's really strange is that she appears to love torturing Willy, yet he would never think of being nasty to her."

"I can't believe a person would let his horse behave the way Sheika does. I don't mean he should beat her with a two-by-four or thrash her with a whip, but a good quick snap with the whip, accompanied by a verbal reprimand ought to teach the horse proper behavior pretty fast. A spoiled horse like Sheika is a danger to itself and its owner," Edgar said.

"Have I ever seen this guy?" I said, trying to pick him out of the many boarders I had met at North Sixty.

"Sure, don't you remember?" Edgar said. "He was the guy that annoyed you while you were showing Fancy at last year's show. He was next to the showring yelling at his horse, and he upset Fancy with all his commotion."

"Oh, yeah, that guy! And that same day his filly kicked him in the stomach, didn't she? He screamed bloody murder when she did it and was doubled over in the driveway for quite a while. Immediately the weanling filly had stood beside him so innocentlike, looking around as if she had no idea what that crazy guy next to her was yelling about. For Heaven's sake, don't tell me he's still yelling at that horse, and she's still beating him up?"

"That's right," said Jim. "I pity him cause she beats him up so much, but it's just getting to be a joke anymore; the minute he takes Sheika out of her stall, he starts yelling, 'HO!' because immediately she starts dragging him down the aisle. Everybody at the barn laughs, but they feel sorry for him, too, cause he always seems to be nursing some kind of cut or scrape from a recent bout with Sheika. He wears bandages like Purple Hearts.

"Yet Willy is a puzzle. If anyone tries to help discipline Sheika for him, he gets offended, insisting he knows what he's doing and that he should mind his own business."

"Gads," I said, shaking my head.

"Oh, and Ed," said Jim, "did you hear the latest about Willy? He's advertising himself as a horse trainer," Jim choked as he led Fancy back to her stall.

"Trainer! Oh, God, what a disaster! He'll kill himself with those kinds of training techniques," Edgar said.

"The whole thing, Ed, is that if he would listen to some knowledgeable horse people, he might be able to handle these animals safely. But he becomes so arrogant when anyone offers help that he almost asks for abuse. And now he's going to train other horses? God help them and him!"

Jim leaned against Fancy's stall and started to laugh. "The other day when I was up at North Sixty, Willy had Sheika out to clip her mane."

"Wonderful. I bet that was a real trip," Edgar smiled.

Jim started to laugh, first low and soft, then louder blasts came until there was no other sound but a faint, strained gasping. Finally he managed to tell the story. "I could've died. Willy had been drinking a can of soda, so when he was ready to clip Sheika, he set the soda can along one of the stall walls. Of course, when Sheika heard the clippers, she went crazy. Willy cried, 'HO!' but Sheika ignored him, reared, danced around and knocked over his soda can. The horse crushed it to a pulp, and the soda leaked out in a big puddle all over the floor." Jim shook his head, his cheeks bursting in remembrance of the event.

"Then he tried calming her down, patting her on the side of the neck. At that she turned right around and bit him on the wrist. I couldn't believe it! There was his wrist bleeding like a stuck pig. He let out one hell of a scream followed by a tremendous roar of, 'HO-O-O-O!' I couldn't stand it; it was pitiful but hilarious because he's so thick-headed and won't listen to anybody's advice.

"But Willy didn't give up. There he was with his wrist bleeding all over the place. He went at her again with the clippers. This time when she spazzed out, she stepped on his foot. She mashed it pretty good. He cursed a blue streak then screamed, 'HO!'"

"What happened then?" I asked.

"The usual. He put her back in her stall and limped away madder than hell. But ya know, it's so damned funny because he has it coming to him. She's not really a mean horse; she behaves fine for me and everyone else. She just needs him to let her know who's boss."

He shook his head, thinking about Willy and his troubles.

I offered some advice, "Say, guys, I think we might notify the Audubon Society of the rare discovery of this Hobird. I mean, we all realize that it does not exist outside the North Sixty Ranch and that it adapts to the most cruel and unjust living conditions ever put to any living creature. Gee, if we could find him a girlfriend, we could breed them and make a flock of Hobirds. Hey, hey, guys: big bucks!"

"Yeah, but who could stand hearing its song, an endless, 'HO-O-O-O!...HO-O-O-O!...HO-O-O-O!'" Edgar laughed.

45

Misty and His Guardian Angel

As we had many times before, we pulled up alongside Fred and Leah Sigley's—our neighbors—barn, and I jumped out first and ran inside. A sudden rustling came from the darkened box stall. Peering into the gloom, I was aware of the barn's musty smell: a mousy fume mixing with the sweet fragrance of grain and hay. Turning over and over in the straw, the pony writhed from the sharp pains of colic. With every violent roll, a new wave of barn scents drifted ominously.

We humans usually sense danger through our eyes and ears. We can sometimes see an automobile accident about to happen or hear a strong wind threatening to topple a tree. We can recognize approaching disaster listening to an argument between friends or hearing an explosion. But we seldom *smell* danger. It was through the sense of smell, however, that I could feel more poignantly a strange, even eerie, anxiety about this pony's condition. The pony, tossing in the straw from side to side to relieve the pain, roiled up odors sharper and more pungent from the rending. And there was a foreboding, an unexplainable apprehension about this bubbling cauldron of smells. I was used to the quiet odors of a barn, not a fulmination of them.

The dapple gray Shetland pony became still when the lights were flicked on. Leah and Edgar walked into the stable. The petite, short-haired, middle-aged woman with a thin-lipped smile stepped beside me and gripped the stall door's edge.

"Misty started rolling again," I said with worry, my gaze following the prostrate pony.

"I know; he's been doing that on and off all evening. I'm sorry to get you guys out here again tonight, but he doesn't seem to be able to shake this colic." Leah's forehead wrinkled into a frown, and she bit her lip. She continued, "Misty's not young, but we can't let anything happen to him because of Trudy. Trudy will die if anything happens to her little pony."

With a grim expression Edgar unlatched the stall door and stepped inside. Misty raised his head from the straw bed and stared.

"It's all right, Misty. I'm just here to help you." He patted the pony's side, bathed in sweat, and held the stethoscope to his flank. "Just want to listen to your gut, old boy," Edgar said in a low deliberate voice. The pony sank his tired head into the straw. Edgar moved the stethoscope from point to point, listening for the gut sounds that meant recovery. If he heard nothing, it meant there was a blockage, and unless the Sigleys agreed to surgery, death was almost a guarantee. He listened intently, his eyes focused on the cobwebs in the rafters.

Awaiting the verdict, Leah clenched the stall door. The pony's condition had deteriorated since we had seen him earlier.

Yesterday, after receiving a frantic call from Leah Sigley that something was wrong with Misty, we hurried to the farm. We had peered into the stall at Misty who, while not eating, was at least on his feet. Although he was kicking at his belly, it seemed like only a mild case of colic that a few shots of painkiller and an anti-spasmodic would cure.

Little Trudy Sigley, the Sigley's five-year-old daughter, had stood brushing her pony, telling it to "whoa" as Edgar made his initial examination of the animal. Her blonde curly head reached just about up to the pony's shoulder. An adorable girl with smooth, chubby pink cheeks, she brushed Misty all over with a soft body brush. Her hand barely fit around the brush, it was so small. Her full attention was on that pony, and the two looked a couple meant for each other, the one standing obediently while the other whisked little brush strokes all over his body.

"What's wrong with Mithty?" Trudy asked her mother, her eyebrows knitted into a Shirley Temple frown.

"He has a little bellyache, Trudy, that's all," her mother reassured.

"Just hold him nice for Dr. Balliet so he doesn't walk away." The pony, so docile, wasn't even thinking of moving, but Trudy felt important and helpful holding him for Edgar. A cat jumped up to the stall ledge, and Trudy scolded it for intruding.

"You're a good nurse," Edgar said to the five-year-old as he injected banamine, a painkiller, into the vein. The pony didn't even jerk his head when the needle hit home.

"Thank you," Trudy said.

"Would you like to be a nurse when you get big?"

"No," she responded in a loud voice. "When I get big, I'm going to be a cowgirl."

"A cowgirl! That sounds exciting!" Edgar smiled. "I bet you and Misty will make a great team." Leah laughed and reminded Trudy to hold onto her pony real tight so that Dr. Balliet could give him another shot. The little girl planted her cowboy-booted feet squarely in the straw, and the small chubby fingers gripped tighter on his halter.

"Is he real sick?" Trudy asked, chewing her lower lip.

"No, he's sick, but not *real* sick," her mother said.

"Will I be able to ride him tomorrow?"

"Maybe, but I think we ought to give him a rest for a while, don't you? You know how you feel when you get sick. You just want to stay in bed and watch television."

"Can we bring in the television for Mithty, too?"

Edgar laughed and put the last syringe in his pocket. Her mother said, "No. Misty doesn't like television—except for westerns. Besides, he doesn't like all the commercials."

"Yuck, I don't blame you, Misty," Edgar agreed, patting the gray pony's neck. "Looks like you'll be up and trotting around in no time; then you can go outside and play."

"Will he be okay?" Trudy asked again. She stood on tiptoe and kissed the pony on the muzzle. He nuzzled and nudged her.

"Yes, he should be just fine in a day or two." Edgar straightened Trudy's cowgirl hat.

"Thank Dr. Balliet for coming out to check Misty this evening, Trudy," said Mrs. Sigley.

"Thank you for checking Mithty, Dr. Belly," Trudy said shyly, letting go the pony and following Edgar to the truck.

And with the cool September wind to our backs, we climbed into the truck. "That medication should take care of his problem, Leah. Keep an eye on him. If he gets worse, just give me a call."

As we had driven down the lane, the barn lights flicked off, and the rays from the outside lamp silhouetted the mother and daughter walking hand in hand back to the house.

A voice jolted me out of my recollection of the day before. It was Edgar. "No gut motility now. Last night his guts were quite active, and he was gassy; now I hear nothing." Edgar was chewing a piece of straw, and his expression was grim. I knew what was coming next. "Doesn't look good, Leah. He's starting to dehydrate. It really doesn't look too good—sorry."

Leah's voice came in spurts, and she gripped the edge of Misty's stall so hard that her knuckles grew shiny white. "My God, what do I tell Trudy? That pony is the most important thing in her life. I don't know what I'll do if I have to tell her Misty will die," she fretted, wringing her hands. "How will I tell her?"

Edgar counseled, "Don't tell her yet, not if you don't have to. I'm going to pump everything I know of into this little guy." He thought. "First, we'll need to put him on IV fluids to take care of the dehydration." Determined, he went to the truck.

The night flowed into the barn and with it the frosty, moist September air. It was 12:30, and all was silent except for the hooting of a barn owl somewhere in the trees. Leah and I stepped outside, needing a reprieve from the grip of death.

A thin voice broke the silence in the stable behind us. "What's wrong with Mithty?" Startled, Leah and I turned, facing Trudy who we thought was asleep in the house. Her blonde hair was tousled, and her cotton nightie, with tiny blue flowers on a white background, was twisted between her legs. Her eyes were wide, and this time they demanded an honest answer.

"Trudy," her mother scolded, "What are you doing?"

"What's wrong with Mithty?" Trudy said again, running over to the stall in her bare feet. Her little face twitched as she saw our expressions.

You can never really trick children unless they allow you to. Did my parents really think that I believed them when they told me one day my Easter chick just "went away"? At that age I hadn't been formally introduced to death, but I was somehow aware that at some time things ceased to exist. Trudy sensed it, too. She knew her pony was in trouble, and she would not settle for a lie.

Running into the stall, she kneeled in the straw beside Misty, stroking his forehead and smoothing the scraggly, bushy mane. "What's the matter, Mithty? Don't you feel good?" The pony nickered, his flank vibrating under the strain.

Leah went into the stall after her but didn't try to take her from her pony's side. She knelt down in the straw. "Misty got worse, Trudy. He really doesn't feel very good now. And he's very tired."

Tears welled up in Trudy's eyes as she pleaded with her mother. "But can't Dr. Belly fix him?" Her face contorted. "Fix him up, Mommy, please."

I bent down in the straw next to Trudy and Leah and stroked Misty on the neck. "Dr. Balliet and I are going to do everything we know to help Misty, Trudy. If anyone can help him, Dr. Balliet can."

The little girl rubbed her eyes on the sleeve of her nightie. "God won't take my good pony away, will he, Mommy?"

Leah avoided the question. She beckoned her daughter to come along and reached out a trembling hand, "Come on, let Dr. Balliet give him his medicine. Besides, Misty needs some sleep; you're keeping him up. Tomorrow morning we'll get right up and check on him."

But Trudy had not forgotten her question. She understood her mother's silence, "He won't take him away, will He, Mommy?"

Leah bent over and picked her up, carrying her quietly out of the stall and barn and into the house. We heard a low, muffled crying until the door to the house snapped shut.

Edgar was rummaging about in the back of the truck.

"What are you going to do now?" I asked.

"Everything," he said, his arms lost in bottles of medicine. "I just took a tap from his abdomen." He raised the test tube, the yellow fluid outlined against the truck's light.

"Hey, it doesn't look bad, does it?" I observed.

"Not so far, anyway—but I've got to give it another ten minutes to settle." He pulled a long tube from a side drawer and placed it, together with a pump and jug of mineral oil, inside a metal bucket. "If the tap is bad, then there is nothing I can do for the poor guy—it means he's already ruptured his gut. But if it's all right, then we'll treat for a blockage and hope he'll eventually pass it." He picked out a bottle of injectable laxative, then hooked up an IV system.

"Here, hold out your hands," he said, wrapping two rubber tubes around my arms and piling two IV bottles and a catheter into my hands. "Go ahead; I'm coming right behind you."

The barn's light glowed a bare stinging swath into the night. It was a harsh, eye-smarting brilliance that dared us approach the reality inside. We knew Misty lay precariously close to that "dreamless sleep" beneath that merciless light. I didn't want to go back in. I could have walked more bravely into the dark surrounding woods, through an unknown maze of trees and vines than into this starkly lit barn.

Summoning all my courage, I parted the bright yellow curtain of light and entered the stable, placing an armful of medicines, tubes and syringes on the floor beside Misty's stall. He was standing now; the painkiller was finally beginning to work.

I let him in on a secret before Edgar came back. "Misty, you're going to be fine if Dr. Balliet has anything to say about it because he's the best veterinarian in these parts." Misty turned a fuzzy head and nickered.

For another hour Edgar worked on the pony, setting up the IV line to drip saline solution into his veins throughout the night. Edgar gave him a large dose of mineral oil and an enema, "to get things moving again," as he always says.

A while later Misty's condition was still grave, but at least Edgar offered every chance for recovery. It would have been so easy to have declared the pony incurable and administered the euthanasia solution, thus protecting Leah and us from any more psychological hurt. But Edgar never gives in to the Shadow without a fight. Only the morning would tell if the pony would live.

Leah came out of the house just as we were about to leave. She seemed resigned to Misty's fate. "Thank you for coming out again tonight. We really appreciate it. Is Misty any better?"

"A bit, but his condition is still very serious. The tap came out negative, so we know he's not ruptured; I just hope he didn't take such a setback that we can't pull him around." Edgar started the truck's engine.

"Please check every hour or so to see if the catheter is still in the vein; I don't want his neck blowing up with fluid."

"How's Trudy?" I asked.

"Upset. God, I hope that pony doesn't die. It took an hour until she fell asleep. I told her I'd wake her when he got better."

"I'll stop here first thing in the morning to check him. If he should get worse in the next few hours, call me."

The harsh barn light chased us down the stony lane toward home. We stared straight ahead into the blackness encasing us like a tomb, but I couldn't shake the image of the pony struggling to live.

That night sleep came uneasily. We had three hours of undisturbed sleep, yet it was a restless, gnawing kind of sleep. By 7:30 in the morning we were once more driving up the Sigley's stony driveway. The lights had grown softer now, mingled with the dawn. A frosty mist rolled over our truck as we pulled up to the barn. We hurried down the dusty aisle to Misty's stall.

Our eyes adjusted to the dim light within, as daybreak began to leak into the stable from Misty's window. I couldn't believe it: miraculously Misty was standing in a corner of his stall munching hay. He turned to look at us, questioning our intrusion so early this fine day. His IV fluids were still running, his neck swathed in adhesive tape to secure the catheter, and he was still tied to the front of the stall. But, incredibly, he was alive.

"He made it!" I shouted, unable to contain myself. I hopped up and down outside his stall. "Good job, Misty!" I grabbed Edgar, who was right behind me, "You, too, Edgar. Good job!" I squeezed his hand. He laughed, noting the surprised expression on Misty's face. He was obviously pleased with himself.

"Wow, a miracle! I didn't know if I would be able to pull him through," Edgar said, shaking his head.

Then I saw movement in a far corner of Misty's stall. "My God! It's Trudy!" I said, and at that moment Leah, housecoat wrapped tightly around her, walked into the barn.

"Yes, she's been here since just after you left last night. I thought I had put her to sleep, but when I went to bed, she must've sneaked out of the house. I came back to check Misty an hour later and found her fast asleep in a corner of his stall." The mother admired her child through the stall bars. "So I woke her up and started to take her back to the house, but she begged and carried on so much that I let her stay.

"I dressed her in her cowgirl outfit, wrapped a blanket around her and tucked her into the straw bed here by Misty. Of course, I've not slept a wink all night; I've been out here with Trudy and Misty."

Trudy raised her head from the straw, bits of it sticking in her golden curls.

"Now what did you want to tell Dr. Balliet when he came back this morning?" Leah reminded the little girl.

Trudy's eyes blinked with sleep, and she raised herself on her elbows, "Thank you for saving Mithty, Dr. Belly. Thank you for saving my pony." She giggled shyly and flopped back onto the straw, tucking the blanket up underneath her chin and wriggling down lower into the soft bed.

"I'm just glad to see he's all right." Edgar stepped into the stall and untaped the pony's neck, removing the catheter from the vein. The pony didn't budge an inch, but all the while the slow eyes assessed Edgar, following his arm as he pressed the base of the stethoscope on the flank.

Edgar rested a hand on the pony's back, as Leah and I watched from outside the stall door. He smiled, "Misty, you'll be all right now." Then Edgar faced us. "His gut sounds are good. This guy will be with us for awhile yet, Leah. Now don't give him any grain for the next twenty-four hours, but hay is okay. He's getting his appetite back, I see."

Misty turned to his hay rack and snatched a mouthful of timothy from between the bars. His furry jaw hitched and chomped the good grass, and his expression, unlike that of last night, spelled contentment and comfort.

"Well, can't do anymore here now that everybody's healthy." Edgar grinned. "Ready, Gay? Got to check on a cow with an R.P. at Topman's."

That picture has become indelibly fixed in my memory: Misty standing in his stall, shifting his weight, and munching the good hay, and his little "pardner" sleeping protectively on the straw bed beside him.

46

Mirkwood

We still live in the same doll house-like cottage we built so long ago, though we recently added an addition that Edgar still claims we don't need. In winter, to reach us, visitors to our place must drive through white and drifting snow casting magical images of light. In spring and summer, visitors to our place must drive over hills tipped yellow with wild mustard and fields of sunflowers. Just outside the town of Northampton, he or she will see a patch of woods perched atop a hillock, an oasis amid a hundred acres of corn, alfalfa and soybean fields. Between two hills lies our fourteen acres of woods and pasture which we named Mirkwood in remembrance of Tolkien's forest.

In fact, sometimes one might think that more idealized forms of the creatures from Tolkien's book do peer at us from behind stumps or glacial boulders as we go about our chores. A more likable Bilbo Baggins might have taken up residence in our woods, especially on a sunny day as cumulus clouds cast giant shadows over the trees. And on pewter-gray days as the snow begins to fall, I imagine as I peer from the picture window trolls and dwarves playing mischievous games in the underbrush.

These days our seven horses whinny greetings to the occasional visiting friend. To us, each horse has his or her own distinct personality, though those who do not speak the language of animals might scoff at such an observation. I recognize in each animal I meet various personality traits similar to those found in humans: jealousy, affection, anger, embarrassment, curiosity and mischievousness.

In fact, our Tennessee walking horses are especially distinct individuals. Nicholas, our thirty-five-year-old gelding, is the herd's conservative, unperturbed member to the end, preferring the quiet dignity associated with "cool" and equine nonchalance to the squeals and heel-flinging behavior of the others. Life to him is idyllic: one morning in the mist-enshrouded pasture passes uneventfully into the next when he can once again stand muzzle-deep in the rich, dew-laden grass. Arthritis has cramped his style somewhat, so that he exerts as little energy as possible. I only ask him for a short, occasional ride around the sheared fields in fall, and during the winter he will oblige with a sleigh ride.

I helped train and teach manners to all our horses. Fancy, the daughter of my first horse, who has an outgoing, extroverted spirit, was my first "child." She loves people and exhibits a kind of fearlessness of humans seen only in an animal that has never been abused or mistreated. Pampered daily from birth, she actually seems to prefer human company over equine. Whenever a car arrives, she challenges it to a race to the end of the driveway, eyeing the vehicular competition as she gallops alongside the fence. Then she squeals, throws her heels over her head, sideswipes the other horses and flourishes her tail as a victory flag. She is a handsome animal with a deep-toned, liver-red coat set off with black legs, mane and tail. With her even temper and pleasant manner, she is one of the finest pleasure walking horses in the area.

Merry, Fancy's mother, died of colic many years ago. She lived into her late twenties and gave us three lovely babies: Fancy, Shadowfax and Julie. We purchased a nice saddlebred mare, too, and she had two foals as well: Lucy and Timmy.

The horses have a warm, draft-free barn in the winter. My best pig buddies, Lowell, Lucille and Ivy Mae, share the barn, too. And we have our own haven as well. On frosty evenings I curl up with the purring cats in front of the blazing wood stove, remembering how Edgar and I labored to drag each rock cemented into the stone hearth from the fields and woods. One quartz rock in particular we dragged from the north corner of the woods. During snowy nights the stove's firelight dances over the rock wall creating surreal patterns. This room is our tranquilizer after a day filled with ailing animal patients and worried human clients. As the telephone becomes silent toward evening, the house cats, Purrl, Kenny, Timmy (named after our first Timmy), the Rexes, Bruce, Milton and Mindy, curl up next to us, no doubt dreaming of caviar heaped high on silver platters.

Off the living room is the den, the base of the veterinary business with its telephone, notebooks, calendars, telephone books and various loose papers, pens and pencils. The computer dominates the room with its ability to reveal, at any moment, the status of a patient's illness or deworming schedule. This room is always in chaos. Around the base of his desk lie Edgar's various veterinary books, journals and other medical magazines, one atop the other. The bookcases stand filled with other books and pamphlets, and my plastic, visible horse, assembled when I was twelve, stands on the top shelf.

Our home, so comfortable and cozy, is our refuge. Yet, even though we might be inside the house at any moment, we feel as though we are a part of the surrounding woods and fields, as if our home had magically erupted from the earth and rocks of the property, thus linking us to its forces and primalness. With the view to the outside, we have invited nature inside to live with us: the beauty of the trees in their changing leaf-clothes, the birds and wild animals that peek curiously at us and the ever-changing design of the weather and cycle of each day.

Conclusion

After nearly twenty years, Edgar and I wouldn't trade our life for anyone's. We cannot imagine working in the middle of a city where the only contact with nature and the outdoors would be watching the pigeons fly from the high-rise office windows to the tenement roof next door. Our feet would shrink from the hot macadam streets and concrete sidewalks. And our insides would turn against fast foods and gooey artificial concoctions sold from aluminum carts. Neither could I walk the big city streets, littered with crushed cola cans and crumpled candy wrappers, in competition with other women promenading their latest fashions: fox-collared coats and three-inch high-heeled boots. And Edgar would be the last person to shop for designer jeans. Similarly, we could not revel in a cyberworld, a virtual reality in which entertainment, imagination and emotion are provided electronically.

No, our life finds us in a very different world, a world at home with nature and her animals, staging for us a daily drama filled, sometimes with sorrow, others, with comedy, but always with scenes of contentment and love. Mother Nature is the director and all her animals and Pennsylvania Dutch owners, like us, are the players.

In nature there is no bitter sarcasm, no vengeance, no self-castigation or malevolence. Instead, there is a logical, fair order of things in which all plants and animals seek their place. Edgar and I always want to be surrounded by this world; we want to be active participants in this environment.

As we drive over green hills and walk through pastures to our patients, we are greeted by clean air and the ice cream breath of the wind. In the summer, locust trees give off a spicy, fresh scent as do the fescue grasses. Wild honeysuckle and lilacs sweeten the days and nights. In the icy mist of winter we drink steaming coffee and taste delicious home-baked goodies from our Dutch clients, sharing their jokes and stories. All makes us grateful for our life and their companionship. And always there is the sweet and mellow scent of our other companions— the barnyard animals, the exotics and pets of every kind.

Instead of the city's cacophony, we enjoy the voices of nature: the low bellowing of contented cows in a pasture, the squealing and grunting chorus of satisfied, nursing piglets, the rustling of fall leaves caught in a whirlwind. We hear crows squabbling at the edge of the woods while a stallion whinnies, beckoning over the fence, to an amorous mare.

We often explore the woods, our feet sinking into the forest mulch where we anticipate meeting with wild animals. We could not imagine shrinking with disgust at walking through a cow or horse pasture, avoiding the manure as a foot soldier avoids land mines. It's all part of the natural order—part of the earth and the way things work.

An afternoon of relaxation and enjoyment for us means lounging on a rocky ridge in bib overalls, overlooking grazing animals. Here we may see a chipmunk, busy feeding her family, who stops at attention, paws crossed and raised in the air, sniffing and staring at this couple who seemingly have invaded her territory. But our sitting on a rock near her in the middle of nature is not really an invasion nor even an intrusion. Though it seems a great portion of the world lives apart from the natural world, we have made it our own habitat. Often, I wonder why it is so many people prefer to sit in a theater, walk the shopping malls in search of the latest fads, watch television or become immersed in social activities involving idle cocktail talk and endless meaningless exchanges. Few folks these days can relax and enjoy themselves as Edgar and I do, listening to the chatter of a squirrel, the song of the nightingale or the rush of wind through a dry, mature wheat field. Yet these are some of the most precious moments of life.

Animals, their owners and the other country folk who are our neighbors are such agreeable friends. My life assisting my husband with his daily rounds has afforded me the greatest opportunities to become acquainted with nature—and, therefore, to understand myself. I know now I am part of the earth, the animals, the forest, the moss that suckles the oak.

A mare and her nursing foal radiate a contentment and tranquillity seldom seen among humans. It is a picture forever engraved on our minds: the foal stands on shaky legs next to the mother's side. Periodically the mother checks her baby, touching her muzzle to the foal's face. Assured of its well-being, she relaxes, head front, with a maternal sigh. Slowly the foal turns around, spreads its front legs, dips its head under and up into the milk-filled udder. Through the air breaks the sucking noises of the foal as the mother tips her hips toward it. Then, Edgar and I turn to each other and smile. This, for us, is peace. Here with the animals, our friends, is the life we both value.